BORN OF
GOD

BORN OF GOD

Sermons from John 1

D. Martyn Lloyd-Jones

THE BANNER OF TRUTH TRUST

THE BANNER OF TRUTH TRUST
3 Murrayfield Road, Edinburgh EH12 6EL, UK
P.O. Box 621, Carlisle, PA 17013, USA

∾

© Lady Catherwood and Mrs Ann Beatt 2011

First published 2011

∾

ISBN-13: 978 1 84871 125 9

∾

Typeset in 11/14.5 Adobe Minion Pro at
the Banner of Truth Trust, Edinburgh

Printed in the U.S.A. by
Versa Press, Inc.,
East Peoria, IL

Contents

☙

Publisher's Foreword

On Sunday morning, 7th October 1962, Dr Martyn Lloyd-Jones began to preach a series of sermons on the early chapters of the Gospel according to John in Westminster Chapel, London. The series was to occupy him at intervals till his retirement in 1968.

His intention, he said, was 'not to give a detailed, consecutive exposition of John's Gospel, but rather to pick out the application of the teaching to the state and condition of the Christian in this world' (Sermon 1: *Why John Wrote His Gospel*). That intention is well exemplified in the 32 sermons in the present volume, preached between October 1962 and June 1963. As will be seen from the list which follows, the expositions focus, with only minor exceptions, on two texts and two areas of teaching which Dr Lloyd-Jones believed to be of vital importance to his hearers: law and grace in relation to the Christian (based on John 1:17), and the assurance of salvation (based on John 1:12–13). All the sermons focus on the life shared by those who have been born of God – his children by faith in his beloved Son. With this emphasis in mind, we have entitled the volume *Born of God*, on the basis of the description found in John 1:13: 'Which were born, not of blood, nor of the will of the flesh, nor of the will of man, but of God'.

We would like to thank Lady Catherwood and Mrs Rhona Pipe for their excellent editing of the sermons for the press.

THE PUBLISHER
April 2011

Dates and Texts of the Sermons

1.	7 October 1962	John 20:30–31[1]
2.	14 October 1962	John 1:5
3.	21 October 1962	John 1:17
4.	28 October 1962	John 1:17
5.	4 November 1962	John 1:17
6.	11 November 1962	John 1:17
7.	18 November 1962	John 1:17
8.	25 November 1962	John 1:17
9.	2 December 1962	John 1:17
10.	9 December 1962	John 1:17
11.	16 December 1962	John 1:17–18
12.	23 December 1962	John 1:17
13.	6 January 1963	John 1:1–18
14.	13 January 1963	John 1:10–12
15.	20 January 1963	John 1:12–13
16.	27 January 1963	John 1:12–13
17.	3 February 1963	John 1:12–13
18.	10 February 1963	John 1:12–13
19.	17 February 1963	John 1:12–13
20.	24 February 1963	John 1:12–13
21.	3 March 1963	John 1:12–13
22.	10 March 1963	John 1:12–13
23.	17 March 1963	John 1:12–13
24.	24 March 1963	John 1:12–13
25.	31 March 1963	John 1:12–13
26.	7 April 1963	John 1:12–13
27.	28 April 1963	John 1:12–13
28.	5 May 1963	John 1:12–13
29.	12 May 1963	John 1:12–13
30.	19 May 1963	John 1:12–13
31.	26 May 1963	John 1:12–13
32.	2 June 1963	John 1:12–13

[1] Dr Lloyd-Jones said that he might equally well have taken as his text John 1:12–13.

1

Why John Wrote His Gospel

And many other signs truly did Jesus in the presence of his disciples, which are not written in this book: but these are written that ye might believe that Jesus is the Christ, the Son of God; and that believing ye might have life through his name (John 20:30–31).

The words to which I call your attention are to be found in the Gospel according to St John, chapter 20, verses 30 and 31. But we might equally well take as our text the twelfth and thirteenth verses in the first chapter of this Gospel: 'But as many as received him, to them gave he power to become the sons of God, even to them that believe on his name: which were born, not of blood, nor of the will of the flesh, nor of the will of man, but of God.'

Now during the following Sunday mornings I propose, God willing, not to give a detailed, consecutive exposition of John's Gospel, but rather to pick out the application of the teaching to the state and condition of the Christian in this world. According to all authorities, this is undoubtedly the last of the Gospels and that gives it particular significance. It has always been recognized that there is something essentially different about this Gospel, as contrasted with the other three – Matthew, Mark and Luke – and it seems to me that the great difference is this: though they are all, of course, portraits of our Lord and Saviour, in John's Gospel there is more application; a greater emphasis is placed on the bearing of all this upon us as believers. That is why it is John's Gospel that records how, towards the end of his ministry, our Lord gave more time and attention to the preparation of his people for the days that were ahead, days in which they would have the problems of life and living apart from his actually being with them in person. In other words, there is fuller teaching about the doctrine of the Holy Spirit in this Gospel of John than there is in any of the other Gospels. And it is to that doctrine in particular that I want to direct your attention.

Now this, I repeat, is the last of the Gospels. It was written to Christian people who had been in the Christian life for some time. A number of years had passed since our Lord's life and death and resurrection. So why was it that John ever wrote this Gospel? That is always a good question to ask about any book in the Bible. We must never think of these writers as literary men. The literary man writes because he enjoys writing and in order to make a living. But these were practical men. They were apostles, they were evangelists and teachers and, in a sense, they only wrote when they had to.

It is perfectly clear why John wrote this particular Gospel. It was written in order to strengthen and to establish and to encourage these first-century Christians, and from that we deduce, of course, that that was what they needed. They were obviously people who had become discouraged in various ways and for various reasons. We know that they were subjected to a great deal of very cruel persecution. The first Jews who believed were persecuted both by their own fellow-countrymen and by the Gentiles. And Gentile believers, too, were subjected to very grievous persecution. So the first believers had these great trials and troubles and that, in and of itself, immediately produced a problem. There is always a tendency on the part of Christian people to think that the moment you become a Christian all your troubles have ended. It is quite wrong to believe that, but people will persist in doing so. The result is that when trials and troubles come, Christians are taken aback, and begin to query the gospel and to wonder whether it is true after all. Now there were people like that in the first century, exactly as there are today.

There are those who think that John's Gospel was written in AD 70. We cannot determine the exact date, but if it was AD 70, then we can quite understand how the first readers felt. The city of Jerusalem had been attacked and destroyed. The Romans ruled everywhere and the Jews had, as it were, been cast out. This was a shattering experience – no question about that. Now that may have been a part of the background to this Gospel, but whether it was or not, there were many persecutions and trials and troubles and difficulties, and that is why this Gospel was written.

You find exactly the same situation in the last book of the Bible, the book of Revelation, written by this same man, John. Why did he write it? Again, it was to comfort the first-century Christians. It was not written for this generation to which you and I belong, it was written to those people, to enable them to face the calamities and terrible trials that had come upon them. They were not only brought before the magistrates and the powers, but large numbers were massacred, put to death in a most cruel manner. It was the 'sport' of the aristocracy of Rome in those times to go to the Coliseum and other places and watch the poor Christians being thrown to the lions in the arena. That is the background.

But there was also something else. The Christians had been taught that the Lord Jesus Christ would come back again into this world to wind up his great work, to put an end to history and to introduce his kingdom. But the years were passing and he had not come. And there were many who were troubled by that – again beginning to wonder whether the message was true or not. They had this great promise, this 'blessed hope', but nothing seemed to be happening concerning it.

And then, in addition, there was false teaching. This is what I want to emphasize most of all because, under the influence of the Holy Spirit, it was undoubtedly the main factor that led John to write this Gospel, as probably it led the others to write theirs. False teaching about what? Well, especially about the person of the Lord Jesus Christ. And, of course, this is basic and central. I need not weary you with a catalogue of the various false ideas that are held today with regard to our Lord. Nearly all of them appeared in the first century. There is nothing new, nothing modern, about wrong ideas concerning the person of the Lord Jesus Christ. Let us remember that. There are many people who think that to say that Jesus of Nazareth was only a man is the hallmark of modernity. But that was said in the first century! All that these foolish people are saying today – and thinking they are very clever and sophisticated in doing so – about the Lord and about the Old Testament, is, indeed, almost as old as the Bible itself. You are not being clever, you are not being learned, when you say such things. You are simply repeating what has been said from the very beginning.

Now this false teaching took many forms, but there were two in particular. First, there were people who said, 'Yes, Jesus of Nazareth is the eternal Son of God, but he only *appeared* to be incarnate. He was never truly man. He did not have a real human body; it was a sort of phantom body.' That was one heresy – Docetism.

The second teaching was the view that Jesus of Nazareth was only a man but that at his baptism the eternal Christ came upon him, entered into him and remained in him until the cross. The moment he was nailed to the cross, the eternal Christ left him, so that it was only the man Jesus who died. Now that was a very popular heresy, and it was taught at that time by a man called Cerinthus. There is a story told about Cerinthus and this very apostle, John. John, one day, was going into the public baths and as he was entering he was told that Cerinthus was there. And John immediately turned around and walked out – he would not even be in the same building as this heretic! John hated this doctrine because it detracted from the glory of his Lord and Master. So that is also the background; this is why John came to write his Gospel. He says, 'These [signs] are written, that ye might believe that Jesus is the Christ, the Son of God; and that [knowing and] believing ye might have life through his name' (*John* 20:31). The church, you see, was being disturbed by these false teachings.

Then on top of all that there were large numbers of so-called 'apocryphal gospels': different people were writing lives, biographies, of the Lord Jesus Christ. These were confusing the members of the early church and were a great problem in the early centuries. The apocryphal gospels were rejected by the church, under the leading of the Holy Spirit, and were never incorporated in our New Testament. But people still get excited about them today. Recently there was enthusiasm about a so-called Gospel of Thomas, and I have been amazed to see Christian people wondering whether they are going to get something new and fresh. Do not waste your time, my dear friends; everything you need to know is here, in the Bible. You need not get excited about any apocryphal gospel. These gospels never add; they always detract.

There is always something that is merely human and imaginative about them. That is why the church in her wisdom rejected them. It is a bad sign when people get interested in these supposed discoveries, as if they are going to get a fresh glimpse of truth. It is all here in what we have before us, you do not need anything more.

In the early church, the effect of all these problems was that Christian people became depressed, they became uncertain and confused, they asked, 'What are we to believe?' And the result was that their enjoyment of the Christian life and their experience of it were suffering. And it was to deal with that very situation that John wrote his Gospel. I do hope we are all clear about this. The Gospels, like everything else in the New Testament, were not written for the world; they were written for believers. Luke tells us in his Gospel, written to this man Theophilus: 'It seemed good to me also, having had perfect understanding of all things from the very first, to write unto thee in order, most excellent Theophilus, that thou mightest know the certainty of these things, wherein thou hast been instructed' (*Luke* 1:3–4). The Gospels were written, in other words, in order to confirm and establish the early Christians and to deliver them from this condition of uncertainty and unhappiness, this kind of lethargy, that would come upon them, and the consequent feeling of hopelessness. Now this is, to me, a vital principle. The Gospels are primarily for Christian people in order that we might have assurance and certainty.

The first thing to which I am anxious to call your attention is the way in which John deals with such a situation: depressed, unhappy, uncertain Christians, people not enjoying the fulness of the Christian life. John looks at these Christians in amazement and says to himself, as it were, 'What can I do with these people? What exactly is the message that they need?'

Now notice what John does not do. He does not merely write a letter of general comfort. I am beginning to think that the modern Christian church is dying of comfort. The idea seems to be current that the main function of Christianity is to give us some comfort. Of course, in an ultimate sense, it does, and it is the only thing that does, but the Christian church is not just a 'nice' place and Christians are not just meant to be 'nice' people. A Christian preacher is not meant to be a 'nice' man who makes people feel a little bit more comfortable and happy while they are in a church. Yet that seems to me to be what is happening. Are you not appalled at the present state of the Christian church, our ineffectiveness, the masses outside, the arrogance and the sin? What is the matter? Why do people not come to church? I must confess that I am more than ever convinced that they do not come because of what they see there. What they see is a number of 'nice' people, who seem to be wanting sentimental and emotional comfort. That is what they see, but that is not the Christian church.

No, the Christian church is meant to be an army with banners! Never was she so needed in the world as she is at the present time. And yet what do people coming to churches find? I am not necessarily referring to this congregation, but to other congregations. There is great value in having a holiday and slipping into churches here and there, little chapels up and down the country, and just seeing what is happening. And if one does, one gets the impression that people go to church in order to be praised, in order to be comforted, in order to be told soothing things. But that is not the business of Christianity and John does not do it.

John does not merely give some general comfort; he does not even make an appeal. No, he gives instruction – 'these are written'. There is much more, he says, that he could write. There at the end of his Gospel he says, 'And there are also other things which Jesus did, the which, if they should be written every one, I suppose that even the world itself could not contain the books that should be written' (*John* 21:25). And, as we have seen, he also writes, 'Many other signs truly did Jesus in the presence of his disciples, which are not written in this book: but these are written' – why? – 'that ye might believe that Jesus is the Christ, the Son of God; and that believing ye might have life through his name.' This Gospel, I say again, is written to Christians.

'But,' you say, 'Christians do believe.'

I know. In a sense, we do. But the question is: Do we *really* believe? John says, in effect, 'That you might really believe and know what it means to believe, and that you might have life through his name.'

'But, surely, Christians do have life?'

Yes, but there is a difference between the life of an infant and the life of an adult. There is a difference between the life of a healthy infant and the life of a marasmic [wasted] infant. There is that little infant, skin and bones and nothing else, but still breathing. You are not pleased, you are not proud. 'It is alive,' you say. Yes, but is that life? Of course not. That is just existence. The child is not meant to be like that. So John writes, I repeat, in order to get the church out of this marasmic, unhealthy, morbid condition, and what he does is give it instruction. First, he writes the doctrine of the person of the Lord Jesus Christ. And, second, he writes of the possibilities for us because the Lord Jesus Christ is who and what he is. That is what you need, says John, so he writes his Gospel. And I am suggesting that the other Gospels were written in exactly the same way. And is not this our greatest need at the present time?

What sort of picture are we presenting to the world? Are we giving the impression that Christianity is the most wonderful and glorious thing that the human race and all civilizations have ever known? Are we giving the impression that when someone becomes a Christian, everything is new and changed and different, that Christians are delivered, emancipated, set free, filled with a glory and a power – is that it? John will go on to say, 'And of his fulness have all we received, and grace for [upon] grace' (*John* 1:16). Are we giving that impression? Now this, to me, is tragic. The world is on fire. It is desperate; it does not know what to do. Here is the only message. But it comes through us, and we have no right to blame the world for judging Christianity through us: it is a perfectly fair thing to do. We are its representatives, we are the guardians and the custodians of the faith. The world is absolutely right to judge this message through us. You cannot expect it to do anything else.

What is the matter with us? That is the question. Why are so many of us depressed Christians? Why do so many of us come to the house of God in order just to get a little fillip or a nice feeling or a bit of encouragement or sympathy? Why is it that so many of us are mechanical in our Christian lives, having to push ourselves, to press ourselves, to remind ourselves that we are Christians? Why do we regard our faith as a matter of duty and feel rather proud of ourselves because we attend a place of worship? Oh, what an utter travesty of Christianity! Do we give the impression that we really are rather proud of ourselves for being in church at this moment instead of going to the seaside – it is obviously going to be a very sunny day and it will be wonderful at the seaside but we have made a great sacrifice, we have come to the house of God – is that the impression we give? Well, if it is, I am not surprised that the majority of people in this country are outside the church. This is all wrong.

Many of those early Christians gladly faced ostracism from their families and nearest and dearest because of what they had found in the gospel. As I have reminded you, they were persecuted, they were thrown into prison, they were ready to face martyrdom, they thanked God that at last they had been accounted worthy to suffer shame for his name's sake. To them, martyrdom, to be allowed to die for him, was the final crown of glory. That was the spirit that conquered the ancient world – there is no doubt about it. That is how Christianity spread. And you and I must come back to this. Our responsibility, I emphasize again, is tremendous at this present time. You and I are going to be judged by God in eternity as to our witness and our testimony in this evil hour in the history of the world, this hour in which we find ourselves. What have we done to bring this gospel to the notice of the masses of the people? What impression are we giving with respect to it and its nature? That is the question, and that is the matter on which we shall all be judged.

What do we need, therefore? Like these people to whom John was writing, we do not need comfort. By that, I mean that we do not need comfort directly. The comfort of the gospel comes indirectly, through the truth, not directly. My primary task here is not to give comfort, it is to introduce you to him, the 'friend that sticketh closer than a brother' (*Prov.* 18:24). If I comfort you, I am acting as a drug to you. So much of what is being preached and put forward today as Christianity is in fact psychology. It is nothing but psychology dishonestly using Christian terminology. It is the psychological treatment of men and women to get them over their fears and phobias and anxieties and sleeplessness and many another problem. But that is not the business of the gospel. John does not send these first-century Christians a little bit of psychology, he does not give them comfort directly and immediately. No, no! That is not the function or the purpose of Christian preaching.

But you listen to this psychology! That is why I am calling your attention to it. I do trust that we are not being misled by this kind of thing. If you listen to it on your television and wireless, or read it, this is what you get: some vague, general, comforting psychological 'talk' supposed to make you feel happy as you go to sleep and to help you to sleep. And there is nothing of this glorious message, so often nothing about the person of our Lord himself, as if Christianity were just some soothing syrup to make life a little bit easier and more bearable. I say again that this is a travesty of Christianity! It is not surprising that the world is as it is. It is not surprising that the Christian church is as she is.

Not only do we not need comfort, we do not need exhortations, we do not even need appeals. Again, there is so much of that today. People are being exhorted to do this, that and the other; they are being appealed to; they are being organized into activities. That is not what we need. All our activities are to be the result of our understanding of the truth. We do not need spiritual clinics. We are all so subjective. We say, 'This sin that's getting me down, this is the problem. What can you tell me about it?' And then I, the preacher, concentrate on this sin and give a little psychological treatment. No, no! That is the wrong way.

The answer to it all is given by John in his Gospel. It is teaching! Doctrine! Do not look at individual problems, get at the ultimate source of the trouble. All these individual problems are nothing but symptoms of a great central disease. So John says: I know your state and condition. I know that you are muddled and confused by these apocryphal gospels and by these heretical teachers. I know that you are discouraged because of your trials and your tribulations. Therefore I want to help you and this is how I will do that: 'In the beginning was the Word, and the Word was with God, and the Word was God.' That is how John does it. And that is the only way. It is the way of every reformation; it is the way of every revival. Teaching! Do you know what is the matter with us? I will tell you. We none of us really believe in the Lord Jesus Christ!

The trouble with all of us is that we do not know enough about him. So John says: The thing you need above everything is to be brought to this knowledge of him – who he is, what he has done and what he has made possible for us.

But notice how John holds together two things – and here is my main emphasis. 'These are written that ye might believe [know] that Jesus is the Christ, the Son of God' – it is the great doctrine of the person and work of the Lord Jesus Christ; yes, but, second – 'and that believing ye might have life through his name.' Or here it is in the twelfth verse of this first chapter: 'As many as received him, to them gave he power to become the sons of God.' 'As many as received him'! There it is. The great objective doctrine. 'Yes,' continues John, in effect, 'but I am not merely going to write to you about him and give you the doctrine concerning him in order that I may fill up your heads with theoretical knowledge – I want you to have *life*.' The two go together – the knowledge and the life. The doctrine and the experience. The understanding and the working out of this understanding in daily life.

Now the moment the knowledge and the life are separated, we are lost. Yet they are being separated. There are some people who put the whole of their emphasis upon the doctrine, the objectivity, the theology, and they stop at that. But their lives are quite useless. Others may therefore say to them, 'All right, you're interested in that, I'm interested in something else.' They want to see what Christian belief does in actual practice, in daily life and living: Is there life here?

But then a large number, the majority, put their emphasis upon the second aspect only and exclude the first. Their whole emphasis is upon life and experience. We are living in a psychological age and we are all so subjective, we are always turning inwards, wanting this and that. We start with ourselves – man as the centre of the universe, so we believe. And this is absolutely fatal because if you set out wanting life only, then all the cults will come and meet you and will say, 'Here it is, here is the very thing you want. Do you want happiness? Do you want a cure for insomnia? Do you want peace? Do you want guidance? Here it is. It is so simple, it is all for you, for nothing.' And people fall for it and accept it.

No, no! The knowledge and the life must never be separated. We must believe and come to know that Jesus is the Christ, the Son of God, and we must give proof that we really do believe it and know it by manifesting life! His life! The thrilling life of God in our own souls and in our ordinary practice and behaviour. That is the thing, says John, that is why I am writing this Gospel to you – that you may know this.

Now at the present time people object to doctrine and do not like the order in which John puts these things. They say that they do not have time to read, that doctrine is too difficult, that they cannot understand it. It seems to me that in a church service people expect an address of just a pleasant little ten or fifteen minutes. No more: they cannot take any more. They do not want high doctrine. They say, 'We want something to help us to live. Life is difficult, you know, we haven't got time to be bothered with all these doctrines of yours. Does it matter what people believe as long as somehow or another they feel that Christ helps them?' That is the argument today. Believe what you like as long as you get some help out of it. We decide what we want, and we must have it, and if we do not get it, we are annoyed and will not take anything else. That is the whole attitude, and it is condemned utterly in the New Testament from beginning to end. Listen: 'Evil communications corrupt good manners' (*1 Cor.* 15:33). If you go wrong about the resurrection, says Paul in 1 Corinthians 15, you will very soon go wrong in your life. If you are not right about the fundamentals of your faith, your whole life will go astray. We must start with doctrine.

Christian people, do you object to doctrine? Do you object to high doctrine about the Son of God, about his person and about his work? Do you think that the Christian church is a place where you just get that little bit of comfort and solace and no more? Is that it? Well, just as we are and with all that we are facing, do you know what John gives us? Listen to this: he gives us the Prologue to this Gospel. Here are modern men and women. They are so proud of themselves with all their learning, all their scientific advances, all their philosophy and so on, and yet when they come to the matter of going to church, they say, 'Now don't give us doctrine and theology, we can't take it. We can't reason. We don't have the time. We want comfort. We want help.'

Yet nearly two thousand years ago, to these hard-pressed slaves and servants, as most of them were, to these people who were being persecuted and were face to face with death, John said: 'In the beginning was the Word, and the Word was with God, and the Word was God.' These mighty paradoxes, this high and exalted doctrine! It is in all the New Testament epistles; it is the same in every single one of them. And I am calling your attention to this because it is the only answer to our condition. We are all suffering from ignorance – ignorance of the Christian faith, ignorance with respect to what we are supposed to believe. That is our main trouble. Our problem is not something subjective, primarily; it is lack of understanding. So we must start with doctrine, and out of that will come the life, the experience, the everything that we need. We cannot get it without taking the apostolic approach.

Now all this is so important because the Christian message is that Christ is the Saviour and that the whole of salvation is in him and comes from him – not primarily in his teaching but by what he did and who he was. This is what makes doctrine so crucial. Christian salvation is not a matter of reading the teaching of Christ and then going out and trying to practise it. That is a denial of the gospel. People who say to me that they can put into practice the Sermon on the Mount are already telling me that they are not Christians. You cannot live the Sermon on the Mount until you are a Christian. You have to be made a Christian first. So we must start with the person of the Lord Jesus Christ, this blessed person himself. He is the Saviour; he is the salvation. It is 'of his fulness' that we have all received and 'grace for [upon] grace' (*John* 1:16). So can you see the importance of doctrine? Was Jesus of Nazareth a man only? Well, if he was, then he cannot be my Saviour. Adam was perfect but Adam fell. Create another perfect man and he will also fail. It takes more than a man to save me. So I am bound to be concerned about the doctrine of the person of Christ.

'But,' someone may ask, 'if he was truly a man, then was he a sinful man? You say that he was a man, you say that the Word was made flesh, and dwelt among us, that he was born of the Virgin Mary. But she was a sinful woman like everybody else; everybody is born in sin and "shapen in iniquity". He was born of the Virgin Mary, was he therefore sinful? Was his human nature sinful?'

Is that an irrelevant question? Is that something that is of no importance to the Christian believer? My dear friend, your whole salvation depends upon these issues. If he was a sinful person, he had to save himself, and no man can save himself. So the Bible is very careful to answer that question and to tell us that he was not sinful.

But then someone may say, 'Was he only God? Were the Docetics right? Was Jesus of Nazareth God with a kind of phantom body? Did he never really become man? Was he never truly "made flesh"?'

Is that an irrelevant question? Let me show you the relevance of all these matters. If our Lord was nothing but God and never became truly man, then how can he represent me? What I and the whole human race need is a representative who is one of us and who understands us, who can take our burden upon himself and can stand as our representative before God. Adam was the representative of the whole of humanity. I need a new representative. Yes, but because I am human, my representative must be human. So I am very concerned about this. I must know whether he was God in a phantom body or whether he truly became incarnate.

Not only that; doctrine helps me in another way. I need someone who can help me in my temptations and in my infirmities. Here we are, like those first Christians, in all the trials and the difficulties of life. As I have been reminding you, they were having a hard time and John says: Here is the doctrine of the person of Christ.

'How did that help them?' you say.

It helped like this: '[He] was in all points tempted like as we are, yet without sin' (*Heb.* 4:15). Our Lord went through it all, he suffered it all, he was truly man. All my comfort in him as a sympathetic high priest vanishes if he was not truly man as well as truly God.

And then there are other questions. When our Lord came into the world, did he cease to be God? There is a heresy that says that he emptied himself of his Godhead, and was no longer eternal God but only a man. I have already touched on the relevance of that to the whole problem of my personal salvation. It is foolish to say that doctrine does not matter to me, that all I need is a bit of direct help and comfort. My answer to all that is, I say again, that salvation all comes from him and through him.

So, then, the first thing I must be certain about is our Lord himself. I must know exactly who he is and what he has done: the meaning of his death, for instance. Was that just the death of a pacifist or of a martyr? Was it just the death of an honest person who was not going to recant and withdraw his teaching? Is that the thing that saves me? Is that the thing that delivers me and reconciles me to God? Was he just a man loyal to his principles and teaching? This is the most vital question under the sun for me as I am concerned about my soul and my salvation. I want life! How does he give me life? You see, every one of these questions is theological, doctrinal. And John deals with them because he knows full well that if men and women are not right and clear in their understanding of the Lord Jesus Christ, they will go altogether wrong. They may find some temporary comfort, or a kind of cult, the 'Jesus cult', even, but it will be of no value to them. You must be right, John says, about this fundamental truth. So he starts with the doctrine.

Now it is not my intention to take you in detail through all the great doctrines. I am just here to show you that unless we have this understanding that John talks about, then we have nothing at all. So let us just glance at it. Let me give you my headings as we close. What should be my chief concern as a Christian? The answer is: To know him, and to know who he is. Now I forget my aches and pains, I forget my insomnia and everything else. If he is what the Bible claims he is, he can deliver me; he can deliver me from anything and everything.

One thing I want to know, then, is: Who is he? And I am given the answer. He is the eternal God! 'In the beginning was the Word, and the Word was with God, and the Word was God. The same was in the beginning with God.' Jesus of Nazareth! Eternal from the beginning, eternally in the presence of his heavenly Father, face to face with God the Father! That is what John tells me. Are you too busy to take it in? How do you think those slaves two thousand years ago took it in? You do not have the time? Of course you have! Apply your mind, my friend.

As you value your life and all your witness in this world and your eternal destiny, make certain that you are secure about these doctrines. Eternal God! Only begotten – coming out of the Father eternally! He is not a creature. Not only that, he is 'the Word of God', which means that he is always the expression of the Godhead. He is always the one who is manifesting and revealing the Godhead.

But what else? He is the Creator: 'All things were made by him; and without him was not any thing made that was made' (*John* 1:3). God's plan, of course, is the ultimate, and he is the ultimate planner of creation. But the executive in creation is the Son of God. This is taught constantly in the Scriptures. You remember that great declaration of this truth in the Epistle to the Hebrews. The writer says, '[God] hath in these last days spoken unto us by his Son, whom he hath appointed heir of all things, by whom also he made the worlds' (*Heb.* 1:2). He is the Creator. He is also the source of all spiritual life and light and understanding. 'In him was life; and the life was the light of men. And the light shineth in darkness' (*John* 1:4–5). Here it is: there is no spiritual life apart from this person. There is no knowledge of God, no eternal life in the soul. 'And this is life eternal, that they might know thee the only true God, and Jesus Christ, whom thou hast sent' (*John* 17:3).

Eternal life is not an experience, primarily. It is to know him and to receive of him. That is how the Bible teaches it. So you do not start with yourself and your experiences; you look at him. It is the knowledge of him that gives you this life. Here he is, then – eternal God! Everlasting Word! Creator! Source of all spiritual power and all spiritual life and existence! And the message is that this one came into the world. The apostle John, speaking of John the Baptist, says: 'He was not that Light, but was sent to bear witness of that Light. That was the true Light, which lighteth every man that cometh into the world' (*John* 1:8–9).

Now, says John, this is what you need to lay hold of, this is what you really must grasp.

You say you have believed it. All right. But do you realize what you are believing? Here is this everlasting God, the second Person in the blessed Holy Trinity. He is 'the only begotten Son, which is in the bosom of the Father' (*John* 1:18). There he is, the Creator of the universe, the source of all life and light and knowledge in a spiritual sense. What is the message? Oh, that this one has come into the world! John is not the saviour. Philosophy – Plato, Socrates, Aristotle, these are not saviours. This one coming into the world! 'The Word was made flesh, and dwelt among us' (*John* 1:14). He came and he lived here for a while. He was still God but he was truly man. He had a human soul; he was one of us. He is truly man; he is truly God. Not man in sinful flesh but in the 'likeness' of sinful flesh. Not born out of ordinary wedlock; born of a virgin, born miraculously, 'conceived of the Holy Ghost'! This is what we are to know. All this is of crucial significance and importance. This one came and was born as a babe in Bethlehem. All this is involved, says John.

And this one who came into the world has gone back. He was here: 'And the Word was made flesh, and dwelt [tabernacled, tented] among us, (and we beheld his glory, the glory as of the only begotten of the Father,) full of grace and truth' (*John* 1:14). This is what we need to know. This is the one who has come to save us. This is our hope. This is my only comfort and consolation: 'I have laid help upon one that is mighty' (*Psa.* 89:19). People cannot help me; they cannot help themselves. No man can ever save himself, no man can atone for his sins or erase his past sins. I do not want teaching only: I cannot apply it. I need someone who can take hold of me. I need someone who can deliver me. I need someone who can put life into me. Here he is! The source of it all. God in the flesh. 'The Word was made flesh, and dwelt among us.'

Now that is the way in which John proceeds to comfort these early Christians, and it is the only consolation that is adequate to our condition. It is the message that we stand urgently in need of. Do you really believe this, my friend? Do you really believe that God 'hath visited and redeemed his people' (*Luke* 1:68)? Do you really believe that the Son of God left the courts of heaven temporarily in order to come down on earth to give you *life*? Is that what we believe? How, then, can we be as we are? Why is it that we are not on fire? Why is it that we are not aflame? Why is it that we are not exulting and glorying? Why is it that we are not manifesting this life? Why is it that we are not lost in a sense of wonder and of love and of praise? How can we take these things so much for granted? How can we regard them as something almost ordinary? How can we talk so much about ourselves and so little about him? How can we talk so much about our needs and so little about his fulness? These are the questions we need to answer.

Do we truly believe in him? Unless we are moved to the depths of our beings by the Lord Jesus Christ himself, how can we say we believe? How can we grumble and complain, how can we be marasmic and almost lifeless, if we really believe this? My friend, turn your eyes away from yourself. Look to him, look at him, and stay there until you have seen him and know him and you are amazed and astonished. And you will find that you will be filled with life, life anew, life that is life indeed, life that is life eternal. The comfort you need, the help we all need, is this: 'In the beginning was the Word, and the Word was with God, and the Word was God . . . And the Word was made flesh, and dwelt among us.' ∾

2

The Light and the Darkness

And the light shineth in darkness; and the darkness comprehended it not (John 1:5).

We have been considering the fact that so many of us who are Christians are failing to show forth the glory and the wonder of the gospel. This is important, not only for our own sakes, but still more because of the whole state and condition of the world that is round and about us. Christians, as is obvious from the New Testament, are meant to be a rejoicing people. They are partakers of this 'so great salvation' (*Heb.* 2:3). They are people, therefore, who should 'rejoice evermore' (*1 Thess.* 5:16). That is the terminology used in the New Testament itself and if we are not in that condition, if we are not giving the impression to the world that we are in this happy position, then we are very defective as Christians and we are missing so much that God offers to us freely through his dear Son, our Lord and Saviour.

So the question is: Why are we not rejoicing? And I have suggested that the first reason – and obviously this is put in the first position by the apostle John – is our failure to realize the truth concerning our Lord and Saviour. We accept it, we say we believe it, but we fail to realize exactly what it is. We somehow tend constantly to lose the thrill and the wonder and the amazement that it invariably produces when it is truly realized. For instance, how many of us can say quite honestly out of our hearts and from our experience at this moment that we feel, like the great apostle Paul, that when we look at this truth, we must simply cry out, 'Great is the mystery of godliness: God was manifest in the flesh, justified in the Spirit, seen of angels, preached unto the Gentiles, believed on in the world, received up into glory' (*1 Tim.* 3:16)?

Now that was the typical reaction of the apostle Paul himself, as it was of so many who we read of in the New Testament – this sense of astonishment that God should be so concerned about us. This is the great theme of John's Gospel: 'God so loved the world, that he gave his only begotten Son' (*John* 3:16). Salvation is in the Son of God. It is not in a man. It is not in a theory. It was the Son of God who came: 'The Word was made flesh, and dwelt among us.' We must recapture that wonder, we must feel about it as the biblical writers felt and as God's people have felt through the centuries. Look at the number of hymns devoted to the person of our Lord, to his praise and to singing his glory. According to John's teaching, this is the first great essential. We do not need some psychological treatment in order to make us happy. What we need is doctrine. We need to know the truth that we say we believe and to take a firm hold of it.

But that is not the only thing. Let us look at it like this. Why did the Son of God ever come into this world? Why was there ever any need for him to do so? Why was it that the world was not saved by the law given through Moses? Why was the world not saved by the teaching of the prophets? Why was the Son of God, the Word, ever 'made flesh'? What accounts for the fact that though this took place, though this is an event belonging to history, the world is indifferent to it? And why is it that we who claim and profess his name are oftentimes so lethargic and unhappy and struggling and striving and failing to manifest forth this sense of wonder and astonishment?

Now that is the second great theme that John immediately puts before us in this introduction, this Prologue, to his Gospel. He puts it very strikingly in the fifth verse: 'And the light shineth in darkness' – under darkness – 'and the darkness comprehended it not.' There is the answer.

The second cause of trouble, in other words, is that there is something wrong with us. We are not only wrong in our failure to understand the Lord Jesus Christ as we ought, but we also fail to realize the truth concerning ourselves, and these two failures, of course, operate together. And that is why the apostle proceeds to give us an explanation and exposition of this whole matter.

Now you notice the dramatic way in which John introduces this subject. There is a kind of abruptness about it, an abruptness that is characteristic of the writing of this particular apostle. He starts with an amazing description of our Lord and Saviour: he is 'the Word of God', the expression, the eternal expression, of the Godhead. He is God. He is God the Son. And yet there is this distinction. He was 'with' the Father, looking into the face of the Father, as it were – this great doctrine of the blessed Holy Trinity. And then the apostle reminds us that 'all things were made by him; and without him was not any thing made that was made'. He was the instrument of creation. And John goes on to say, 'In him was life; and the life was the light of men.' He was the author, the origin, of all life. But, particularly, he is the light of men, the one who gives us all spiritual knowledge and understanding. It is through him that we received, at the original creation, the image of God. And the apostle John is glorying in all this. But suddenly there comes this fifth verse: 'And the light shineth in darkness; and the darkness comprehended it not.' And immediately a question is raised: What is this darkness? Where has it come from? And thus the apostle introduces this theme, this essential theme, concerning the nature of man.

Now the argument can be put like this: there are two things that are basic to our full enjoyment of the Christian gospel. The first is what God has done in his Son; the second is our need for all that – the biblical doctrine of man in a fallen, sinful state, the biblical doctrine of sin. And the two obviously go together. If we have an inadequate doctrine of sin, we shall never see our need for the coming of the Son of God. That is the trouble with people who do not believe in the deity of Christ and regard him as just a teacher and an exemplar. Their real trouble is that they do not see that they need something more than a teacher. They say, 'All we need is instruction, education and knowledge.' And they say that because they are defective in their understanding of themselves and of the condition of humanity.

Now this is the picture that John gives us. There is the original creation – the creation of man in particular. He has been made lord over creation; he has been endowed with faculties that are part of the image of God. He has a mind; he has reason; he has understanding; he has self-knowledge; he is capable of fellowship and communion with God. Now that is the light. Christ is the light of all people. It is because we are made in the image and likeness of God that all that was true of man at the beginning. Man had light and he enjoyed the light, and so he enjoyed fellowship and communion with God. But then immediately we realize that that is no longer true of men and women, that is no longer true of the world. This world is no longer paradise. It is no longer a place of light. There is an entirely new situation.

The characteristic of the world at the present moment is darkness. John tells us that that is indeed the trouble, that this light about which he has been speaking is now to be found shining in darkness. And there at once he puts before us the whole position. 'All things were made by him; and without him was not any thing made that was made.' It was made perfectly; God looked upon it and saw that it was good. It was all a manifestation of this light and this life. But it is no longer like that; it has become darkness.

So here we are face to face with this great basic teaching that runs through the whole Bible. Why is the world as it is? Why is there this darkness? Now that is the question that should be engaging the thinking of all people who are concerned about the days in which we are living. And there is only one adequate answer: the fall of man. This is something that is universal. We are so accustomed to dividing up the world into countries and nations and continents that we tend to forget the much more important and vital fact that the whole world is one. Underneath all the divisions and the distinctions there is one common element, this element of darkness, this element of failure, this element of utter confusion. The differences in civilizations and cultures and anything else you can think of, no matter what it may be, do not make the slightest difference at all. There is this universal element of disturbance, turmoil, ignorance and lack of ease. And, I repeat, the only adequate explanation is the biblical doctrine of the fall of man.

Here is man, created perfect, having the light. He does not have it now – why not? It is because there has been a fall; and that is what is described at the very beginning of the Bible, in the third chapter of the book of Genesis. You just do not begin to understand world history, apart from anything else, if you do not believe that. You do not understand the world today, you do not understand the meaning of the contradiction that is in life at this present time, unless you accept that. Why is it that all the efforts of man to lift himself up always fail? It is because the whole world of man has fallen, fallen away from God. And so it is now true to say that the light that is in Christ is shining in the midst of darkness. The prophet Isaiah says, 'For, behold, the darkness shall cover the earth, and gross darkness the people' (*Isa.* 60:2). It is all implicit in this fifth verse of John's Prologue. Suddenly, having been talking about the light and the life, John introduces this element of darkness, and the darkness is only to be explained in that way. We need not go into the details now because what I am concerned about is that we should realize something of the consequences of this darkness that has come into the lives of men and women and into the life of this world. There has been a universal fall, so that all nations, all people, all cultures, are fundamentally in the same position and are suffering from the same central need.

The question before us, therefore, is this: What does this darkness mean? 'The light shineth in darkness,' says John. All who are familiar with the Bible will be very familiar with this term. It is used by all the biblical writers. This same John, writing to Christians, says in his first epistle, 'The darkness is past' (*1 John* 2:8). 'You have come out of it,' he says, in effect, 'because you are Christians.' The apostle Paul is equally fond of this term. He says: 'Ye are all the children of light, and the children of the day: we are not of the night, nor of darkness' (*1 Thess.* 5:5). Writing to the Ephesians, he talks about 'the unfruitful works of darkness' (*Eph.* 5:11) and says, 'Ye were sometimes darkness, but now are ye light in the Lord' (*Eph.* 5:8). I could go on – there is almost no end to the number of quotations – 'darkness' is the universal description in the New Testament of the state and condition of human beings by nature.

Let me, then, try to divide this subject by putting it like this. People as they are by nature, as they are born into this world, are in darkness;

the whole world is in this darkness. Here we are in the darkness that is round and about us, and this light is shining into the darkness. So what is this darkness? It is essentially, of course, the darkness of ignorance. We talk about people being 'enlightened' and we say that we can 'throw light' on to a subject. That is just a metaphorical way of saying that 'darkness' means a fundamental ignorance, a lack of knowledge. And this is the whole trouble with the world at this moment. This is the only explanation of our present problems and difficulties.

What is man, by nature, ignorant of? John says: 'No man hath seen God at any time; the only begotten Son, which is in the bosom of the Father, he hath declared him' (*John* 1:18). The fundamental trouble is ignorance of God. There is no excuse for that, as Paul shows so plainly in Romans, where he says that man, if he had eyes to see, would understand from creation alone that God is. God's 'eternal power and Godhead', Paul says, should have been obvious: 'For the invisible things of him from the creation of the world are clearly seen, being understood by the things that are made, even his eternal power and Godhead; so that they are without excuse' (*Rom.* 1:20). Paul means that God has revealed himself by everything that he has made. He reveals himself in nature, in the flowers, in the leaves, in all creation. You cannot say that all this has come about by accident and chance – all this perfect order and arrangement, the design, the pattern, the repetition, all that people call 'the laws of nature'.

Now the alternative to believing in God the Creator is to believe that this world is the result of accident and chance, that these things just happened. But how can chance produce such regularity? No, no! There is only one answer – there is a great mind behind it all and that is God, the mind of God, as John has been telling us in the Prologue. 'All things', he says, 'were made by him; and without him was not any thing made that was made.' But the world is unaware of this. It does not even learn the lesson that creation should teach it.

And, in the same way, if men and women could see clearly, if they exercised their powers as they were meant to, they would be able to deduce from providence that there must be a God at the back of everything. And the same is true of history. The history of the Jews, in particular, simply cannot be explained except in these terms. But people do not realize that. Therefore, 'they are without excuse' – and the apostle Paul means that they should realize it, but they do not. They are unaware of the fact that God is over all, they do not know about the character of God – his mighty power, the eternity of God, the holiness of God, the majesty of God. They do not know that God is the Judge eternal and that the world is God's world. They always think in terms of themselves. They think it is their world. And so they imagine that it is only what they do in the world and to the world that counts and makes any difference. But that is the fundamental fallacy.

Men and women thus looking at themselves as lords and gods have been trying throughout the running centuries to solve their problems by means of civilization. But because this is not their world, they do not succeed, they cannot. Already they are wrong! They do not realize that God has made the world in a given way, that he has made it to work on certain rules, that it is bound to function in that way and cannot function in any other way. And people are thus struggling against the law of nature and of their own being, and they find themselves in endless confusion and frustration. There is no hope for the world until they realize the truth about God: that he is over all, that he remains the same, that his laws and principles remain the same and that everything is subject unto him. How much time and thought and attention do you think is being given to that aspect of the matter in this world in which we find ourselves?

But then men and women are equally ignorant about themselves. This, to me, is the great tragedy of the present time. Those who are trying to exalt themselves are at the same time insulting themselves, and they are doing this by not realizing their own true greatness. They are proud of the fact that they are just animals. That is the amazing thing! It is a curious fact that they should be proud of their theory of evolution, which states that human beings have evolved from nothing up through the animals, that they are just a particular branch of the anthropoid and so on. They are proud of this and do not realize that in that pride they are insulting themselves. They do not know that man has been made in the image of God and is different from all else in creation. They do not realize that the Father, Son and Holy Spirit spoke among themselves and said, 'Let us make man in our image, after [according to] our likeness' (*Gen.* 1:26). There is this uniqueness about man. He has a soul. He is not just an animal and he is not just in this world to enjoy himself. No, no! 'The chief end of man is to glorify God and enjoy him for ever' (The *Westminster Shorter Catechism*). He was made as a companion for God, and God made him lord over all. God gave him some of his own prerogatives and powers. That is man! But modern men and women do not think of themselves like that and it is not surprising, therefore, that their world is in darkness and in terrible trouble.

Men and women think of themselves only as animals, and they think, therefore, of satisfaction for the animal part of their lives. Their real interest in putting an end to war is so that they may have peace to go on sinning. That is why they are against war – it just disturbs their good times, it is an interruption, a nuisance. And work is becoming a nuisance, too. What men and women want is money in order to enjoy themselves and anything that interrupts that enjoyment is annoying, hence most of our troubles at this moment. All this is the result of the fact that people do not realize the truth about themselves – that each person has a soul and belongs to God and the spiritual realm, that they are to be above and over all these things instead of living to them and being governed by them. They are in the dark about themselves as much as they are about God, and they do not know how to live, therefore; they have no idea of true living. They regard the worship of God as a bore, as dull and uninteresting. There are many who regard it as stupid and an anachronism and would think that we are fools to gather in a building such as this at this hour.

And, in the same way, men and women are utterly and completely in the dark about the world and its history, about the meaning of the world and the meaning of time. They do not know that God has made this world for his own glory, for his own purposes, that he set the process going, this process of time. The world is not just something that happens by accident. Everything is part of a plan and on a definite programme and the time element is of the most urgent importance.

In their ignorance and darkness people do not realize that there is an end to this time process and that beyond that there is the judgment of God. Man has wandered away; he has fallen from his original position where he shared the mind of God and the secrets of God and where he had understanding. He has lost it and is thus in the dark about God and himself, the world in which he is living and the destiny and the object of it all. All this is what John is saying in this one verse: 'The light shineth in darkness.'

And there is something, it seems to me, that is even more serious. It is true of man not only that is he in the dark, but that the darkness is also in him. And this is the most terrible thing of all. He is in an atmosphere of darkness, yes, but the atmosphere has penetrated into him. John pays very special attention to this in his Prologue, as I shall show you.

'What do you mean,' says someone, 'by saying that the darkness is in man?'

I mean, partly, that man shows that the darkness is in him by the very way in which he thinks; his whole process of thinking has become dark. There is a verse that puts this perfectly: 'And God saw that the wickedness of man was great in the earth, and that every imagination of the thoughts of his heart was only evil continually' (*Gen.* 6:5). The darkness has entered into the very mind of man. The human mind, which was originally light and enlightened and could think in a straight and right manner, is no longer capable of that. Read again that vivid and terrifying passage from the first chapter of the Epistle to the Romans. I have heard preachers say that that portion of Scripture should never be read in public. What utter nonsense! I would almost say that today it should be read every Sunday in order that we may begin to understand the world in which we are living. You read all this in your newspapers, do you not? Well, here it is, the Bible has prophesied it. The Bible knows all about it and says: This is your world. It is a world in which people's minds are twisted and perverted.

Think of the instrument that God has given man – the brain, this power to reason and comprehend and understand – but look at the uses to which man is putting it. That is because the darkness has entered into the very mechanism of human thinking and reasoning and understanding, and so men and women are playing and toying with evil thoughts, evil imaginations and evil desires. The whole world is in a state of moral confusion because of the darkness that is in man. Our Lord himself was constantly emphasizing this. He said that it is not that which goes into the mouth that defiles a man but that which comes out of him: 'For from within, out of the heart of men, proceed evil thoughts, adulteries, fornications, murders . . .' (*Mark* 7:21). 'For I know that in me', says Paul, '(that is, in my flesh,) dwelleth no good thing' (*Rom.* 7:18). That is man as the result of the fall; the darkness has entered into him: 'For ye were sometimes darkness' (*Eph.* 5:8). Not only were you in the dark, but your mind and your thoughts were dark.

But the darkness is equally clear in the realm of what man likes and loves, in the realm of the affections. John puts it like this: 'And this is the condemnation, that light is come into the world, and men loved darkness rather than light, because their deeds were evil' (*John* 3:19). They loved it! There is no question at all about it. The world loves its way of life. It loves its sin; it delights in it; it boasts of it; it gloats over it. Again, that is because the darkness has entered in. Here is man, a creature made in the image of God, given an original righteousness, holy, innocent, without any sin or blemish, thinking the thoughts of God and communing with God in the garden. But look at people today. Look at what they lust after and crave for. Look at what they delight in. The darkness has entered into the human constitution. It affects not only the mind, but the heart, too.

And in exactly the same way, the darkness affects what man does; it affects the will. 'And God saw that the wickedness of man was great in the earth' (*Gen.* 6:5). Now that horrible description refers to the time before the Flood. Man, made perfect, had degenerated to that condition and then the world was destroyed, but a family was saved, and on it goes. But very soon the world was back in the same condition. In that first chapter of the Epistle to the Romans the apostle Paul is simply giving a terrible summary of history. Look at the darkness in Sodom and Gomorrah. Look at this darkness in the modern world; look at it in the great cities; look at it in the villages at the present time, in this land and in other lands. Here it is – we are back in the second half of Romans 1. Why? Because that is the sort of life that men and women are living. Their wills are twisted and perverted. There is nothing in them that has not fallen and is not being vitiated by this darkness. 'The light shineth in darkness.' Is that not true at this moment? Is not the light of this gospel shining in a dark land at this present time? Throughout the whole world we see nothing but this darkness, this 'gross darkness' (*Isa.* 60:2), over the eyes of the people, and the consequent muddle and confusion and even hopelessness and despair.

But there is something that is even worse than all I have said. The most terrible thing about the darkness that has entered into human beings is that it makes them incapable of recognizing the light even when it is shown to them. It is bad enough that they should be thinking and desiring and willing as they do, but the terrible thing is that even when the light comes, they cannot see it. That is the meaning of this verse, 'The light shineth in darkness; and the darkness comprehended it not.' I am reading the Authorized [King James] Version. You will find that modern versions, the Revised Standard Version and the New English Bible and others, translate this verse as 'the darkness overcame it not', or something like that. But I want to argue for the correctness of the translation given by the Authorized Version: 'comprehended', or 'apprehended', gives, I believe, the true meaning because it brings out this terrible further consequence of the fall of man.

The translation 'comprehended' is also in line with what we are told in verses 10 and 11. John is saying the same thing in all three verses. 'The light shineth in darkness; and the darkness comprehended it not' – there is the general statement. Then he divides it up in verses 10 and 11: 'He was in the world, and the world was made by him, and the world knew him not' (verse 10) and, 'He came unto his own' – the Jews – 'and his own received him not' (verse 11). The three statements go together. Why make a different point in verse 5 and say that the darkness did not 'quench' it, or the darkness did not 'overcome' it, or the darkness did not 'master' it? That is an extraneous thought. John is trying to show us that though the light is there, the world, in its darkness within and without, does not recognize it and is incapable of seeing it.

Now, of course, translating verse 5 in this way also puts it in line with the teaching that we get much more explicitly elsewhere, in a passage, for instance, such as 1 Corinthians 2:7–8: 'We speak the wisdom of God in a mystery, even the hidden wisdom, which God ordained before the world unto our glory: which none of the princes of this world knew: for had they known it, they would not have crucified the Lord of glory.' There it is in a perfect form. The tragedy, says the apostle, is that though God's own Son came into the world, his people, because they were in darkness and darkness was in them, could not recognize him, could not see it, could not get it. You would have thought that the Pharisees and scribes, of all people, would have recognized him, but they were the ones who did not. The light was shining before them, but they, 'the princes of this world', were utterly incapable of recognizing and appreciating and receiving the light. And this, of course is the verdict upon our world at this present time. The vast majority of people in this country do not believe this gospel. Why not? Well, they say, because of their 'enlightenment', because they are educated and cultured. But the real answer is that they are blind. They do not believe because the darkness that is in them makes them incapable of believing. They cannot recognize the light even when it shines before them in the face of Jesus Christ.

But, even worse, men and women in darkness not only cannot recognize the light, they hate and despise it. Look again at John 3:19–20: 'This is the condemnation, that light is come into the world, and men loved darkness rather than light, because their deeds were evil. For every one that doeth evil hateth the light, neither cometh to the light, lest his deeds should be reproved.' Now this is the extraordinary thing. Do we realize the depth of sin and iniquity? Are you not now beginning to see why the Word had to be made flesh? What is the point of giving teaching to people who hate the light? No, no! Knowledge and instruction can never save such people.

Read the pages of these four Gospels and you will find that when our blessed Lord was here, people said, 'Thou hast a devil' (*John* 7:20); 'He hath Beelzebub' (*Mark* 3:22); 'This man blasphemeth' (*Matt.* 9:3) – the Son of God in all his perfection, in all his glory, the Word made flesh shining in his glory! The apostles, who had been enlightened, said, 'And we beheld his glory, the glory as of the only begotten of the Father, full of grace and truth' (*John* 1:14). But the Pharisees said, 'This fellow! Away with him! Crucify him! He's a blasphemer, get rid of him.' Not only did they not recognize the truth, they hated it, they despised it. Listen to the way the apostle Paul puts this: 'But the natural man' – that is, man as he is born into the world, man in the darkness – 'receiveth not the things of the Spirit of God: for they are foolishness unto him: neither can he know them, because they are spiritually discerned' (*1 Cor.* 2:14). And is that not still the trouble?

The problem is not merely that men and women do not recognize the Lord and his teaching and his salvation, but that they despise it. They despise the blood of Christ in particular and pour contempt upon it. They hate the doctrine of the atonement. They look at the doctrine of the rebirth with disdain. They regard it as utter folly and will not have anything to do with it. If you give people moral and ethical teaching, they will say they are very interested. Why? Ah, they think they can keep that, but they know that the truth about the Lord condemns them and they hate it and finally reject it.

And here it is all before us in the Prologue: 'The light shineth in darkness; and the darkness comprehended it not . . . He was in the world, and the world was made by him, and the world knew him not. He came unto his own, and his own received him not.' And so the Lord said in his high-priestly prayer, 'O righteous Father, the world hath not known thee' (*John* 17:25). And the world does not know his people. It does not recognize them. It has persecuted them throughout the centuries. Our Lord said, 'I am come in my Father's name, and ye receive me not: if another shall come in his own name, him ye will receive' (*John* 5:43), and that is what the world has been doing. It idolizes its great men, its statesmen, its philosophers, its kings and queens and princes. But when the Lord of glory comes, it does not receive him. And that is entirely owing to the fact that it is dark and in the darkness. Men and women are in the dark and the darkness is in them, in the very vitals of their being. But the extraordinary and the glorious thing that we are told is this: 'The light shineth in darkness.' It goes on in spite of the darkness. And it is the only light. There is no philosophy or human teaching that can deal with such a predicament, and we have it on record that 'the world by wisdom knew not God' (*1 Cor.* 1:21).

The Greek philosophers were seeking him, 'if haply they might feel after him' (*Acts* 17:27), but they could not find him. The greatest brains have never arrived at God: they never will. There is only one light that can give us light on God. 'No man hath seen God at any time; the only begotten Son, which is in the bosom of the Father, he hath declared him.' He alone can declare him, and he alone can give us light on every problem that we have. And this has been true from the beginning. Man rebelled against God and fell and became enshrouded by darkness and the darkness entered his own soul. But, thank God, God came down into the garden in the cool of the evening and gave the promise of the seed of the woman that should bruise the serpent's head (*Gen.* 3:15). The light was shining in the darkness of a fallen Eden.

What is the Old Testament? Oh, it is nothing but the light shining in the darkness. Look at Noah in the days before the Flood, for one hundred and twenty years building his ark, pleading with these people; look at Lot grieving in Sodom and Gomorrah. What is this? Oh, it is the glimmer of light, the light of Jesus Christ shining in the darkness. Noah, Lot, Abraham, the patriarchs, the whole nation of Israel, the prophets – it is the light shining in the darkness. There was no other light, but the light went on shining, the light from Christ. It is all from him and it is all about him. He is the light: 'In him was life; and the life was the light of men. And the light shineth in darkness' – and on it goes.

And eventually Christ comes, and he says, 'I am the light of the world: he that followeth me shall not walk in darkness, but shall have the light of life' (*John* 8:12); and, 'Yet a little while is the light with you' (*John* 12:35). And then he goes, but he leaves a body of people, twelve ordinary, uneducated men, and he says, 'Ye are the light of the world' (*Matt.* 5:14). I am making you the light of the world. You will reflect me. I will fill you with my Spirit and you will shed forth this light that is mine. You are the light of the world because I am the light of the world.

And Christ has gone on shining. There on the road to Damascus he shone into the heart of a rebel called Saul of Tarsus, who hated him, blasphemed him, who thought he was all wrong and did his best to exterminate his cause. But suddenly the light shone into Saul's heart, and so he says: 'For God, who commanded the light to shine out of darkness, hath shined in our hearts, to give the light of the knowledge of the glory of God in the face of Jesus Christ' (2 Cor. 4:6). It takes light from heaven to enlighten our darkness, to give us understanding and knowledge, and this light comes from the blessed Light. And he is still sending his light. God sent his Holy Spirit upon the church in order that she might be made an agency for disseminating the light, shining it forth. And you and I as Christian people are those who have received the light, who have been enlightened: 'For ye were sometimes darkness, but now are ye light in the Lord: walk as children of light,' says the apostle Paul (Eph. 5:8).

Is it not obvious that we must understand these matters if we are to enjoy the full blessings of this great Christian gospel of salvation? Why is it, I ask again, that we are not thrilled at the thought of this salvation? Why does this not bring us to our feet? Why does this not fill us with such a sense of exultation and rejoicing that we can scarcely contain it? Why is the church lifeless and lethargic? I have suggested to you the two main reasons: we have not beheld sufficient of his glory and we have never realized the depth of the iniquity and the darkness out of which he has rescued us.

A light view of sin always leads to a superficial salvation and to a superficial Christian life. You have got to measure the heights of his glory, you have got to measure the depth of your own natural iniquity and darkness. And as you get the two, you will then begin to see something of the wonder of his grace. May God enable us to realize that if we are Christians it is because the light is shining into our darkness, the darkness that was so deep that we could not even recognize the light, the darkness that was so deep that it made us hate the light, the darkness that was so deep that it made us reject the light. But the light is shining. It has penetrated the darkness and has given us this blessed illumination, and we have come to know him, whom to know is light and life and glory. ❧

3

The Relationship of Law and Grace

For the law was given by Moses, but grace and truth came by Jesus Christ (John 1:17).

I am calling your attention to this passage, the Prologue to John's Gospel, let me remind you, because it seems obvious to me that somewhere or another we in the Christian church are failing, that somehow or other we have gone astray. Far too often we give the impression that the main effect of Christianity upon us is to make us miserable and to take something from us. As a result, the world appears to be happier than the church, a view that, of course, is misleading and wrong. Therefore it behoves us to examine ourselves to discover the cause of our condition. Are we rejoicing in the Lord? Can we say that we have all things and abound because we are in him? My suggestion is that if that is not our state and condition, it is essentially due to our failure to realize the truth concerning our Lord and what he has made possible for us by his work on our behalf. So we are examining this and we have seen that the apostle John divides it up in various ways.

The first aspect we had to consider was an inadequate view of the person himself, the person of our Lord. It is almost incredible, but it is so true, that there are many of us who, though we are Christians, somehow seem to forget that the Son of God has literally come into this world in order to save us and to give us a share in this great salvation. Then we came to the second aspect, which is emphasized in the fourth verse: 'In him was life; and the life was the light of men.' He is the light. But we also saw this: 'And the light shineth in darkness; and the darkness comprehended it not.' Though the Word was made flesh and dwelt among us, the world did not recognize him or receive him. 'He came unto his own' – the Jews – 'and his own received him not.' And this was because of the darkness, the darkness in which they dwelt and the darkness that was in them. This is still the trouble with the world today and the extent to which you and I are failing to recognize his glory and to realize what he has done for us and to rejoice in it – that is the measure of the darkness that still remains in us.

But now we come on to a different aspect of this matter, another theme, another subdivision. Here is the fundamental problem: not merely why the world does not recognize him, but why we do not. Why is the church not filled with life and power and vigour and joy and thanksgiving and praise? We have looked at two of the reasons and now we turn to the third, which is our failure to see what he has done for us in terms of the law – and that is the very matter that is dealt with in the seventeenth verse of the Prologue. In a prologue you introduce the themes, which will later be worked out in greater detail, and that is exactly what the apostle John does at this point. One of the major themes of his Gospel is our failure to realize what the Lord Jesus Christ, the Son of God, the eternal Word, has done for us in terms of the law – or our relationship to the law.

The first thing we must do is look at our text and make quite certain that we are clear as to its meaning. 'For the law was given by Moses, but grace and truth came by Jesus Christ.' This is a verse that is often misunderstood, and the first thing we must emphasize, our first principle, is that this statement is not meant to depreciate the law, or to dismiss the law, as if it were of no value. There are many who have interpreted this verse in that way. They maintain that John is saying here that the law is of no value at all. 'Forget it,' they say, 'forget all about it. Dismiss it! In this Christian era, the law should not be mentioned. Preach Christ and nothing else. Drive the law right out of court so that it is never mentioned again.' But that is not what this verse means.

Another common misunderstanding is the idea that the contrast that is in the verse is an absolute contrast. There are those who interpret it as meaning that there was no grace in the law given by Moses, there was no truth, and it is only in Jesus Christ that we have grace and truth.

They press the antithesis, the contrast that the apostle is making, to that extreme limit.

Now why do I say that it is wrong to throw out the law? The answer is that the law, after all, is God's law, not human law. It was not Moses' law but was simply given by Moses, through Moses. It was not something that he conjured up. There are people who believe that, I know, but John did not, and neither do we. We believe the Scriptures, which tell us that God gave the law to Moses. Moses was taken up on to the mount and he was given the law in all its details. Not only that, we are told very plainly in more than one place in the Scriptures that the law was mediated by angels. God used the angels to give the law to Moses. Writing about the law, the apostle Paul says: 'It was added because of transgressions, till the seed should come to whom the promise was made; and it was ordained by angels in the hand of a mediator' (*Gal.* 3:19). We must not depreciate the law. The giving of the law was in many ways the pinnacle of everything that happened in the Old Testament. It was God dealing directly with his servant through the instrumentality of the angels. And Moses, having received the law in this way, passed it on to the people.

The author of the Epistle to the Hebrews points out exactly the same truth when he exhorts the people to hold on to the things that they have heard. He puts it like this: 'For if the word spoken by angels was stedfast, and every transgression and disobedience received a just recompence of reward; how shall we escape, if we neglect so great salvation?' (*Heb.* 2:2–3). Now that is his way of referring to the law – it was 'the word spoken by angels' and it was steadfast. Why? Because this law, mediated in that way, was God's law. So never speak lightly of the law. I say again that the last thing that John ever intended was to dismiss the law or to speak lightly of it as if it were of no value at all.

But not only that, there is, after all, in the law itself an element of grace and of truth. What is the meaning of the burnt offerings and the sacrifices and all the ceremonial of the law that was given by God to Moses for the people? What is the meaning of the tabernacle and the temple, all the furniture, all the dress and all the symbolism? Why was a lamb slain morning and evening? Why the blood of bulls and of goats, and the ashes of an heifer? There is only one answer and explanation, and that is the element of grace. These were all shadows pointing forward to the great Antitype, to the coming of the Messiah, the Christ, the Deliverer.

You must not say that there is no grace in the law. There is. There is grace and truth in the law. It was meant to convey that. We must never press the antithesis, the contrast, to a ridiculous extreme. No, no! That is not what John intended. John does not want so much to bring down the law, to depreciate it, as to show the superiority, the greatness, the glory and the all-sufficiency of this blessed one who has come, our Lord and Saviour. So John contrasts Moses with Jesus Christ. You do not dismiss the dawn because it is not midday sunshine. How ridiculous it would be to do that. The law is simply the difference between the partial and the complete, between the preparation and the fulfilment. The law was given; grace and truth came in all their fulness in and through the Son of God.

In other words, John is saying here what the author of the Epistle to the Hebrews says in his first two verses, where he introduces his theme in much the same way: 'God, who at sundry times and in divers manners spake in time past unto the fathers by the prophets, hath in these last days spoken unto us by his Son.' It is God who spoke in those 'divers manners' and in different times and forms and ways. Do not forget that! It is always God speaking. Then he spoke in that way but now he has spoken once and for ever and perfectly in his Son. But you do not deride the former or despise it. No, no! What John calls us to do is to realize that when the fulness has come, we do not remain with the shadow and with the type. That is John's first reason for contrasting the law with the grace and truth of Jesus Christ.

But John also has a second reason, and that is to correct the misuse of the law, a misuse of which the Jews, in particular, were so guilty. Indeed, that was the problem with the Jews and was their main reason for rejecting the Son of God. They rejected him because they held on to the law and somehow felt that he was violating it. John knows that. To the Jews, the real stumbling-block to faith in Christ was the law, the law of God. But they misunderstood it, they misinterpreted it.

And therefore John is anxious that they should become clear in their thinking with regard to the law, what it was meant to do, its function and purpose and its whole relationship to the gospel and this new dispensation. So he takes up the whole question of the law that was given through Moses and the grace and truth that came by the Lord Jesus Christ.

There, then, is the meaning of the text. And now, having defined its terms, let me go on to the second principle, which is this: the importance and the value of all this for us.

'But why do that?' says somebody. 'The times are much too serious for us to spend our moments in some theoretical discussion about law. I find the world very difficult to live in. I'm surrounded by the world, the flesh and the devil. I have my temptations, I see the whole world on fire, and are you just going to indulge in some theoretical consideration of law and grace? Oh, my dear sir, you are a century, at least, behind the times. We're not living in those halcyon days of mid-Victorianism when everything was so quiet and peaceful and people had the leisure to deal with these theological and doctrinal problems.'

But I want to show you that this subject is most relevant to you. In Jesus Christ there is an absolute fulness, and you and I are meant to be receiving of that fulness. That is the way to live in this world. The only people who have ever conquered this world and mastered life are the people who can say with John, 'And of his fulness have all we received, and grace for grace.' So if you are finding life difficult, if you are failing and if you are unhappy and defeated, I will show you that it is because somewhere or another you are getting muddled about this whole business of the law. There is nothing more practical than this issue. It was practical then; it is practical now. I put it like this: Why is it that we are not more thankful to God for what he has done for us in the Lord Jesus Christ? Why is it that we are not always filled with a sense of praise and thanksgiving? What is the matter? I suggest that it is all due to this failure on our part to realize the truth of the text that we are now considering.

Now this failure happens in two main ways and I want to put them before you. Let us examine ourselves, each one of us, as to which group we belong to. The first danger, the first tendency on our part, always, is the one I have already been referring to, namely, to dismiss the law and not allow it to do its work in and upon us. I believe that this is a particular danger in the case of those of us who call ourselves evangelical. I think that the most common misunderstanding to be found among evangelicals is the view that tells us to dismiss the law, the view that says that we do not want the law, that we should not preach it any longer, because we are in the New Testament and are preachers of grace, preaching Christ only and offering salvation in his name. Let me show you the fallacy there: it is the terrible fallacy of regarding grace as something that dismisses the law altogether.

Grace was never meant to dismiss the law, and it must never be so regarded. Now I have the authority of the great apostle Paul for saying this. If ever there was a preacher of grace it was the apostle Paul, yet this is the great point he makes in the first section of his Epistle to the Romans, especially in the first three chapters, where he deals with the whole problem of the law. He has to deal with it in connection with both the Jews and the Gentiles.

People were getting muddled about law and grace and Paul shows them that they are now saved by grace. He then imagines a Jew saying, 'Very well, then, you are saying that the law was of no value, that it was a mistake and didn't do any good.' And the apostle replies like this: 'Do we then make void the law through faith?' And he is horrified at the suggestion. 'God forbid,' he says: 'yea, we establish the law' (*Rom.* 3:31).

Let us take that statement in Romans 3:31 in context. After Paul has outlined the great way of salvation, he says:

Where is boasting then? It is excluded. By what law? of works? Nay: but by the law of faith. Therefore we conclude that a man is justified by faith without the deeds of the law. Is he the God of the Jews only? is he not also of the Gentiles? Yes, of the Gentiles also: seeing it is one God, which shall justify the circumcision by faith, and uncircumcision through faith. Do we then make void the law through faith? God forbid: yea, we establish the law (Rom. 3:27–31).

'Do not imagine for a moment,' says the apostle, in effect, 'that my argument, my reasoning, means that I am making the law void, saying there is nothing in it and it is of no value, that you should forget all about it and dismiss it. Never!' he says. 'God forbid! We are establishing the law.' What does Paul mean by that? Let me put it like this – and this is the real exposition of John 1:17. Grace can only be measured truly in terms of law. You will never know the real value and meaning of grace until you have understood the teaching concerning the law. In other words, you and I will never know what the grace of God in the Lord Jesus Christ has really done for us until we realize deeply that it has saved us from the condemnation of the law. That is the only way to measure grace. I say again that we cannot appreciate grace except in terms of our understanding of our position under the law. Now let me hold before you the perfect statement of that. The best exposition of it that has ever been given is the incident that is recorded in Luke 7:36–50. In these verses Luke tells us that our Lord was invited into the house of a Pharisee to have a meal. He was sitting down, or reclining, upon a couch when a woman, a great sinner in the town, came along and began to wash his feet with her tears and to wipe them with her hair. The self-righteous Pharisee was amazed at this and said to himself, 'If this man were a prophet, he would know exactly what this woman is, and what she has been, and he would not allow her to touch him, or even to come near him, leave alone do what she is doing now. This man cannot be a prophet.' Our Lord realized what was in that Pharisee's mind, and said: 'Simon, I have something to say to you.'

'Master, say on,' said Simon.

Then our Lord began to speak about two debtors – this is most important teaching, which is often misunderstood. We read:

There was a certain creditor which had two debtors: the one owed five hundred pence, and the other fifty. And when they had nothing to pay, he frankly forgave them both. Tell me therefore, which of them will love him most? Simon answered and said, I suppose that he, to whom he forgave most. And he said unto him, Thou hast rightly judged. And he turned to the woman, and said unto Simon, Seest thou this woman? (Luke 7:41–44).

And then our Lord drew the contrast between Simon and the woman. Simon had invited our Lord to a meal but had not received him with the customary politeness. He had not anointed his head with oil, and he had not given him water to wash his feet, or welcomed him with a kiss. But the woman, there she was, kissing his feet, washing them with her tears, wiping them with her hair and then anointing them with the most precious oil. This amazing contrast!

And what is this contrast due to? Our Lord gives this explanation: 'Wherefore I say unto thee, Her sins, which are many, are forgiven; for she loved much: but to whom little is forgiven, the same loveth little' (*Luke* 7:47). What does he mean? It looks at first as if he is saying that the more you sin, the better it is, because the more you sin, the more will be forgiven you, and the more you are forgiven, the more you will love. 'Now,' says our Lord, in effect, to Simon, 'this woman is treating me like this and in a manner so different from you because she realizes the greatness of my forgiveness to her. You have treated me as you have done because you do not realize my great love to you in the forgiveness of your sins.' So is he putting a premium on sinning? Is he saying that it is a good thing for us to sin heavily and deeply in order that we shall have more forgiven, and therefore love more?

Of course, the idea is a sheer impossibility. No, our Lord is teaching that it is the realization of the need for forgiveness of sins that matters. The woman realized that she had been forgiven, but Simon, being a proud Pharisee, did not see any need for forgiveness. He had never led the adulterous life of this woman; he had been a very good and respectable man, like the Pharisee in the parable in Luke 18. That man gave a tenth of his goods to the poor, he fasted twice in the week – he did not see any need for forgiveness. That Pharisee never asked God for anything. He said, 'God, I thank thee, that I am not as other men are.' And Simon, not having seen the need, had not received forgiveness, and so he did not love.

But that does not mean that he did not need to be forgiven; it does not mean that he was not a sinner. Of course he was. He was a greater sinner than the woman because of his spiritual pride, which is the greatest sin of all. 'The failure to realize his sinfulness, that is the trouble,' said our Lord, in effect. 'People do not love me because they do not realize what I have done for them.'

Here, then, is the whole point: What is the state of your love and mine for the Lord? Do we love him? Do we rejoice in him? Can we say with Peter, 'Whom having not seen, ye love; in whom, though now ye see him not, yet believing, ye rejoice with joy unspeakable and full of glory' (*1 Pet.* 1:8)? This blessed Saviour, the Word who was made flesh and died for us – to what extent do we love him? The answer is: to the extent to which we realize the greatness of the forgiveness that we receive in him and through him. And what makes us realize the depth and the greatness of this forgiveness? There is only one answer. It is our consciousness of our sinfulness and of our need of forgiveness. And the thing that gives us that is the law! Nothing else.

So we will never appreciate grace until we have understood the teaching of the law and have seen ourselves under the law. Those who dismiss the law will never know much about grace. Part of our trouble is that we have dismissed the law. And because we have done that, we have never realized our true need. We are too healthy. We talk too glibly about 'loving the Lord'. But that is not a glib thing, it is something very deep, it is the sort of thing that makes somebody do what that woman did in Simon the Pharisee's house. It is the profoundest emotion conceivable. We talk about loving the Lord, we repeat the phrases, but I am asking, my friends, are we not too light-hearted as we say this? Have we ever known deep repentance? Have we ever known sorrow for sin? Have we ever known the plague of our own hearts? Those who have are the people who love the Lord. That is what our Lord taught in the parable that he uttered in Simon's house: 'But to whom little is forgiven, the same loveth little.' And I repeat that nothing gives us a realization of how much has been forgiven us except seeing ourselves under the condemnation of the law of God.

Do not dismiss what was given through Moses. You will never know much about grace if you do. To dismiss the law shows a complete misunderstanding of it. The trouble with us is that we have been healed too quickly, too lightly, we are in too much of a hurry. We want relief and we want peace. No, no! The trouble with us is that we have substituted believism for faith; we have rushed to grace before the law has done its work upon us. We are impatient with the law. We want Christ presented positively. We want to come immediately to the gospel. We do not want introductions. And because we do not want introductions, we have no gospel, finally. No, no! We must be clear about this: there is only one way to know and to appreciate the grace of God in Jesus Christ, and that is to know the depth of iniquity that is brought out by the law given through Moses. Therefore, I say, let us examine ourselves. As you face this great Prologue of John, do you find yourself saying, 'Well, am I Christian at all? I don't thrill as I think of him. I can't say I love him like that. I can't say that I'm living to him and to his glory. What's the matter with me?' If you are saying that, then examine yourself in terms of law. Have you been healed too quickly? Were you forced or pressed to some decision before you really knew your need of Christ? It is the one to whom much is forgiven who loves much. If our love is small, it is because we do not feel we have been forgiven much, and we do not feel that because we have never seen our need of forgiveness. And we have never seen our need of forgiveness because we have never listened to the law that God gave through Moses. That is the trouble.

And it works out, of course, in exactly the same way in our whole attitude towards sanctification. If we enter into this Christian life in the wrong way, we will probably continue in the wrong way and, again, we do that by avoiding the dictates of the law. In other words, is there not a tendency in us to regard sin as primarily a nuisance? What is our definition of sin? Is it not that it is something that spoils life for us? Do we not always tend to think of it in a purely subjective manner as this thing that gets us down and makes us unhappy? 'If only I could get rid of it!' That is our approach to sin, is it not? We start with ourselves; we end with ourselves. But the law makes us think of sin as it is in the sight of God. 'Against thee, thee only, have I sinned, and done this evil in thy sight,' says David (*Psa.* 51:4). He had committed adultery and he had murdered a man. But what worried him was not that the sin had made him miserable. 'Before thee . . .' That was the point! It was that God hated the sin, and David had sinned against God! That is one trouble, therefore.

And another trouble with our attitude towards sanctification is that we desire to be happy rather than holy. We want happiness, so we go to our meetings, our conferences, our conventions, to get 'it'. What is 'it'? It is the happiness of getting rid of our problems. A book that has had a great influence has a significant title: *The Christian's Secret of a Happy Life*.[1] That is it! 'Happy life'! Come along, I will tell you. I can make you happy quite easily. You need not wade through your Bible, you need not understand theology, you need not go this long, roundabout way via the law. Here you are: 'The Christian's secret of a happy life'. But happiness does not come first.

What does come first? Holiness! The moment you put happiness in the title, you have already gone wrong; 'the Christian's secret of a holy life' is what we need to know. Notice how our Lord himself puts it in the famous Beatitudes: 'Blessed are they . . .' Who are the happy ones? 'Blessed are they which do hunger and thirst after' – happiness? No, no! 'Blessed are they which do hunger and thirst after *righteousness*: for they shall be filled' (*Matt.* 5:6), not the people who are seeking happiness, and saying, 'Oh, I wish I could get rid of this sin, I wish this or that would go, then I would be perfectly happy.' That is the whole trouble – I so often have to deal with it. People come to me and give me the impression that if only they could get rid of this one sin, they would be perfectly happy. They have never seen themselves as sinners; they have never understood righteousness. It is not the one sin that matters but your whole condition before God. It is not happiness, primarily, that you need but holiness, righteousness, godliness, justice, truth. 'Grace and truth came by Jesus Christ.'

Eventually, in terms of sanctification, this misunderstanding of the law works out into what is called 'antinomianism', which means that you do not recognize any law at all. You say, 'It doesn't matter very much what I do: I'm under grace. I'm saved. I'm a Christian. I'm all right now. "Grace and truth came by Jesus Christ." The law is finished. We don't talk about law any longer: we're in the New Testament now. Don't bring law in again.' Very many Christians think like that, and act

---

[1] *The Christian's Secret of a Happy Life* was written by Hannah Whitall Smith and was first published in 1875.

accordingly, so there is a lowering of their lives, a living in a worldly manner. The world enters in and everybody feels it is all right. 'Grace! We are under grace!' But that is sheer antinomianism.

Antinomianism is that terrible misunderstanding of grace that says, 'Because you are saved, you are always saved and it does not matter what you do.' The first two statements are right – because you are saved, you are always saved – but if you go on to say, 'Therefore it doesn't matter what I do', then the question is: Are you saved at all? Because people who are saved know what they are saved from, they know what they are saved for and they know that their supreme desire is to serve God, to honour him and to magnify and to glorify his great and holy name.

Dismissal of the law leads to terrible consequences at every point –in our coming into the Christian life and in our continuing in the Christian life. It always leads to a superficial, glib, lightly happy Christian life, which has a false joy. There are people who say, 'I've never had a doubt ever since I was converted.' Some of them very much need to have doubts. When you examine their lives, you see the contrast. How can they be happy like that in view of the things they do and say? There is a false joy as well as a true joy, and the way to get rid of that is to examine yourself in the light of the law. So the first misunderstanding that leads to the failure to realize the truth of John 1:17 is a tendency to dismiss the law altogether.

Before I close, let me just say a word on the second misunderstanding, which is the tendency to mix law and grace. The first person says, 'Grace gets rid of law'; the second person mixes grace and law. That, too, is bad and brings us into trouble because the moment we begin to mix grace and law, we have no joy at all. Of the two misunderstandings, it is the better. It is better to have no joy at all than to have a false joy. It is better to be miserable than to assume that you are all right when you are not. Those who mix the two have no joy because they are constantly slipping back under the law in their thinking, in their outlook.

There are many Christians who oscillate between law and grace instead of holding the difference clearly in their minds. How do they do that? Well, here are some instances. If you ask them what it is that makes a person a Christian, they will be perfectly clear about it. They realize that they are saved only by the Lord Jesus Christ and his perfect work on their behalf. Then they suddenly fall into sin and they are wretched, they are unhappy. You can do nothing with them. Why? Because they have left the grace position and have put themselves back under the law. They raise the whole question of their justification, they doubt whether they have ever been forgiven – because they have fallen into sin. Now what is happening there is that they are mixing grace and law. They have gone from the grace position to the law position, and Christians must never do that. They are 'under grace', not 'under law'. I will explain that more fully later on; I am just giving illustrations here.

The same confusion sometimes happens in the matter of prayer. Sometimes, when we are given some dim realization of who and what God is and we are honest with ourselves, or when we have been searched by a sermon or by a book that we have been reading and feel unclean and unworthy, we may say, 'How can I possibly go to God and talk to him and enter into his holy presence?' And we feel we cannot pray. But this is, again, because we have gone back to law and have forgotten that we are under grace; we have mixed up grace and law.

The third example is in connection with sanctification – and this is very subtle. Here we are in the Christian life, we have believed the right things and yet we are somehow unhappy. There is a contradiction within us, we are lacking in joy and there is a failure in our life. Then somebody comes to us and says, 'Now it's quite simple. You will be all right, your problem will be solved. Listen to me, just do this . . .' And we are ready to listen. But, again, that is nothing but going back under the law. The cults teach that kind of approach, do they not? The cults can always solve our problems for us quite easily. We have only to do one thing and everything will automatically be put right. Quite simple! Short cut, and there we are. But the moment I accept that, I am back under law because any teaching that comes to me and says, 'Only do this and you will be all right', is always the law. That was exactly what the false teachers were saying to the members of the church at Galatia. They said, 'Yes, you are Christians, but if you really want to have the fulness of blessing, you must submit to circumcision. Just add on circumcision and you will have it all.'

There is only one answer to that kind of teaching: 'Stand fast therefore in the liberty wherewith Christ hath made us free, and be not entangled again with the yoke of bondage' (*Gal.* 5:1). You must not add on anything. If you try to add anything at all to faith in Christ, you have detracted, you have taken from it. Did the apostle not say that? 'Behold,' he said, 'I Paul say unto you, that if ye be circumcised, Christ shall profit you nothing. For I testify again to every man that is circumcised, that he is a debtor to do the whole law' (*Gal.* 5:2–3). So if you say, 'I've only this one thing to do and then I will be completely sanctified', or, 'If I just do this one thing, then I will get this blessing', then it is *you* who are doing it, and the moment you say, 'I will do it', you are back under the law and you have mixed up grace and law. And all who do that find themselves in perpetual misery. They take up teaching after teaching, always trying to get this 'it', this wonderful experience, this short cut that is going to put everything right. But they never get it because they have gone back under the law. No, it is not like that. It is 'of him' that we receive the fulness, and it is always of him. It is bad and wrong and foolish to mix up grace and law just as it is to dismiss the law, to deride it and to say we have nothing to do with it.

There, then, are the two chief misunderstandings with regard to this whole question of the relationship of law and grace. And, God willing, having shown how this applies to us and how relevant it is to our daily life and living and experience, we will go on to try to define the function and the value of the law, both positively and negatively. 'Stand fast therefore in the liberty wherewith Christ hath made us free, and be not entangled again with the yoke of bondage.' ∾

4

The Function of the Law: Revealing the Truth about God

For the law was given by Moses, but grace and truth came by Jesus Christ (John 1:17).

We have seen that one of the major causes of our failure to realize the blessings of the Christian gospel is that our understanding of the law of God, and of our whole position relative to it, is totally inadequate. Moreover, I have suggested that we will never really know the blessings of grace until we learn how to estimate them in terms of law.

We have been looking at this subject from the standpoint of Christian people in particular but I want to emphasize that in many ways there is no more urgently important question for everybody in this and every other land. To have a right understanding of the law of God is not only vital for individual Christians and for the life of the Christian church, which is so ineffective, but it is equally vital for the life of the whole nation with all its moral and industrial problems and the lawlessness that is becoming increasingly manifest. And surely everybody must see how vital it is in the whole international situation. Why have we had the crisis of this past week?[1] Why are the nations of the world trembling as they are this morning? What is the cause of all this? Well, I want to suggest that ultimately the cause of all these problems is a failure to understand the truth concerning the law of God. This is not some theoretical question; it is the most practical, the most urgent, question facing the world today. It is of vital importance throughout the whole of life, for Christians and for non-Christians.

[1] The Cuban missile crisis. This sermon was preached on 28 October 1962.

I come now to this aspect of the question: What is the real function of the law of God? What is the value of law? Or, looking at it specifically from the Christian standpoint, let me put the question like this: Why is a preliminary law-work always essential in the matter of salvation? Why must Moses always come before the Lord Jesus Christ? 'The law was given by Moses, grace and truth came . . .' Moses first and the Lord Jesus Christ following. Or let me put it still more plainly: Why did God ever give this law through Moses? That is the fundamental question. It is a fact of history that Moses did not concoct this law or think it up and elaborate it. Moses received it. You find the account in chapters 19 and 20 of the book of Exodus. Moses went up the mount and he was given the law. Then he came down and promulgated the law to the people, never claiming that he had thought it out, but saying that he had received it from God, that it was God's law. So the vital and fundamental question is: Why did God ever give this law to this race of people?

The answer, of course, is really given quite clearly in the law itself, in the Ten Commandments. The point I want to emphasize is that those Ten Commandments were given in two tables and there is an obvious difference between them. The first table starts with God himself; the second deals with human relationships – 'Honour thy father and mother', and so on. Then we must notice how our Lord answered the scribe who asked him, 'Which is the great commandment in the law?' Our Lord's reply was: 'Thou shalt love the Lord thy God with all thy heart, and with all thy soul, and with all thy mind. This is the first and great commandment. And the second is like unto it, Thou shalt love thy neighbour as thyself' (*Matt.* 22:36–39). That is in precisely the same order and that is the first point that I want to establish.

It is very important at this moment in the history of our world to recognize the order of these two tables, the order also given by our Lord in his reply to the scribe. The order is: God first, fellow human beings second. Now we might very well spend all our time just considering this point because the whole trouble of the world today is that it has forgotten that order and, indeed, has reversed it and at times even totally forgotten the first table. It would be simple for me to show you how all our major

problems emanate entirely from just this failure to observe the order
– the first and the second, the chief and the one that follows.

The reasons that are generally given for this failure and confusion
are more or less as follows. We are fond of saying that we are practical people, and we contrast ourselves with our forefathers who lived
a hundred years ago. We say, 'Those people, of course, lived in the
halcyon days of the mid-Victorian period and had time and leisure.
But life is different now. It is so busy and everything is involved and
complicated.' And we say that we have no time to bother about theology and doctrine and dogma. We must have something practical; we
want something to help us.

'Ah,' says the hard-headed man of the world, imagining that he is
being clever, 'I've no time for all these theoretical matters and these
definitions and theological points of yours. What I want is something
to help me to live. I need something to help me to get on with my fellow men and women. What I want is some practical word that will
solve this tension in the world and enable the nations to live together
in peace and concord and amity. This is no time for theology and doctrine. Give us some practical word of help, something that will enable
us to get through it all.' That is his great demand.

Notice that practical help is put over and against doctrine and dogma
and theology. And there, I am suggesting, is the whole essence of the
trouble. Of course we need help. We all need help. The nations need
help. But the first thing we must learn is that we must be helped in
God's way. The difficulty about this so-called practical approach is that
it always starts with ourselves and with other people. We say, 'Here is
my problem. Here are my difficulties. I want this and I want that. I
want guidance. I want help. I want healing.' We are subjective and we
come filled with ourselves. We try every agency. Then we say, 'I wonder
whether God can help me?' God comes last. In desperation we finally
turn to him in prayer. This is what we have always done. This is what
we do during every war.

There is a story from the last war[1] about a group of men who had
been torpedoed. There they were in their little lifeboat, and they had

[1] The Second World War

been in the boat, perhaps, for many days. The food had gone, the water was finished, and face to face with death they did not know what to do. Then somebody said, 'I wonder whether prayer would help us?' They had not thought of it before. You start with yourselves, with your problems and your difficulties, and then at long last, in desperation, you think of God. That is the human order, is it not? That is the world's order. Of course, during the last war, when things were going very badly, there was a national day of prayer. But only when things were desperate. We did not keep on holding it. We only turn to God in dire need. God is the last resort, not the first. We reverse the order completely. And it is exactly the same in all inter-relationships, whether between individuals or between nations. We always start with our problems and their settings and we try to solve them in our own way. And when we have utterly failed, then, and then only, do we think of God and turn to him. That is the major explanation of the whole state of the world at this very minute, internationally and nationally.

What is wrong with this approach? Let me try to show you something of the complete fallacy of this way of thinking. Apart from anything else, it is doomed to failure at the very beginning. Say you start with the second table rather than the first, insisting that your major problem is your neighbour. 'There we are,' you say, 'my neighbour and I, and we are disagreeing. We are quarrelling and life has become tense. There is that nation, here is this nation; here are the two big powers and there is the Iron Curtain. The tension! The problem is the problem of neighbourliness, friendliness, how to get on together. Fellowship!' That is what the world is saying. Everybody is looking at the second table of the law. But what a futile procedure that is.

As we have seen, our Lord puts the second commandment like this: 'Thou shalt love thy neighbour *as thyself.*' The very terms in which the commandment is expressed show how completely impossible that is. We are told that if only we love our neighbours as ourselves, all our problems will be solved, the armaments will be abolished and we will all live happily ever after. Yes, but you see what that presupposes? It presupposes that I love myself truly. I am to love my neighbour *as* I love myself. But how can I love myself unless I know the truth about myself? How can

I love myself, still less my neighbour, until I am aware of what I really am and what I really need, until I know the ultimate cause of all my troubles? So if you start with the second commandment, it immediately puts you into a difficulty: What is the truth about yourself? There is only one answer to that question, and only one place where we will ever find that answer. Where is that? Oh, it is in the first commandment.

I only discover the truth about myself when I stand face to face with God. The whole trouble in life is that we fail to do that. Instead of starting with God, I start with myself. And, of course, starting with myself, I am concerned about my own interests. There is nothing wrong with me, it is always somebody else who is wrong. Look at the cases in the courts. Never the husband, always the wife. But the wife says it is always the husband. It is always somebody else. Look at the nations. Each one accuses the other. They are doing it now; they have been doing it during the past week. They all start with themselves. And the moment you start with yourself, you have already gone wrong. We are no judges of ourselves. And this is because we are so anxious to be on good terms with ourselves. We are all experts at this book-keeping that we do: we always balance our accounts. We put the good against the bad, underestimating the bad and overestimating the good. We always produce a most wonderful balance sheet!

But the moment you start with yourself, you open the door to selfishness, self-centredness, self-justification; you always open the door to envy and to jealousy, to hatred, to malice, to spite, to war. 'From whence come wars and fightings among you?' asks James in his epistle. He answers, 'Come they not hence, even of your lusts that war in your members?' (*James* 4:1). It is as simple as that. But the world does not recognize that because it always starts with the second table instead of the first. It starts with human beings and their relationships instead of starting with God. I say again that we cannot love our neighbours as ourselves until we are right about ourselves. It is a sheer impossibility. Our central trouble is that we do not know the truth about ourselves.

Now this failure is something that we have already discussed. When we considered John's statement about the light shining in the darkness, we saw that the scriptural teaching is that not only are we surrounded by darkness, but there is darkness inside us. Our minds are darkened. We do not think straightforwardly and clearly. We have become perverted. In other words, we are all of us, however great our intelligence, governed much more by our desires than by reason. That is the whole trouble in the world today. During the last hundred years, men and women, turning their backs upon God, have increasingly said that all that people need is education. Then they will use their minds; then they will banish war. But better education has not brought about peace. Why not? Because there is in each of us something profounder and more elemental, something stronger than reason, and that is these drives, these passions, these desires. How can we be blind to this? Reading a newspaper ought to be enough to convince us. Crime is not confined to the ignorant and illiterate. You find it in all ranks and stations of society. Yet we fondly think that by starting on the human level, we can solve our problems.

But we are failing. We are bound to fail. We cannot solve our problems. I am here just to press upon you that our business as Christian people is to enlighten the world with respect to this, to say that their whole approach is wrong. We must tell them that they are reversing the order, that they are starting with the second table of the law instead of with the first and so are bound to go wrong. You cannot love your neighbour as yourself until you are clear and right in your understanding with regard to yourself. And the only way you can ever get an understanding of yourself is by standing in the presence of God. This is where the law comes in; this is why God gave it.

So what was the purpose of the law? What was its function? Let me subdivide it like this: God first of all gives the revelation of himself so that we may see ourselves in his light and in his sight; then he proceeds to tell us the truth about ourselves. In other words, I am suggesting that one of the greatest needs of the world at this moment is to be introduced to the Ten Commandments in the right order. I find there are many foolish people about who are picking out just one of the commandments and saying, for instance, 'Thou shalt not kill', as if that were the whole of God's law. It is not. It belongs to the second table, not the first – such people are already wrong. No, no! You take the order as God gives it. In other words, our greatest need is to know the truth about God.

Does it surprise you that we are spending this Sunday morning in discussing this subject? Is anybody here disappointed that I am not telling President Kennedy or Mr Khrushchev what they should do? But that is not why I am here, that is not the preaching of the gospel. That is the church abrogating her true and primary function. I do not know enough about the situation, nor does anybody else who is in a pulpit this morning, whatever his position in the church. Anything that is said is all guesswork. What I am here to do is to say that the world is as it is, and every individual is as he or she is, because we are all ignorant of God.

What, then, are the facts? The first thing God tells us is that he is the only God; there is no other. 'The LORD our God is one LORD' (*Deut.* 6:4). And he does not recognize any other. The children of Israel in their folly were constantly making gods, making idols and worshipping them and adopting the gods of the other nations. This always brought them into trouble and they were always being called back to the realization that there is only one true and living God.

And then let us remember that he is an almighty God. This is how we are told about God's power: 'But the seventh day is the sabbath of the LORD thy God: in it thou shalt not do any work' – why not? – ' . . . for in six days the LORD made heaven and earth, the sea, and all that in them is, and rested the seventh day' (*Exod.* 20:10–11). This is God's world. It is not our world. It is not an accident. It is not something that has evolved out of some primitive slime. No, no! It is the creation of the almighty God. He made it for himself. It belongs to him. The world is as it is today because men and women think it is their world. It is not! The almighty Creator is illimitable in his powers. He reminds these children of Israel: 'I am the LORD thy God, which have brought thee out of the land of Egypt, out of the house of bondage' (*Exod.* 20:1). And he brought them out, as the Scripture tells us, 'with an high hand' (*Exod.* 14:8). They had nothing: it was his power that brought them out.

The world needs to remember that God is an almighty God. The people of the world are drunk with power because they can send men into space and make rockets that may land a man on the moon. The world thinks it has power but in the sight of God we are but as grasshoppers, and even smaller! The almighty God! Oh, that these giant nations would realize that this morning, that they might be humbled and tremble in his presence! 'The LORD reigneth; let the people tremble' (*Psa.* 99:1).

And God is not only the Creator and artificer, he is the sustainer of the whole universe. If God ceased to sustain this universe, it would collapse in a moment. Read Psalm 104 at your leisure and there listen to that good man who wrote these words as he tells you that if God withdrew or withheld his spirit from animals for a second they would die, everything would collapse. God keeps it all going. His providence is over all. He reigns and rules over all. He permits many things. Very often we do not understand his permissive will but that does not mean that he is not in control and is not over all. He is an almighty and eternal God manifesting his almightiness in these various ways.

And then we are reminded that God is spirit. That is why we must not make any representation of him. If you try to materialize him, you will detract from his glory, you will deny him. You must not make your graven images; you must not bow down to them afterwards and think that you are doing God honour. God is spirit. God is everywhere and you cannot localize and materialize him. That was a constant fallacy on the part of these children of Israel and others.

But, above all, we are reminded that God is holy. Surely his prime object in giving this law to Moses was that he might remind the people that he is a holy God. It is repeated everywhere: 'Ye shall therefore be holy, for I am holy' (*Lev.* 11:45). What does that mean? Well, who can define or attempt to describe holiness? It is beyond us. 'God is light, and in him is no darkness at all' (*1 John* 1:5). 'God cannot be tempted with evil, neither tempteth he any man' (*James* 1:13). 'For our God is a consuming fire' (*Heb.* 12:29). No evil, no sin, nothing unworthy can come near him. God is everlastingly holy, eternal purity. We cannot conceive of this. How glibly we talk about God. We do not realize that he is a holy God who hates sin and evil and all that belongs to that realm.

And then we are reminded that God demands worship of us; he demands, indeed, our total allegiance: 'Thou shalt have no other gods before me' (*Exod.* 20:3). You must not put any god by the side of God. You must not put yourself there and worship yourself and your achievements, making a god of yourself. You must not put your husband or wife there. You must not put your children there. I have known many people who have worshipped their children; their children were their gods, they lived for them. There are people who worship their possessions, their money, their social status; they live for these things. When they do this, they are making idols. They are putting something by the side of God and worshipping it. But God prohibits that. 'Thou shalt not make unto thee any graven image, or any likeness of any thing that is in heaven above, or that is in the earth beneath, or that is in the water under the earth' (*Exod.* 20:4). 'Thou shalt not take the name of the LORD thy God in vain; for the LORD will not hold him guiltless that taketh his name in vain' (*Exod.* 20:7).

I say again that God demands our total allegiance. Notice this extraordinary term in Exodus 20:5: 'I the LORD thy God am a jealous God.' God will not tolerate any other god. Why not? Because there is no other god. It is a lie. He is the true God as well as the living God. All the idols – they have no power, they have no life. 'Eyes have they, but they see not . . . they have hands, but they handle not' (*Psa.* 115:5, 7). None of the things that men and women are worshipping today can help them. How did these things help them this last week? If these bombs had been let off, if a war had come, what would have been the value of the gods that the people are worshipping – their pleasure and their amusement, their wonderful lives? They are no good. They have no life. They are not true. They have no power to sustain us. God does not tolerate them. God is a jealous God in the sense that he alone is God and there is none other beside him. Our Lord was making the same point in answering the scribe who came with his clever question. The scribe wanted to know which was the first and the chief of the commandments. This was your clever 'modern' man trying to trip our Lord. There were some 614 distinct points in the law and the scribe said, 'Which is the first commandment of all?' These people spent their time in arguing this point. Listen, said our Lord, I will tell you: 'Thou shalt love the Lord thy God with all thy heart, and with all thy soul, and with all thy mind, and with all thy strength' (*Mark* 12:28, 30). Not with a little bit but with the whole. It is not these minutiae and details of the law that matter, it is your total relationship to God. You must love him, and you must love him with the whole of your being. He has made you. He owns you. Your life and your destiny are in his hands. He wants the totality of your personality, he wants the whole of you – nothing less.

God is a jealous God. You do not put yourself first and then, when you are in trouble, run to him and give him just a portion, the tail end of your life. No, no! It does not work, my friends. And that is why so many foolish people who run to God frantically in prayer when they are in trouble find that they do not get help. Then they say that there is no God. But they do not understand, they do not know the truth about God. They need to read the Ten Commandments again.

But, on top of that, remember that God is a just God and a righteous God, and he is a God who judges.

Thou shalt not bow down thyself to them, nor serve them: for I the LORD *am a jealous God, visiting the iniquity of the fathers upon the children unto the third and fourth generation of them that hate me; and shewing mercy unto thousands of them that love me, and keep my commandments. Thou shalt not take the name of the* LORD *thy God in vain; for the* LORD *will not hold him guiltless that taketh his name in vain* (Exod. 20:5–7).

Modern men and women do not like that; they do not believe it. They say, 'God is love. We believe in the God of the New Testament, the God of the Lord Jesus Christ. We don't believe in that God of Sinai.' But the answer to that is that the Lord Jesus Christ did believe in the God of Sinai! He said that he had not come to change the law. He said, 'One jot or one tittle shall in no wise pass from the law, till all be fulfilled' (*Matt.* 5:18). He did not come to destroy the law and the prophets but to fulfil them. And he spoke of a God who is just and righteous and holy and who judges. God is a judge and he does punish the iniquity and the transgressions of men and women.

Now this is where all this doctrine is so practical. God is judging the world at this present hour. Why do you think we have had two world wars in the twentieth century? How do you explain the present tension? Why should this century be as terrible as it has been? To me, the only adequate explanation is that it is a part of God's wrath upon sin, it is God visiting the iniquity of people upon themselves and upon their descendants. The world in its cleverness has turned its back upon God for the last hundred years and when people do that, God abandons them to their own devices, their own results. Part of that is war and rumours of war, lust and passion let loose, immorality and vice on our streets and in our cities, everywhere. It is a part of God's punishment of sin that he withholds his restraining grace and allows men and women to reap the consequences of their own folly and apostasy. He is a judge. He is a righteous judge. He is a holy and a just judge. He punishes in this life.

But it is still more vital for us to realize that there is to be a judgment and a punishment at the end of all. God made this world, he set it going and he will bring it to an end. And the world will come to an end in an act of judgment. The message of the whole Bible is that God will send his Son back into the world to judge it in righteousness. And he will judge the world on what? On its relationship to him. That is the one test. Not on what I thought about peace and war, not on my opinion on the Cuban crisis, not on what I think of what is happening in India – no, he will judge me on what I have done face to face with him. 'The chief end of man is to glorify God and to enjoy him for ever' (*Westminster Shorter Catechism*). And if I have not, if I have lived my own selfish, narrow, petty life and have not lived to his glory and have not loved him, I am condemned.

But, thank God, there is this element of mercy here in the Ten Commandments: 'shewing mercy unto thousands of them that love me, and keep my commandments' (*Exod.* 20:6). Yes, if we but obey him, if we listen to his voice, if we respond to his appeal, there is mercy, abundant mercy. The God who gave the law sent his only Son, 'full of grace and truth'. But, remember, his mercy is for those who love him and keep his commandments. It is not something you take, and say, 'God is love, I can do what I like.' No, no! You see that Christ has redeemed you in order that you may serve God, and you give yourself to him and begin to live to his glory.

And my last word on this great subject is that God has revealed that he has a purpose for this world. Here it is at the very beginning: 'I am the LORD thy God, which have brought thee out of the land of Egypt, out of the house of bondage' (*Exod.* 20:2). This means that though the whole world has sinned against God – we find the record of that in the book of Genesis – God has not abandoned the world. He has a plan. He has a purpose. He takes hold of a man called Abraham, brings him out of Ur of the Chaldees and turns him into a nation. This is the nation through which God is going to redeem the world, and out of which, eventually, his Son will be born as Saviour of the world. So when this people were in trouble in the bondage of Egypt and were without hope and on the point of being destroyed once and for ever, God, in the fulfilment of his plan and purpose, brought them out, conquering their enemies. Pharaoh and his hosts and his chariots were drowned in the Red Sea and the people were taken to the land of Canaan.

And that is God's message, I believe, for this world today. He is preparing his own people for the glory that is coming. All Christians are citizens of the kingdom of God, they belong to God's people, and God has a plan and a purpose for them, which nothing can frustrate. Let every enemy arise, communism, capitalism, any other *ism*, let them all stand up against God. As he destroyed Pharaoh and his hosts in the Red Sea, he will destroy every enemy, and his kingdom shall reign over all. There is a time coming when 'the earth shall be filled with the knowledge of the glory of the LORD, as the waters cover the sea' (*Hab.* 2:14).

> *Jesus shall reign where'er the sun*
> *Does his successive journeys run;*
> *His kingdom stretch from shore to shore,*
> *Till moons shall wax and wane no more.*
>
> Isaac Watts

God the Almighty will bring his people to his goal in spite of every enemy and every opposition. My friends, do we know this God? Are we subject to him? Are we living to the glory of this God? Do we love him? Do we find our all in him?

The first table of the law holds us and the whole world face to face with the everlasting God, the Father of our Lord and Saviour Jesus Christ. Let us bow before him in our hearts, in our spirits, in our souls, and plead with our fellow men and women to do the same ere it be too late. ॐ

5

The Function of the Law: Revealing the Truth about Ourselves

For the law was given by Moses, but grace and truth came by Jesus Christ (John 1:17).

W e have been considering the fact that we will never understand the grace and truth that came by Jesus Christ until we are clear in our understanding of what the law did to us, what it said to us and the position into which it put us. This is a vital matter, which is why we are discussing it at some length. In our last study we began to look at the function of the law. First and foremost, its purpose is always to remind us that we are face to face with Almighty God. The law delivers us out of a morbid subjectivity and self-concern and puts us into the context of a relationship to him.

And then the law goes on to tell us something about the character of God. As I have reminded you, the law is given in two tables. The first states that God is a holy God, a just and a righteous God. He is a God who punishes sin and iniquity. He is a God who has a great purpose for his people. So we must worship him, and worship him only. We must not take his name in vain; we must not take his day in vain. We must just live to glorify God. That is the first table of the law, and it is essential that we should understand what it says. We will never know what God has done for us in and through the Lord Jesus Christ until we have grasped the teaching of the first table of the law. That is the measure of this 'grace and truth' that have come through the Lord Jesus Christ.

But we do not stop at that; there is a second table to the law and it is vital that we should go on to consider it. It is there that we find God's demands of us in relation to other people. The second table of the law tells us that there are certain other aspects to God's law, which all arise from the commandments in the first table. It is because God is God, and God has made and owns the world, that my relationships to my fellow men and women ever come into being and are important. My attitude to others is governed by my attitude to God. I must not take my fellow men and women as people in and of themselves. They must be regarded as people who, like myself, are under God, and I must view them in that way from the beginning to the very end. So we are given the demands of the second table:

> *Honour thy father and thy mother . . . Thou shalt not kill. Thou shalt not commit adultery. Thou shalt not steal. Thou shalt not bear false witness against thy neighbour. Thou shalt not covet thy neighbour's house, thou shalt not covet thy neighbour's wife, nor his manservant, nor his maidservant, nor his ox, nor his ass, nor anything that is thy neighbour's* (Exod. 20:12–17).

Those are the commandments that are to be found in the second table of the law, and it is important that we should realize why we are to observe them. God gave them in this way: 'Ye shall be holy; for I am holy' (*Lev.* 11:44). We are to be a holy people because we are the people of a holy God, not because we are interested in holiness in and of itself. That has been the error made by so many. It is the danger inherent in monasticism and in the lives of the so-called 'holy men' of Buddhism and Hinduism and various other religions. But not here. It is not the cultivation of your own soul in and of itself that matters but that you may be worthy of your Father who is in heaven. That is the biblical emphasis from beginning to end. And I am concerned to emphasize that the demands of this second table of the law are still there and are as applicable today as they have ever been. God still demands holiness of everybody. He demands it of Christians; he demands it of non-Christians. He is the maker and the creator of all, he is the governor of all, and he issues this command to all people.

There is a false idea that would have us believe that the teaching in the second table only begins at the giving of the law to and through Moses at Mount Sinai. People seem to think that the law only began then. But that is quite wrong. This law was originally given to man and made a part of his very nature and constitution when God first created him. What happened in the giving of the law on Mount Sinai was that God was reminding his own particular people of this fact and stating it explicitly. The apostle Paul is so concerned about this point that he devotes a bit of an argument to it in the second chapter of his great Epistle to the Romans, and it is important that we should look at that. This idea that the law, the Ten Commandments, was only for the children of Israel is, I repeat, a central fallacy, and the apostle here in Romans 2 makes that perfectly clear. He puts it like this:

[God] will render to every man according to his deeds: to them who by patient continuance in well doing seek for glory and honour and immortality, eternal life: but unto them that are contentious, and do not obey the truth, but obey unrighteousness, indignation and wrath, tribulation and anguish, upon every soul of man that doeth evil, of the Jew first, and also of the Gentile; but glory, honour, and peace, to every man that worketh good, to the Jew first, and also to the Gentile: for there is no respect of persons with God. For as many as have sinned without law shall also perish without law: and as many as have sinned in the law shall be judged by the law; (for not the hearers of the law are just before God, but the doers of the law shall be justified. For when the Gentiles, which have not the law, do by nature the things contained in the law, these, having not the law, are a law unto themselves: which shew the work of the law written in their hearts, their conscience also bearing witness, and their thoughts the mean while accusing or else excusing one another) (Rom. 2:6–15).

Here Paul is saying that these Gentiles did not have the law. By this he means that, being Gentiles and not Jews, they did not receive the law as it was given explicitly by God to Moses on Mount Sinai. But Paul says that this makes no difference because, though they were never given the law on tables of stone, the same law is written in their hearts, and they prove that by their consciences.

The argument is that God, when he originally made man, made him righteous. He put a righteousness into him, and there is a remnant and a relic of that righteousness in every human being. That, in a sense, is the meaning of the conscience. The law of God is written in the heart of every human being and it is meant to be observed. All that God was doing through Moses at Mount Sinai was reminding his own nation of this. The law was in their hearts, it was in the hearts of Jew and Gentile, but because of sin and evil and because of their turning their backs upon God, they had forgotten it and were negligent. So God said, in effect, 'I am going to remind you of my law; it is in your hearts, but that is not enough, I am putting it before you.' He underwrote it, as it were, and held it there before them so that it would be unmistakable.

But, remember, the law is all the time written in the hearts of all people, both Jew and Gentile, and that is why I say that it still holds. It is as obligatory now as it was when man was originally created. It is urgently important for us all to remember and to realize that this law still holds today. We are living in an age when men and women are trying to explain away the law. They say that they do not believe in discipline and so on; they all do what they like and what they think is right. But that is a violation of this fundamental law of our very being and constitution. 'Thou shalt not kill. Thou shalt not steal. Thou shalt not commit adultery . . .' The commandments are all there, and in our consciences we know they are there. To deny them is to deny our own consciences. When any of us violates any one of these laws, we know we are wrong. We try to explain this psychologically and so on, but that is just our attempt to answer and to silence our consciences: 'Their conscience also bearing witness, and their thoughts the mean while accusing or else excusing one another.'

The second table of the law, then, we can summarize like this: 'Thou shalt love thy neighbour as thyself', and it is a part of God's demand of us. Why do we not appreciate the grace of God in Christ Jesus? It is because, in the first place, we do not realize that we are meant to glorify God with the whole of our being. Second, it is because we do not realize that we are meant to love our neighbour as ourselves. When we face these two tables of the law, we see our failure. However respectable and good and nice we may be, have we lived to the glory of God? Do I love the Lord my God with all my heart and soul and mind and strength?

Do I love my neighbour as myself? It is as we face this that we see our failure and sinfulness, and we see the need of grace and what grace in Christ has done for us. That is where the law comes in. We will never appreciate grace until we see the working of the law.

But let us go further. The law of God was given to carry that even a stage further – that is, to convince us of our terrible sinfulness, to bring our sin right home to us. It is the most difficult thing in the world, is it not, to convince us of our sin and of our sinfulness? There is nothing any man or woman hates more than that. We are always so ready to defend ourselves, we are experts at it. The term used now is that we are all experts at 'rationalizing' our sins. We can explain them away; we can excuse them. This is quite obvious. We accuse and judge other people, as Paul says in Romans 2:1–3. We condemn another person for doing something but when we do exactly the same thing, ah, well, of course, circumstances were rather different!

Do you remember the old story of David falling into a grievous sin over Bathsheba? God sent the prophet Nathan to talk to him about it and Nathan, very cleverly, instead of putting it directly to David, told him a parable. He said, in effect, 'This is the sort of thing that is happening in your kingdom, this is what a man has done against another man.' And David rose up in righteous indignation, though that was simply a rich man taking another man's only lamb. David said that this heinous sin must be punished in a most terrible manner. And then Nathan looked at him and said: 'Thou art the man!' David had not stolen a lamb from another man, he had stolen another man's wife and in addition had murdered that man. David could see the sin in somebody else but he could not see it in himself. That is the trouble with all of us. We find it extremely difficult to see our own sinfulness, and because of that we have never realized the greatness of God's grace in Christ Jesus. It is those who have seen their utter sinfulness who rejoice in the grace of God and who live to praise God. Our failure in the Christian life is therefore mainly due to our failure to realize our sinfulness, and that is why the law was given.

We all, of course, if we are intelligent people, have some idea of the darkness we have been talking about. If you have ever read any philosophy, you will know something about the darkness of human nature and of life in this world. If you have read books on morality and ethics, then you must know something about darkness. If people have any code of honour or of morals, they will be aware of the extent to which human nature is deficient in these areas. Psychology? Yes, psychology tells us something about this darkness. Psychology analyses and probes human nature, the psyche, this essential thing that is in a human being, and discovers many foul and ugly and hidden things. Let us grant that much even to Freudian psychology. It gives a very poor picture of human nature, does it not?

In these ways we can know something about our sinfulness, about the darkness, but that is not enough. And it is not enough because we are still protecting ourselves – we are generally talking about somebody else. The last people to see the truth about themselves are generally the psychologists. They understand everybody else but never themselves, poor fellows. And so you find the psychologist announcing that a Christian should never suffer from insomnia and never have a nervous breakdown and then you hear that the great psychologist has gone down with both. That is just typical. Psychology and philosophy are all right as far as they go but they do not go far enough. They cannot penetrate this self-defence mechanism that we are all so expert at putting up. There is only one thing that can do this, and that is the law of God. Here is the divine X-ray that reveals everything, that leaves nothing hidden.

But how does the law penetrate our defences? There is a great deal of teaching on this subject in the New Testament, particularly in the epistles of the apostle Paul. He was a Pharisee, an expert in the law, and more than any other man had an understanding of the meaning and the purpose and the function of the law of God. Paul was its greatest exponent. What, then, does he tell us? He tells us that the law is of value in that it defines sin. And sin needs to be defined. Every law does that up to a point, does it not? That is why we need laws. Who can decide whether or not your next-door neighbour's wireless is too loud? You have to define levels of noise. Whose right of way is it when you are driving your car or walking? The law has to establish boundary lines. One man says, 'It's my right', the other man says that it is his. The decision cannot be left to the individuals concerned because they will always twist things to suit themselves. So the law comes in, and it defines sin.

Listen to the apostle saying something about the function of the law: 'Therefore', he says, 'by the deeds of the law there shall no flesh be justified in his sight: for by the law is the knowledge of sin' (*Rom.* 3:20). Now I will not stay to give a full interpretation of that verse now, that must come later. My point is that Paul is saying that the law cannot save anyone. Why not? Because it was never meant to. Its purpose is to define sin – 'by the law is the knowledge of sin'. Or take it again as Paul puts it in Romans 4:15: 'Because the law worketh wrath: for where no law is, there is no transgression.' You cannot prosecute a man unless you have a law under which to prosecute him. When you take him to the court you say, 'Under such and such an act, section . . . sub-section . . . this man . . .' Where there is no law, there is no transgression. The function of law is to identify, to define, sin, to tell us exactly what it is. You have this again in Romans 7:8: 'For without the law sin was dead', and Paul says this in other places in that chapter.

Now all this means that the question of our sinfulness is not just a matter of a vague feeling that we are not what we ought to be. That is all right – we are not what we ought to be. But as long as we leave it at that, we will never do anything about it. When the law comes to me, however, it does not just look at me and say, 'You are a sinful creature.' Instead, it says, 'You are guilty of this and that and that and that.' And that is what we do not like. 'Oh, yes,' I say, 'of course I'm ready to admit I'm not a hundred per cent saint.' Everybody is ready to say that. People think that is a wonderful thing to admit. But if you look at them and say, 'Quite right, my friend, you are not only not a hundred per cent saint, but I happen to know that you are guilty of this and that', they will hate you for it. Of course they will. It is all very well to say to me that I am not the man I ought to be and that there are certain things in me that are wrong, but the moment you become specific, I object. But that is exactly what the law does: it says that I am guilty in particular.

The law does not just come and say, 'Now you must be good, you must love God and you must love other people.' Knowing us as it does, it says, 'You must not steal this person's property. You must not take the law into your own hands and kill that person who has annoyed you.' That is all that the commandment 'Thou shalt not kill' means; it has nothing to do with nations. God commanded the very nation to whom he said, 'Thou shalt not kill', to exterminate the Amalekites. That is where these pacifists go so wrong. That commandment, like each of the Ten Commandments, is an individual matter. The law particularizes; it does not leave us with a general statement. Sin is not just a matter, I say again, of a general feeling. The law holds us down to particulars. It comes to us and says, 'I have a number of questions to put to you.' It is like the policeman who says to us, 'I have a number of questions that I want to put to you. Where were you at such and such a time and what were you doing?' So that is the first way in which the law penetrates our defences. The law convinces us of sin by defining sin.

But let me hurry to the second point, which is that the law brings out the whole element of desire in connection with sin, and here is a terrible thing. The apostle Paul uses the words 'concupiscence', 'coveting' and 'lust'. Oh, he says, this is the whole trouble: 'What shall we say then? Is the law sin? God forbid. Nay, I had not known sin, but by the law: for I had not known lust, except the law had said, Thou shalt not covet' (*Rom.* 7:7). This is one of the greatest functions of the law, and it is just here that it convinces everybody. There are people who say, like the Pharisee of old, 'God, I thank thee, that I am not as other men are . . . even this publican. I fast twice in the week, I give tithes of all that I possess' (*Luke* 18:11–12). There's nothing wrong with me. I've never done anything wrong.

Wait a minute, says the law. 'Thou shalt not covet.'

Our blessed Lord himself was the first to expound this truth, and this is where he was always able to convict the Pharisees. This is why the Pharisees and scribes and the others conspired together against him and eventually crucified him. Our Lord could make a Pharisee feel that he was a terrible sinner, and he did it like this. Listen to our Lord in the Sermon on the Mount:

Ye have heard that it was said by them of old time, Thou shalt not kill; and whosoever shall kill shall be in danger of the judgment: But I say unto you, That whosoever is angry with his brother without a cause shall be in danger of the judgment: and whosoever shall say to his brother, Raca, shall be in danger of the council: but whosoever shall say, Thou fool, shall be in danger of hell fire.

Then listen:

Ye have heard that it was said by them of old time, Thou shalt not commit adultery: but I say unto you, That whosoever looketh on a woman to lust after her hath committed adultery with her already in his heart (Matt. 5:21–22, 27–28).

Our Lord is saying: You have misunderstood the law. You think it is only dealing with actions and you have never realized that it deals quite as much with thoughts and with desires and aspirations. You may not have done these things actually, in practice, but have you thought of them? Have you done them in your heart? If so, you are guilty.

The law also brings out this whole matter of coveting. And that was the terrible discovery that the apostle Paul himself made. Listen to him: 'I had not known sin, but by the law: for I had not known lust, except the law had said, Thou shalt not covet. But sin, taking occasion by the commandment, wrought in me all manner of concupiscence. For without the law sin was dead' (*Rom.* 7:7–8). To covet is as damnable as to steal. An evil desire is as bad as an evil deed. This is something that the law alone can bring home to us. I know that from the standpoint of the law of the land and general morality and ethics that is not true, but we are not dealing here with human law. We are dealing with the law of God, and men and women in the presence of God, and God is able to read the thoughts and the intents of the heart. 'For the word of God is quick, and powerful, and sharper than any twoedged sword, piercing even to the dividing asunder of soul and spirit, and of the joints and marrow, and is a discerner of the thoughts and intents of the heart' (*Heb.* 4:12).

Nothing is hidden from God. He is concerned about thoughts and desires; he is as concerned about coveting as about sinful actions – and it is there in the Ten Commandments. That is where these Jews were so blind – 'Thou shalt not covet thy neighbour's wife'! It is not only that you do not actually try to take her, you must not even covet her, nor anything that belongs to your neighbour. You do not love your neighbour properly if you covet, let alone take, anything that he or she possesses. So the law brings this home to us and here it convinces us of our sinfulness – the element of desire and of coveting, concupiscence, lust, passion.

Oh, says David, after he was brought to an understanding of this commandment, 'Behold, thou desirest truth in the inward parts' (*Psa.* 51:6). My trouble, says David, after his terrible crime, is not only that I have committed adultery and murder, the real trouble with me is that I ever had that desire, it is this rottenness that is in me! 'Create in me a clean heart, O God' (*Psa.* 51:10). I do not want to be right merely in action, I want a new heart. I want a heart that will hate this kind of thing! David realizes that God will be satisfied with nothing less than truth in the inward parts. And again David is able to say: 'If I regard iniquity in my heart, the Lord will not hear me' (*Psa.* 66:18). Though I may be outwardly very respectable and moral, if I am harbouring sin in my heart, I know that God will not hear me. I must not regard iniquity in my heart and fondle it. The desires must be cleansed. Now it is the law alone that will bring us to this kind of condemnation and show us the truth about ourselves. So you see the madness of getting rid of the law.

The third point, the next function of the law listed by the apostle Paul in Romans 7, is this: the law goes on to bring out what he calls the exceeding sinfulness of sin. Listen: 'Was then that which is good made death unto me? God forbid. But sin, that it might appear sin' – that is it, the camouflage taken away, the veil drawn back, sin exposed! There it is for what it actually is – 'working death in me by that which is good; that sin by the commandment [by the law] might become exceeding sinful' (*Rom.* 7:13). What is Paul talking about? Well, I must try to expound it to you. It took me many Friday nights to do that not so long ago in this pulpit. There were many of you not here at that time; I am sorry for you, as you will not be able to follow the argument properly, but let me try to give you a summary!¹ Paul is saying that as the result of the fall and as the result of sin, man is as bad as this, he is as evil as this, he is as rotten and as sinful as this – that he even twists the law of God to serve his own lust and passion and sinfulness. Paul puts it like this: 'For when we were in the flesh, the motions of sins, which were by the law, did work in our members to bring forth fruit unto death' (*Rom.* 7: 5). Notice that the motions – the movements, the impulses, the workings – of sin were 'by the law'. In effect, Paul is saying, 'You know, before my conversion' – and it is true of all people who are not Christians – 'the effect that the law had upon me was not to make me better, it was to make me worse. The very law of God with its commandments stimulates, energizes, rouses the passions that are in us.' And Paul goes on to explain this:

But sin, taking occasion by the commandment, wrought in me all manner of concupiscence. For without the law sin was dead. For I was alive without the law once: but when the commandment came, sin revived, and I died. And the commandment, which was ordained to life, I found to be unto death. For sin, taking occasion by the commandment, deceived me, and by it slew me.

What, then, is Paul's conclusion? It is this:
Wherefore the law is holy, and the commandment holy, and just, and good. Was then that which is good made death unto me? God forbid.
There is nothing wrong with the law. So why did the law make me worse than I was? Well, the apostle says:
But sin, that it might appear sin, working death in me by that which is good (Rom. 7:8–13).
In other words, it comes to this: man is in such a rotten condition as the result of sin that, even when you tell him not to do things, what is really happening is that you are arousing his desire to do them all the more. And is that not true? We all know that it is. Paul gives the reason in his Epistle to Titus: 'Unto the pure all things are pure: but unto them that are defiled and unbelieving is nothing pure; but even their mind and conscience is defiled' (*Titus* 1:15). It works out like this: the very

---

¹ The reference here is to the Friday night series on Romans.

law of God that was given to men and women to keep them from sin made them sin all the more because it had the effect of stimulating these passions and evil desires that were within them.

I have said often from this pulpit that there is nothing that I know of that is so wrong and dangerous as the so-called moral teaching that is being given in schools today – the so-called 'sex instruction'. The Victorians, we are told, hid this subject, they made a secret of it, and thereby the thing became a great problem. But now we know from psychology that we must be frank about these things, bring them into the open! So you tell the young people about them. And what is the result? The medical officers of health of most of the boroughs of Great Britain are giving the results at the present time – an appalling increase in venereal diseases in adolescents. Why is this? It is because teachers have been telling the children and young people about these things.

The motives of these teachers are very good, of course. It is to teach about the harm, the danger and the results. But people thought that young people, merely as a result of being told, would respond by saying, 'We'll never do this, we wouldn't dream of it!' How ignorant these teachers are of Romans 7! By giving young people the information, they are arousing their curiosity, they are awakening and stimulating their interest. 'The motions of sins, which were by the law' – even the law drove me to sin, says Paul, because I was rotten. It was not that there was anything wrong with the law, the rottenness was in me. I am so rotten that I twist even God's law and make it serve my own lust and my own evil desire.

Now if that is true of the law of God, how much more true is it of the moral and ethical teaching of men. No, no! 'Unto the *pure* all things are pure.' But who is pure? Before our eyes, statistics are proving the truth of Romans 7 but the philosophers and scientists, all the people controlling the Home Office, do not know the law of God, they do not know Romans 7 – and hence the moral muddle and the moral problem that is facing this country today.

So I end with this: the law not only shows us the exceeding sinfulness of sin as nothing else can, it also shows us all to be ultimately guilty and condemned before God. Paul says:

Now we know that what things soever the law saith, it saith to them who are under the law: that every mouth may be stopped, and all the world may become guilty before God. Therefore by the deeds of the law there shall no flesh be justified in his sight: for by the law is the knowledge of sin. But now the righteousness of God without the law is manifested, being witnessed by the law and the prophets; even the righteousness of God which is by faith of Jesus Christ unto all and upon all them that believe: for there is no difference: for all have sinned, and come short of the glory of God (Rom. 3:19–23).

There is nothing in the universe today that condemns everybody, but the law of God. Moral teaching condemns certain people – the night life of London – but it leaves us untouched in our respectability. Yes, yes! But the law of God when it comes along condemns and convicts every one of us. Covet! Desire! Evil thoughts! Imaginations! Who is there who is not guilty? 'There is none righteous, no, not one . . . all the world may become guilty before God . . . For all have sinned, and come short of the glory of God' (*Rom.* 3:10, 19, 23).

I have known people who have said that they do not see the need of Christ, they have never seen the need of grace, they have never done anybody any harm, they have always lived good lives. But these people have never listened to the law; they have never known anything about coveting; they have never examined their hearts. They are not only denying the Scriptures, they are utterly ignorant of themselves. They, of all people, are the greatest sinners because there is no greater sin than never to have seen your need of the blood of Christ to cleanse you and to save you. That is why people are deficient in their appreciation of the 'grace and truth' that came through Jesus Christ. Never having realized their own ugly, foul, black hearts, never having realized the exceeding sinfulness of sin, they have never known anything about this wondrous grace of God in Christ Jesus.

Do not dismiss the law, my friend, if you want to know anything about grace. Let the law speak to you. And though you may have been a Christian for years, if you are not convicted of your sin and do not feel that you are foul and unclean, then I despair of you.

Oh for a heart to praise my God,
A heart from sin set free,
A heart that always feels thy blood
So freely shed for me.
                    Charles Wesley

This is the main function of the law – to bring our sin home to us, and the exceeding sinfulness of that sin. ∾

6

The Law and the World

For the law was given by Moses, but grace and truth came by Jesus Christ (John 1:17).

We are continuing our study of this crucial verse because, as I have been trying to explain and expound, it gives us a kind of key, not only to the understanding of this Prologue of John's Gospel, but also to the whole of the Christian gospel, the Christian life and outlook. The greatest trouble with all of us, indeed, with the whole world, is our failure to realize what God has done for us in and through his dear Son, our Lord and Saviour Jesus Christ. That is what the Christian church is about – it is about him.

So even on a Remembrance Day such as this,[1] the church, when she behaves as the church, does not talk about people, she talks about God, she talks about the Son of God, who was made man for us and for our salvation. As we have been seeing, we can only appreciate men and women truly as we look at them in the light of God and his most holy law.

We will never know other people truly until we know ourselves. We are to love our neighbour as ourselves, and we will never know ourselves until we look at ourselves in the sight of God and in the light of his law.

God gave this law through Moses. He had already put his law into the heart of man when he made him but because of the fall and sin and rebellion, men and women forgot the law and wandered away from it, so God explicitly gave it again in the Ten Commandments. We are

---

[1] Remembrance Day or Armistice Day (11 November) commemorates the dead of two World Wars and subsequent conflicts.

therefore trying to see the importance of this law. We have seen that it is very definitely important from the Christian standpoint. Our whole conception of salvation depends upon it. If we have not known some preliminary law-work, then our idea of grace is very defective. It is only those who have seen themselves condemned under the law who rejoice in the grace of God in Jesus Christ our Lord. We have seen, too, that Christians need the law as regards their sanctification. Nothing but the law reveals unto us the depth of sin and unless we know something about that, we cannot possibly appreciate as we should the glories and the wonder of the grace of God. This law-work is essential and we dismiss the law only at our peril.

But now I am anxious to look at this matter with you in a more general manner because this is a message for the whole world as well as for the church. The law of God speaks to the whole of humanity. And never was its message needed more than it is today. What can we do better, therefore, on a day such as this – Remembrance Day – than consider something of what the law of God has to say? I lay down the fundamental proposition that the whole trouble in the world at this moment is due, ultimately, to neglect of the law of God, a neglect sometimes based upon sheer ignorance but at other times due to the arrogance of unbelief and the deliberate rejection of the Bible, which is the Word of God. That neglect is the one single cause of man's falling away from God and consequent falling away from what he was originally and from what God intended him to be.

Now let us try to work out that fundamental principle along a number of lines. What does neglect of the law of God lead to? First of all, it leads to a general apostasy, and that, speaking generally, is the position of the world today. The world is in a state of apostasy, which means that it no longer lives its life in terms of God, it no longer believes in him and its life is no longer centred on him.

I know that thousands, perhaps millions, of people in this country on this Remembrance Sunday will be taking part in some sort of a religious service, but we are not misled by that kind of thing. Most of it will be sheer paganism. People attend services and sing hymns but they do not believe in God. They do not worship God every day of their lives; they do not pray privately; they do not read the Word of God.

No, the world itself is in a state of apostasy. At times it likes to persuade itself that it believes in God but the very fact that it does that only at times is in itself the greatest possible insult to the almighty God, who demands, as we have seen, that we should worship him with all our heart and all our soul and all our mind and all our strength – not just now and again because of some special occasion. There is no greater hypocrisy than that. But this is the condition of the world and the Bible throws light upon the consequences.

What happens when men and women cease to believe in God and cease to worship him and to live to his glory? They then begin to believe in themselves and set themselves up as gods of some kind. The devil knows this very well. That was why the original temptation was such a temptation. 'Yea, hath God said ye shall not eat of every tree of the garden?' said the serpent to Eve (*Gen.* 3:1). And then he went on to say, in effect, 'Of course, God said that because he knows very well that the day you eat that fruit you will be enlightened, you will be like God himself – and that is what you should be.' And Eve fell to the temptation, and humanity has fallen to it ever since. The moment men and women cease to subject themselves to God, they set themselves up as gods. They are all worshipping themselves today and have been for most of the last century.

Of course, the result is conflict. The moment people set themselves up as the ultimate authority, they are filled with pride and with self-worship. As the Scriptures show us everywhere, the heart of the devil, the original rebel against God, was lifted up with pride. That is why he fell. The whole trouble with the devil is self, it is pride, and all who listen to him are in the same condition. And the inevitable consequence is clashes and collisions; each god wants to be supreme, each one wants to rule. That is why every sinner is a tyrant. You can see this even in a little child. He wants his own way. He is intolerant. He will not be disciplined. He wants what he wants. That is the result of sin.

And this pride shows itself in the whole of life. You find it in individuals, in groups and in nations. It is the cause of industrial strife; it is the cause of the tension between the nations, these rival blocs, these great giants. One goes higher, so the other must get higher, and here is the inevitable clash. Pride! Inflated with pride! That is the cause of war. Ultimately, the cause of war is not political or economic but is purely theological. War is entirely due to sin. There is no other explanation. 'From whence come wars and fightings among you?' asks James, and answers his own question: 'Come they not hence even of your lusts that war in your members?' (*James* 4:1). Lust is the cause of war, and lust is the creature of pride and of self-worship.

But further than that, this falling away from God, this apostasy, leads to an entirely false view of everything. It gives us a false notion of life, of history and of human greatness – and to me this is one of the most tragic things in connection with life in this country at this present time. It is true of all countries. The whole notion of life and of living and of the purpose and function of history has become lost. This is the tragedy of people in sin. They think they are exalting themselves but they are actually debasing themselves.

'What do you mean?' asks someone.

What I mean is that there is surely nothing quite so tragic at the present time as the way in which people are thinking increasingly in terms of merely existing. Had you noticed that? Existence is the great thing now. So in our own time and generation, and especially since the last war, we have seen how some of the most precious things in life have gradually been going.

Let me illustrate what I mean. The whole notion of heroism is going. You do not hear much about heroism these days. Why not? Because people are much too interested in preserving their own lives. The important thing today is to extend the length of our lives in this world. The idea that there are certain causes that are worth fighting for, certain things that are worth dying for – that has gone. There are slogans saying this – I am only using this as an example, I am not concerned to be political – but a slogan such as, 'Better red than dead', sums up what I am saying. There it is: the terrible, the awful, thing is to be dead. Existence is what is important, even if you exist as a slave. 'Better exist as a slave than die as a free man.' And that idea has come in because men and women have lost the sense of their own greatness; they are content to live in chains as long as they can just go on existing.

Romance has gone, too. I understand from the newspapers that this is evidencing itself in the theatres – the so-called 'kitchen-sink drama'. There is no romance there; there is no life. It is just sordid existence. But people are no longer interested in life and in principles. They want to perpetuate this horrible, foul existence. What a tragedy it is! Now the cause is purely theological. This is one of the consequences of turning away from God. Of course, those people who were alive a hundred years ago, who regarded themselves as great thinkers and scientists, they began all this, but they had no idea where it was going to end. If you turn away from God in an attempt to elevate yourself, you will ultimately debase and lower yourself, and you will have no respect for yourself. Man becomes just an animal, a beast, and nothing matters but food and drink and sex and existence. So romance has gone out of the window, and idealism and heroism and all things that make life worth living.

And as for the whole notion of a purpose in history, of 'One far off divine event, to which the whole creation moves'[1] – nothing is heard about that nowadays. You get these immoral pessimists, these people who teach experimental marriage and so on, just trying to get existence perpetuated and increased. Oh, what a fall! What a tragedy! It is a direct fall, which happens because men and women are ignorant of the law of God and do not know him and, therefore, do not know their own true value.

So there is the principle in general. But let me go on and illustrate it in other respects. Another consequence of forgetting or ignoring the law is that people fail to realize that unrighteousness is always the inevitable consequence of ungodliness. There is a great statement of this in Romans 1:18: 'For the wrath of God is revealed from heaven against all ungodliness and unrighteousness of men, who hold the truth in unrighteousness.' Note the order: ungodliness first, unrighteousness second. That is a most important point, and I would venture to assert that the failure to realize and to remember this has been one

[1] From *In Memoriam A.H.H.* by Alfred, Lord Tennyson.

of the major blunders of the last hundred years. Those great Victorians, so-called, are the criminals, they are the people who did the damage, they are the ones who should be pushed off their pedestals – these supposed great thinkers, the Darwins, and the Huxleys, and the Spencers, and those who followed them, and the timorous church leaders who were so uncertain of their faith that they did not denounce them as they should have done but allowed their teaching to permeate even into the message of the Christian church.

What was the teaching of these Victorians? The idea was this: though you shed the supernatural and the miraculous, and though you no longer believe in God in any real and living sense, you can nevertheless hold on to all the incomparable moral, ethical teaching of the Bible. So they all began to say that you could hold on to the teaching of the Old Testament and the Sermon on the Mount while no longer believing in the deity of the Lord Jesus Christ, in his miracles, in his atoning death and in his literal, physical resurrection and so on. They shed the theology but they said that you could still retain the morals and the ethics. So the great characteristic of the end of the last century was the formation of societies to reform morals and to keep this and that pure. The church and her message went down and down and societies came up on all sides. And people really believed it could be done, that you could divorce morals from religion. But today it is tragically and painfully evident that that simply cannot be. It is impossible. The last hundred years has really proved that.

You cannot separate godliness and morality. Understanding this is an essential part of understanding the age in which you and I are living. The moment you shed godliness, you will get unrighteousness – 'all ungodliness and unrighteousness of men' – the one invariably follows from the other. Let me show you how it is inevitable. The tragedy is that people are so ignorant of the Bible. It is all here, the first principles are here. But in their wisdom people have ignored these and have said that education and moral culture can do everything that is necessary. But they cannot because, to start with, you are left without a standard. Where do you get your standard from? If you banish God, if you banish the Ten Commandments, what standard do you have?

The answer is, of course, that you have no standard except each person's opinion, and one opinion is as good as another. Why, then, should we recognize any moral standard at all? And the result is that we have rival schools of moral teaching. There is a teaching called *hedonism*, which says that the important thing is pleasure; we are all meant to enjoy ourselves. The cult of pleasure and happiness – that is right which gives me and others the greatest amount of happiness – has been taught quite seriously. The claim is made that happiness, surely, should be put first. We are all meant to be happy – why shouldn't we be? So happiness is the supreme goal.

Others advocate *utilitarianism*. They say that the best you can hope for in a world like this is to keep things going, to keep them working. You do not ask whether a thing is good or bad, right or wrong, but whether, on the whole, it works. That was the philosophy of John Stuart Mill, and the Victorians half-worshipped him. He was not a Christian, he was scarcely a theist. He taught that what counted was anything that helped, anything that worked. So there is another theory, another standard.

A slight modification of utilitarianism is *expediency*. Advocates of this belief hold that there are no such things as absolute standards. We have to judge what is likely to work and the end justifies the means. An end that is desirable justifies the use of almost any means to get there. This has been a very popular view. Not only is it the theory of the Jesuits, it has also been adopted by nations and within society. It has been very popular in social work, for instance. And what is the consequence? Some people have worked it out in this way: if the end justifies the means, then 'might is right'. If my might will enable me to arrive at a desired end, then that is all right. Expediency was really the philosophy of Hitler, though it did not begin with Hitler. It is the philosophy of fascism. Believing that this system is the right one, you must impose it upon people. There have been terrible consequences, with deliberate lying and deceit defended as legitimate instruments of state, as we have seen in the case of Hitler and others. There is an old saying, 'All's fair in love and war.' But it is not. That is a lie. All is not fair in love and war. There are absolute standards there as well.

Now I am simply using these illustrations to establish my point that the moment you turn your back upon the law of God, you have no standard at all, and because you have no standard, then ultimately you will have no righteousness. Another way it works out is this: because of the absence of standards, there is no longer a belief in discipline and, especially, the whole notion of punishment goes. If you do not have a standard, how can you exercise discipline? And what makes things still more complicated is that because of the absence of certain fundamental, eternal, absolute standards dictated by the law of God, a kind of sliding scale develops. This is an acute modern problem.

Have you noticed the change in the moral standards of society, even during our own lifetime, say, during the last twenty years? What was frowned upon by everybody twenty years ago has now become the thing to do. Have you noticed a change creeping into the language of the newspapers – I am told it is still worse in novels – and in the ordinary language and demeanour and behaviour of people on the streets and everywhere else? Have you noticed the things that are now allowed without anybody turning a hair? There were standards among statesmen fifty years ago. They no longer obtain. A man could not hold office in the Cabinet if he had been divorced. He can now!

I am just showing you that the moment you abolish the law of God, you not only have every person with his or her own standard, you also have changing public standards. So the question arises: What is right? Each generation apparently has the right to determine what, if anything, is right. This was the great argument that was put forward at the time of the Wolfenden Report[1] – that we must be governed, always, by the majority opinion at the time. So today we must not be governed by acts that were passed in previous generations and were based upon the law of God. No, no! That is all wrong! Morals are decided by counting heads. The result is that there is no standard of good and evil, right and wrong; and there are certain people who actually agree with the words, 'Evil, be thou my good.'[2]

---

[1] The Report of the Parliamentary Committee on Homosexual Offences and Prostitution, September 1957.

[2] From *Paradise Lost* by John Milton.

It seems to me that we are very rapidly reaching a stage in which anything that is clean and pure and romantic is dismissed as outmoded, dowdy, and out of date. Unless there is something wrong and unclean about a thing, it is of no value, it is not artistic. And that view is being applied not only in the realm of art, but all along the line. One of the consequences is that punishment is, of necessity, regarded as harsh and cruel. How can I punish somebody for doing something if I have the feeling within me that in ten years' time everybody will be agreed that it is not wrong at all? I have no right to punish, so I do nothing, and there is no punishment.

The final result is an ultimate lawlessness, and I think we are rapidly approaching that state. It is very interesting to watch this sort of 'rake's progress'. First of all, people rebel against the idea of sin. When it promulgates its law, the Bible talks about sin. But people object and argue that there is no such thing. They say, 'There may be law-breaking, there may be crime, but sin is a horrible notion, get rid of it.' But now we have reached a stage in which they are also getting rid of crime. There is no such thing as crime – it is all a matter of disease! So in the courts it increasingly happens that the expert medical witness is the most important person, and the judges are naturally troubled because they no longer have any law to administer. An expert witness comes along and says, 'This man was not responsible, he didn't know what he was doing'; or, 'He couldn't help himself, that's how he was made.' And that is it. Do not talk about perversions, they say, there is no such thing, and do not call anything 'unnatural' because what you say is unnatural is natural to this man. You have no standards. It is all a matter of our make-up, our medical condition, the balance of our glands. You first of all get rid of sin, and then you get rid of crime. In the end, people do what they want to do – complete lawlessness and chaos.

But let me show you this along another line. I do trust that I am making it abundantly clear that law is absolutely essential, and that the moment we turn our backs upon the whole concept of law as we find it in the Bible, we are heading for disaster. Now many evangelical people have encouraged a disregard for the law. They say, 'Don't preach the law any longer. Don't condemn, don't denounce, just say, "Come to Christ." So they have been aiding and abetting this whole tendency to do away with law, which leads to the modern chaos. Let me show you this by putting it in the form of a principle. When men and women turn their backs upon law, they always develop a dislike of negatives, and a corresponding dislike of details. The whole notion has been that all we need to do is inculcate and develop a good outlook and right spirit in general. We do not need to be told in detail to do this and not to do that. That is insulting. We must never say, 'Thou shalt not', but rather we should simply always be saying, 'Now isn't this wonderful? Isn't this right? Isn't this good?'

This principle of turning away from negatives and details has been applied all along the line. Look at it, for instance, in education. We are told that we must no longer teach the three Rs and compel children to learn by rote, to repeat and repeat until what they are learning has become fixed in the memory. We are told that that is absolutely wrong. Nor must we discipline children or compel them to learn in a mechanical manner in order to get their minds stored with facts. All that is being frowned upon. I remember quite well the introduction of the Montessori system, which teaches that instead of drumming information into the child and exercising discipline, you get the child interested in numbers and words and history and so on, and you give explanations. You must not treat children like machines, no, you are to develop their interest and draw out understanding. Well, these ideas have been applied increasingly for the last forty years, and we are all familiar with the results. We find businessmen complaining that their clerks are incapable of simple arithmetic and that they are ignorant of spelling and grammar.

What has gone wrong? It is all due to a failure to understand the true condition of the child. The child is not meant to understand. Childhood is the time when the memory is keen and active and can absorb facts. It does not matter whether or not the child understands them, understanding comes later. What is essential is that children should be given facts so that when they are grown up they will be able to employ or develop reason, using the facts they have stored, which now become of inestimable value. As it is, children are able to talk learnedly as if they understand, but they do not; they are talking theories and they lack a basic knowledge of facts. This is but one example of the modern dislike of the negative and the detail. We are being told that all that humanity needs is a good spirit in general, and we are now witnessing the consequences.

Now the answer to all this is seen in the law, which, knowing us as we do not know ourselves, is always specific. The law always comes down to details, and it is very interested in negatives. That is why people hate the Ten Commandments: you shall not kill; you shall not steal; you shall not commit adultery. 'Insulting!' they say. Is it? No, no! The law knows us and it knows that we are always ready to develop a wonderful general spirit as long as we have liberty to fail in detail and practice. The law does not allow us that liberty. The law pins us down; it examines us on specific issues and questions. The law does not ask, 'Are you a good man?' It asks, 'Are you doing this? Are you doing that?' And this is essential. It is the only way of instructing us. We can never learn truly in any realm or department without getting down to the details.

I do not know what the modern theory is on learning a musical instrument such as the piano but I would advocate that children be made to practise their scales and not start with the masterpieces. Get down to it, the finger exercises, get all this mechanical part done first, so that in the end you do not have to think about that and can give your mind to interpretation. If you start with interpretation before you are right on your mechanics, the inevitable result will be chaos, it will be discord. And this is what is happening today in the whole of life.

But let me go on to another aspect of this denial of the law. All this, in the end, leads to a failure to see the need of authority and the need of sanctions. A law without sanctions is of no value, so the law always has to have its sanctions. When God said that if people did certain things, he would punish them, he did punish them. He did not merely say it, he did it. We have a statement of this in Hebrews 2:2: 'If the word spoken by angels was stedfast, and every transgression and disobedience received a just recompence of reward; how shall we escape, if we neglect so great salvation?' God laid it down that if people did certain things, they were to be stoned to death. Read your Old Testament history and you will find that this happened. What God said, God did. God warned his own people and when they disobeyed, he punished them, as he had said he would. He drove them out of paradise; he drove them into the captivity and the bondage of Egypt; he drove them into Babylon. Law always carries sanctions. Law, the whole concept and notion of law, carries the notion of authority, which applies the law and metes out the punishments pronounced by the law. But all this is most unpopular in this age and generation to which we belong, and that is why the world is as it is.

The world, in a sense, is suffering from a false view of love and grace. The whole trouble is that it has forgotten the first half of our text. The second half says, 'Grace and truth came by Jesus Christ.' People say, 'That's it! All that's needed is to preach Christ, to preach him as an example, preach him as a moral teacher, preach him as "the pale Galilean", preach him as a most wonderful person. That's all you need. Drop your law.' So they have left out, 'The law came by Moses.' The world thinks it believes in love. That is why it no longer worships God. Love is the universal solvent; everybody believes in it. And that is why they do not really believe in God. It is because in God there is always law.

And starting there, with a false notion concerning God and his righteousness and his holiness and his determination to punish evil, the world goes on to a false view of human nature. The idea today, is it not, is that people are fundamentally good. That is why they do not like the biblical teaching about sin; that is why they ridicule some of the hymns. There was a theologian, so called, in this century, who ridiculed Charles Wesley's hymn for saying:

> Just and holy is thy name,
> I am all unrighteousness;
> Vile and full of sin I am.

He said, 'You must not say that! When you apply for a job, you don't say that to your prospective employer, so why should you say it to

God?' And people say, 'That's Old Testament teaching, that's Moses; "grace and truth . . ." Human beings are essentially good.'

And because of these two views – that God is love only and that people are essentially good – it is said that all that is necessary to put the world right is to show men and women the good way to live and give them a picture of life as it ideally should be. That includes, of course, the banishing of war and the forming of a great council of nations – the League of Nations, the United Nations Organization, call it what you will. Then the nations will destroy all their armaments and they will all live happily together. What a wonderful picture! 'All that's necessary,' it is said, 'is to put that concept before men and women.'

Of course, this was done after the First World War and after the Second World War. I remember the idealism, particularly after the 1914–18 war. There was not so much after 1945; people were beginning to learn, unconsciously. But after the First World War there was the League of Nations, this glorious idea. Peace between the nations of the world must be maintained. Nobody could refuse to believe in it and to practise it. Set it before the nations that God is love and that people are essentially good. They are bound to rise to it. Appeal to them. Be reasonable. Do not say, 'Thou shalt not', but say, 'Isn't this wonderful? Surely this appeals to you?'

And the leaders of the nations tried that approach with Hitler. Afterwards that was called appeasement. But they believed it then. 'Surely,' said Mr Neville Chamberlain, 'if I only meet him and talk to him man to man . . . I'm a businessman and I've never yet failed when I meet a man across the table. It's all very well sending diplomatic notes but I'll go to him. I'll sit down with him and appeal to him. He's bound to listen.' And Chamberlain believed it! He was quite honest; he was perfectly sincere. It was his theology that was wrong.

And then, after putting the great ideal before the nations, you give them an example, a great moral example. During the period between the two world wars, when war broke out between Japan and China concerning Manchuria, there was a Christian leader who called for people to volunteer to go and sit down between the two rival armies. He really believed that this wonderful moral example would put an end to the war! Today people are urging Britain to disarm unilaterally. Why? 'Well,' they say, 'if Great Britain showed that moral example, it would shake the nations. They would all destroy their armaments immediately.'

Now I am not here to preach politics but I am here to preach theology and all I am saying is that that is devastatingly, hopelessly bad theology! Moral example! Do people rise to moral example? If they did, they would all have risen long since and followed Christ. But they do not because human nature is fundamentally evil and because men and women do not know that they need sanctions, that they need law. 'The heart is deceitful above all things, and desperately wicked: who can know it?' (*Jer.* 17:9).

The Bible puts it like this: ultimately there is nothing so wrong as to appeal in Christian terms to people who are not Christians. A man or woman who is not a Christian cannot be expected to live the Christian life, and to ask anyone to do so is to deny the truth of the Bible. To preach grace and truth to people who have never known condemnation is absolutely fatal. But that is what the world has been doing; that is what the idealist is doing.

This is the ultimate heresy of pacifism. It expects Christian conduct from people who are not Christians. It believes you can apply the principles of the teaching of Christ to people who are not regenerate. This view is rank heresy. That is not to say that war is good; war is an evil. But the Bible teaches that until men and women come under grace, you must keep them under law. That is why there are kings and queens and emperors and governments. That is why the apostle writes to the Romans: 'Let every soul be subject unto the higher powers. For there is no power but of God' – the apostle Paul is including the Roman emperor there, remember; he is including pagan states – 'the powers that be are ordained of God . . . for he [the magistrate] beareth not the sword in vain' (*Rom.* 13:1, 4).

Law must be enforced; it must be applied; it must have sanctions. And the Bible says that people are so rotten, so evil – it is the law that reveals the extent of this evil, as we have already seen – that it is no use appealing to them. They have their own standards. They do not agree with the law, they do not agree that that is the ideal. The majority of people in this country today do not regard the Lord Jesus Christ and his way of life as being ideal. Of course not; they like this sordid horror that I have been referring to and will not rise to the example of Christ and follow him. No, they are so rotten that they must be kept in order. They must be punished. The law must be applied. They must be hurt. It is the only thing they understand. They do not have it in them to respond to the glories of God. You need emperors, you need kings, you need 'the powers that be'. You must have a sword. Evil must be restrained, otherwise the world would become nothing but sheer chaos. That is the biblical teaching. That is the essence of this whole matter of law.

'The way of transgressors is hard' (*Prov.* 13:15) – and it must be made hard. That is one of the ways whereby we eventually have some hope that men and women will be ready to listen to the message of grace and truth that has come in and through our Lord and Saviour Jesus Christ. It was only when the Prodigal Son found himself in the far country with the husks and the swine that he began to realize the truth concerning himself. And human beings are still like that. I regard these two world wars as a part of God's punishment upon them for their apostasy. And there will be more and more until the final return of Christ and the ultimate judgment.

That is the position as regards the world. But for the individual, the message is this: Realize the truth of all this. Cease kicking against the pricks (*Acts* 9:5). Cease fighting against the law of God. For God will enforce his law. He has sanctions, he has the power, and he will see that his law is carried out. And the final verdict upon lawlessness and unbelief and rebellion is eternal banishment from the presence of God. When men and women realize that, then, and only then, are they ready to listen truly to the message that tells them that 'grace and truth came by Jesus Christ'.

Christian people, I have taken you through this in the hope that you in turn will preach it to your neighbours, to those who work with you in offices, to those with whom you mix. I hope you will put it in this way so that they will not be misled by this false idealism that masquerades as Christianity but is a denial of biblical teaching. I trust you will enable them to see that Christianity is not some vague, flabby sentimentality, but is based on law, on justice, on truth, on righteousness, leading to the grace of God in Jesus Christ, our Lord. May God enable us to do so. ❧

7

The True Nature of the Law: The Schoolmaster

For the law was given by Moses, but grace and truth came by Jesus Christ (John 1:17).

We have been looking at the function and purpose of the law and have still not finished with this subject because there is one further, vital misunderstanding that we must consider. Why did God ever give this law to the children of Israel through Moses? That is the statement: 'The law was given by Moses.' As we read in Galatians 3:19: 'It was ordained by angels in the hand of a mediator.' But why was this?

We have already had many answers to that question, but I ask it afresh in order that I may put it like this: the whole trouble with the children of Israel, both in the Old Testament and especially at the time when our Lord came into the world, was due to the fact that they misunderstood and misapplied and abused the law of God. That is why so much attention is paid to the law in the pages of the New Testament. Our Lord himself deals with this. He says, 'Think not that I am come to destroy the law, or the prophets: I am not come to destroy, but to fulfil' (*Matt.* 5:17).

That is why discussions concerning the law are recorded in the book of Acts and that is why it is, in a sense, the major theme of the epistles to the Romans and to the Galatians, and why it is inevitably discussed in many other epistles also. It is all due to the fact that the people had misunderstood the meaning and the function of the law and thereby had abused it. This was the main cause of their trouble and of their tragedy.

So it is to this question of why the law was given that I am now anxious to call your attention, because the problem of the law still obtains. There are many people in trouble about their spiritual experience simply because they are abusing the law or misunderstanding it in some shape or form. One constantly finds in pastoral experience that when Christian people are in trouble, it is very often simply because they have again gone back under the law and have been guilty of this abuse that was so true of the children of Israel. There are others who are uncertain whether they are Christians at all and it has always been for this selfsame reason. So it is important for us to have a clear conception of the relationship of law and grace, the very issue put before us in John 1:17.

Let me put it in the form of an assertion or a principle: *the law was never given as a possible way of salvation.* Now there, at once, we come face to face with the cardinal error of which the Jews were guilty. Having misunderstood the function and the purpose of the law, they were regarding it as a way of salvation. They believed that by the observance of the law, by carrying it out, they could justify themselves before God and could work up a righteousness that would satisfy his demands. That was their initial and their continuing error. And, I repeat, there are many today who are in exactly the same position. They do not always put it in terms of 'law', of course, but it is the principle that matters. All those who think that they can make themselves Christian are guilty of this same error, and that includes all who think that Christians are to be defined as men and women who live good lives, or do a lot of good, or sacrifice themselves for the sake of others. Anybody who thinks that he or she can ever satisfy God and be accepted by him and get into heaven on the basis of his or her own actions is immediately guilty of this particular error. That is, I say again, to believe that you can justify yourself by the deeds of the law. And it is amazing to notice how common this basic attitude still is.

This error takes many different forms. You will find certain people described as outstanding Christians but when you come to examine them and their beliefs, you find that they do not believe in the Lord Jesus Christ – some even deny his deity. So why are they regarded as Christians? Because of the good work they are doing! They have made sacrifices, they are serving humanity, they are trying to put into practice the ethic of Christ. But they do not rely upon his death and upon his blood: in fact, they dismiss and denounce it. Now to think like that is to misunderstand the whole point and giving of the law.

But, even beyond that, there is a very definite teaching, sometimes known as Dispensationalism, which propounds exactly the same error. This teaching would have us believe that the gospel of the grace of God did not begin until the death and resurrection of the Lord Jesus Christ. It says that during his lifetime he did not speak about grace at all but preached 'the gospel of the kingdom', as Dispensationalists call it, which was a kind of legal doctrine by which people were to be saved, and it was only when our Lord was rejected as the Messiah that the whole notion of the gospel of the grace of God came in. Proponents of this view tell us that if you wish to look for the gospel of the grace of God, you must not go to the Gospels but to the epistles, and particularly to the epistles to the Ephesians and Galatians. And then they say that in the future, after our Lord has returned to this world and set up his kingdom, the gospel of the grace of God will no longer be preached. People will then again be saved by this gospel of the kingdom – no longer by grace but by some works of theirs and their obedience. In other words, Dispensational teaching has several types of gospel and the gospel of grace is only a kind of interim gospel.

But Dispensationalism radically misunderstands the whole question of the law. It states that there was a time, and will again be a time, when men and women can be saved by their own actions, by their conformity to law, that it is possible for us to be saved apart from and without the grace of God in and through our Lord and Saviour Jesus Christ. Dispensationalists put it bluntly like this: if the Jews had only believed and accepted the teaching of the Lord concerning his kingdom, then the gospel of grace would never have been needed at all and would never have come in. But that, to me, is the most basic misunderstanding that can ever be conceived. So you see the importance of looking at this whole issue of law and grace.

What, then, is the answer to such a teaching? It is, I repeat, that the law was never given as a possible means of salvation. We must once and for ever get rid of the idea that God, through the law, was trying an experiment – for that is what that teaching really comes to. It maintains that God, having said various things to the children of Israel, then said to them, in effect, 'Well, here it is, I will put it to you in the form of a law. If you keep that law and live it, you will be saved.' An experiment! But the people failed.

Let me give you the evidence on which I make this assertion that God never gave the law as a possible way of salvation. It is quite abundant. Let us take it first of all as it is put to us by the apostle Paul in his Epistle to the Romans. He deals with it in chapter 9 and it is also the point of the first three chapters, where Paul shows that justification is by faith only. He says: 'Therefore by the deeds of the law there shall no flesh be justified in his sight: for by the law is the knowledge of sin' (*Rom.* 3:20). But here it is, still more explicitly, perhaps, in chapter 9, where the apostle shows this basic, tragic error of the Jew:

What shall we say then? That the Gentiles, which followed not after righteousness, have attained to righteousness, even the righteousness which is of faith. But Israel, which followed after the law of righteousness, hath not attained to the law of righteousness. Wherefore? Because they sought it not by faith, but as it were by the works of the law. For they stumbled at that stumblingstone (Rom. 9:30–32).

They did indeed and that has been the stumbling-block ever since. Then Paul goes on in chapter 10 to work out the same point:

Brethren, my heart's desire and prayer to God for Israel is, that they might be saved. For I bear them record that they have a zeal of God

– zeal was not their trouble; they were trying to please God, they wanted to be just with him and blessed by him –

but not according to knowledge, For they being ignorant of God's righteousness, and going about to establish their own righteousness, have not submitted themselves unto the righteousness of God. For Christ is the end of the law for righteousness to every one that believeth. For Moses describeth the righteousness which is of the law, That the man which doeth those things shall live by them (Rom. 10:1–5).

There, then, we have before us the perfectly plain statement that the whole trouble with the Jews in their rejection of Christ was their misunderstanding of the law. They said, in effect, 'God has given us the law and by our keeping of that law we are justifying ourselves in the sight of God; by keeping the law we are becoming righteous and saving ourselves.' As Paul puts it: 'They were going about to establish their own righteousness.' And that is why they would not submit to the righteousness of God. But the teaching of Christ about the whole purpose of his coming, everything that he said and did, condemned this view. In him, and in him alone, is salvation. Again, this is put very clearly in that great statement in Galatians 3:8: 'And the scripture, foreseeing that God would justify the heathen through faith, preached before the gospel unto Abraham, saying, In thee shall all nations be blessed.' The point that the apostle explicitly makes here is that God did not give the law as a means of salvation. He had already preached the gospel to Abraham.

There are many people who say that the gospel only starts after the Lord Jesus Christ came into this world, and dispensationalists, as I have said, would even postpone it until his resurrection. But the answer is that it all began with Abraham, indeed, even before Abraham. The gospel began back in the Garden of Eden, and you will find it in Genesis 3:15. But the promise of grace as a way of salvation came explicitly at the time of Abraham: 'So then they which be of faith are blessed with faithful Abraham' (*Gal.* 3:9). It was through his seed that this blessing was going to come.

Now the apostle Paul was so troubled by the misunderstanding of this truth, particularly by the people in the churches of Galatia, that he goes further and argues it out extensively. He says:

Brethren, I speak after the manner of men

– he is saying, in effect, 'Now in order to make this plain and clear to you I am going to use an illustration. I am going to put it in very simple terms.' So he goes on –

BORN OF GOD

*though it be but a man's covenant, yet if it be confirmed, no man disan-
nulleth, or addeth thereto.*

Even when a man makes a covenant, Paul explains, it is valid in law
and nobody ventures to disannul it or to add to it. Even with a human
document such as a will, nobody dares put it on one side or add to
it. There it is; it is to be observed and it will be observed. Now, listen,
Paul says:

*To Abraham and his seed were the promises made. He saith not, And
to seeds, as of many; but as of one, And to thy seed, which is Christ.*

In other words, the promise of salvation in Christ by grace was made
to Abraham. This difference between 'seeds' and 'seed', Paul says, shows
that God was telling Abraham that it was through one man, Christ,
who was to come out of his loins, that this great salvation would come
to all nations. And Paul continues, working out his illustration:

*And this I say, that the covenant, that was confirmed before of God [by
God] in Christ, the law, which was four hundred and thirty years after,
cannot disannul, that it should make the promise of none effect.*

Now you see the argument? Back in the time of Abraham, God had
made his covenant, he had made his statement that salvation was to
be by grace, and by grace alone, and that it was to be through this
'seed' that was to come, the Lord Jesus Christ. Now, then, Paul says,
that is the covenant. I have reminded you that even with an ordinary
human, earthly covenant nobody ventures to disannul it or to add to
it, so how much more so in the case of God. If God made his covenant
there with Abraham, the law, which came 430 years later, cannot
disannul it, or put it on one side, or make the promise of none effect.
Then Paul says:

For if the inheritance be of the law, it is no more of promise.

If God had said, 'I am going to give you the law, keep it and it will
save you', then it would mean that he was going back on, and annulling,
his promise, because he had already said that salvation was by grace,
and by grace alone. The idea is monstrous!

[96]

Well, says the Jew, if you are saying that, then why did God ever give the law? If you are saying that it is not given as a means of salvation, what is its purpose?

Wherefore then serveth the law?

Here is the answer. My first principle is:

It was added because of transgressions

– because of the sinfulness of the people –

till the seed should come to whom the promise was made; and it was ordained by angels in the hand of a mediator. Now a mediator is not a mediator of one, but God is one.

Do not worry about that now.

Is the law then against the promises of God?

That is the crucial question.

God forbid

– the suggestion is unthinkable. It is a terrible thing to say. The God who has given the promises is the very same God who has given the law, so it is impossible that the law can be against the promises of God –

for if there had been a law given which could have given life, verily righteousness should have been by the law.

If any law could have produced righteousness, then that would undoubtedly have been the way.

But the Scripture hath concluded all under sin, that the promise by faith of Jesus Christ might be given to them that believe.

Now, then, listen:

But before faith came, we were kept under the law, shut up unto faith which should afterwards be revealed. Wherefore the law was our schoolmaster to bring us unto Christ . . .' (Gal. 3:15–24).

Now I am concerned to establish that the apostle has taken all that trouble to tell us that God never gave the law as an experiment, he never offered it as a possible way of salvation. That, says the apostle, would mean that God was going back on his own covenant, or on his own oath, on his own word. He had already preached the gospel to Abraham and, because he is God, he cannot go back on it. So whatever else you may think about the law, you must never regard it as a means whereby you can put yourself right with God.

To complete the argument, we put it like this. The Jews not only misunderstood the whole function and purpose of the giving of the law, but that, in turn, led them to misunderstand its demands; hence our Lord's exposition of the law in the Sermon on the Mount: 'Ye have heard that it was said by them of old time . . . But I say unto you' (*Matt.* 5:27–28). In other words, the only way the Jews or anybody else can ever persuade themselves that they can be righteous and just in the sight of God by observing the law is by paying attention only to the letter of the law, ignoring the spirit. Our Lord was constantly drawing attention to that. Not only did he deal with it in the Sermon on the Mount, but we also find it in Matthew 15 and in Mark 7, where he says, in effect, 'You have put your traditions before the law; you say that as long as a man does not do this or say that, he is all right. But that is what *you* say – God has not said that.' The Jewish leaders were substituting their own reading of the law for the actual demands and dictates of the law of God.

So that is my first principle. The law was never given as a possible means of salvation. Let me press this home particularly to those of us who are evangelical. It is, I repeat, our desire to safeguard the doctrine of justification by faith only that often makes us say that we have nothing to do with the law and preach Christ only. But that is the mistake. We are correcting the fallacy of the Jews in a wrong way. That is to misunderstand the whole object and purpose of the giving of the law. Let us, then, continue with our consideration of what that purpose is.

My second principle is that over and above what the law does to convict us of our sin and to show the exceeding sinfulness of sin, *it was given to show the utter and complete impossibility of salvation by the law.* Now I am not trying to be paradoxical but I am putting it like that in order to emphasize this point. Not only was the law *not* given as a possible means of salvation, it was given in order to show that salvation by keeping the law is impossible. Let me give you my authority for that: '*For what the law could not do, in that it was weak through the flesh*, God sending his own Son in the likeness of sinful flesh, and for sin, condemned sin in the flesh' (*Rom.* 8:3). Here is a crucial statement. The law could not save men and women and, of course, God knew that before he ever gave it. So that finally disposes of dispensationalist teaching, does it not? God knows everything. He knows the end from the beginning. Nothing is hidden from him. God knew that the law could not save anybody: 'what the law could not do'.

But why could the law not save anybody? Because, says Paul, 'it was weak through the flesh'. Now I think that means three main things. First, the law could not save anybody because of the exalted character of its demands. The Jews, as I have just told you, thought they were keeping the law; the apostle Paul used to think that he was keeping it. In that bit of autobiography in Philippians 3, he says, '. . . touching the righteousness which is in the law, blameless' (*Phil.* 3:6). When he was a Pharisee, he really thought he was keeping the law of God. All the Pharisees thought that. What was the matter with them? They had never realized the real demand of the law of God; they were reducing everything. They had turned the law of God into something that they could keep, and that is what every self-righteous, self-justifying, respectable person who does not believe in Christ is still doing. People set up their own little standards, which they know they are already keeping, and therefore they think that everything is all right. Yes, but as Paul says, that is not the righteousness of God. That is your own righteousness. You say, 'As long as I don't do this or that, and as long as I do good, I'm surely satisfying God.' But that is not what God says.

What does God say? He says: You must love me with all your heart and all your soul and all your mind and all your strength. And then, having done that, you must love your neighbour as yourself (see *Matt.* 22:37–40). That, and nothing less than that, is the demand of God's law. It is no use your arguing; that is what God has said. You may be entirely respectable and a very nice and good person, but are you loving God with the whole of your being? I can prove to you that you are not.

You are loving yourself because you are pleased with yourself, you are proud of yourself and your actions and you do not see your need of the Lord Jesus Christ. You are a terrible sinner. You are, of all sinners, perhaps the greatest. There is no greater sin than spiritual pride, self-satisfaction, feeling that the Son of God need never have come because we have never sinned, we have never done any wrong.

And why do people say that? It is, I repeat, because they have their own definition of sin. They have never committed murder, they have never committed adultery, they have never got drunk. But as for backbiting, pride, jealousy, envy, snobbery – they do not regard those as sin. They have their own definition of sin, but it is not God's. They have never realized the exalted character of the law. The law demands that we love God with the whole of our being and our neighbour as ourselves, and that we live to his glory. It is interested, as we have seen already, in motives and desires. Oh, 'Thou shalt not covet', the words that got Paul, eventually. It is in the law, my friend, and if you covet, you are a sinner.

Then let me give you another indication of the demands of the law. I have put it in general, but Paul summed it up like this: 'Love worketh no ill to his neighbour: therefore love is the fulfilling of the law' (*Rom.* 13:10). If you are not full of love, you have not fulfilled the law; love is nothing less than the fulfilment of the law. Let us consider some other statements made about the law. 'I testify again to every man that is circumcised, that he is a debtor to do the whole law' (*Gal.* 5:3). The whole of it! And if you want a final word, James will give it to us. The Epistle of James is the epistle that all self-righteous people should always be made to read. If you are finding it difficult to convince them of justification by faith, make them read James. That sounds odd, does it not, but listen, this is what James says: 'For whosoever shall keep the whole law, and yet offend in one point, he is guilty of all' (*James* 2:10). If you keep 99.999 per cent of the law, it does not save you! If there is the slightest failure, he says, you have failed in the lot. That is the demand of the law! It requires an absolute perfection of obedience, and nothing less. There are no loopholes, there are no qualifications, there are no 'get-outs', as we say. It is all or nothing. There, then, is the law. Who can keep it to that extent! By its own character and by its own demands it shows quite clearly that it was never meant to justify anybody.

The second meaning of these words, 'What the law could not do, in that it was weak through the flesh', the second reason why the law cannot save us, is that the law leaves it to us. The law comes to us and says, 'There it is, that is what you must do, and *you* must do it.' But I am weak, 'weak through the flesh'. I am sinful. Not only that, there is this other contradiction in me. That is the great theme of Romans 7. The apostle Paul says:

For we know that the law is spiritual: but I am carnal, sold under sin. For that which I do I allow not: for what I would, that do I not; but what I hate, that do I. If then I do that which I would not, I consent unto the law that it is good . . . For I know that in me (that is, in my flesh,) dwelleth no good thing: for to will is present with me; but how to perform that which is good I find not (Rom. 7: 14–16, 18).

Notice that we are not simply asked to give our assent to the law, we are not asked to admire it and say, 'It's wonderful! That's what we ought to do.' I am not asked to praise the law – I am asked to perform it.

For the good that I would I do not: but the evil which I would not, that I do (Rom. 7:19).

And is that not true of every one of us?

I find then a law, that, when I would do good, evil is present with me. For I delight in the law of God after the inward man: but I see another law in my members [in my body], warring against the law of my mind, and bringing me into captivity to the law of sin which is in my members. O wretched man that I am! who shall deliver me from the body of this death? (Rom. 7:21–24)

There it is; the law leaves it to us. I say, 'The law of God – yes, I see it's good, it's wonderful. I'm going to keep that law. I want to keep it.' Then I begin to try, and I fail; the law in my members is dragging me down. I want to, but I cannot. When I look at something objectively, I know that it is wrong, and I know I should not do it, but that is the very thing I do! That is the whole of life; that is experience. I am so constituted that 'in me dwelleth no good thing'. So there is this perpetual contradiction. In other words, the law simply tells me what I must do. We have already seen that it does something even worse. Because we are sinful, it actually inflames our passions and makes us sin all the more – not because there is anything wrong with the law but because there is so much wrong with us.

Was then that which is good made death unto me? God forbid! But sin, that it might appear sin, working death in me by that which is good; that sin by the commandment might become exceeding sinful (Rom. 7:13).

And, lastly, the third meaning is that the law was never meant to save because it never offers us any help at all. To tell a man or woman what to do is not enough. Do we not all know that? That is the whole tragedy of life; we cannot do what we want to do. Yet the law simply says, 'Do this'! And I cannot do it. The law leaves me entirely to myself. Now this is the truth that the apostles were given to understand. We see this in a wonderful statement in Acts 15:10. The apostle Peter is at the conference that the early church held in Jerusalem in order to discuss this very matter. 'Now therefore', Peter says, 'why tempt ye God, to put a yoke upon the neck of the disciples, which neither our fathers nor we were able to bear?' There were people who were trying to say that the Gentiles who had become Christians must be put under the law, that they must be circumcised and so on. 'Look here', says Peter, in effect, 'don't insist on that, it's an impossible yoke. No one has ever been able to keep it.'

So I sum up by saying that no one was ever meant to be saved by the law. Indeed, the law was given in order to show that nobody ever could be saved by this means.

So I come to my third and last principle in answer to the question: Why was the law given? What was the real, fundamental object that God had in mind in giving it? This is my next step in my argument of three principles. My first principle is that the law was given because of sinfulness and was never given as a possible means of salvation. My second principle is that the law was given to show the sinfulness of sin. My third principle, to which we now turn, is that *it was given 'to lead us to Christ'!* Now you see why I am so concerned about this verse of ours: 'The law was given through Moses, but grace and truth came by Jesus Christ.' You understand why I am so anxious to show that we should never dismiss the law or condemn it or ridicule it and say it does not matter and that as Christians we must think nothing of it because we now believe in Christ and grace. You see how wrong that is? The law was given, ultimately, in order that it might bring us to Christ. It was given that we might know our utter helplessness and hopelessness and our ultimate, complete inability to save ourselves.

The difficulty with all of us is that we will never admit that we cannot do things. The reason why we do not believe in Christ and accept his salvation is that we still think we can save ourselves; every one of us needs to be knocked down before we can be raised up. Remember the statement that was made by ancient Simeon to the mother of our Lord: 'This child is set for the fall and rising again of many in Israel' (*Luke* 2:34). We must become utter paupers, we must realize our final helplessness, before we will ever accept grace, and the only thing that brings us to that position is the law of God. This is the only thing that convinces and convicts us. The moment we understand the true nature of the law, we see our complete hopelessness, as I have been indicating to you. One hundred per cent obedience! Impossible! Here am I with this 'law in my members' and my divided self. Impossible! I might as well give up at once. The law, when it does its work in me, makes me desperate, it makes me cry out:

> *Not the labours of my hands*
> *Can fulfil thy law's demands;*
> *Could my zeal no respite know,*
> *Could my tears for ever flow,*
> *All for sin could not atone;*
> *Thou must save, and thou alone.*
>
> Augustus M. Toplady

But let me put it in the magnificent language of the apostle Paul in the Epistle to the Galatians: 'But before faith came, we were kept under the law, shut up unto the faith which should afterwards be revealed'

(*Gal.* 3:23). That is why the law was given. As we have seen, that is the end of Paul's argument. He said that the law was not given to put aside the doctrine of grace that God had preached to Abraham through the gospel. Of course not! That would have meant there was a contradiction in God. It was not meant to disannul the promise.

What was the law for, then? Oh, it was meant to shut us up to the promise. It was meant to show men and women that they could never do anything at all to save themselves. They are hemmed in, they are shut in to this promise of God, which was made originally to Abraham and now has been fulfilled in the coming of the Son of his love and the Son's perfect work on our behalf. They are 'shut up'! Oh, I rather like this translation; it is rather good. I had never thought about it until this minute. Do you know what the law says to you? Shut up! Shut up about your self-righteousness and all your goodness and your great sacrifice. Shut up! Not only do not try to go on doing things like that to put yourself right with God, but stop talking, put your hand over your mouth, get down into the dust and ashes. The most respectable person in the world, the most moral, ethical individual, you, too, get down and put on your sackcloth and ashes. Shut up!

But then in Galatians 3:24 Paul adds this further statement: 'Wherefore the law was our schoolmaster to bring us unto Christ.' And this is still the case. I assert again that no one ever truly comes to Christ except he or she be brought by this schoolmaster. I do not understand a conversion and a regeneration that says, 'I know nothing about repentance.' I do not find such a gospel in the Scriptures. If you say, 'I came to Christ because I wanted to be blessed by him, because I wanted this, that and the other', and have never come to him as a desperate sinner, then you have not come to him at all. The law is our schoolmaster to bring us to Christ that we might be justified by faith. That is why it was given. That is the inspired account of the reason for the giving of the law. Therefore we must never dismiss the law. Do not misinterpret John 1:17. Do not kick the law out. Do not depreciate it. That is not John's purpose at all. He is showing that it was meant to bring us to Christ and to the glories of what Christ has given us. Its purpose was to emphasize the pre-eminence of Christ.

So, then, the right reaction to the error of the Jews, and to all who are trying to justify themselves by their works, is not to dismiss the law but to use it rightly. If I preach the law in such a way that somebody goes home thinking, 'Very well, all I've got to do is live like that and I will be a Christian', then I have preached the law badly and wrongly. But if I have preached the law in such a way as to make somebody say, 'I'm completely and entirely hopeless and unless I can be saved by someone outside myself, I'm done for', then I have preached it properly. That is the answer to the Jews. It is not to reject and never preach the law, but to preach the law properly. Let me again quote the apostle Paul:

But we know that the law is good, if a man use it lawfully

– people were trying to bring the law back but Paul says: No, you are bringing it back in the wrong way –

knowing this, that the law is not made for a righteous man, but for the lawless and disobedient, for the ungodly and for sinners, for unholy and profane, for murderers of fathers and murderers of mothers, for manslayers, for whoremongers, for them that defile themselves with mankind, for menstealers, for liars, for perjured persons, and if there be any other thing that is contrary to sound doctrine; according to the glorious gospel of the blessed God, which was committed to my trust (1 Tim. 1:8–11).

That is the right use of the law, and that is the way in which we should look at it. I am concerned about this not primarily as a matter of theology; I am concerned about it primarily as a pastor. Almost every Sunday someone who is in trouble about this will come to me and say, 'But my past life, my sin . . .' And the moment I hear that, I know that that person has a problem with understanding this question of the law. I say, 'You are confessing to me that you are a sinner?'

'Oh yes, I'm terrible . . .'

I say, 'But that is your right to justification by faith.'

'But if you only knew . . .'

I say, 'It doesn't matter what I know or what I don't know: Christ died for the ungodly, he justifies the ungodly.'

And when I see people hesitating and wondering whether they can be forgiven, then I know that they still have a hankering notion somewhere that if only they had lived a better life, then all would have been well. And if only they could get rid of this sin, or if they could stop committing it, all would be well. That means that they are still under the law. It means that they are guilty of this initial error of regarding the law as a means of salvation and of deliverance.

My dear friend, are you clear about this? 'By the deeds of the law there shall no flesh be justified in his sight: for by the law is [simply] the knowledge of sin' (*Rom.* 3:20). The law will convict you, it will knock you down, it will shut you up, it will leave you in complete and entire helplessness, and by so doing it is acting as the schoolmaster, the pedagogue, to lead you to the only one who can save you, our Lord and Saviour Jesus Christ. 'For the law was given by Moses, but grace and truth came by Jesus Christ.' ❧

8

The True Nature of the Law: A Fingerpost to Grace

For the law was given by Moses, but grace and truth came by Jesus Christ (John 1:17).

We have been considering the real function and purpose of the law. And we have seen that it was meant to reveal God to us, the character and the holiness of God, and our relationship to him. It was meant, likewise, to reveal God's demands of us, to show what it is that God expects of us, in order to bring us to a state of conviction and to show us our need of what God alone can give us. It was also meant – and for the same end, of course – to bring out the exceeding sinfulness of sin, to show that sin is not something light and superficial but deep down in the very depths of our being.

And that led us to the point at which we arrived last time, namely, that we are entirely and completely hopeless and helpless. We finished on this note – that the real business and function of the law is to be our schoolmaster to lead us and to bring us to Christ. It was never intended to be a way of salvation. Or, to take a term that the apostle uses in Galatians 3, it was meant to 'shut us in', to 'shut us up' unto Christ, to shut every door, every way of exit and of escape and to hold us there face to face with him.

We are now in a position, therefore, to make this assertion: that the most important thing to grasp about the law is that it is a pointer, a fingerpost, to grace. This is a fundamental assertion. *The law points to Christ.* Moses points to the Lord Jesus Christ and indicates to us why our Lord had to come. In other words, there is no better prolegomenon, or introduction, to the gospel than the law. That is what its function really is. It is the introduction to grace, to the coming of our Lord and Saviour Jesus Christ. We are now on the doorstep, as it were, of the season of Advent,[1] and that is the way to approach it. That is precisely, of course, what John is doing here, at the beginning of his Gospel. He tells us how 'the Word was made flesh' and, in connection with the law, he tells us why the Word was made flesh. I will go further – he tells us why the Word had to be made flesh if man really was to be delivered and to be saved.

Now that is the essence of the relationship between law and grace, between Moses and Christ; so you see why I have been at such pains to impress the point that it is entirely and utterly wrong to regard them as opposites. You can also see how wrong it is either to dismiss the law or to overestimate the function of the law and to rely upon it and to regard it as a means or a way of salvation. The vestibule is not the house; the introduction is not the subject itself; the preliminary is not the actuality. There is this relationship: on the one hand, the two must never be separated but, on the other hand, the law must not be exalted into a central position as a means of salvation and deliverance. We arrive, then, at this most important position – that the law points to, shuts us up to, Christ. That is what the law can do, that is what it must do, but that is the utmost of what it can do. You remember that phrase we looked at last time: 'what the law could not do' (*Rom.* 8:3). It can do certain things, but nothing beyond those.

So, in the light of this idea that the law is the introduction, the pointer, to grace, let us once more look at the relationship between the law and grace, and let us illustrate this in different ways. The first is this. The law actually, in and of itself, did point to grace. Even when it was first given to Moses through the medium of angels, the law, as God gave it, contained within itself this element of grace. Now where do we see that? Well, we see it in the ceremonial law – and this is something that we should never forget. God not only gave Moses the Ten Commandments and the moral law, he gave him, at the same time, what is called 'the ceremonial law'; it is part and parcel of the same revelation, the same preparation.

[1] This sermon was preached on 25 November 1962.

A Fingerpost to Grace

In the ceremonial law we read a lot about burnt offerings and meal offerings, about sacrifices and the blood of bulls and of goats, and about the ashes of an heifer and various washings and so on. Today people very often struggle as they read the end of the book of Exodus and the book of Leviticus and parts of Numbers, and they say, 'We can't understand all this. We don't know what it's all about. Has it got any-thing to do with us? Is it just some detailed instruction for the children of Israel at that time, very largely a matter of public health or something like that?' And the answer to this confusion is simply that the object and purpose of the ceremonial law was to show the absolute necessity of *grace*. The provision of these laws indicates that God himself was teaching those children of Israel and showing them the only way in which they could approach him. He had told them that they were his people, that he demanded a certain type of conduct and behaviour from them. Then he gave the ceremonial law, and in it he was providing a way to enter into his presence.

But what I am emphasizing is that it was God himself who provided the ceremonial law. The people did not imagine these things. Moses did not invent them. Moses was taken up the mount, and all this was revealed to him in detail. Then he was told to go down and to do everything according to the pattern that had been shown him. So there is a very real significance in all that he was told and in all that he had to do and that the children of Israel had to carry out. And the ultimate meaning of it all is that it shows the way in which God is to be approached.

But there is also something else in the ceremonial law. Why do the people have to take these animals? Why do they have to put their hands on the head of the bull? And why must it be slain and its blood collected and then presented to God by the high priest – what is the meaning of it all? Why does a lamb have to be slain and presented morning and evening? What is the purpose? And there is only one answer: this is the way in which God tells the children of Israel that they need forgive-ness. And you notice that it is God himself who provides the way and the means and the method. Now that is all *grace*. But all that is also a part of the law. That is why this putting of law and grace as complete antitheses is always wrong. There is grace in the law. The law indicates the need of grace; this is a part of the law's own message. It is interesting to observe how, in all this ceremonial, the children of Israel are being told and reminded of the fact that ultimately they are dependent upon the grace of God. They have been given the commandments, these are the things to do, and yet at the same time God says, in effect, 'Now, as you will fail to observe them, here is my provision'; and they had to carry out the details of that ceremonial law. So we find that the law, in and of itself, contains this element of grace.

But still more: the law, in a prophetic manner, points to grace by making it quite plain and clear that all these burnt offerings and sacrifices and everything else to which I have referred, were not ends in themselves. These, we are told, are but *types*, but *shadows*. They perform a function, yes, but their main function is to point to something that is yet to come. These are all simply for the time being, as the author of the Epistle to the Hebrews puts it. You will find rich teaching about this in Hebrews chapters 7 and 9. Here it is, for instance, in chapter 9:

Which was a figure for the time then present, in which were offered both gifts and sacrifices, that could not make him that did the service perfect, as pertaining to the conscience; which stood only in meats and drinks, and divers washings, and carnal ordinances, imposed on them until the time of reformation (Heb. 9:9–10).

That is a perfect summing up of it all. All these are for the time being, they are simply sufficient 'until . . .' That is what I mean by this prophetic element. The paschal lamb slain when the children of Israel were about to leave Egypt for Canaan, the blood of that lamb painted on the doorposts and lintels of their houses, that is something in and of itself. Yes, but its main function is to point to the Lamb of God who is going to come. And so with every single burnt offering and sacrifice and every provision that has ever been made – they are all of them pointing, indicating, showing, that the great antitype is still to come. They are the shadow, not the substance; they are the preparation, not the reality itself. So the law thus points to grace in a prophetic manner. It says: This is the arrangement for the time being.

In the ceremonial law you have Moses pointing to Christ; you have the law pointing to grace. And one of the great errors, indeed, the greatest error, of the children of Israel was that they so constantly failed to remember that. They tended to regard their offerings and sacrifices as sufficient in and of themselves. They thought that as long as they made their offerings and their sacrifices, there was nothing more to be done. That was the error against which the prophets were constantly protesting.

The message of the prophets has often been misunderstood by today's so-called higher critics. They say that there was a feud between the priests and the prophets and that the proof of that is the way the prophets kept on saying that God did not want burnt offerings and sacrifices, and that this was not what he had told the people to do when he brought them out of Egypt at the beginning. And they add that there are also the great statements to this effect in certain prophetic psalms, such as Psalm 50, where God declares that he does not need offerings and sacrifices, 'For', he says, 'every beast of the forest is mine, and the cattle upon a thousand hills' (*Psa.* 50:10). And from that it is deduced that there was outright opposition between priest and prophet. But, of course, that is a complete misunderstanding.

What the prophets were saying was this: God had certainly ordained these offerings and sacrifices but he had never said that they were sufficient in themselves, he had never said that they completed the work, he had never said that they were a substitute for heart worship and a real submission to him and obedience to him. But the people of Israel were saying that obedience did not matter very much. It did not matter what they did as long as they presented their burnt offerings and sacrifices; that would make everything all right and God would be well pleased. That attitude was what the prophets denounced.

Now you see the importance and the relevance of that for us? That is our habitual Protestant criticism of Roman Catholicism and every other form of Catholicism, is it not? Our criticism is that they argue like this: 'Do what you like but go and confess it to the priest and you will be all right. It doesn't matter what you do as long as you confess. As long as you take your offering and your sacrifice all is well.' And we also, as Protestants, are in reality no different. We think that good acts balance bad acts, that if we make generous contributions to funds, we cover our deficiencies in other respects. To think like that is to put our reliance upon the burnt offerings and the sacrifices, to regard them as acting, as it were, *ex opere operato*, which is the false view of sacraments. It is to believe that there is magic in the water, magic in the bread and the wine, magic in any good act, which automatically sets us free. I say again that the law must never be regarded as sufficient in and of itself. I am also arguing that the law contained all this immediately. It said: You need forgiveness, you need God to provide a way of forgiveness. This just covers your sin for the time being. You are kept, you are waiting for something, for someone who is yet to come.

Thus the law itself pointed to Christ, to grace. And, indeed, there was a specific statement to this effect, which God told Moses to give to the children of Israel: 'The LORD thy God will raise up unto thee a Prophet from the midst of thee, of thy brethren, like unto me; unto him ye shall hearken' (*Deut.* 18:15). There is Moses, the one to whom and through whom the law was given, saying: This is all right, but I am simply pointing to this other Prophet who is to come. He is the one to whom you must listen.

There, then, is our first principle, but let me state a second. The law pointed to grace not only in and of itself; it also pointed to it in its teaching, in its implications. This is a most important matter. The law shows us the absolute need of grace, and that is where any notion that we can ever justify ourselves by works or by keeping the law is so absolutely fatal. How does the law show this need? It does it by telling us that it must be honoured because it is God's law. The moment we realize the meaning of the law, we see that it is something that must be honoured in every detail. The moment men and women really understand the law, they cease to talk about goodness, they cease to be interested in good and kind deeds and actions, important though they are; they realize that the law of God makes an absolute demand, that God will be content with nothing less than one hundred per cent fulfilment.

Our Lord puts this very clearly in the Sermon on the Mount in that crucial verse: 'Think not that I am come to destroy the law, or the prophets: I am not come to destroy, but to fulfil. For verily I say unto you, Till heaven and earth pass, one jot or one tittle shall in no wise pass from the law, till all be fulfilled' (*Matt.* 5:17–18). There is the key statement in this respect and a very vital one it is. The law is the law of God. It is not our idea of righteousness or decency or goodness that matters, but God's demand and God's request, and it is an absolute demand. There it is, thundering to us, 'This do, and thou shalt live' (*Luke* 10:28), and at once it makes us see that we are all guilty, we are all condemned before God. Now this is always the introduction to the gospel. Perhaps one of its most characteristic statements is found in Romans 3 – and this is how Paul always introduces the gospel:

Now we know that what things soever the law saith, it saith to them who are under the law: that every mouth may be stopped, and all the world may become guilty before God. Therefore by the deeds of the law there shall no flesh be justified in his sight: for by the law is the knowledge of sin.

The law convicts! It shows our failure. But then here comes the gospel:

But now the righteousness of God without the law is manifested, being witnessed by the law and the prophets

– the law and the prophets witness to the gospel –

even the righteousness of God which is by faith of Jesus Christ unto all and upon all them that believe: for there is no difference: for all have sinned, and come short of the glory of God; being justified freely by his grace through the redemption that is in Christ Jesus (Rom. 3:19–24).

Now that is a perfect statement of this whole relationship between law, prophets and grace. The main point is that the law by its teaching, and the implications of its teaching, shows us the utter, absolute need of grace. 'There is none righteous, no, not one . . . and all the world may become guilty before God' (*Rom.* 3:10, 19). The law makes me see that I need to be forgiven by God, and that is its great function and its work. This is always the first point in conviction, this is the essential preliminary to any real understanding of the whole doctrine of

salvation – that I am a failure, that I am guilty, that I am lost and need
to be forgiven. In other words, as the hymn puts it, here I am:

> Nothing in my hand I bring;
> Simply to thy cross I cling.

I am helpless, I am hopeless, I need to be washed, so I fly to this
fountain:

> Helpless, look to thee for grace.
>
> Augustus M. Toplady

Helplessness is an introduction to grace.

The law shows us our absolute need of grace: that is the first thing that
we see and deduce about the teaching of the law as an introduction,
as a pointer, to grace. But then let me give the second thing. The law,
in its teaching, shows abundantly clearly that nothing but grace can
save us and suffice us. Here, again, is this great, crucial matter, here,
really, is the origin of the Protestant Reformation. This is the big truth,
this whole doctrine of grace. This was the grand rediscovery that was
made by Luther and the other Reformers in the sixteenth century. And
the point I am concerned to emphasize is that there is nothing that so
demonstrates and proves to the hilt our complete and entire depend-
ence upon grace as the law of God. That is why I say that the law is the
introduction to grace – indeed, that it is the one introduction.

Now the whole trouble which so many people encounter in this
whole question of Christian salvation is very largely due to the fact
that a true law-work has never been done in them. They have never
fully understood this teaching concerning the law. But once the law has
done its work upon men and women, it makes them see that nothing
but grace can possibly save them. This is the great contention that is
made in the second chapter of Paul's Epistle to the Ephesians. And
having made this point, the apostle then repeats it:

> But God, who is rich in mercy, for his great love wherewith he loved us,
> even when we were dead in sins, hath quickened us together with Christ,
> (by grace ye are saved;) and hath raised us up together, and made us sit
> together in heavenly places in Christ Jesus: that in the ages to come he
> might shew the exceeding riches of his grace in his kindness toward us

through Christ Jesus. *For by grace are ye saved through faith; and that not of yourselves: it is the gift of God: not of works, lest any man should boast. For we are his workmanship, created in Christ Jesus unto good works, which God hath before ordained that we should walk in them* (Eph. 2:4–10).

Now why does the apostle make so much of that? Why does he go on repeating that 'by grace are ye saved' and the negative, 'not of works', and so on, with the final, 'we are his workmanship'? Well, he is just establishing this great fact that our salvation is only and entirely because of the grace of God. This is absolutely fundamental and crucial. Anybody who is not a Christian in this congregation at this moment is certainly in that condition because he or she is still relying upon himself or herself. You are relying upon your goodness or your works or your deeds in some shape or form. The stumbling-block is *grace*. Grace means that we receive salvation for nothing, that we can do nothing. But that is what we do not like. We feel that there is value in our goodness; we feel that surely there is some point in our being moral. We say, 'Are you telling us that we, who have always been brought up in a church and have always lived good and religious lives, that we are in an identical position this morning to that of the worst blackguard in London, who has never been inside a chapel?'

The gospel says: Yes, you are, there is no difference at all!

We say, 'What about all our reading of the Bible?'

The Bible says: There is no value in it if you are relying upon it.

'All the good we've done?'

Useless! Filthy rags! Worthless! This is the great teaching of the New Testament.

Now that was always the stumbling-block with the Jews; they could not believe it. The idea that they and the Gentiles were equally dependent upon the grace of God was, they felt, an insult. It was a mockery of God's own law given to his people. Because that was what Christ taught, they regarded him as a blasphemer. They could not follow it. The Gentiles were not only pagan, they were dogs. They were 'strangers from the covenants of promise' – outside the covenants – 'having no hope, and without God in the world' (*Eph.* 2:12). How could they be in the same position as God's own people, the godly Jew, the religious Jew? And yet, as I have shown you from the quotation from Romans 3, the apostle's whole argument is that there is no difference. 'There is no difference', he says, 'for all have sinned, and come short of the glory of God' (*Rom.* 3:22–23). Everyone is reduced to a common denominator.

And what proves that there is no difference? It is the law. That is the whole argument the whole time. It is the law that shows us our utter hopelessness and helplessness. And if we have not seen it, I say again, it is because we have not understood the law: the law has not done its work upon us; the schoolmaster has not really taught us. That is where law is still so absolutely essential. It is the one thing that makes us realize that we are utterly dependent upon grace alone. How does the law do this? Well, we have already seen it. Let me just remind you. We are not only guilty in the sight of God, but we are completely without strength, completely helpless, and therefore completely hopeless.

In that second chapter of the Epistle to the Ephesians the apostle Paul gives an amazing summary of our complete helplessness. What is the truth about us? Well, he says, it is that we are all living 'according to the course of this world' (*Eph.* 2:2). We are dominated by the devil: 'Among whom also we all had our conversation in times past in the lusts of our flesh, fulfilling the desires of the flesh and of the mind; and were by nature the children of wrath, even as others' (*Eph.*3:3). That is where we were, says the apostle; that is where everybody is. He puts himself, you notice, in with them. We are all guilty before God. But we are not only guilty – it does not stop at that. We are debased; we are perverted. We are governed by these 'lusts', as Paul calls them, which are not only in the flesh, but also in the mind. We cannot get out of this; we are all the creatures of lust.

'But,' says somebody, 'I've never committed adultery – that's lust.'

It is lust, I agree, but what about 'the desires of the flesh and *of the mind*'? Temper, anger, is a lust quite as much as adultery, and so are jealousy and envy and spite and ambition. These are the things that keep people awake at night. If they prevent you from sleeping, it means you are governed and controlled by them. We are all guilty of these lusts, every one of us. We are not only guilty, we are perverted; our very nature is rotten.

But it is even worse than that; we are all dead! 'You hath he quickened, who were dead in trespasses and sins' (*Eph.* 2:1). Spiritually dead! Do you know God? Is he real to you? If he is not, it is because you are dead! You say, 'I've lived a very good life.' All right; I am not asking you that. The question is: Are you spiritually alive? The sign of spiritual life is that you know and love God. The little infant loves the parent; it has not got much understanding but, instinctively, it loves. So does the person who is alive spiritually. So the test we apply to ourselves is this: Do we know God? Do we know the Lord Jesus Christ? Are they real to us? Do we love God? That is the Lord's own test. If we do not, it means we are spiritually dead. And what is the point of all your good works and deeds when you are dead? They are all artificial flowers. There is no life, there is no value, in them. The apostle Paul came to see this himself. All that he had trusted in, he says, he counted as dung: 'that I may win Christ, and be found in him, not having mine own righteousness, which is of the law, but that . . . which is of God by faith' (*Phil.* 3:8–9). Now it is the law that opens our eyes to that. Our works are never sufficient. God demands perfection.

So here I am. I am guilty. I am helpless. I am weak. I am hopeless. I am here and can do nothing. If I spend the rest of my life fasting and sweating in a cell in a monastery, living a religious life, so called, I will be none the better at the end. That is what Luther had to discover. And it is the law that brings that out. We see this summarized perfectly in Romans 7. With his mind, Paul says, he sees the value of the law of God, he wants to keep it. But then, he says, 'I see another law in my members' (verse 23). 'For that which I do I allow not . . . but what I hate, that do I' (verse 15). And here I am: 'O wretched man that I am!' (verse 24). That is the cry for grace. The law puts me flat on my back. I cannot stir; I cannot move; I am dead in trespasses and sins. The law proves the utter, absolute necessity of grace before I can be saved.

Thus we have seen that the law, by its teaching, shows us, first, our need for grace and, second, that nothing but grace can save us. The third point I make is this: the law by its teaching defines what grace is.

Grace is the free, unmerited favour of God. Grace is kindness shown to the utterly undeserving. Grace says that salvation is entirely due to and because of what God is. It is all the result of God's nature. It is nothing in me at all. So if I try to bring in anything of myself, I am denying grace. There have been many who have done that. That is the whole tragedy of Roman Catholic teaching. Roman Catholics talk a lot about grace: they even say that grace is in the water with which a child is baptized; they say it is in the bread that becomes transubstantiated, and in the wine. Transmissible grace! Yes, but they also insist upon your good works. They call it 'synergism', 'working together with'. I must work with grace. No, no! That is a denial of grace. Grace means that salvation is altogether and entirely due to God, that it is of him from beginning to end, that I make no contribution at all.

'But surely', you say, 'my believing does it?'

No, no! If you say that your believing saves you, you are denying grace. And do you still want to do that, having seen that you were dead? Can the dead do anything? We are not told that we are very ill, we are told that we are *dead* in trespasses and sins. And dead means dead! The dead can do nothing; therefore it must be all of God. 'Not of works, lest any man should boast' (*Eph.* 2:9). If you turn your faith into works, you are denying grace. No, no! 'For by grace are ye saved through faith; and that not of yourselves: it is the gift of God' (*Eph.* 2:8).

The law shows me that I cannot make any contribution to my salvation. If my best contribution is as 'filthy rags', if my best contribution is as 'dung', what is the value of it? In any case, I am dead, spiritually dead! The law proves to me the nature of grace, and grace is, as I say, the free, unmerited favour of God. The apostle describes it at length:

But God, who is rich in mercy, for his great love wherewith he loved us, even when we were dead in sins, hath quickened us

– we need to have life put into us, to be quickened like a child in the womb who does not do anything about it, but is quickened –

together with Christ, (by grace ye are saved;) and hath raised us up together, and made us sit together in heavenly places in Christ Jesus

– why? –

that in the ages to come he might shew the exceeding riches of his grace in his kindness toward us through Christ Jesus (Eph. 2:4–7).

What does this 'grace' mean? It means that our salvation is entirely due to God's own nature. It is because he is kind, it is because he is love, it is because there is no limit to his graciousness.

Now let us be clear about this. God did not send his Son into this world as a response to our cry. No, no! He even created the cry within us! God does not *respond* to us; it is God who causes us to respond to him. It is God who acts first, last, always. Our salvation is entirely and altogether of God. Grace means that we are saved not because of anything that is in us but in spite of everything that is true of us. It is because of his love, his kindness, his compassion, his mercy, this grace of his, 'the exceeding riches'. God was moved by nothing except his own glorious nature – and that is grace.

Let me give you another great statement of all this:

For when we were yet without strength, in due time Christ died for the ungodly. For scarcely for a righteous man will one die: yet peradventure for a good man some would even dare to die. But God commendeth his love toward us, in that, while we were yet sinners, Christ died for us. Much more then, being now justified by his blood, we shall be saved from wrath through him.

But listen:

For if, when we were enemies, we were reconciled to God by the death of his Son, much more, being reconciled, we shall be saved by his life (Rom. 5:6–10).

That is the truth about us – guilty, perverted, enemies of God, hating God; even dead, helpless, hopeless, lifeless. God has done it all. That is his grace. And all this that is so true about us is established by the law of God given through Moses to the children of Israel, the law that was originally written in the human heart. The law defines grace. Salvation must be altogether and entirely in God and of God because there is nothing left in me to bring it about.

And this leads to the fourth point, which is that the law, by its teaching, indicates and predicts what the grace of God in Christ does for us, what it must do for us. In other words, the law anticipates for us prophetically what the message of the gospel must be – and this is very wonderful to me. Do you want to know what the gospel of Jesus Christ is? I can tell you. What does the law say I need first and foremost? The answer is *forgiveness*. The gospel announces the forgiveness of God.

But does the law stop at that? Does it say that I only need forgiveness? No, it does not. For the law not only convicts me of my guilt, it shows me that my nature is twisted and perverted and rotten; it shows me that there is no good thing in me; it shows me that I am dead. So what must I get in the gospel? What is the gospel going to give me? Oh, forgiveness first, but then new birth, a new nature, new creation! The gospel proclaims it, but the law has demanded it. This gift of grace that the law points to is essential because I need not only to be forgiven but to be able to dwell with God and to walk with God and to commune with God and to obey God, and I need a new nature that will love the light and hate darkness, instead of the nature that I have, which loves the darkness and hates the light. So the law prophesies that that will be the second element in the gospel preaching. And it is.

And the third and the last thing that the law tells me I need is power. I now see the meaning of the law and its spiritual character, 'but how to perform that which is good I find not' (*Rom.* 7:18). I now have the new nature, I have understanding, but how to live this life? So I am told that I need some power within me, and the gospel tells me that the Spirit of God will come and dwell in me and will be a power in me: 'Unto him that is able to do exceeding abundantly above all that we ask or think, according to the power that worketh in us' (*Eph.* 3:20). 'Work out your own salvation with fear and trembling. For it is God which worketh in you both to will and to do of his good pleasure' (*Phil.* 2:12–13).

Here, then, we see this most interesting relationship between the law and grace, between Moses and the Lord Jesus Christ. Do not separate them, my friends, do not regard them as antitheses, do not kick away the law. No, no! You see how essential the law is! It is a fingerpost to grace. It points to Christ. It points to the gospel. It shows me my utter, absolute need of grace. And then it shows me the grace of God in Christ and what the gift of his grace is. Pardon! 'Ransomed, healed, restored, forgiven'! Reconciled to God, made a child of God, the Spirit of God dwelling in me as a tabernacle and working in me mightily and preparing me ultimately for the presence of God, for the perfection of heaven and the holiness of his holy presence. 'The law was given by Moses, but grace and truth came by Jesus Christ.' 'The law was our schoolmaster to bring us unto Christ' (*Gal.* 3:24). The law shuts us up unto Christ. The law is the introduction to Christ. The law calls for grace, anticipates it and leads me to submit myself utterly and completely to it. For being dead I must be quickened, and it is God who creates within me the very realization of my need.

> *Let not conscience make you linger,*
> *Or of fitness fondly dream;*
> *All the fitness he requireth*
> *Is to see your need of him.*
> *This he gives you,*
> *'Tis the Spirit's rising beam.*
>
> Joseph Hart

Our salvation is entirely and only and absolutely and all in all of God. 'By grace are ye saved.' Glory be to God who, in his infinite and eternal grace, has visited and redeemed his people. ∾

9

The Christian's Relationship to the Law

For the law was given by Moses, but grace and truth came by Jesus Christ (John 1:17).

We have discovered that if we have a true understanding of the biblical teaching with regard to the law of God given through Moses to the children of Israel, then we have the only true introduction to the gospel of the grace of God in and through our Lord and Saviour Jesus Christ. As we have been seeing, the law indicates that we need forgiveness, renewal and power, and grace answers that. 'All the promises of God in him are yea, and in him Amen' (2 *Cor.* 1:20). Grace is the answer to the needs that are in man in his fallen state and condition, as proved and demonstrated by the law. And the glory of the gospel is that it does indeed deal with every one of these conditions, and infinitely more. That is why the apostle John puts it as he does, in the form of a contrast: 'The law was given by Moses' – it did what it had to do, but it could do no more than that; but, thank God – 'grace and truth came by [and through, and in] Jesus Christ.'

Now we are advancing step by step and stage by stage, and the position we are in at the moment is that we are able to ask this important question: What, then – in the light of the coming of the Son of God and the grace and truth of God in him – is our relationship as Christian believers to the law of God?

Now I take it – indeed, this is my experience and I think it would be the experience of all pastors – that there is no question of there being anything of greater practical importance than just this very issue we are now considering. Why? It is because it affects our position at every point and at every stage. It is the failure to understand the exact nature and function of the law that keeps many from belief in the Lord Jesus Christ as their personal Saviour and Redeemer. The greatest enemy of justification by faith is justification by works. In other words, it is the law once more. People have not understood the message of the law. But, as we have seen, the moment they do understand it, they can no longer rely upon their own works. So I repeat that from the standpoint of evangelism and of our very introduction into the Christian life, there is no more important question than this.

But it does not stop at that point. There are many Christians who are in trouble because they get into a confusion and somehow or another put themselves back under the law. Some of them do this when, having fallen into sin, they are immediately distressed, wondering whether they are Christians at all. Then another trouble is the attacks and the assaults of the devil. He is ever ready to come when we do fall into sin, and he tries to get us back again into bondage. Trouble also arises in times of false teaching. The epistles to the Romans and to the Galatians deal with that, and it is teaching that is very badly needed at the present time. Teaching is also of vital importance in the whole question of assurance of salvation. Very many Christian people lack assurance because they are not quite clear on this question of their relationship to the law of God. And it is equally vital to be clear on this issue in the whole matter of our sanctification. There are people who are in error over sanctification, and are guilty of antinomianism, simply because they have not understood their relationship to the law of God. There, then, are some of my reasons for saying that this is one of the most practical matters that we can ever consider together.

As I have been indicating all along, as in all these issues, there are two dangers: one is that we may not go far enough in our understanding; the other is that we may go too far. It is always one or the other. We either stop short of where we should be or else we go beyond it – and the devil sees to that. He holds us back or he drives us too far forward. He makes us uncertain about a doctrine or he makes us so press it that it becomes a veritable hindrance to us. I could illustrate that at great length. We are people of extremes. Here, then, is the difficulty. So let us see what our relationship, as Christian believers, is to the law – and all I must do to deal with this is to put certain texts before you that make this relationship abundantly plain and clear. Let me put them in the form of three headings.

First: 'For Christ', says the apostle Paul, 'is the end of the law for righteousness to every one that believeth' (*Rom.* 10:4), and he goes on to expound that in the remainder of that tenth chapter. But that is only one of the statements. Paul has already been saying the same thing to these Romans. Here it is, for instance, in chapter 3:

Therefore by the deeds of the law there shall no flesh be justified in his sight: for by the law is the knowledge of sin. But now the righteousness of God without [apart from] the law is manifested, being witnessed by the law and the prophets; even the righteousness of God which is by faith of Jesus Christ unto all and upon all them that believe: for there is no difference: for all have sinned, and come short of the glory of God; being justified freely by his grace through the redemption that is in Christ Jesus (Rom. 3:20–24).

Now that is a very wonderful statement of the same truth. Indeed, the apostle has written this Epistle to the Romans solely to make this point plain and clear. Here it is in chapter 1: 'For I am not ashamed of the gospel of Christ' – Paul is using that figure of speech called *litotes*: he means that he is very proud of the gospel – 'for it is the power of God unto salvation to every one that believeth; to the Jew first, and also to the Greek.' But this is the real reason: 'For therein' – in this gospel – 'is the righteousness of God revealed from faith to faith: as it is written, The just shall live by faith' (*Rom.* 1:16–17). This is what the apostle glories in; this is what led to his conversion. This is obviously, therefore, the whole basis and foundation of the Christian gospel. And the Epistle to the Romans is nothing but an exposition of this fact that the righteousness of God is revealed, a righteousness that is by faith. That is the whole purpose of that epistle, as it is, indeed, of the Epistle to the Galatians and of many of the other epistles. So here, then, is the basic statement, and here is the first thing that as Christians we must lay hold of in our understanding of our relationship to the law.

For all Christians, the problem is how to get hold of righteousness. We cannot stand in the presence of God unless we are righteous. God is righteous, God is holy, how can we stand in his presence? We must be clothed with a righteousness, how can we get it? That is the question. It is Job's old question: 'How should man be just with God?' (*Job* 9:2). In the law God has told us the type of righteousness he demands. He says: If you manage to produce that kind of righteousness, then I will receive you. 'For Moses describeth the righteousness which is of the law, That the man which doeth those things shall live by them' (*Rom.* 10:5). But we find we cannot do them, so here we are, condemned by the law. And here is the answer: 'Christ is the end of the law for righteousness to every one that believeth.'

Now, then, what does Paul mean? Let us put it like this. Here we are, entering the season of Advent.[1] Why did the Lord Jesus Christ, the Son of God, ever come into this world? The answer is that he came in order to become 'the end of the law for righteousness to every one that believeth'. I make bold to assert that you cannot really understand the incarnation and the message of the four Gospels unless you are clear about the law. I shall have more to say about that next Sunday morning but I leave it as a principle just now. The Lord Jesus Christ came into the world to take over from us this whole burden and problem of the law and our relationship to God. He came because it was a burden we could not bear. He came because, as Paul tells us, 'All have sinned, and come short of the glory of God' (*Rom.* 3:23); 'For by the law is the knowledge of sin' (*Rom.* 3:20). So he came in order to take upon himself this whole question of obtaining a righteousness that would satisfy God. That is what is meant by the words 'the end of the law for righteousness'.

'Christ is the end of the law' – how? In two main ways – and this is the glory of the gospel; this is the first principle of the teaching of the gospel; this is the basis on which we stand. First, he gave the law a perfect obedience, and the law demands this, as we have seen. As the apostle proves to the Galatians, and as James says still more strongly, 'For whosoever shall keep the whole law, and yet offend in one point,

[1] This sermon was preached on 2 December 1962.

he is guilty of all' (*James* 2:10). So we are all guilty. But our Lord failed in no respect. He honoured God's law and he fulfilled it absolutely. And he did that, remember, for us! He came as our representative. He is the new man, the second Adam, the last Adam, also, and the last man, and he rendered a perfect obedience to God's law. That was essential.

But, second, something else was equally essential. Not only have we failed to keep and honour the law of God, we have broken it. As we have seen, we are guilty before it, and the law is thundering out its penalty upon our transgressions and our sins. The penalty demanded by the law is there looking upon us and it must be exacted in every single detail – these are fundamental and basic points with regard to the gospel. So when the law pronounces its punishment upon sin, that punishment is to be carried out – it must be. And this is the glorious message of the grace of God, this is what John is saying: 'The law was given by Moses, but grace and truth came by Jesus Christ.' He means that our Lord not only carried out the dictates of the law to all perfection, but also bore the penalty of the law for his people. He is the 'end' of the law for righteousness to all who believe. To nobody else, but that is what he is to believers.

The message of the grace of God to us in Christ Jesus is that as our representative the Lord Jesus Christ has borne the punishment and God gives us his righteousness. And this is what should make Christian people rejoice. That is why Paul is so proud of his gospel. A righteousness of God, from God, is given to us by faith. We receive the righteousness of the Lord Jesus Christ. Paul was constantly writing about this, and it is not surprising. This was the thrilling discovery that he made on the road to Damascus, a discovery that changed his life. There he had been, sweating and trying, and suddenly he saw it was all wrong and he was hopeless. Then he received this great righteousness. Listen to him writing to the Philippians:

Yea doubtless, and I count all things but loss for the excellency of the knowledge of Christ Jesus my Lord: for whom I have suffered the loss of all things, and do count them but dung, that I may win Christ, and be found in him, not having mine own righteousness, which is of the law, but that which is through the faith of Christ, the righteousness which is of God by faith (Phil. 3:8–9).

And he has got it! That is why Paul is rejoicing.

So here is our first general principle, therefore: Christ is the end of the law for righteousness as far as we are concerned. What does that mean in practice? Let me put it to you in a number of practical deductions. The first is this: We must always think of salvation in terms of the law and our relationship to the law. Does that surprise you? It is a contradiction of so much popular evangelistic preaching today, which says: 'Have nothing to do with the law; just offer Christ.' No, no! You will never understand Christ if you are not clear about the law. We must never think of salvation in any terms save in terms of the law. I mean by that, never think of salvation in terms of your feelings. That is the bugbear, is it not? We say, 'What do I feel like? I don't feel I'm saved. I don't feel I'm a believer.' That is the trouble with many people. They rely upon their feelings, their inward moods and states. They confuse assurance of salvation with salvation itself, so they are in trouble. Start always by looking at salvation in terms of the law.

The crucial question for every one of us as we are by nature is not what we may or may not feel, but our whole state and condition under the law of God. That is the serious thing; whether I am happy or miserable is comparatively irrelevant. It is the same with the law of the land, is it not? It is not what you and I feel that matters; the question is: Have we broken that law or not? You may say that you felt very ill when you knocked into somebody else's car but that will not help you. The problem is that you have broken a law, you have knocked into the man's car and you are liable. Your feelings are irrelevant. The law is objective. Let us view salvation like this. What damns us is not what we feel. The Pharisee had very wonderful feelings, had he not, in our Lord's picture of the Pharisee and the tax-collector? The Pharisee felt that everything was all right. Oh, how deceptive feelings are! When you think you are wonderful, you are hopeless. No, no! Salvation must always be thought of in terms of the law. It is objective. Salvation is a matter of your standing, your whole position before God.

But then, having said that, I hasten to say this: while the first deduction is that we must always think of salvation in terms of the law, the second is that we must never think of salvation in terms of *our* having to keep the law in any form or way. Why not? There is no contradiction here; it is a logical sequence. It is because Christ kept it. This is where grace comes in, telling us that he stood in our position, positively and negatively: 'Christ is the *end* of the law for righteousness to every one that believeth.' That is justification by faith: that you recognize the full demands of the law and then see that he has satisfied them for you. It is entirely a matter of faith, says Paul in chapter 10 of the Epistle to the Romans. The whole trouble with the Jews was that they sought this righteousness not by faith but by the works of the law. And the result was that they were outside, though they were Israel, whereas the Gentiles were inside. So there is my second deduction.

We must never look at or rely on anything we are or anything we do – never! You may have been converted fifty years ago, and you may have grown in grace and developed tremendously, but I say to you at this moment, if you are relying on anything in yourself, anything you are, anything you have done, you have, as it were, left the position of grace and are back under the law. The apostle puts it like this in Galatians 2:21: 'I do not frustrate the grace of God: for if righteousness come by the law, then Christ is dead in vain.' We are justified by him and his righteousness at every point and at every stage. This is the message of grace: God in his infinite grace and goodness looks upon believers not as they are, but as they are in Christ. He does not see us, he sees him, and we are in him.

But come to the second general principle, which is that Christ has delivered us from being *under* the law: 'For sin shall not have dominion over you: *for ye are not under the law*, but under grace' (*Rom.* 6:14). Now, again, let us be clear about this. It is a definition of the first principle, but in more detail. It just means that he has delivered us from the condemnation of the law. Our whole position and relationship to God is no longer determined by law but by the Christ who has fulfilled the law for us. Here, again, is a point that we must have abundantly clearly if we are truly to rejoice as we ought in this great salvation. So let me read these great texts to you. We have seen the first: 'Ye are not under the law, but under grace.' Then listen to it in Romans 7:

Know ye not, brethren . . . how that the law hath dominion over a man as long as he liveth? For the woman which hath an husband is bound by the law to her husband so long as he liveth; but if the husband be dead, she is loosed from the law of her husband. So then if, while her husband liveth, she be married to another man, she shall be called an adulteress: but if her husband be dead, she is free from that law; so that she is no adulteress, though she be married to another man, Wherefore, my brethren, ye also are become dead to the law by the body of Christ; that ye should be married to another, even to him who is raised from the dead, that we should bring forth fruit unto God (Rom. 7:1–4).

That is a tremendous statement. But go on to Romans 8:

There is therefore now no condemnation to them which are in Christ Jesus, who walk not after the flesh, but after the Spirit. For the law of the Spirit of life in Christ Jesus hath made me free from the law of sin and death [the law which pronounces my death] (Rom. 8:1–2).

Or take another great statement in Galatians 2:19: 'For I through the law am dead to the law.' What an important statement! Paul does not just say, 'I am dead to the law', but, 'I *through the law* am dead to the law, that I might live unto God.'

So what does all this mean? Let me summarize it. We are told that we are no longer under the law because we are 'dead to the law'. The whole relationship that existed between us and the law no longer obtains because the Lord Jesus Christ has, in the way I have indicated, fulfilled it, both positively and negatively. So as far as we are concerned, when we are in him, the law has nothing to say to us; it has nothing to say to him. He came, he was 'made of a woman, made under the law' (*Gal.* 4:4), and while he was in this world he was under the law; but the moment he died and rose again and ascended, he was finished with the law. And when we are in him, we are dead to the law, dead in this matter of our status and standing and relationship to God depending upon our fulfilling the law. That has been done for us.

I am fond of quoting a hymn of Augustus Toplady that puts this perfectly:

> *The terrors of law and of God,*
> *With me can have nothing to do;*
> *My Saviour's obedience and blood*
> *Hide all my transgressions from view.*
>
> Augustus M. Toplady

That is it! And we must say that. If you understand this teaching, you are bound to say it. You can say, 'The terrors of law' – the terror of God himself in his holiness – 'and of God, with me can have nothing to do.' Why? Because – 'My Saviour's obedience and blood hide all my transgressions from view.' The law can say nothing to me. I am already in the position of having fulfilled its every demand in Christ. Therefore, it has no terror for me. Augustus Toplady was not alone in putting that doctrine into a hymn. Charles Wesley lived at the same time as Augustus Toplady. Though the two men differed violently on a fundamental doctrine of the Christian faith, Wesley could say this:

> *No condemnation now I dread,*
> *Jesus, and all in him, is mine;*
> *Alive in him, my living Head,*
> *And clothed in righteousness divine,*
> *Bold I approach the eternal throne,*
> *And claim the crown, through Christ my own.*
>
> Charles Wesley

They are both absolutely agreed. This is the position that every Christian should be in. 'No condemnation'! 'There is therefore no condemnation to them which are in Christ Jesus' (*Rom.* 8:1). We are no longer under the law. Until we believe on the Lord Jesus Christ we are all under the law, but because he has carried it out perfectly we are no longer in that position. We do not have to rise through it and above it to stand before God; he has put us above it. We are indeed 'dead to the law'.

So let me come again to the practical deductions. The first is that we must therefore never listen to the accusations and queries of the devil, for he does tempt and condemn us all, and he tries to have us believe that we are not Christians at all. If he does not tempt you like that, my friend, I am afraid there is something wrong with you. He has tempted the greatest saints in that way. That is the difference between a true assurance and some psychological condition. The devil comes, he is 'the accuser of the brethren' (*Rev.* 12:10), he is the adversary, and he tries to make us believe that we are not Christians, especially when we fall into sin. Now we must never believe him: we must know how to answer him. Christians are tempted in this way but they have the answer. That is the Christian position.

Second, we must never allow ourselves to feel condemned. The Christian must never be dejected in this sense. We are told to examine ourselves. You may say that if you examine yourself, you will feel very miserable. Quite right. But the point is, you must not stay in your misery. Here, again, is the difference between true Christians and the people who only think they are. People who think they are Christians and who are relying on their works, can be made utterly dejected by the devil, but he will never make Christians dejected because they say, 'Quite right, I admit I'm a failure, but my righteousness is in him, not in myself.' So they have the answer. They must, therefore, never lie down in condemnation.

Or, in the third place, and to put it still more practically, we must never query or doubt our salvation simply because we may fall into sin, or because we may fail. That is a point at which so many get tripped up and caught. They fall into sin and they say, 'Oh, it's impossible that I'm a Christian. If I were, I wouldn't do this – how can I have done it? And now here I am, I'm under condemnation. I'm guilty.' And they are afraid to go to God. But that is to fail to understand this whole matter of our relationship to the law. The law will speak against you but you can answer it and say, 'Christ has answered for me. He has died for this sin as well as all other sins. Therefore I'm free.'

So my fourth practical deduction is that it is the duty of Christians to have assurance of their position; it is the duty of Christians to have the joy of salvation and to rejoice in Christ Jesus. Obviously! Here is the teaching, this is the message of grace – that I am not under the law, that in Christ I am dead to the law. So if I see this and believe it, I must rejoice! What can hinder my assurance?

'Ah,' you say, 'but you don't know the state of my heart!'

My friend, if you are still holding on to the state of your heart in this matter, you have not understood this message concerning your relationship to the law.

'But,' you say, 'if you only knew what I did and what I've done, and what I'm likely to do and what I'm still doing.'

I do not care what you have done! It is all in Christ or you are not in Christ at all. And that is the basis of assurance. And it is the business and the duty of Christian people to have assurance. It is a matter of teaching; it is a matter of understanding.

'Ah,' you say, 'but I don't feel . . . '

I do not care what you feel. I started by saying that you must regard salvation objectively in terms of law and your relationship to God, and your standing. Christ has fulfilled it for you. Very well, rejoice! That is the argument, and it is an inevitable one. We must all come into the position of being able to say:

> Jesus, thy blood and righteousness
> My beauty are, my glorious dress;
> 'Midst flaming worlds, in these arrayed,
> With joy shall I lift up my head.

Nikolaus von Zinzendorf
trans. John Wesley

That is how you arrive at assurance. You see yourself under the law, then you see him fulfilling it all, and you rejoice in him, and in him alone. Very well, there is the second great general principle.

Now come to the third: *Christ, through the Spirit, enables us to fulfil the law*. I imagine that at this point some people are uncomfortable and dislike what I am saying.

'But you said just now,' they may object, 'that Christ is the end of the law. I have nothing to do with the law now.'

You must not say that and you must not speak like that. Let me show you why. Christ, through the Spirit, enables us to keep and to fulfil the law, and if you do not regard this truth as being as glorious as the first two, I would suggest to you that there is something wrong with your whole view of salvation. This is as wonderful, if not more wonderful, than the other principles. There is no better test, therefore, that we can apply to ourselves than just to ask: Do we rejoice to know that it is the business of grace to enable us to fulfil the law?

Grace, in other words, must never be thought of in law-less terms. You must never think of the grace of God as just a way of escape, just a way of forgiveness, just that which always sets us free. But that is what we like to think, is it not? That is what we want. We like to think of grace as that which comes to us and says: 'In a sense, go and do what you like, sin as much as you like. It is all right: you are not under law, you are under grace.' But that is a most terrible thing to say. That is a violation, a travesty, of the doctrine. That is antinomianism, which is the greatest curse imaginable. Indeed, let me put it like this to you: If grace does not enable me to keep and to live the law of God, then it means that the devil has triumphed over God!

'How do you get that?' asks someone.

I get it like this. What the devil did in the fall was not merely to make man disobey God, but also to make a slave of him, and to make him incapable of obeying God and honouring God's law. Salvation means that the works of the devil are to be entirely undone and nullified; it therefore includes this: man must be given ability to live and to keep the law of God. If salvation just means that we are forgiven but we can still go on failing, then the devil has succeeded. But he has not! By the grace of God, the devil has been defeated and utterly routed. The Lord Jesus Christ did not come into this world by the grace of God simply to give us forgiveness. He did that, thank God for it. If we are not forgiven, we have nothing and we are altogether and entirely hopeless. That is my first need but it is not my only need.

Christian people, let me say it again, it is the season of Advent. Why did the Christ, the Son of God, leave the courts of heaven and come into this world? Listen: 'And she shall bring forth a son, and thou shalt call his name JESUS' – why? – 'for he shall save his people from their sins' (*Matt.* 1:21). Not merely from the guilt of their sins, but from their sins. Let us never forget that. Indeed, our Lord says it himself in the Sermon on the Mount: 'Think not that I am come to destroy the law, or the prophets: I am not come to destroy, but to fulfil' (*Matt.* 5:17). Listen again to the apostle Paul, the great advocate of justification by faith only, the man who tells us we are dead to the law and no longer under it: 'Do we then make void the law through faith? God forbid: yea, we establish the law' (*Rom.* 3:31). Never interpret grace as that which gets rid of the law or makes nothing of it or makes it void – never.

Again, as I have already quoted, Paul says, 'For sin shall not have dominion over you' – why not? – 'for ye are not under the law, but under grace' (*Rom.* 6:14). Notice what he is saying: Because you are not under the law now, but under grace, sin shall not have dominion over you. It is a part of the purpose of the incarnation. Listen to Paul again:

For what the law could not do, in that it was weak through the flesh, God sending his own Son in the likeness of sinful flesh, and for sin, condemned sin in the flesh: that the righteousness of the law might be fulfilled in us, who walk not after the flesh, but after the Spirit (Rom. 8:3–4).

It is quite unmistakable. Listen to it again in Romans 13:

Render therefore to all their dues: tribute to whom tribute is due; custom to whom custom; fear to whom fear; honour to whom honour.

He is writing to Christian believers –

Owe no man any thing, but to love one another: for he that loveth another hath fulfilled the law. For this, Thou shalt not commit adultery, Thou shalt not kill, Thou shalt not steal, Thou shalt not bear false witness, Thou shalt not covet; and if there be any other commandment, it is briefly comprehended in this saying, namely, Thou shalt love thy neighbour as thyself. Love worketh no ill to his neighbour: therefore love is the fulfilling of the law (Rom. 13:7–10).

The Ten Commandments still apply and you and I must keep them. This is an exhortation to Christian believers. Love! Love one another. Why? 'Love is the fulfilling of the law.' We are meant to keep all these commandments and grace enables us to do so.

Or let me give you a final quotation, a remarkable statement of Paul to Titus:

For the grace of God that bringeth salvation hath appeared to all men, teaching us

– what does it teach us? –

that, denying ungodliness and worldly lusts, we should live soberly, righteously, and godly, in this present world; looking for that blessed hope, and the glorious appearing of the great God and our Saviour Jesus Christ; who gave himself for us

– why? –

that he might redeem us from all iniquity, and purify unto himself a peculiar people, zealous of good works (Titus 2:11–14).

I am saying that Christ through the Spirit enables us to fulfil the law. That is Christianity. It is not, 'Do what you like, sin as much as you like, grace covers you.' It is the opposite of that. You are forgiven and therefore, by the power of the Spirit, live the law, keep it, please God.

And so my last word is this: grace gives us the power to keep the law, and grace alone does that. Listen to the apostle writing in Romans 7: 'Wherefore, my brethren, ye also are become dead to the law by the body of Christ; that [in order that] ye should be married to another, even to him who is raised from the dead, that' – what? – 'we should bring forth fruit unto God' (*Rom.* 7:4). You were married to the law and you brought forth nothing but dead works. You are married to Christ now – what is to be the result of the marriage? All this wonderful fruit of good works, keeping the law, doing what God intended from the very beginning of his creation. There it is, and he enables us.

Listen to the sixth verse of that same chapter: 'But now we are delivered from the law, that being dead wherein we were held; that we should serve in newness of spirit, and not in the oldness of the letter.' So we still keep the law but we keep it in a new way. We were trying after the letter, we are now doing it in the spirit. Or take Romans 14:17: 'For the kingdom of God is not meat and drink; but righteousness, and peace, and joy in the Holy Ghost.' Or again, 'Now the Lord is that

Spirit: and where the Spirit of the Lord is, there is liberty' (*2 Cor.* 3:17) – and that is written in the context of the law. We have liberty. We are not striving hopelessly to keep the letter; we are keeping the law with liberty, with abandon and with joy.

So listen to the way in which it is put by John in a most astonishing statement in his first epistle. Again, this is written to believers: 'For this is the love of God, that we keep his commandments: and his commandments are not grievous' (*1 John* 5:3). The difference between non-Christians and Christians is this: here are non-Christians really hating the law of God. They try to keep it and fail, and they find it a terrible burden; it is 'grievous'. What of Christians? Well, to Christians, his commandments are not grievous. Christians love the law of God. They want to keep it; they are given power to keep it.

There is the relationship of the Christian to the law. The non-Christian is like the child struggling at his exercises on the piano, having to go through them mechanically and forced to practise against the grain. It is the difference between that and a master concert pianist who plays with ease and with grace, who does not have to think about it at all, who now has it as a part of his very nature, and there he is, concentrating only on interpretation. 'His commandments are not grievous.' Christ has sent his Spirit into us, the Spirit that was in him is in us, and therefore we must 'reckon ourselves to be dead indeed unto sin, and alive unto God, through our Lord Jesus Christ'. We must 'walk in newness of life', as risen from the dead. We are put into a position in which now, by the power of grace, we are enabled to live and to practise the law of God, to be what man was intended to be in his original creation.

Let us never forget these three principles: '*Christ is the end of the law* for righteousness, to every one that believeth.' He therefore *delivers us from being under the law*, and makes us dead to the law in the sense of trying to keep it in order that we may be righteous and justify ourselves. He delivers us from its condemnation. But, thank God, through the new birth and the indwelling Spirit, *he enables us to keep the law ourselves and to honour it*: 'That the righteousness of the law might be fulfilled in us, who walk not after the flesh, but after the Spirit' (*Rom.* 8:4).

Never think of salvation except fundamentally in terms of law. But then have your right distinctions and you will avoid the twin errors – justification by works, and antinomianism, which brings the grace of God into greater disrepute than perhaps anything else. 'The law was given by Moses, but grace and truth came by Jesus Christ.' Blessed be the name of God! 'Thanks be to God for his unspeakable gift!' ∾

10

The Abundant Riches of His Grace

For the law was given by Moses, but grace and truth came by Jesus Christ (John 1:17).

For some time now we have been examining this great and most important statement in the Prologue of John's Gospel. We are doing so in order that we may truly understand and appreciate as we should what the blessings of grace, the grace of God in Jesus Christ our Lord, really are and what they bring to us. We have been at pains to emphasize that this statement, this text, does not in any way detract from the value of the law. We have seen that the law was given by God and that it has a very special function in the purpose and plan of salvation of Almighty God but we have also seen that the law was only preparatory, that it was a kind of signpost or fingerpost pointing to Christ. To use that great expression of the apostle Paul, it was our 'schoolmaster to bring us unto Christ'. We are now drawing certain deductions from what we have seen. The question that must always arise in our minds as we face this text is: Why did John put it in this particular way? And the answer is undoubtedly that he wants to show the superiority of grace.

Now John is anxious to say that you do not need to detract from law to show the superiority of grace. He wants to show that grace and truth have come in the Lord Jesus Christ and therefore these Christian people to whom he is writing should be rejoicing and glorying in it. He writes his Gospel in order to remind them again of the things they had already believed but were not fully comprehending. Let me, therefore, put it as a question at this very moment. Do we rejoice in grace as we ought? It is an appropriate question to ask during this season of Advent. Does the grace of our Lord Jesus Christ really fill us with a sense of joy and of praise unto God? Does it lead us ever to say, 'Thanks be unto God for his unspeakable gift' (*2 Cor.* 9:15)? That was how John was anxious to present the gospel to these people. In his first epistle, he puts it in much the same way. He says, 'That ye also may have fellowship with us: and truly our fellowship is with the Father, and with his Son Jesus Christ.' And then he says, 'And these things write we unto you, that your joy may be full' (*1 John* 1:3–4). That is why he wrote that epistle. John wants to know that Christian people really are rejoicing in the blessings of grace. He is saying: We are not under law any longer; we are under grace now. And he wants us to understand this and to know exactly what we have inherited.

In other words, the Lord Jesus Christ came into this world in order to bring grace and truth. This is the whole meaning and purpose of the incarnation. John wants these people to enter into the full enjoyment of this, and his way of putting it here is to contrast it with what the law had done. The law did many wonderful things, as we have seen, things that are absolutely essential, but it could but point. And what it pointed to has come, says John, so let us enter into the possession, the enjoyment, of it; let us experience this as we were meant to.

Having, then, shown the function and the purpose of the law, and having seen where the Christian believer stands with respect to it, we are now in a position to look at grace more positively, to see what it is that it really brings to us and why we should all be rejoicing in it. Here is the way that John does this – he says: The law was wonderful but it only went so far, and grace and truth have come. The author of the Epistle to the Hebrews says very much the same thing. He writes, 'He [our Lord] is the mediator of a better covenant, which was established upon better promises' (*Heb.* 8:6). Indeed, you can say that the whole of that great Epistle to the Hebrews is nothing but a commentary on John 1:17. So is the Epistle to the Romans; so is the Epistle to the Galatians. These men are all saying the same thing. Their epistles are grand expositions of this one text that we are examining so carefully and minutely.

'A better covenant,' says the author of Hebrews, 'established upon better promises'. What does this mean? Well, let us ask the question:

Wherein does grace excel over the law? What are these 'better promises'? What is this 'better covenant'? What makes John delight to be
able to say, 'The law was given by Moses, but grace and truth came by
Jesus Christ'? What is this plus? What is this extra? That is what we are
going to find out. To use the language of that hymn of Charles Wesley
we have just been singing, I want to tune your hearts. I have a feeling
they need to be tuned. Singing expresses the state of the soul. Where
were the trumpets as we sang that last hymn? Where was the triumph?
Our hearts need to be tuned! That is the way we show that we have
grasped this message, that we have realized it and are rejoicing in it.
God's people are meant to be a rejoicing people. We are not meant to
be uncertain and hesitant and unhappy and doubtful and tentative.
Not at all! That is the whole message of the New Testament.

So what is this contrast, what is this 'better thing' that grace has
brought? For now, let me just concentrate on two aspects. The first
great contrast between grace and law is that grace *gives*. The law gives
nothing. The law makes demands. The law presents a bill. The law says:
'Here is the account, are you ready to settle it?' But grace is altogether
different. That is why everybody likes John 3:16: 'God so loved the world,
that he gave . . . ' He is not making a demand in Christ, in Advent, and
in the whole message of the gospel. It is giving. 'He gave . . . he sent'!
These are the terms that are used.

Now this is most important. There is nothing legalistic about grace,
whereas law, of course, is essentially legalistic. That term that the apostle uses in Romans 6:23 is, again, such a wonderful expression of this
very point: 'The *wages* of sin is death; but the *gift* of God is eternal life
through Jesus Christ our Lord.' Wages – exact calculation, the result
of what has been done. And there it is: it is a ledger; it is bookkeeping;
it has the sort of exactness that is always the characteristic of law. But
when you come to the realm of grace, you are in a new world altogether.
You do not talk about wages here. This is the gift of God!

Our Lord himself established that point once and for ever in his great
parable of the labourers in the vineyard. The owner of that vineyard
had promised the men who had gone in at the beginning of the day
that he would give them a denarius for the day's work. And then, later

on, he engaged some more men, promising to pay them 'whatever is right'. And there were some people who were only engaged at the eleventh hour. When the time came to settle, the men who had been working from the first hour were amazed when they were paid one denarius, exactly the same amount as the men who had only worked for the last hour. They said: 'This is unjust, it's unfair. We've been toiling through the heat and burden of the day, but these men have come in at the last hour and you've given them exactly what you've given us. This isn't right.'

Now why did our Lord speak that parable? He had only one object: it was to tell the people that they were no longer under law but under grace. The owner says, in effect: 'Have I not a right to do as I please? You have had your just wages, you have had what was promised you in your contract. You have no right at all to complain. You said you would do this work for one denarius; you have done the work – here is your denarius. Can I not do as I like with my own?' (See Matthew 20:1–15.) I am the one who gives grace, says our Lord. He gives a day's wage to those who have only worked for an hour. That is the contrast between grace and law; it is the difference between demanding and giving.

But I want to emphasize that grace not only gives, but gives freely. Here is the great note, of course, of the whole of the gospel, perhaps stated more perfectly than anywhere else in Romans 3:24, where the apostle Paul puts it in such a striking manner: '*Being justified freely by his grace* through the redemption that is in Christ Jesus.' Freely! The apostle has already shown that nobody can pay anything. 'All have sinned, and come short of the glory of God' (*Rom.* 3:23); 'And all the world may become guilty before God' (*Rom.* 3:19); 'There is none righteous, no, not one' (*Rom.* 3:10). When we were utterly helpless, penniless, hopeless, God justified us 'freely'.

I must not stay with this – we considered it last time – but, my dear friends, are you happy about justification by faith only? Do you realize that you are forgiven in spite of what you are? Do you realize that Augustus Toplady describes the position of everybody when he says:

> *Nothing in my hand I bring;*
> *Simply to thy cross I cling.*

'Justified freely'! 'Come ye to the waters . . . yea, come, buy wine and milk without money and without price' (*Isa.* 55:1). That is it! That is the Christian salvation. The evangelical prophet Isaiah had been given a glimpse of it. So do not look at your own blackness and unworthiness and what you have not done. It does not matter. You would never have enough to pay. You come as a pauper. Everybody does. It is the free gift of God! It is *free* grace! That is the glorious message of Christian salvation.

But let me move on to another aspect. Grace not only gives, and gives freely, it also gives very richly – and I want to emphasize this. You find it here in verse 16 of this Prologue of John's Gospel: 'And of his fulness have all we received, and grace for grace' – which means, grace upon grace upon grace. There is no end to it; it comes as an endless stream, wave upon wave upon wave. This is a way of expressing the freeness, the richness, of God's grace. This is the great theme, in a sense, of the whole of this Gospel of John. You have it again in Jesus' words to the woman of Samaria: 'Whosoever drinketh of this water shall thirst again: but whosoever drinketh of the water that I shall give him shall never thirst; but the water that I shall give him shall be in him a well of water springing up into everlasting life' (*John* 4:13–14).

> *Plenteous grace in thee is found,*
> *Grace to cover all my sin;*
> *Let the healing streams abound,*
> *Make and keep me pure within.*
> *Thou of life the fountain art,*
> *Freely let me take of thee.*
>   Charles Wesley

Or, to take another expression, this time from John 6: 'Jesus said unto them, I am the bread of life: he that cometh to me shall never hunger; and he that believeth on me shall never thirst' (*John* 6:35). That is it! All this is but an expression of this richness of the giving of grace. But I must take you to Romans 5 because it is in many ways the most wonderful expression of all this teaching. Here it is worked out in detail by the apostle Paul, who is simply expounding these glorious statements of our Lord. Let me pick out certain verses for you.

Verse 15: 'But not as the offence, so also is the free gift.' Paul is saying that there is a kind of opposite in this: 'the offence' – 'the free gift'. But he says that you do not stop at that, it is not that the two are exact. The grace of God does not just balance our transgressions and our sin. No, no! The whole point is that there is a superabundance about grace. The free gift does not correspond in that respect with the offence. 'For if through the offence of one many be dead' – now, listen – '*much more* the grace of God, and the gift by grace, which is by one man, Jesus Christ, hath *abounded* unto many.' There it is. Paul wants to bring out this notion of grace that is abounding. You immediately think of John Bunyan, do you not: *Grace Abounding to the Chief of Sinners*. But look at the next verse.

Verse 16: 'And not as it was by one that sinned, so is the gift.' The gift, Paul says, does not correspond in degree to the sinning. One man sinned – that was Adam – and certain consequences followed. One man, Christ, has done what was necessary for our salvation – and certain consequences follow. This appears to be an exact parallel. But it is not. The apostle says, 'Not as it was . . . so is the gift' – why? – 'for the judgment was by one to condemnation, but the free gift is of many offences unto justification.' Much more, again, you see.

Verse 17: 'For if by one man's offence death reigned by one; *much more*' – here is the point – 'they which receive abundance of grace and of the gift of righteousness shall reign in life by one, Jesus Christ.' The same point.

Verse 20: 'Moreover the law entered, that the offence might abound. But where sin abounded, grace did *much more* abound.' Now the translators were in difficulties there. It is almost impossible to translate the apostle's words, 'grace did much more abound'. The sin abounded as the result of the law, but grace superabounded. That is what Paul is really saying.

Verse 21 'That as sin hath reigned unto death, even so might grace reign through righteousness unto eternal life by Jesus Christ our Lord.'

Now there it is. There the apostle brings out in his own perfect manner the 'much more', the 'abounding', the 'superabounding'! Grace gives! Grace gives freely! And, oh, the riches of God's grace!

But let us go on. Listen to the apostle in 2 Corinthians 8:9: 'For ye know the grace of our Lord Jesus Christ' – this is the kind of grace that I am talking about, he says – 'that, though he was rich' – what is the measure of that 'rich'? Oh, it is the riches of God, it is eternal, it is everything – 'yet for your sakes he became poor' – there is the measure of this superabundance of grace – 'that ye through his poverty might be [made] rich.' I say that grace gives. What does it give? Well, it gives that! He left the courts of glory, he left all the signs of this glory, he was born as a babe in a stable and of parents who were so poor that they could not afford a lamb but could just give turtle doves when they came to present their offering (*Luke* 2:24). That is the measure of the riches of the giving of grace.

And, again, in the next chapter, the apostle bursts out, 'Thanks be to God' – for what? – 'for his unspeakable gift' (*2 Cor.* 9:15). No language can describe it; the gift is so great, it baffles all the vocabularies. It is an unspeakable, an inexpressible, gift. That is the measure of the giving of grace.

And then – I could keep you endlessly with this because, as I say, it is the great theme of the New Testament – listen to a particularly wonderful statement in the Epistle to the Ephesians: 'In whom we have redemption through his blood, the forgiveness of sins, according to the riches of his grace' (*Eph.* 1:7). The 'riches of his grace'! But here the apostle is only starting and he always works up – the more he says a thing, the more he sees the wonder of it. There it is in the first chapter of Ephesians, but listen to the second chapter: 'That in the ages to come he might shew the exceeding riches of his grace' (*Eph.* 2:7). You see, first of all, 'according to the riches of his grace', and then it becomes 'the exceeding riches of his grace'. But even that is not enough. When we go on to the third chapter, we find he puts it like this: 'Unto me, who am less than the least of all saints, is this grace given' – what for? – 'that I should preach among the Gentiles the unsearchable riches of Christ' (*Eph.* 3:8). 'Riches . . . exceeding riches . . . unsearchable riches'! That is it – you cannot measure it, it baffles all attempts.

And so here we have this great teaching before us, put in this striking manner by the apostle John in the Prologue of his Gospel: 'Of his fulness have all we received, and grace for [upon] grace.' There is no end to it. Here is this everlasting life that goes bubbling up; it is all the result of the freeness by which grace gives us these benefits from God. And James is not to be outdone in this matter. He says: 'If any of you lack wisdom, let him ask of God, that giveth to all men liberally, and upbraideth not' (*James* 1:5). God does not merely give, he gives *liberally*.

But let me hurry to another aspect – the manifold and varied ways in which grace is given to us. Here I quote from the apostle Peter: 'As every man hath received the gift, even so minister the same one to another. As good stewards of the *manifold* grace of God' (1 *Pet.* 4:10). It is a 'manifold' grace; it is a variegated grace, endless in its expressions and in its forms. What does Peter mean? We cannot hope to deal with it exhaustively, but let me give you just a glimpse into this manifold grace of God.

Have you ever considered *restraining* grace? Have you ever thanked God for the way in which he restrains you? What would we all have been if he had not restrained us? What would we still often do if he did not restrain us? Grace not only urges us forward, at times it also holds us back. A man once wrote this:

> *How oft to sure destruction*
> *My feet had gone astray,*
> *Wert thou not, patient Shepherd,*
> *The guardian of my way.*
> Lawrence Tuttiett

The hand that is placed upon us, that holds us back when anger or temper or resentment or something else threatens to engulf us, the hand of God quietly, gently laid upon us, pacifies us and keeps us calm and quiet and holds us back. I sometimes think that when we do arrive in the glory and look back upon the journey, we shall thank God for his restraining grace as much as for anything else. Have you not been conscious of it – how God has suddenly held you? You cannot explain it in any other terms. You were on the point of something – you were held back. Read Psalm 73 – that man gives wonderful expression to it there: 'But as for me . . . my steps had well nigh slipped' (verse 2). He had almost . . . but not quite! He was led to go to the house of God, and there he was given the understanding that he needed. The restraining grace. That is one way of looking at grace.

But think of *supporting* grace: the supporting grace of God in trials and troubles and tribulations. Oh, is there anything more wonderful than this! I suppose the classic description is the one that is given by the great apostle Paul in 2 Corinthians 12. Three times he prayed that the 'thorn in the flesh' might be taken away. He felt that he could not go on, that he could do nothing: how could he with this thorn in the flesh? But notice the answer: 'My grace is sufficient for thee' (2 *Cor.* 12:9). And Paul felt that it was. So he was able to say, 'When I am weak, then am I strong' (2 *Cor.* 12:10). I glory in infirmities now, says Paul, because in infirmities I understand the supporting grace of God in a way that I never could otherwise.

> When darkness seems to hide his face,
> I rest on his unchanging grace;
> In every high and stormy gale
> My anchor holds within the veil:
>   On Christ the solid rock I stand,
>   All other ground is sinking sand.
>
> Edward Mote

Do you know the supporting grace of God, my friends? 'He giveth liberally.' It is grace upon grace; it is abounding; it is abundant grace. Do you know it in the hour of trial and troubles, when you are surrounded and almost overwhelmed? Are you aware that you are being held, supported, sustained?

Or think of it in terms of temptations – temptations within and temptations without. James has a great statement with respect to this in that fourth chapter of his epistle. He is talking about the lusts that are in the flesh, which lead to war and various things like that, and he says, 'Ye adulterers and adulteresses, know ye not that the friendship of the world is enmity with God?' – he does not mean literal adulterers and adulteresses but all who are committing spiritual adultery by being worldly minded – 'whosoever therefore will be a friend of the world is the enemy of God. Do ye think that the scripture saith in vain, The Spirit that dwelleth in us lusteth to envy?' (*James* 4:4–5).

But what can we do about it? Who are we to stand against all this? Here is the answer, in verse 6: 'But he giveth more grace. Wherefore he saith, God resisteth the proud, but giveth grace unto the humble.' Though we are fighting the world, the flesh and the devil, God gives not merely grace, but more grace, sufficient grace, more than enough for whatever our circumstances or position may chance to be. So that we should make a prayer like this:

> *O Lamb of God still keep me*
> *Close to thy wounded side;*
> *'Tis only there in safety*
> *And peace I can abide.*
> *What snares and foes surround me,*
> *What troubles strive within;*
> *The grace that sought and found me*
> *Alone can keep me clean.*
>
> James George Deck

And it will! I say again:

> *Plenteous grace with thee is found,*
> *Grace to cover all my sin;*
> *Let the healing streams abound,*
> *Make and keep me pure within.*
>
> Charles Wesley

And it will! This wonderful, supporting grace of God.

And then let me give you another glimpse, another aspect, of God's variegated, manifold grace: *the keeping and the preserving grace of God.* 'Being confident of this very thing, that he which hath begun a good work in you', says Paul to the Philippians, 'will perform it until the day of Jesus Christ' (*Phil.* 1:6). It is the great theme of Philippians. 'I know both how to be abased, and I know how to abound . . . I can do all things through Christ which strengtheneth me' (*Phil.* 4:12–13). His grace is sufficient, says Paul to the Corinthians, as we have seen. 'My God shall supply all your need,' he says, again to those Philippians (*Phil.* 4:19). Quite so, says Augustus Toplady:

> *The work which his goodness began*
> *The arm of his strength will complete;*
> *His promise is Yea and Amen,*
> *And never was forfeited yet.*
>
> *Things future nor things which are now,*
> *Nor all things below nor above,*
> *Can make him his promise forego,*
> *Or sever my soul from his love.*
>   Augustus M. Toplady

The grace that buys us will keep us and preserve us. 'Neither shall any man pluck them out of my hand,' says our Lord (*John* 10:28). If grace ever lays hold of you, it will never let you go. There is no 'falling from grace'. The 'final perseverance of the saints' is guaranteed by the enabling, preserving, keeping grace of God.

There is also God's *prevenient* grace, a grace that goes ahead of us and prepares the way for us, so that when we arrive at a position, we find that grace has been there before us. The psalmist is always celebrating that particular fact.

Grace, then, gives to us in a variegated, an almost endless variety of ways. That is one great contrast – the law demands; grace gives. And, oh, the giving of grace! My dear friends, are you receiving grace upon grace? That is what we are meant to do. That is why John wrote his Gospel. That is the whole point of the Prologue. The rest of the Gospel is an exposition of this abundant, superabundant, abounding grace – do we know it? Are we receiving it? Are we rejoicing in it as we ought? What does Christmas, what does Advent, mean to us? Do we realize that Christ came in order that we might be enjoying this grace? Or do we feel we are left to ourselves and that we are holding on to our bit of Christianity desperately, just managing? Oh, shame upon us! 'My grace is sufficient for thee'! And it is more than sufficient, it is more than we can ever need. There is no end to it; it springs up like a fountain into everlasting life.

But let me hurry on to say just a word on the second great contrast between law and grace. Grace not only gives: it also *reigns*: 'That as sin hath reigned unto death, even so might grace reign through righteousness unto eternal life by Jesus Christ our Lord' (*Rom.* 5:21). This is another great theme of the New Testament. But what does Paul mean by 'reign'? He means that grace has power in it. The whole trouble with the law is that it lacked power: 'What the law could not do, in that it was weak through the flesh, God sending his own Son in the likeness of sinful flesh, and for sin, condemned sin in the flesh' (*Rom.* 8:3). The law is all right, it makes its statements, but it can do nothing: it cannot give us power; it cannot help us. 'Do this,' it says, and it leaves the doing to me! But the glorious thing about grace is that it reigns, it has power. That is the meaning of reigning, is it not? There is no point in a monarch who does not have power. A monarch cannot reign without it. The whole essence of reigning is that there is power, there is authority and ability to do things; a monarch's word is a command; it is imperative, and must be carried out.

What does grace do? Here I only want to emphasize one aspect in order to interpret more fully my concluding words last time. Grace is that which enables God's great plan and purpose to be carried out in us. What is that purpose? It is 'that he might redeem us from all iniquity, and purify to himself a peculiar people, zealous of good works' (*Titus* 2:14). Last week I ended by saying that to the Christian the commandments of God are not grievous (*1 John* 5:3). The grace of God in Christ has come not merely that we might be forgiven, not only that we might be justified, but to enable us to live the life that God would have us live, to keep the commandments of God. That is the purpose. And grace enables us to do this. That is why, to the Christian, the commandments are not grievous.

Let me show you what I mean. Grace, I repeat, is powerful; it reigns. How? Well, Ephesians 2 tells us that it 'quickens' us. In that chapter, the apostle Paul introduces the whole notion of grace and he puts it like this: 'But God, who is rich in mercy, for his great love wherewith he loved us, even when we were dead in sins, hath quickened us together with Christ, (by grace ye are saved;)' (*Eph.* 2:4–5). It is grace, he says, that does this. Grace is the dynamic power. You were dead, you were buried in sin, then you were 'quickened' – by grace! Grace reigns, so it puts life into the dead, brings us to our feet and raises us up with Christ. It quickens us and regenerates us. Then it goes on to sanctify us. It enables us to live according to God's holy law; it explains why the law is not grievous.

Now let me show you the meaning of the statement in Hebrews 8:6 concerning the 'better covenant', which has now been given: 'But now hath he obtained a more excellent ministry, by how much also he is the mediator of a better covenant, which was established upon better promises.' What does the writer mean? Wherein lies the superiority of grace over law? It is here. Where does the new covenant excel over the old? Why do we glory that we are now not in the old dispensation but in the new? Why do I say I am Christ's man, not Moses' man? Here is the answer, here is the great difference:

Not according to the covenant that I made with their fathers in the day when I took them by the hand to lead them out of the land of Egypt;

– that is the covenant God made through Moses, that is the law –

because they continued not in my covenant, and I regarded them not, saith the Lord. For this is the covenant that I will make with the house of Israel after those days, saith the Lord.

– now here it is –

I will put my laws into their mind, and write them in their hearts (Heb. 8:9–10).

That is a description of Christianity. Christianity does not do away with law – and you see why I have been contending for that all along? The Christian does not say, 'I've nothing to do with law, I'm a Christian now.' No, what Christianity, what the grace of God, does is put the law of God into your mind and into your heart. This is the difference. The law is now within us and not without us. The law given through Moses was on 'tables of stone'. It is no longer there; it is inside us. So Paul, in writing to the Corinthians, can put it like this:

Ye are our epistle written in our hearts, known and read of all men: forasmuch as ye are manifestly declared to be the epistle of Christ ministered by us, written not with ink, but with the Spirit of the living God; not in tables of stone, but in fleshy tables of the heart (2 Cor. 3:2–3).

It is exactly the same truth. The law of Moses was outside us, written on stone. There it was, thundering at us and saying, 'This do, and thou shalt live' (*Luke* 10:28). But it is now inside me. That is the difference between grace and law. And what a wonderful difference this makes. According to the apostle John, the difference is that a Christian cannot continue living a life of sin. Had you realized that? Listen: 'He that committeth sin is of the devil' – when John says, 'committeth sin', he means going on living in it, lying down in it, being mastered by it, sin being a habit – 'for the devil sinneth from the beginning. For this purpose the Son of God was manifested, that he might destroy [undo] the works of the devil.' Listen: 'Whosoever is born of God doth not commit sin' – now obviously that does not mean that he never falls into sin, otherwise there is not a single Christian in the world. It means that whoever is born of God does not go on committing sin. Why not? – 'for his seed remaineth in him: and he cannot sin, because he is born of God' (*1 John* 3:8–9).

Now that passage is not teaching sinless perfection, but it is teaching that the seed of God that is in Christians means that they cannot go on being slaves to sin; they are born of God and the seed remains in them and keeps them from that state of sin. The law, in other words, is now in them, not outside them. This is how Paul puts this in Philippians 2:12–13: 'Work out your own salvation with fear and trembling.' Why? Oh, 'For it is God which worketh in you both to will and to do of his good pleasure' – to do his commandments, his law. That is it. He enables us to do it by working in us.

Or look at it like this: 'I will put my laws', says God, '*into their mind*' – and this is most wonderful. It means that we understand God's law. The trouble with people under the law is that they are like children. The child hears the parent saying, 'You mustn't do this; you must do that.' So he does not do this or that, perhaps, but he is resentful. He does not understand the reason. He does not see the purpose of the instruction. He thinks he ought to be allowed to do anything he wants to do. The parent says, 'No!' and the child gives obedience, but oftentimes grudgingly and complainingly and feeling it is hard and all wrong. That is men and women under the law. But the moment the law is written in the mind, one understands. When we get older, we thank our parents for their prohibitions as well as for their encouragement; we thank them for the discipline they exercised, for the things they taught us not to do and the things they taught us to do. 'When I was a child . . . I thought as a child.' But not now I have become a man (*1 Cor.* 13:11). So the law written in the mind gives us understanding and enables us to see that what matters is not the letter of the law but the spirit. That is a most wonderful discovery. As long as you are looking at the mere letter, you hate it, but once you see the spirit and the object and the purpose, you begin to enjoy it.

'I will put my laws into their mind' – why? First, in order that I may understand that God's laws are quite inevitable because of the character of God. Let me say it with reverence, God had to give the Ten Commandments. The Ten Commandments are a transcript of God's own holy character. So one is not surprised at them. One does not resent them. One sees that they are what they are because of the character of God; one sees that they are absolutely, essentially right. If the whole world kept the Ten Commandments today, there would be paradise. And it is the law written in the mind that enables me to see that.

Then, second, the law written in the mind enables me to see that therefore I ought to rejoice in these commandments of God. 'We are his workmanship,' says Paul in Ephesians 2:10, 'created in Christ Jesus unto good works, which God hath before ordained that we should walk in them.' In other words, you have been born again in order that you might live this life. You thank God that it is such a wonderful life. You no longer complain. You say, 'It's marvellous that I'm now to live that kind of life!' You do not resent it; you rejoice in it. We can sum it up like this: 'Be ye holy; for I am holy' (*1 Pet.* 1:16). The moment men and women see that, they no longer resent the law. God is saying: 'I want you to live like this because this is what I am. I am holy, so be holy.' So you do not kick against the gospel and say that it is narrow and prohibitive. You say: This is God's life and I am to live God's life.

And then, in the third place, there is this marvellous argument of the *hope*. 'Every man that hath this hope in him', says John, 'purifieth himself, even as he is pure' (*1 John* 3:3). If you really believe you are going to heaven, if you want to go to heaven, well, then, says John, surely to be eligible you must begin to prepare to go to heaven. The real trouble with a man who says he wants to go to heaven and yet is living to the full in this life, and wants to live this life, and feels Christianity is narrow, his real trouble is that he is a fool who cannot think straight. So if you resent the commandments of God, do not talk to me about heaven, do not talk about spending your eternity looking into the face of God! 'He that hath this hope in him *purifieth himself* even as he is pure.' That is the result of the law written in the mind.

In other words, God is saying: I will write my law in their minds and in their hearts. I will give them a new disposition. I will give them a heart of flesh instead of a heart of stone. I will make them desire to keep my law. I will make them love my law. They will no longer hate the law when it condemns them. When they fall into sin and the law condemns, they will say, 'Absolutely right. I've been a fool, I shouldn't have done that. I'm unworthy – oh, how can God forgive me!'

True Christians never argue with the law when it condemns them. They admit it. They confess it. They humble themselves and repent with a godly repentance. Yes, when men and women are born again, they say, 'That law of God, of course I will keep it. I will keep it in order to please God. He sent his only Son from heaven to earth for me. Christ, who was so rich, became poor that I might live, and all I am to do now is show him that I love him and that I want to thank him. How can I do that? By keeping his commandments, by living the life that he wants me to live.' God says, 'I will put my laws into their mind, and write [imprint] them in their hearts' so that they will understand my law and love it and rejoice in keeping it.

So there it is, hurriedly and inadequately. That is the superiority of grace! It gives in abundance. It enables me to live this abundant life. It gives me power. It reigns and it will go on reigning until all the people of God are spotless and pure, without any wrinkles, glorified and perfect and well-pleasing in the sight of God, who is no longer ashamed to call them his people, nor is Christ ashamed to call them his brethren. My dear friends, are we rejoicing in grace? Are we able to say, 'The law was given by Moses but, thank God, grace and truth have come by Jesus Christ'? Can we say that we have been bathed by the showers of God's supporting grace? Is that our position? It is meant to be. It is the whole meaning of Christmas and the incarnation, the death on the cross and everything. Oh, let us pray God to open our understanding by his Holy Spirit that we may see the triumphs and the glories of the grace of God! ∞

11

Truth in Its Fulness

For the law was given by Moses, but grace and truth came by Jesus Christ. No man hath seen God at any time; the only begotten Son, which is in the bosom of the Father, he hath declared him (John 1:17–18).

*W*e continue with our study of the seventeenth verse, but the eighteenth verse, as I hope to show you, is a kind of explanation of the latter part of verse 17. We have spent our time in considering Moses and the Lord Jesus Christ in terms of the contrast between law and grace. But you notice that there is a further contrast in verse 17. There is a comparison here between law and truth, in exactly the same way as there is between law and grace, and now we come to work out this second contrast.

It is very important, once more, to bear in mind that John puts it like this not to disparage the law or Moses, but simply in order to show the superiority of grace and truth and of the Lord Jesus Christ. I keep on repeating this because I am well aware of the fact that so many think that now that we are in the Christian dispensation, we are to disparage law, to dismiss it, to say that it does not come in at all. I think we have seen abundantly clearly the error of any such teaching. John himself is very careful to prevent our falling into such error. For instance, in chapter 5 we read: 'Search the scriptures', or, 'You do search the scriptures' – whichever you prefer, it does not matter – 'for in them ye think ye have eternal life: and they are they which testify of me' (*John* 5:39). Our Lord is referring there, of course, to the Old Testament Scriptures, and indicates clearly that they refer to him and testify of him.

Our Lord goes on to put this still more clearly: 'For had ye believed Moses, ye would have believed me: for he wrote of me' (*John* 5:46). It is obviously wrong, therefore, ever to speak disparagingly of Moses and the teaching of the law. The purpose of verse 17 of the Prologue is not to dismiss the law as useless, but just to show that the law, though it was given by God and given in a very glorious manner, was nevertheless incomplete. It was not perfect; it lacked the fulness that is to be found in our Lord Jesus Christ alone. That is the spirit in which John writes these words. The law, I repeat, was given by God, and in a glorious manner. It had a specific work to do and it did that work, but nevertheless it was only preparatory. And this applies not only to grace but, equally, to truth. So we are now going to show the ways in which the law was incomplete when put by the side of the truth that has come in its fulness in and through our blessed Lord and Saviour.

First, we shall consider in general the incompleteness and imperfection of the law from the standpoint of truth and of the revealing of truth. And then, second, we shall look at the law as it was incomplete in one particular and most important respect. Now when we consider the first point, we find that this is adverted to very frequently and is made quite plain in the New Testament itself. For instance, one respect in which we see the incompleteness of the law is that the truth that is conveyed to us by the law was conveyed by *types* and *shadows*. These are the terms that are used by the New Testament writers in order to bring out this aspect of the truth, and it is remarkable to notice this terminology. Take, for instance, the apostle Paul's words in Colossians 2:16–17: 'Let no man therefore judge you in meat, or in drink, or in respect of an holyday, or of the new moon, or of the sabbath days: which are a shadow of things to come; but the body is of Christ.' The difference between law and truth is the difference between a type or a shadow, on the one hand, and a body – the substance, the reality – on the other.

But let me give you some further examples of the kind of statement found in Colossians 2:16–17. Take Hebrews 8:4–5. Here the writer is showing the contrast between the two covenants, in all aspects, even including their administration. He says:

For if he [our Lord] were on earth, he should not be a priest, seeing that there are priests that offer gifts according to the law: who serve unto the example and shadow of heavenly things, as Moses was admonished of God when he was about to make the tabernacle: for, See, saith he, that thou make all things according to the pattern shewed to thee in the mount.

The same terms are used: it is 'the example and shadow of heavenly things', not the great reality itself. The same point is made in Hebrews 9, where the author says that everything that happened under the law in the first tabernacle

was a figure for the time then present, in which were offered both gifts and sacrifices, that could not make him that did the service perfect, as pertaining to the conscience; which stood only in meats and drinks, and divers washings, and carnal ordinances, imposed on them until the time of reformation (Heb. 9:9–10).

It was temporary, it was transient, just a matter of types and illustrations and shadows. Then there is a further statement in Hebrews 10:1: 'For the law having a shadow of good things to come, and not the very image of the things' – now there it is explicitly – 'can never with those sacrifices which they offered year by year continually make the comers thereunto perfect.'

So here is an important difference between the law and the truth, and that is really the exposition of John 1:17: 'The law was given by Moses, but . . . truth came by Jesus Christ.' It is the difference between a picture or a hint or an illustration, and truth itself. Everything under the law was a mere representation – and therein lay its real limit. 'It is not possible', says Hebrews 10:4, 'that the blood of bulls and of goats should take away sins.' They were never meant to; they could not. They were but shadows, adumbrations, anticipations of that which was to come in its fulness in and through our Lord and Saviour himself. That is the first contrast: he is the great antitype himself, he is the truth, he is the substance, or, to use the language of Hebrews 10:5, he is the 'body', the reality itself that was thus hinted at and pointed to by the types and the shadows. So the New Testament refers to him as the truth, and he does so himself: 'I am the way, the truth, and the life' (*John* 14:6). He is 'the light of the world' (*John* 9:5). Our Lord is the incarnation of truth. In and of himself, he is the truth.

Perhaps we can best fix this in our minds by reminding ourselves of the language used by John the Baptist: 'The next day John seeth Jesus coming unto him, and saith, Behold the Lamb of God, which taketh away the sin of the world' (*John* 1:29). Here is the difference. It is no longer a case of lambs provided by men – one every morning and evening, and the paschal lamb and so on; they are only pictures and illustrations. Here is the Lamb pointed to by all the others, the Lamb of God himself, the Lamb whom God is providing, and providing not merely to cover over sins in the way those others did. Their blood merely covered over sins for the time being until the time of reformation should come and now that this time has come, here is the Lamb of God who really does take away the sin of the world. That is John the Baptist's proclamation. So the incompleteness of the law from the standpoint of truth is seen in the contrast between truth conveyed through the law, which is a matter of hints and glimpses and suggestions, and the truth that arrived in all its fulness and in all its glory in the person of God's Son.

But let me hurry on to a second way in which we see the incompleteness of the law and the fulness of truth that is in Christ. The author of the Epistle to the Hebrews starts his great letter by saying this: 'God, who at sundry times and in divers manners spake in time past unto the fathers by the prophets . . . ' In the past, he says, God revealed the truth to the fathers through the prophets in many parts and portions and in many ways. And how true that is! What you have in the Old Testament is a little bit here and a little bit there; that is its characteristic. The whole thing is incomplete. It is very interesting at this Advent time to look at the prophecies concerning our Lord and to see how one aspect was given here and another aspect there: the place he would be born in, the time when he would come, certain things that were going to happen; 'sundry times', 'divers manners'! One prophet given this detail, another that. That is the whole characteristic of the law – taking the law to cover all of the Old Testament, Moses and the prophets, all of them together.

And in this incompleteness we see another vital difference because our Lord himself is the truth. 'In whom', says the apostle Paul to the

Colossians, 'are hid all the treasures of wisdom and knowledge' (*Col.* 2:3). It is all in the person of our blessed Lord and Saviour. It is not just a hint; it is not just this or that little aspect. He is the truth in all its fulness. He is the light of the world. There is nothing incomplete. No longer parts and portions, bits and pieces, but the whole, in this one person.

Then let us look at another contrast. What we really have in the Old Testament is promises. They are very wonderful promises. They are, indeed, 'exceeding great and precious promises' (*2 Pet.* 1:4). God gave his people these promises from the very beginning, starting in the Garden of Eden (*Gen.* 3:15), and he went on giving promises. Yes, but it was never more than promises. That is the astounding fact. That is what we as Christian people should always bear in mind. Listen again to the way in which the author of the Epistle to the Hebrews puts this in chapter 11 when he gives this gallery of the great saints of the Old Testament. He says, 'And these all, having obtained a good report through faith, received not the promise' – they did not receive the fulfilment of the promise, that towards which the promise was pointing – 'God having provided some better thing for us, that they without us should not be made perfect' (*Heb.* 11:39–40). So they were left merely with the promise, the hope, the possibility, and they held on to that. That is the meaning of faith; it is 'the substance of things hoped for, the evidence of things not seen' (*Heb.* 11:1).

These Old Testament men and women of faith received the promises, and they lived by them and looked forward. But it never got beyond that. That is why it is right to say, 'The law was given by Moses, but grace and truth came by [our Lord] Jesus Christ.' How? Well, let the apostle Paul again put that in his own way: 'All the promises of God in him are yea, and in him Amen, unto the glory of God by us' (*2 Cor.* 1:20). He is the fulfilment of every promise. Go through the Old Testament, make a list of every single promise: you will find that he is the answer to every one, the promises have been fulfilled. That is the difference. The law through Moses, great as it was, given by God with glory, was, nevertheless, only the promise, the possibility, the hope. Now it has arrived.

And the last difference can be put in this way: it is the contrast between Moses himself and our blessed Lord and Saviour. It is interesting to see the way John puts this. 'The law was given by Moses' – two things, law and Moses – 'grace and truth came by Jesus Christ.' So there is a comparison not only between the law and grace, and between the law and truth, but also between Moses and the Lord Jesus Christ. And that is done quite deliberately because it does help to bring out the pre-eminence, the superiority, perfection, completeness that is in the New Testament gospel. In other words, the contrast in this whole matter of truth can be put very well in terms of the contrast between Moses and the Lord himself.

What is this contrast? Let us again allow the Epistle to the Hebrews to answer the question. If you know how to use your Bible, you will not need so many commentaries! The Bible is the best commentary on the Bible. Listen to the way Hebrews puts it:

Wherefore, holy brethren, partakers of the heavenly calling, consider the Apostle and High Priest of our profession, Christ Jesus; who was faithful to him that appointed him, as also Moses was faithful in all his house. For this man was counted worthy of more glory than Moses,

– why? –

inasmuch as he who hath builded the house hath more honour than the house. For every house is builded by some man; but he that built all things is God. And Moses verily was faithful in all his house, as a servant, for a testimony of those things which were to be spoken after; but Christ as a son over his own house; whose house are we, if we hold fast the confidence and the rejoicing of the hope firm unto the end (Heb. 3:1–6).

Now there is the full statement with regard to this matter. The difference between Moses and our Lord is the difference between a house and the builder of the house. When you say that the builder of the house is superior to the house, you are not making fun of the house, you are not saying the house is useless or worthless, you are not dismissing it. Of course not. It is a relative difference. The law is God's law and it is still there but we have something greater. That is what John is saying. The difference is thus between the house and the one who had the mind and the understanding and the ingenuity to plan and produce his specifications – the creator, the architect, the artificer, the builder.

A second way in which the author of Hebrews puts this contrast between Moses and our blessed Lord is this: it is the difference between a servant and a son. Moses, great man though he was, was only a servant, and the greatest servant is inferior to the son, even when the son is a babe. In the Old Testament, Moses stands out pre-eminently as the great servant, yes, but what is a servant, even on tiptoe and in the moment of his greatest exaltation, when you put him by the side of the son? And this Son happens to be the maker of all things, and therefore God. 'Every house is builded by some man; but he that built all things is God.' That is what we have already been told about the Son: '[God] hath in these last days spoken unto us by his Son, whom he hath appointed heir of all things, by whom also he made the worlds' (*Heb.* 1:2). What we have received through Moses is what we receive through a servant; what we receive through the Lord Jesus Christ is received through the Son of God himself. So here it is: 'The only begotten Son, which is in the bosom of the Father, he hath declared him' (*John* 1:18).

And the last way in which the Epistle to the Hebrews works out the contrast is this: it is the difference between a testimony to the truth or a teaching about the truth, and the truth itself. 'Moses verily was faithful in all his house, as a servant, for a testimony of those things which were to be spoken after' (*Heb.* 3:5). Moses could not go beyond that. He was a pointer, a testimony, a witness. He points us in the direction. He says that the truth is going to come. But in our Lord we have the truth in all its fulness. He is the truth and, as I have reminded you, he proclaimed this on more than one occasion. He is 'the light of the world' (*John* 9:5). Or, as John puts it here in this Prologue, '[He] was the true Light, which lighteth every man that cometh into the world.'

There, then, is the general difference that is indicated by our text. But now let us turn to the particular application for, obviously, that is what John has in mind. When he talks about truth, he says: I am really talking about the truth concerning God. 'The law was given by Moses, but grace and truth came by Jesus Christ. No man hath seen God at any time; the only begotten Son, which is in the bosom of the Father, he hath declared him.' So the particular application is with regard to the whole matter of the truth concerning God. That is ultimate truth. That is really what we mean by truth. It is the knowledge of God. And this is what makes John rejoice. This is why he indulges in this comparison. He says, in effect, 'At last it is possible for us to have this knowledge.'

So John starts by saying, 'No man hath seen God at any time.' He is not referring only to seeing God with the physical eye. John is not merely saying that no one has actually seen the form or the shape of God because God is Spirit. That is included but he goes beyond that. He is saying that no one has any true knowledge of God – seeing in that sense. When we do not understand something, we say, in our common parlance, 'I don't see that.' And it is the same here. When John says, 'No man hath seen God', he means that no one has ever seen the truth about God in its fulness; it is impossible. Now here the contrast with Moses is particularly helpful. Moses brings out this aspect of the truth in a very glorious manner because in every respect he came nearer to seeing God than anybody else did.

The philosophers have not come anywhere near to seeing God. They simply speculate; they know nothing at all. Is that an exaggeration? No, it is not! Philosophers know nothing about God – how can they? There is a limit to their capacity, and God is infinite. Philosophers think that they can deduce certain things, but they have no authority, they have no sanction whatsoever, for their deductions. All that is groping after the truth, seeking God 'if haply they might feel after him' (*Acts* 17:27). That is all they can do, as Paul told the Athenians. That is why we should pay no attention at all to what any philosopher who is not a Christian may say about God. It is useless, absolutely worthless. It is simply what that philosopher thinks. Philosophers are sinful, finite people and by definition are incapable of knowing God. That is why they change their ideas and their gods from time to time, and that is why, when they talk in interviews on the television, they all contradict one another. Buddhism, anything else you like, all these false religions, are human philosophies, every one of them. They are simply specula-tions based upon nothing whatsoever except the opinion of mortal, fallible human beings.

But when you come to Moses, you are looking at somebody who is in an entirely different category from the philosopher. Moses never sat down and began to write in this way: 'This is what I think, this is what I say about God.' That was not his position at all. Moses was a man who received a revelation. What truth was given to him? The full answer is in the book of Exodus. First of all, Moses went up Mount Sinai, and there he received the law from God, as he received much else. There, we are told, God spoke to Moses 'face to face' (*Deut.* 5:4). But be careful about that, because I will show you in a moment that he did not actually see the face of God. 'Face to face' is but an expression. It means that God spoke to Moses in a very intimate manner. He addressed Moses and Moses knew that God was speaking to him. He came into the presence of God, hence this radiance in his face to which Paul refers in 2 Corinthians 3.

The point, however, is that Moses went up the mount and he was there with God for forty days receiving the revelation, God giving him a knowledge of truth that he might impart it to the people. We see it perfectly in the Ten Commandments but there was a great deal of information that was given in addition to that. So here is something that puts Moses in a category of his own. And not only Moses, but all the prophets also: 'No prophecy of the scripture is of any private interpretation . . . but holy men of God spake as they were moved by the Holy Ghost' (*2 Pet.* 1:20–21). This is revelation! Moses had it in this supreme manner. The prophets went into a kind of ecstasy when the divine afflatus came upon them. But Moses spent the forty days with God on Mount Sinai, face to face, as it were, in that strange intimacy.

But more than that was given to Moses. Take that extraordinary incident recorded in Exodus 33, where Moses, with a strange boldness, makes his request, 'Shew me thy glory.' And God answers him and says that he cannot do exactly what Moses asks: 'For there shall no man see me, and live' (*Exod.* 33:18, 20). The sight is more than anyone can stand. However, though that is not possible, God says he will do this for Moses:

I will make all my goodness pass before thee, and I will proclaim the name of the Lord *before thee; and will be gracious to whom I will be gracious, and will shew mercy on whom I will shew mercy . . . Thou canst not see my face: for there shall no man see me, and live.*

And then God says:

There is a place by me, and thou shalt stand upon a rock: and it shall come to pass, while my glory passeth by, that I will put thee in a clift of the rock, and will cover thee with my hand while I pass by: and I will take away mine hand, and thou shalt see my back parts: but my face shall not be seen (Exod. 33:19–23).

Now that was a remarkable and extraordinary thing. Moses was given a glimpse of the glory of the incomprehensible God! Yes, but he just saw him 'passing by', as it were – the 'back parts' of God! He did not see the face of God. Oh, he saw the glory – there is no question of that. Not in the fulness of the expression of it, but the mere hem of the glory of God, something unusual, something amazing. So Moses was given that revelation of the truth concerning God; yes, but you see the limitation. And so he was never able to do more than bear witness, bear testimony, to the truth, to point to it and to repeat what he had been told in the great revelation.

And this limitation is true of the whole of the Old Testament. Our Lord says about Abraham: 'Abraham rejoiced to see my day: and he saw it, and was glad' (*John* 8:56). Yes, but he only saw it 'afar off'. This is true of all these Old Testament characters and it is also true of what we are told about God in the law. In the law I see something of the character of God. I see his holiness, his righteousness, his justice – that is what I see supremely. And it caused men then to quake, as it causes them to quake even at this present time. This is true of all the prophets. The apostle Peter uses an extraordinary phrase with respect to this: 'Of which salvation the prophets have enquired and searched diligently, who prophesied of the grace that should come unto you: searching what, or what manner of time *the Spirit of Christ which was in them did signify*, when it testified beforehand the sufferings of Christ, and the glory that should follow' (*1 Pet.* 1:10–11). In other words, these prophets were vehicles of the truth. God was giving truth through them. But they did not understand it; they were enquiring; they were trying to understand. When is it going to happen? What is going to happen? How is it going to happen? Though they were giving the truth, they were amazed at it and were trying to grasp it.

And as our Lord himself says, this partial sight was true of John the Baptist, who was the last of the great line of prophets. Of John the Baptist our Lord said, 'Among those that are born of women there is not a greater prophet than John the Baptist' (*Luke* 7:28). And yet the truth about John the Baptist is this – we have it here in this first chapter of John's Gospel: 'There was a man sent from God, whose name was John. The same came for a witness, to bear witness of the Light, that all men through him might believe. He was not that Light, but was sent to bear witness of that Light' (*John* 1:6–8). That is it. He could not go beyond that. We have it again in verse 15: 'John bare witness of him, and cried, saying, This was he of whom I spake, He that cometh after me is preferred before me: for he was before me.' You see the limit? But then our Lord puts it still more plainly, perhaps, in the fifth chapter, where he says this of John:

He was a burning and a shining light: and ye were willing for a season to rejoice in his light. But I have greater witness than that of John: for the works which the Father hath given me to finish, the same works that I do, bear witness of me, that the Father hath sent me (John 5:35–36).

Now there it is. Moses, the great law-giver, all the mighty succession of prophets, even the last, the forerunner, the herald, John, they all simply witness to the truth. They have had a glimpse of the back parts, as it were, but no more. They give us valuable information, they teach us the truth concerning God in parts and portions, but they do not go beyond it. But now 'grace and truth' have come through Jesus Christ. Listen to the way the apostle John puts it here in the Prologue: 'No man hath seen God at any time; the only begotten Son, which is in the bosom of the Father, he hath declared him.' Now there is great trouble about the translation[1] here and one cannot settle it definitely, but there is very good authority for saying that it should be read like

---

[1] The difficulty referred to relates to the underlying Greek text. The best evidence seems to favour retaining the reading 'only begotten Son'.

this: 'No man hath seen God at any time; the only begotten God, who is in the bosom of the Father, he hath declared him.' He is 'the only begotten'. He is 'the only begotten God' for, 'the Word was God'. He is God, eternal God the Son.

And in order to make that statement still more powerful, John says, 'which is in the bosom of the Father'. To be 'in the bosom' means a nearness, an intimacy; it means that you receive secrets. To people in your bosom you tell things that you do not tell the world. Moses was taken up on to the mount, yes, but he was not allowed to be in the bosom of the Father, he was put in the cleft of the rock and the hand was upon him. But here is one who is in the bosom of the Father, the only begotten, beloved Son of God, the intimate sharer of all the secrets of God from eternity to eternity, the one who knows everything.

Now our Lord repeatedly spoke of this contrast. Listen to the way he puts it to Nicodemus: 'Art thou a master of Israel, and knowest not these things? Verily, verily, I say unto thee, We speak that we do know, and testify that we have seen; and ye receive not our witness' (*John* 3:10–11). Or take it like this in John 3:13: 'No man hath ascended up to heaven' – your great philosophers are earthbound, of the earth, earthy. Who are they to speak about God? What do they know about him? The blasphemy of their speculations should be denounced by us! They have not ascended into heaven! But God is in heaven, not on the earth. God is not a man who can be analysed and dissected as we analyse one another's thoughts. 'No man hath ascended up to heaven, but he that came down from heaven, even the Son of man which is in heaven.' He is speaking on earth but he is still in heaven. He has come from heaven; he is still in heaven. He has looked into the face of God. He is in the bosom of God. Here is the one who speaks with authority.

And so we find later on in the Gospel that our Lord says, 'Verily, verily, I say unto you, Before Abraham was, I am' (*John* 8:58). You are relying on Abraham, he says. You keep on saying, 'Abraham, our father'. You say you know a lot because you are Abraham's children. Of course, you do know a lot, you know more than the Gentiles, but listen: 'Before Abraham was, I am'! I always have been; I always will be.

Or take it again in John 10:30: 'I and my Father are one.' There is nothing beyond that. But perhaps this helps still more: our Lord has just been telling his disciples that he is going to leave them, and they are very upset and very troubled, so he says, 'Let not your heart be troubled: ye believe in God, believe also in me . . . ' And then Philip, poor Philip, still not happy, still not satisfied, says, 'Lord, shew us the Father, and it sufficeth us.' He is saying: 'We are troubled about your going, but though you are going, show us the Father and it will be sufficient for us.' Then we are told, 'Jesus saith unto him, Have I been so long time with you, and yet hast thou not known me, Philip? he that hath seen me hath seen the Father; and how sayest thou then, Shew us the Father?' (*John* 14:1, 8–9). 'The only begotten Son, which is in the bosom of the Father, he hath declared him.'

But let us go on and listen to the apostle Paul expounding this teaching. He, who has been made an apostle that he might pass on the truth, puts it like this: 'But we all, with open face, beholding as in a glass' – what? – 'the glory of the Lord, are changed into the same image from glory to glory, even as by the Spirit of the Lord' (*2 Cor.* 3:18). Or take his description of our Lord in 2 Corinthians 4:4: '. . . lest the light of the glorious gospel of Christ, who is the image of God' – the express likeness of God – 'should shine unto them.' And then comes the great statement in verse 6: 'God, who commanded the light to shine out of darkness, hath shined in our hearts' – what for? Here is the answer – 'to give the light of the knowledge of the glory of God' – in the 'back parts'? No – 'in the face of Jesus Christ.' No longer a glimpse of the passing glory but 'in the face of Jesus Christ'. 'He who hath seen me hath seen the Father.'

Again, the author of the Epistle to the Hebrews puts this truth in a most amazing statement. He talks of this Son in whom God has now spoken to us as 'being the brightness of his glory, and the express image of his person' (*Heb.* 1:3). There is nothing beyond that! He is the exact likeness, imprint, image, of God himself! It is all there in him. 'For in him dwelleth all the fulness of the Godhead bodily,' says the apostle Paul in Colossians 2:9. And that is what John is saying. 'The law was given by Moses, but grace and truth' – the truth about God and the knowledge of God – 'came by Jesus Christ. No man hath seen God at any time; the only begotten Son, which is in the bosom of the Father, he hath declared [exegeted] him.' He has expounded him. He has brought him forth. He has led him out to us. In him we see God and in him we know God; in him we have a full expression of the glory of God. It is in him we know God and the character of God, the power of God, the glory of God, the love of God, the being of God, the longsuffering of God, the justice of God, the righteousness of God, the truth that is God!

How does our Lord exegete God? How does he declare him? Well, our Lord declares God in his teaching: 'Holy Father', he says – lest people have sentimental notions of God's love. 'Our Father which art in heaven, Hallowed be thy name' (*Matt.* 6:9)! And then, thank God, our Lord teaches us about the character of God in the parable of the prodigal son.

The Pharisees thought they knew a great deal about God, they were students of the Old Testament Scriptures, but they were blinded and they did not understand God. So when they saw Jesus Christ mixing with tax-collectors and sinners, they said, 'Behold . . . a wine-bibber, a friend of publicans and sinners!' (*Luke* 7:34).

Oh, says our Lord, you know nothing about God. So he tells the parable of the prodigal son (*Luke* 15:11–32). He says: That is what God is like. His child has become a prodigal, he has become a vice lover; nevertheless, the father heart of God wants his child back. He is waiting for him, looking for him, runs to meet him and embraces him – that is God! Teaching! 'He hath declared him.' You do not find things like that in the Old Testament; here is something that comes only from the Lord Jesus Christ himself.

But then our Lord also reveals the truth about God in his life. In his actions, in all his behaviour and demeanour, he reveals God. Look at his kindness, his compassion. Look at his heart of love. Look at his readiness to stop to heal some poor sufferer or somebody who is in trouble. He never despises anybody. 'A bruised reed shall he not break, and smoking flax shall he not quench' (*Matt.* 12:20). He says: That is how I am; that is how God is.

But, oh, above everywhere else, our Lord reveals God on the cross. If you want to know anything about the justice, and the holiness, and the righteousness of God, go and look at the cross on Calvary's hill. But, thank God, you will see at the same time the 'love so amazing, so divine', and the compassion, and the pity, and the mercy. You will see it all streaming from the face of Jesus Christ upon the cross. 'He hath declared him' – in his teaching, life and living, in his death and resurrection, in everything. Here is the full and final revelation of God.

But we also see in our Lord the truth about God with respect to God's wisdom, and especially in this matter of salvation. 'We preach Christ crucified,' says Paul, 'unto the Jews a stumblingblock, and unto the Greeks foolishness' – why? Because he is 'the power of God, and the wisdom of God' (*1 Cor.* 1:23–24). In the Old Testament you can see hints of the way of salvation. I see the paschal lamb and it tells me something. I do not understand how, but God is going to provide some blood that will spare me. That is all; it is a picture. All right, I will trust, but I do not see, I do not know. And so with all the types and shadows. But when I come to look at him, I know why Paul says to the Corinthians, 'For I determined not to know [and preach] any thing among you, save Jesus Christ, and him crucified' (*1 Cor.* 2:2). It is because here it all is – the way of salvation, justification by faith only, not by my works, not by my goodness – all we have been seeing in these studies. What the law cannot do, Christ has done. He is the fulfilment of it all, in every respect.

Let me put it in this quotation from 1 Corinthians 1:30: 'But of him are ye in Christ Jesus, who of God is made unto us wisdom, and righteousness, and sanctification, and redemption.' It is all there, in him. That is the wisdom of God. Christ has been made wisdom, and there is the wisdom: justification in Christ, sanctification in Christ; more – being 'in Christ'. As I was in Adam, I am now in Christ. The church is the body of Christ. Did Moses teach that? Did the prophets teach that? Of course not. They could not have done. But here it is in Christ. The truth has come in him. 'Now ye are the body of Christ, and members in particular' (*1 Cor.* 12:27). He is the head and we are merely parts and portions.

Not only that; it is in Christ that we see God's great plan and purpose for all the ages. Listen to Ephesians 1:10: 'That in the dispensation of the fulness of times he might gather together in one all things in Christ, both which are in heaven, and which are on earth; even in him.' He alone reveals this. It was never clearly seen before. There are hints, there are suggestions, but here it is stated fully and explicitly and openly.

So I end by putting it to you like this. Our Lord said, 'I am the way, the truth, and the life: no man cometh unto the Father, but by me' (*John* 14:6) No one! You cannot come to the Father except by Christ. Oh, you can arrive at partial knowledge of God along other ways, by the law of Moses and so on. You may know him as the great Creator, you may know him as the great Judge, and in many other ways, but you will never know him as your Father. There is only one way of knowing that and it is in Christ; he alone gives me this knowledge.

Did you ever notice the contrast between the Old Testament and the New, between Moses and Christ? Here it is. This is the highest point the Old Testament can rise to: 'Like as a father pitieth his children' (*Psa.* 103:13). 'Like as'! Does our Lord teach us to say, 'O God, who art like a father'? No! 'Our Father'! 'Abba, Father'! He gives us the Spirit of sonship, 'the Spirit of adoption, whereby we cry, Abba, Father' (*Rom.*8:15). We no longer worship a God afar off. He is a God afar off, 'dwelling in the light which no man can approach unto; whom no man hath seen, nor can see' (*1 Tim.* 6:16), the everlasting and eternal God. But in Christ I – even I – can venture unto him and say, 'My Father' and, with others, 'Our Father'!

The law was given by Moses but the truth about God, the truth of God as Saviour, who adopts me into his family, and makes me his child, and enables me to worship him not in fear and terror but to approach his throne with boldness and confidence and to say, 'Abba, Father', this knowledge has come to me in and through the Lord Jesus Christ and through him alone. He is 'the only begotten Son, which is in the bosom of the Father', and he has declared him unto us. ∾

12

The Incarnation

For the law was given by Moses, but grace and truth came by Jesus Christ (John 1:17).

In our study of this verse we have seen very clearly that the law points to both grace and truth. We can go further – we have indeed been going further – and can say that the law not only points to grace and truth, but *demands* them if we are to be saved. But now I want to go a step further still and say that the law demands that grace and truth should *come*, that they should come in a person, and in the exact way and manner in which they did come when the Son of God entered into this world.

We have seen that John 1:17 is full of contrasts and in our last study we considered the contrast in general between Moses and the Lord Jesus Christ. In addition to the points we have enumerated, we can add this: that Moses was not essential to the law. The law was given through Moses but it could have been given through many others. Some representative, some kind of mediator or leader was necessary, and God chose Moses. But he was not absolutely essential, though he was a great and an unusual man. When we looked at that first verse in the Epistle to the Hebrews, we saw that God gave the revelation under the Old Testament dispensation in many forms and at many times. He had a succession of prophets and to each one was given a part and a portion. Now in not a single case was the particular prophet essential. These people were used by God to be the vehicles and the channels through whom the revelation was given, and thus we find a great variety in their characters, in their abilities, in their offices and in their works.

But now, when we come to this other realm, we find that grace and truth 'came' through Jesus Christ, and I want to try to demonstrate that grace and truth could *only* come through him, and only in the particular, precise way and manner in which they did come. Moses: not essential; Jesus Christ: absolutely essential. Apart from him, grace and truth could not have come at all.

Now the question is: Why? And the answer can be put in general in one sentence. The law, by revealing our state and condition and needs, shows that nothing but the incarnation, and all that followed it, would suffice. The law, by exposing the exceeding sinfulness of sin, and our guilt and our impotence and so on, demands the God-man. It demands the incarnation and everything that followed it. It demands what is put here in these words: 'The Word was made flesh, and dwelt among us.' It demands that the Son of God should come from the everlasting glory in the precise manner in which he came and that he should do all that he did do. Let us, then, try to analyse this and to examine it together.

My first task is to explain why the truth had to come in this particular way, through Jesus Christ. In our last study we saw clearly that he alone – 'the only begotten Son, which is in the bosom of the Father', in the most intimate relationship, sharing all the secrets and having complete and entire knowledge – he alone could exegete, expound, draw out, the Father to us. No man could ever do this. No man has seen, or ever can see, God in any sense at any time. This seeing is not merely physical; it includes a real knowledge and understanding of God and of his being. That is where all philosophy is ultimately not only foolish but arrogant. It attempts something that by definition is a sheer impossibility. But here we see that the Son came. He is the 'fulness' of the Father, and therefore he really can tell us the truth about God. In other words, God alone can reveal God. 'Canst thou by searching find out God?' (*Job* 11:7). 'The world by wisdom knew not God' (*1 Cor.* 1:21). Of course not! It cannot. Not only are we sinful, we are finite, and God is infinite. So we start with the essential postulate that it is only the only begotten Son, who is in the bosom of the Father, who can declare him.

But immediately, you see, a problem arises. In the Old Testament we read, 'There shall no man see me, and live' (*Exod.* 33:20). Men and women cannot look upon God and still go on living, because God is God. This is a problem that is postulated by the law, which, having revealed to us something of the being and character and holiness and justice and righteousness of God, tells us that it is idle to try to arrive at a knowledge of him; it shuts us up entirely to a revelation by God himself. But here is our difficulty – we cannot look upon God and live. Let me emphasize this point by showing you how this gives a real key to the understanding of the incarnation and shows us why it was absolutely essential that truth had to come, why truth cannot merely be stated. Truth must come; it must appear. We will never know God until in some shape or form or manner we see him. Yet we cannot look upon God as we are by nature and live.

Let me give you some illustrations to emphasize why it was absolutely essential that the Son of God should be born as a babe in Bethlehem, why 'the Word' must be 'made flesh' before we could have any knowledge of the truth. The Bible itself gives some very interesting glimpses into this problem. Look, for instance, at what happened on the Mount of Transfiguration. Our Lord took with him Peter and James and John and went up on to that mountain, and he was transfigured before them so that his very clothes became glistening white, brighter than anyone could ever bleach them. There he was, suddenly transfigured, and his glory began to appear, and this is what we read – it is only Luke who gives us this detail and it is a very important one – 'But Peter and they that were with him were heavy with sleep' (*Luke* 9:32). Why was this? Oh, this dazzling glory was having that effect upon them. Then I read again: 'While he thus spake, there came a cloud, and overshadowed them: and they feared as they entered into the cloud' (verse 34). Now the effect of a mere glimpse of the Godhead, of the glory of God, had this effect upon the disciples. They became drowsy and heavy and sleepy and filled with fear, and the cloud came, as it were, to help them by standing between them and the sight. That is one example.

But let me give you another. You remember what happened to the apostle Paul when – still Saul of Tarsus – he was travelling on the road to Damascus. He was a self-confident man, an able man, a man well versed in the Scriptures, a man who taught about God and thought he knew God. But one glimpse of the glorified Lord Jesus Christ strikes him helpless, blinds him, and there he is, lying on the road. What is it? Oh, he has just had, with the naked eye, a glimpse of the glory of God in the face of Jesus Christ.

And then let me give you one further illustration. In the book of Revelation, at the very beginning, John tells us how the revelation, the vision, came to him, and this is what he says: 'And when I saw him, I fell at his feet as dead' (*Rev.* 1:17). He was given a vision of the glorified Lord in this symbolic manner but the effect upon him was that he was almost killed. 'There shall no man see me, and live.' And yet we must see God, as it were, because we will never know the truth apart from that, and we need to know the truth. And the answer? It is the incarnation. Here *is* God, but in the flesh! We cannot add to Charles Wesley's perfect expression of it:

> *Veiled in flesh the Godhead see;*
> *Hail the incarnate Deity.*

There it is! 'Great is the mystery of godliness: God was manifest in the flesh' (*1 Tim.* 3:16). 'In him dwelleth all the fulness of the Godhead bodily' (*Col.* 2:9). So at one and the same time there is a revealing and a veiling, and it is all for our benefit. We could not stand the direct sight – it would kill us. And yet we must have this sight, we must have this knowledge. It is only 'the only begotten Son, which is in the bosom of the Father' who can declare him. And he has come, and in a way that we can bear, that we can stand. There is this sense in which we are seeing God, and yet live, because he came veiled in the flesh. His coming, then, makes the revelation possible to us and, as we are told at the beginning of Matthew's Gospel, he is 'Emmanuel . . . God with us' (*Matt.* 1:23). 'The Word' – which is God – 'was made flesh, and dwelt among us.'

Here, then, is the first matter that we must grasp and realize: the truth had to come in this way. The truth about God cannot be adequately stated in propositions. Revelations of it, parts and portions, bits and pieces, as we have seen, were given in old times, but, oh, it was not enough, it was not adequate, it was just something to encourage the people and to lead them on. Then he comes! And he had to come in this particular way, otherwise the coming would have blinded us again. So we are driven to the incarnation. The law demands the incarnation, otherwise we can never have any knowledge of this truth, which is God.

But, second, let us look at the incarnation in terms of grace – let us see why grace also had to come in this particular manner. The key here, the way to expound it, is to look at the apostle Paul's statement in Galatians 4:4: 'When the fulness of the time was come, God sent forth his Son, *made of a woman, made under the law.*' There it is. That is the exposition. God sent his Son in that particular way – but why? Why are both absolutely essential? The answer is still that the law demanded them, the law insists upon them – that is, if we are to be saved from the law. He must be both 'made of a woman' and 'made under the law', in order, as verse 5 goes on to tell us, 'to redeem them that were under the law'. What does it mean?

Let us work it out. Why were the two aspects necessary? The answer can be put like this. First, our representative must be human, must be a man. Why? Because we are human. Now we do not always appreciate the meaning of this point as we should. Here is the problem: it is man who has fallen; it is man who has become sinful; it is man who is in disgrace. It is the human race itself that fell in man. And so the law rightly demands the punishment of man. And, in a sense, the devil likewise insists that our representative should be man, for the following reason. It was God who made everything and the supreme point of God's creative work was the creation of man. Man was made in the image of God, he was the acme of God's creation. And God looked upon it all and saw that it was good – which may be translated as God looking upon it all and being proud of it and pleased with it. But the devil comes in and he tempts man, and man falls. And apparently what God has done, God's supreme achievement, has turned into a failure. And the devil immediately begins to taunt God with this: This man that you have made, look at him! Made in your own image, the crowning act of your great purpose in creation, there he is! Behold him!

And, therefore, for God to be justified and to be vindicated, it is absolutely essential that whoever comes to redeem and restore humanity must be a man. A mere declaration of forgiveness on the part of God would not solve the problem. It not only would not solve it from the standpoint of the law, it would not satisfy it from the standpoint of the devil. Were God merely to look upon man in his fallen state and say, 'In spite of what you have done and what you are, I forgive you', the devil would still have triumphed. The devil would still say, 'That is all right, you have forgiven him, but look at him. He is still a wreck. He is still hopeless. He is still far removed from what he was at the beginning.' That is why these people who would explain the death of Christ upon the cross in terms of moral influence alone have never understood the very first beginnings of the gospel. They have never even understood the incarnation, leave alone the atonement.

In the same way, were God to send some angelic representative into this world, that would not be adequate, either. Because man has failed, man must succeed. God is not vindicated, God cannot answer and silence the devil and his taunts and his jeers, until he has produced a man who is perfect and does not fail. So our representative, our redeemer, must be a man, he must be 'made of a woman', and he must truly be made of a woman, he must truly become a man.

A God appearing in an outer case of flesh, as some of those early heretics thought – those Gnostic heretics, Docetists, they are called, who said that our Lord's body was a mere appearance – again missed the whole point. That would never have satisfied the devil. The devil would have said: 'Yes, you had to send your Son and put a shell of flesh upon him because you knew that no man could ever stand up to me and to my temptations. You put up man as your supreme achievement; very well, show me that a man can really stand and triumph and prevail.'

So it is essential that the redeemer should be 'made of a woman', that he should truly have a real human nature, as you and I have, that he should not be God in an appearance of flesh. If he is to do a work for us, to satisfy God on our behalf, he must be one of us. That is why those verses from Hebrews 2 are so crucially important:

For it became him [God], for whom are all things, and by whom are all things, in bringing many sons unto glory, to make the captain of their salvation perfect through sufferings (Heb. 2:10).

'Many sons'! He is the leader of these many sons.

For both he that sanctifieth [the Lord Jesus Christ] and they who are sanctified [those who believe] are all of one: for which cause he is not ashamed to call them brethren (Heb. 2:11).

Then follow the quotations that establish that truth. But listen to verses 14 and 15, which put it still more explicitly:

Forasmuch then as the children are partakers of flesh and blood,

– that is to say, those of us who are Christians, we are the children and we are partakers of flesh and blood –

he also himself likewise took part of the same; that through death he might destroy him that had the power of death, that is, the devil; and deliver them who through fear of death were all their lifetime subject to bondage.

And the writer puts this negatively in the next verse:

For verily he took not on him the nature of angels;

– which could be translated, 'he stretched not out his hand to help angels' –

but he took on him the seed of Abraham (Heb. 2:16).

The same point is still being emphasized.

Wherefore in all things it behoved him to be made like unto his brethren, that he might be a merciful and faithful high priest in things pertaining to God, to make reconciliation for the sins of the people. For in that he himself hath suffered being tempted, he is able to succour them that are tempted (Heb. 2:17–18).

Now that is an absolutely essential and vital doctrine. We need someone to represent us, to save us, and he must be a man. Because we are flesh and blood, because we are human, he must be identified with us. And so it is essential that he should be made of a woman, that 'the Word' truly should be 'made flesh'.

But, second, it is not enough to say that he must be made of a woman. We must add that he must be made under the law. Why? Because as our representative he must satisfy all the demands that are being made upon us. That is the exposition of John 1:17. Though he is God the Son, as a man he was subject to the demands of the law. And these demands were all observed in connection with him: when he was born, the offering of the turtle doves, the circumcision; when he was brought up as a Jew, he attended the synagogue and was made familiar with the demands of the law. The law makes these demands on us and therefore must make them on him, otherwise he is not our representative. It was essential that he should keep this law and keep it perfectly. He could not have delivered us from the curse of the law if he had not rendered perfect obedience to the law. He was not keeping the law for himself, but for us, as our representative. As the second Adam, as the 'last man', he rendered perfect obedience to the law of God.

So that is the first part of our problem, but it still leaves the other, and this, as I said, is that we are all guilty, we are all under the condemnation of the law. Here it is, thundering against us and making its demands that 'the soul that sinneth, it shall die' (*Ezek.* 18:4, 20). And if that happens to us, it is the end of us and we are eternally estranged and alienated from the presence of God. But he comes as our representative, made of a woman, made under the law. Why? Because he must bear this penalty of the law. Again, in that one chapter, Hebrews 2, we are given the perfect explanation:

We see Jesus, who was made a little lower than the angels

– that is to say, he was made flesh. He did not come as an angel. He had come as an angel many times in the Old Testament but now he comes as a man. What for?

for the suffering of death,

– we see him now –

crowned with glory and honour; that he by the grace of God should taste death for every man (Heb. 2:9).

He had to be made of a woman, he had to be made under the law, otherwise he could not have borne our guilt and the punishment of the law upon it and could not have died. Because God cannot die, he had to be made of a woman, he had to be made flesh and he had to be made under the law.

Here, then, is this astounding thing: the law demands the incarnation. Our Lord must be a man, otherwise he is not subject to the law, he cannot honour it positively and negatively and answer all its demands; and if he does not do that, he does not save us. The incarnation is absolutely essential. Without it, neither the law nor the devil would ever have been satisfied.

But, of course, I cannot stop there. Our representative had to be God, he had to be divine, because if he had not been God as well as man, he would not have saved us, even though he had died upon the cross and been buried in a grave. If he had been man only, the guilt and the weight of our sins would have crushed him. Our burden would have killed him and destroyed him. In the sense of his eternal separation from God, death would have been too much for him. But he was God as well as man, and this is the meaning of the incarnation – at once God and man, 'Word made flesh'. He did not cease to be God but he was made flesh in addition. He took our human nature, as we have seen from Hebrews 2:14. The only begotten God, who was still in the bosom of the Father, was here on earth and dwelt among us.

Now the importance and the significance of the fact that our Lord is God as well as man is that because of this, he is able even to deal with the problem of death. Listen to how he puts it himself in this selfsame Gospel of John: 'Therefore doth my Father love me, because I lay down my life, that I might take it again. No man taketh it from me, but I lay it down of myself' (*John* 10:17–18). No man can ever use language like that! Where are these ridiculous people who say that what was happening on the cross was that men were taking his life from him? They have not begun to understand it! The whole error of pacifism is that it completely misunderstands what happened on the cross on Calvary's hill. 'I have power to lay it down, and I have power to take it again. This commandment have I received of my Father' (*John* 10:18). No one else could speak like that, no one else could look into the face of death and say: I will deal with you, I will go through you and emerge on the other side! When he was here in the flesh, our Lord was Lord even of death. This is a most important point – and the New Testament goes on emphasizing it, therefore. Listen to the apostle Peter expounding it in his sermon in Jerusalem on the day of Pentecost: 'Him, being delivered by the determinate counsel and foreknowledge of God, ye have taken, and by wicked hands have crucified and slain: whom God hath raised up, having loosed the pains of death: because it was not possible that he should be holden of it' (*Acts* 2:23–24). Of course, everyone dies. Peter goes on to say that the patriarch David was with us, but he is dead. But this man, though of the seed of David, could not be held by death. Then there is another statement in which Peter quotes Psalm 16: 'Because thou wilt not leave my soul in hell, neither wilt thou suffer thine Holy One to see corruption' (*Acts* 2:27). That is why – because he is 'the Holy One', because he is God as well as man. And he had to be God as well as man in order that he could bear this guilt and the law might do its work, that the law might be honoured.

Yes, but our Lord needs power to go through death itself and emerge triumphant, and he does because he is God. Later on, when Peter is preaching to the crowd outside the Beautiful Gate of the temple, he describes him as 'the Prince of life' (*Acts* 3:15). Here is one who is the maker and the author of life and who is therefore stronger even than death itself. And so it is not surprising that the apostle Paul, when he comes to write to the Christians in Rome, says, 'Concerning his Son Jesus Christ our Lord, which was made of the seed of David according to the flesh; and declared to be the Son of God with power, according to the spirit of holiness, by the resurrection from the dead' (*Rom.*1:3–4). This establishes that he is God, otherwise he would never have risen. Sin would have finished even him though he had been perfect man as Adam was perfect. And so, again, the apostle, in writing to the Corinthians, says, 'Death is swallowed up in victory' (*1 Cor.* 15:54). Of course! Because he is the master and the conqueror even of death.

The Epistle to the Hebrews puts it like this: 'And it is yet far more evident: for that after the similitude of Melchisedec there ariseth another priest, who is made, not after the law of a carnal commandment, but after the power of an endless life' (*Heb.* 7:15–16). Here is his secret, this is the explanation of the work that he does that none other can do. 'For such an high priest became us, who is holy, harmless, undefiled, separate from sinners, and made higher than the heavens' (*Heb.* 7:26). And there is only one who can answer to all this, the one who is God as well as man. 'For the law maketh men high priests which have infirmity; but the word of the oath, which was since the law, maketh the Son, who is consecrated for evermore' (*Heb.* 7:28). Therefore 'he ever liveth' (*Heb.* 7:25). But listen to our Lord himself speaking to John in the vision in the book of Revelation: 'I am he that liveth, and was dead; and, behold, I am alive for evermore, Amen; and have the keys of hell and of death' (*Rev.* 1:18). He is the master. He is the victor. He is the one who can bear the full weight of the demands of the law and die but rise again, conquering even the last enemy. He was made sin for us, and yet he rises triumphant o'er death and o'er the grave.

We are establishing this thesis: that the law demands that grace should come and that it should come in the way in which it did come, that the eternal God should become a man, that the Word should be made flesh, that our Deliverer is theanthropic – God-man, both God and man, two natures, but one person. And as a further point, I suggest this to you: that our Saviour must be both God and man in order that you and I might receive the fruits of salvation. How? Well, like this. The law has postulated that we need a new nature, we need a new heart, a new outlook, a new life, and it is in and through him that we receive it. He is the beginner and the regenerator of a new humanity; he is 'the firstborn among many brethren' (*Rom.* 8:29).

To be saved, you and I need to be partakers of the divine nature. But how can that ever happen? It is impossible as we are. The divine cannot mix with that which is sinful. The answer is that we receive his nature, the nature of the God-man. We receive it from the Lord Jesus Christ; we are born of him and we come out of him. As one human nature started in Adam, another started in him. That is the new life, the new nature we receive, and that is why 'he is not ashamed to call them brethren' (*Heb.* 2:11). Salvation does not mean that our old human nature is improved. It means that we receive a new nature, that we are born again.

But salvation goes beyond that. The New Testament tells us that we are 'in him', that we are joined to him, that the church is the body of Christ and that we are 'members in particular' (*1 Cor.* 12:27). How can this possibly be? And, again, there is only one answer: it is because he is God and man. If he had not become man, we could never be joined to him, but as the God-man, the mediator, we can. He is the Head, we are the members, and we receive our humanity, our strength and our everything in and through him. And so you see the wonderful picture that Paul paints in the Epistle to the Ephesians where, having said that Christ is the Head of the body, he goes on, 'From whom the whole body fitly joined together and compacted by that which every joint supplieth, according to the effectual working in the measure of every part, maketh increase of the body unto the edifying of itself in love' (*Eph.* 4:16). This is salvation! This is how the devil is answered. We are in him, and from him we receive power, strength, nutriment, sustenance. Everything comes to us from him, it flows from him, the living Head, through us all.

Or, if you prefer it another way: 'When he ascended up on high, he led captivity captive, and gave gifts unto men' (*Eph.* 4:8). Having completed the work, he was able to send down the gift of the Holy Spirit. And the marvellous and the wonderful thing is that the Spirit that was given to him without measure is exactly the same Spirit that is given to us. Given to him without measure, given to us in measure, but the same Spirit. The Spirit that was in him is in us; '. . . as he is, so are we in the world' (*1 John* 4:17). Now this would never have happened if he had not become man as well as God. This is the ultimate result of the incarnation and his death and all that followed from it.

And, lastly, I hold before you this most comforting thought about our Lord as our great sympathetic High Priest. The author of the Epistle to the Hebrews keeps on repeating it:

Wherefore in all things it behoved him to be made like unto his brethren, that he might be a merciful and faithful high priest in things pertaining to God, to make reconciliation for the sins of the people. For in that he himself hath suffered being tempted, he is able to succour them that are tempted (Heb. 2:17–18).

Listen again: 'We have not an high priest which cannot be touched with the feeling of our infirmities; but was in all points tempted like as we are, yet without sin' (*Heb.* 4:15). If he had not become man, he could never have been tempted. 'God cannot be tempted with evil, neither tempteth he any man' (*James* 1:13). But here is one 'tempted in all points like as we are'. Why? Because he became man, he became flesh, he was incarnate – subject to temptations, under the law, made of a woman. And the author of Hebrews goes on repeating it and glorying in it. And then he puts it like this:

For every high priest taken from among men is ordained for men in things pertaining to God, that he may offer both gifts and sacrifices for sins:

– he must be one –

who can have compassion on the ignorant, and on them that are out of the way; for that he himself also is compassed with infirmity. And by reason hereof he ought, as for the people, so also for himself, to offer for sins (Heb. 5:1–3).

And the argument is that the Lord Jesus Christ has done all this for us. He knows our frame because he has been in it. He knows the heat of temptation, the difficulty of battling against the world and the flesh and the devil, because he has been here himself and has been subject to it all: 'in all points tempted like as we are, yet without sin'. He knows our ignorance; he knows our frailty. He has mixed with men and women. He himself limited his own eternal knowledge while he lived here in the flesh. And so when we go to the throne of grace, we can go with boldness and with confidence 'that we may obtain mercy, and find grace to help in time of need' (*Heb.* 4:16).

> *In every pang that rends the heart*
> *The man of sorrows has a part.*
>
> Michael Bruce

He has been here. He knows. 'The Word was made flesh, and dwelt among us.' From every standpoint, the law demands the incarnation. He must be man – he must be 'made of a woman' and 'made under the law'. And yet he must be God. He is both. So the law was given by Moses but, thank God, grace and truth came through, or by, or in, Jesus Christ. Jesus – man; Christ – the anointed of God, the eternal, everlasting Saviour.

That, as I conceive it and understand it, is the way in which we should think of Christmas and its meaning. Is it not tragic that it becomes sentimentalized? My dear friends, this is a time to think, even before singing. There is no value in your singing unless it is thoughtful. That is why we will have a service here tonight and not a carol service, so called. These matters are to be understood! And if our singing is not the result of our understanding, it is almost a mockery, and perhaps something even worse. 'The law was given by Moses, grace and truth came . . .' They had to come, it is the only way in which we can ever know grace and its blessings, and ever come to know and to rejoice in him and to glorify him for ever. 'Thanks be unto God for his unspeakable gift'! 'Great is the mystery of godliness: God was manifest in the flesh.' ∽

13

Facing the Future

In the beginning was the Word, and the Word was with God, and the Word was God. The same was in the beginning with God. All things were made by him; and without him was not any thing made that was made. In him was life; and the life was the light of men. And the light shineth in darkness; and the darkness comprehended it not. There was a man sent from God, whose name was John. The same came for a witness, to bear witness of the Light, that all men through him might believe. He was not that Light, but was sent to bear witness of that Light. That was the true Light, which lighteth every man that cometh into the world. He was in the world, and the world was made by him, and the world knew him not. He came unto his own, and his own received him not. But as many as received him, to them gave he power to become the sons of God, even to them that believe on his name: which were born, not of blood, nor of the will of the flesh, nor of the will of man, but of God. And the Word was made flesh, and dwelt among us, (and we beheld his glory, the glory as of the only begotten of the Father,) full of grace and truth. John bare witness of him, and cried, saying, This was he of whom I spake, he that cometh after me is preferred before me: for he was before me. And of his fulness have all we received, and grace for grace. For the law was given by Moses, but grace and truth came by Jesus Christ. No man hath seen God at any time; the only begotten Son, which is in the bosom of the Father, he hath declared him (John 1:1–18).

I am drawing your attention to this whole passage because I want to try to show you that in addition to the explicit, particular message that this great portion of Scripture has to give us, which we have been considering together at our leisure, there is also implicit in it a general message that is of the greatest possible importance for us. And this morning I call attention to this passage in particular as today happens to be the first Sunday of a new year.[1] Here we are, looking into an unknown future, and I am anxious to show that there is only one way in which one can really look with confidence and assurance into this future with all its possibilities in a world such as this. It is a world, as we all know, of problems, of pain, of sin, of evil, of perplexity, and, above all, of uncertainty. It is futile and foolish to attempt to prophesy the future. Indeed, from the Christian standpoint, it is even sinful to desire to know too much about it. Rather, the whole position of the Christian, as I want to try to show you, is entirely different from that which is so characteristic of the world outside Christ.

Now there is only one way, I repeat, to face the future in a Christian manner and that is to be sure of the things that we believe. There are certain fundamental postulates as far as Christians are concerned. If they know them and recognize them and live upon them and by them, they can face the future, whatever it may chance to contain, without any fear or foreboding; they can face it quietly and calmly, with a sense of peace and joy. For Christian men and women, there is the possibility of finding a position of rest from which and out of which nothing can ever move them or disturb them. These postulates are to be found implicitly in this great Prologue to John's Gospel and it is to them that I now want to call your attention.

Of course, as we look at the Prologue, we shall discover that it is nothing, in a sense, but a summary of the whole message of the Bible. The great and unique characteristic of the Bible is that though it consists of sixty-six books, it has but one message and that message is to be found everywhere, right through all the various books. It appears in different forms, of course. Sometimes you have to look for it, at other times it is put plainly before you and is quite unmistakable, but it is always essentially this one great message. I am arguing, therefore, that at a juncture like this in our history – in our story as individuals, as a church, as part of the church universal – there is nothing more important for us than that we should be absolutely certain of these

[1] 1963.

fundamental postulates. If we are not, then not only will our future be uncertain and probably unhappy, but we are really not thinking in a Christian manner and we are not functioning as Christian people.

Christianity is not some vague feeling. The Christian life is a life that is based upon truth. We have been considering that: 'The law was given by Moses, but grace and *truth* came by Jesus Christ.' We must get hold of this truth. It is not my business to make you feel happy just while you are in this building and then to let you go back to the world as you were before, with the feeling gradually evaporating. That is psychology, which is almost the exact opposite of Christianity. Christianity is this – that we understand this truth, that we know what it is, and that, therefore, whatever may happen to us, we can apply it. It is *truth*, which has to be applied and which can be applied as we have the operation of the Holy Spirit of God actively within us.

So I am going to remind you of some of these fundamental, primary principles that are all put before us here in the Prologue. The first one is that this is God's world. 'In the beginning was the Word, and the Word was with God, and the Word was God. The same was in the beginning with God. All things were made by him; and without him was not any thing made that was made.' Here is a good place to start, is it not? This world in which we find ourselves, with all its contradictions and all that is so true of it, is God's world. This world is not the result of an accident, it is not the result of chance or something fortuitous. It has not somehow just come into being out of the interaction of blind, impersonal forces.

The prevailing popular idea about the world, of course, is that it is an accident. That is the position of your so-called scientific humanists – indeed, of most humanists. By 'world', I mean the actual physical structure and all the history and everything else. The view is that there is no meaning in it, no purpose. It has come into being in an accidental manner; anything can happen to it at any moment and you never know what will happen next. So there it is, you just hope for the best. You hope that things will continue in a tolerable, fairly comfortable manner as long as you happen to be here but there is no sense or rhyme or reason in it.

Now I do not want to waste your time with this view of the world, but that is the position of the vast majority of people who are not Christians. Whether they be scientific humanists, or historians such as the late Mr H. A. L. Fisher who, having spent his lifetime studying history, said that he had come to the conclusion that the world had no obvious purpose, no meaning and no design. Of course, it is natural that people who do not believe in God should come to such a conclusion but as Christian people we are here to assert that that is not the case. The world is God's world. It is not meaningless, therefore. Its very creation was the result of some purpose and there is a meaning to it all, a meaning to the whole universe, to history, to everything that happens. That follows immediately from the whole notion of creation by Almighty God and it is a very comforting thought.

There is nothing more terrible than to feel that you are simply the victim of chance or fate, of blind, impersonal forces, that there is no object at all in life and no purpose, either to the individual or the universe or the entire human race. Nothing, I repeat, is so frustrating as to feel that the whole of life is meaningless. But here is a great fundamental postulate that says that is not the case. God! God creating! And clearly he had an object and a design and a purpose in the very act of creation – the creation of the universe itself, human beings included.

Even though you and I may not always understand what is happening in our world and lives, it is a good thing to know that there is a purpose, that there is a meaning. That is the whole position of a child, is it not? The child does not understand things that happen but he has confidence in his father and mother, he believes that they know, that they understand, and he therefore stops worrying, leaves the outcome to his parents and so finds peace. And that is our position. Though we may not always know or understand the meaning, we know that there is one because it is God's world, created by him.

And another way I would put this same point is this – and I thank God for this perhaps more than for anything else – it is not our world. For it is as bad to think that it is our world as to think that it is a meaningless world. Man, of course, has inflated himself and has exaggerated his power simply because he has made a few discoveries. I do not want to detract from his greatness but at the present time there is nothing so foolish as this self-confidence. How little he knows! Yet he thinks that it is his world! He thinks that he can manipulate it, that he can order it, that he can develop it, that he can reform it – and we see the results of his efforts! But it is not his world, and thank God, I say again, that it is not. Thank God that the world and its future are not subject to human knowledge and human control and human power. This, again, is a very comforting thought.

What if the future were in human hands? We have had some very good evidence in this present century of what man tends to do when he gets power and control. Christian people, do you not find it rather an exhilarating thought that this world is not our world? Thank God that not only is it not an accident, but it is not man's design, it is not man's creation, it is not man's possession, it is not under his power and control. It is beyond him and outside him. And as we see human beings today in their miserable failure, as Christians we should thank God that the world is God's world, that it is he who brought it into being, who said, 'Let there be light.' There it is, in the first chapter of Genesis. 'In the beginning God'! And in the first chapter of John: 'In the beginning was the Word'!

Now here is the point at which, as Christian people, we should always start. Right away we are differentiated from those who are not Christians. We start with this primary concept that the whole vast and complicated universe, history and all that we are aware of and in which we are involved, has come from God, belongs to God, has a purpose and is in the hands of God. That is the first postulate, which we should never lose sight of whatever may be happening.

But come to a second, which I think must follow immediately. Having laid down as primary that this is God's world, we must hasten to indicate also the doctrine concerning God's *permissive will*. I am deliberately confining myself now to what we have in this particular section of John's Gospel and here, at once, I find this doctrine. Having read, 'In him was life; and the life was the light of men', I then read this: 'And the light shineth in darkness; and *the darkness comprehended it not*.' Whether you interpret 'comprehended' as meaning 'mastered' or 'apprehended' does not matter; it cannot be decided, probably both are true. But what I am emphasizing is the existence, the fact, of the darkness. Here is a most important point.

In the light of my first postulate, people may say, 'Ah, well, that's all right, that's a very comforting thought, but aren't you indulging in a little bit of psychology and wishful thinking? You're turning your back upon the facts. You say it's God's world and with the poet you say, "God's in his heaven, all's right with the world", but it's not true, all's wrong with the world. You've just been indulging in a poetic fancy and in a little Couéism,[1] making yourself feel very happy. You say it's God's world, but look at it, look at the darkness. How do you reconcile what you've been saying about God and his control over this world with the facts that are there staring us in the face?'

Well, fortunately, this passage deals with that whole question; the existence of 'the darkness' is one of its primary postulates. There is a darkness, and the Bible does not try to hide it. Indeed, the Scriptures put it before us very plainly and clearly. But they help us to understand this darkness by introducing us to the great doctrine of God's permissive will. If God is all powerful and has made everything out of nothing, you must account for the existence of the darkness, the evil, and the Bible has its great doctrine concerning that. This is a profound mystery. But what the Bible does tell us is that clearly God permitted evil to exist.

Now as to why God permitted evil, we do not know. We can speculate. But, remember, it is nothing but speculation. All the Bible tells us is that God did permit it in his own inscrutable will. If you want a little speculation, then I put this for your consideration: that the very notion of perfection involves, of necessity, the idea of freedom of choice and of will. Everything that God made, therefore, both angels and human beings, had freedom of choice – and that freedom involves the possibility of a wrong choice. And there you see the possibility of evil. Do not pay too much attention to the speculation, however, but look at the great fact that God with his infinite, almighty power

[1] A psychotherapy that used auto-suggestion; for instance, the repetition of the words, 'Every day and in every way I'm getting better and better.'

permitted the appearance and the entry of evil. And in that way he displayed something of his own eternal glory. He could have made a mechanical universe that could never have gone wrong. He did not do so, especially when he created man and the great angelic beings. They were not to be mere machines, they were to be personalities, and that is where this whole notion of freedom comes in and the possibility of wrong and of wrong choice.

God, then, in order to show forth the perfection of his creation, opened the possibility of the entrance of evil. Not that he created it, but he permitted it. There is a great deal in the biblical history that brings this point out very clearly. Not only are there hints in the biblical teaching with regard to the origin of evil but, as you read the Old Testament history, you constantly find that God, who could have stopped and prevented things, allowed them to happen. This is obvious in the case of many individuals; it is obvious in the whole case of the children of Israel, that nation of Israel. So, then, we deduce this doctrine that God does allow certain things to happen that are evil and harmful and unpleasant for us. Now, again, to me this is a most comforting thought and a most comforting doctrine as we face an unknown future. You must look at it in the right way. The fact that these things happen does not mean that they are beyond or out of God's control. It does not mean that for a moment. It means the exact opposite. It means that God is allowing them, permitting them.

Obvious illustrations spring to mind, do they not? A very good way of teaching people to do something – particularly those who think they know all about it before they have had their first lesson – is just to let them 'have a go', as we say. If you are teaching somebody to ride a bicycle and he says, 'I know all about it', then the thing to do is to take your hand off the saddle and let him fall; then he will begin to learn. You permit him. That does not mean that you lost control. You could have kept hold of the saddle but you did not. Similarly, when things go wrong, it means that for the time being God is not exercising the control. He is permitting, allowing. He has his own great and inscrutable purposes for this, and undoubtedly one of them is the very one I have hinted at – that this is one of his ways of instructing us.

I could illustrate almost endlessly from the Old Testament history. God gave his laws to his people but they would not listen, so he allowed them to get into trouble. He allowed them to discover that 'the way of transgressors is hard' (*Prov.* 13:15). He allowed their enemies to rise against them. Has it not often amazed you that the children of Israel, God's own people, were there in the captivity of Egypt, or suffered defeat at the hands of the Babylonians? Why did God not defend his own people? The answer is that he permitted their enemies to conquer them, though they were his own people. He allowed it; it was for their own good. That is a great illustration of his permissive will.

But now I want to draw a more general lesson because, again, it is, to me, a comforting one. Here is the conclusion: Do not be surprised at what may happen. There is, perhaps, no greater misunderstanding of the Christian message than that foolish belief that says that the moment you become a Christian nothing will ever go wrong for you again. That is not Christianity. The Christian message teaches almost the exact opposite. Look at our Lord himself, look at the treatment he received when he was in this world. This Word, the Word made flesh, 'hath not where to lay his head' (*Matt.* 8:20). Look at the things that happened to him! And he said to us, 'The servant is not greater than his lord' (*John* 13:16). God permitted evil to operate against his own Son; he permits it to operate against us. So as you face the unknown future, do not be surprised at what may happen.

But, still more important, never despair because of what happens, never feel hopeless. In other words, if during this coming year you or I find ourselves beginning to say, 'Why has this happened to me? Is there no God after all? Is the gospel true?', then we have already forgotten about God's permissive will. We have that childish, magical notion of God that thinks that because God is all powerful, and we are his children, nothing wrong can ever happen to us. It is not true! Remember this doctrine of God's permissive will and when things go quite against all that you would have desired, say to yourself: I don't understand this but, though I don't understand it, there must be some object or purpose. 'All things work together for good to them that love God, to them who are the called according to his purpose' (*Rom.* 8:28).

This is one of the great antidotes to despair, to a sense of hopelessness, to a sense of futility. This doctrine of God's permissive will is an essential doctrine for Christian people. It is often the one thing that stands between us and final despair and hopelessness.

Then the third principle that I find here is this: God is concerned about this world. That is the whole point about the Prologue. 'There was a man sent from God, whose name was John . . .The Word was made flesh, and dwelt among us.' God sent him. 'The law was given by Moses' – God gave the law to Moses – 'but grace and truth came [from God] by [through] Jesus Christ' – all along. This is, therefore, the doctrine that teaches us that God is concerned about this world. Here is our only hope. We would not be here at all but for that and we would have no hope as we face the future. The essence of the Christian message is that God has not abandoned this world in spite of what is true of it. This is the great truth emphasized by John everywhere. 'God so loved the world, that he gave his only begotten Son' (*John* 3:16) – that is it.

God's world, yes, but it has sinned, it has rebelled against him, it has fallen, it is cursed, it is evil, it is foul, it is full of darkness. Perfectly true. But the answer is that in spite of this God is still concerned about it. He could have blasted it to nothing at the beginning. He could have destroyed it in a flash. He could have turned his back upon it and said, 'If you think you can get on without me, well, do so!' God did that up to a point and then there was the Flood. But the Flood, again, is just a proof of this doctrine that I am inculcating. God has not abandoned the world. He appears to have but he has not. He intervenes at his own point, in his own time, showing his interest, still, in the world. He has not finally let it go.

But we do not leave this point as a negative. God's concern about the world does not only mean that he has not turned his back upon it. His concern is very positive. God has a plan and a purpose for the world. And that is where you see the blindness, not only of the scientific humanist, but also of the secular historian. These historians study secular history and say that they see no plan, no purpose, no end, that it is not leading to anything. But when you read your Bible, you come to a very different conclusion. Here you see a thread, an objective and a plan; it is here from beginning to end. There is one great unfolding and developing purpose. This is the great message of this Prologue as it is the great message of the whole Bible.

The Bible is the history, the explanation, of God's plan of salvation. That is what it is all about. And here it is: 'The Word was made flesh, and dwelt among us.' God sent his own Son into this world and this is shown to us everywhere in the Prologue. We have this mention of Moses: 'For the law was given by Moses . . .' God gave it. But the very existence of Moses and the children of Israel, to whom Moses had the privilege of passing on the law, is just a demonstration and a proof of God's plan. It was God who created that nation and his purpose was not, as the people thought, that they might have a good time and be blessed but that through them and by means of them he might address the whole world and, eventually, through them send his only begotten Son into the world. That was the object. 'Unto them were committed the oracles of God', as the apostle Paul says (*Rom.* 3:2). Why? Well, they were witnesses, and the only witnesses, to God and to his truth.

As we read through the whole of the Old Testament, we see nothing but the unfolding of this great plan of God: calling a nation, bringing them out of captivity, giving them the law, taking them to the Promised Land, giving them kings, sending them prophets. All along it is nothing but the activity of God. And here, again, is this great comfort that we have. It is a proof that God is concerned about the world, that he has a plan and a purpose for it. Nothing is plainer.

But then when we come to Jesus Christ – 'grace and truth came by Jesus Christ' – we see yet more clearly God's great concern for this world. He has now shown his interest even in this way. There is nothing higher than this. 'God *so* loved the world, that he gave his only begotten Son.' The astounding fact is that the Word, who was 'with God' and 'was God' and 'was in the beginning with God', this Word, 'was made flesh, and dwelt among us'. The Word entered into the human scene, took unto him human nature, became one of us. And this, I say again, indicates one big thing – God's concern for, and interest in, this world. This is the fact of which, as Christians, we must always remind ourselves.

People look at history as they find it in their newspapers and secular history books and say, 'There's no sense, there's no meaning, everything is going round and round, in fact, things are getting worse.' No! I say that the answer is this: Look at that but look beyond that. Look at this other history, God's history, and there you see nothing so clearly as this great plan and purpose of God, indicative of his concern about the world. This is a part of the Christian hope, and there is no hope apart from it. The world has no hope. It clutches on to anything. It is even mad enough to make New Year's resolutions, mad enough to think that the coming of a new year is going to make a difference, mad enough to think that a new political party in power will make a difference. All these are the straws that the world clutches on to in its utter hopelessness and despair. This is all because it does not know that God is concerned about it.

But let us go on. My fourth proposition is that God's purpose and plan for the world is sure and certain, in spite of everything that is true of the world. And this is, to me, the final comfort. Listen: 'He was in the world, and the world was made by him, and the world knew him not. He came unto his own, and his own received him not.' Here, then, is the comfort.

'Comfort?' you say. 'But that is surely refusal.'

I agree. But that is where I find the comfort. I am told that this Son of God, through whom everything was made, was actually in the world, came into it and dwelt among us. 'The world was made by him, and the world knew him not.' Then, to drive it right home to us: 'He came unto his own' – he came to his own possessions and his own people – 'and his own received him not.' Now this is what we must grasp: it is his world, yet the world did not recognize him. In particular, he came to the nation of the Jews, he came out of them. He was a Jew 'of the seed of David according to the flesh' (*Rom.* 1:3). He came to his own people as well as to his own possessions, and his own people despised him. They rejected him. They crucified him. That is the sheer, stark fact by which we are confronted. And yet that is perhaps the greatest comfort of all. In spite of this, he came, and is still operating in this world, and will come again.

Salvation is in spite of us, not because of us. That is why the final heresy, I suppose, is the teaching that there can be justification by works. There is nothing so unchristian as to believe that God blesses you because you are such a good person. On the first Sunday morning of the year, let us get rid of that idea. Do you think that you are a Christian because you are such a good person? Are you looking for God to bless you because you do so much good and have never done anybody any harm? If so, I must just tell you, before you go any further, that you are about as far removed from being a Christian as anybody can be. There is infinitely greater hope for the most hopeless drunkard or prostitute than for you. We are saved in spite of ourselves! 'He came unto his own, and his own received him not', but that does not make any difference; the plan of God goes on.

Here, again, how easily I could give you illustrations from the Old Testament. Look at those miserable children of Israel – how else can you describe them? But they are no worse than miserable Christians, they are no worse than the miserable Christian church today. There they were, God's people, but look at their behaviour – grumbling and complaining, going after the gods of other nations, wanting to live as other nations, always trying to contradict God and to frustrate his plan. They did everything they could to ruin it and it was in spite of them that God's Son ever came into the world. God's plan never depended upon the children of Israel; he carried it out in spite of them and in spite of their opposition and recalcitrance and utter stupidity. And that is what we are told, by implication, in this great Prologue that we are examining together: 'He came unto his own, and his own received him not.'

'Well, that's the end,' you say. 'God's plan is finished. God sends his own Son into the world, to this marvellous creation, which was marred – and what's the use? He was rejected.'

Nonsense! God's plan does not depend upon us, it depends upon God himself. He brings it to pass in spite of human folly, in spite of our utter futility. And notice the steps and the stages – they are all fixed. That is the wonderful thing about this plan of God. There is no obstacle here. God's plan cannot be stopped by a bit of snow or ice, it cannot be stopped by a breakdown on the line. God sends his express through and it is always to the moment, never a second late! Read the Old Testament, my friends; look at what was happening before the Flood. Everything seemed to be out of control but God had his moment planned. He knew exactly when the Flood was coming. He told Noah to start building that ark, and the Flood came at the appointed second. Noah! Abraham! Moses! John the Baptist! Each makes his appearance at the exact moment prepared by God. It was not because the people had reached the point when they were ready to receive and listen. No, no! It was always when things were at their very worst. Look at Moses, born in the utter hopelessness of Egypt when his people were slaves and serfs in captivity. It does not matter what is happening, God's plan works, and works at the exact moment designed for it, because it is from God and from God's power.

And here we are, in the Prologue, and immediately I begin to read, 'There was a man sent from God, whose name was John.' But, you notice, he was *sent*. And here it is at the beginning of the third chapter of Luke's Gospel:

Now in the fifteenth year of the reign of Tiberius Caesar, Pontius Pilate being governor of Judaea, and Herod being tetrarch of Galilee, and his brother Philip tetrarch of Ituraea and of the region of Trachonitis, and Lysanias the tetrarch of Abilene, Annas and Caiaphas being the high priests, the word of God came unto John (Luke 3:1–2).

'I don't care about those names,' says some clever person. 'I want the truth. Who or what are those names to me? I'm not interested!'

Are you not? Well, if so, it is because you are blind spiritually. Why do you think we are given those names? What is their significance? Why does Luke trouble to tell us that it was when all those men were in office in different parts of the world that the word of God came to John the Baptist? There is only one answer, and a commentator has put it perfectly. He said that that list of names is a list of the greatest pack of blackguards that perhaps the world has ever seen in control of the destinies of nations! That is when the Word came. Not when the world was evolving and the nations were led by great idealists and moralists.

No, no! When affairs were in the hands of these blackguards, God sent his word to John the Baptist, his servant.

And so it is always. 'The Word was made flesh.' When was the Word made flesh? 'When the fulness of the time was come' (*Gal.* 4:4). That is always the way. And that is where I see our final hope and consolation. Everything that the world and the flesh and the devil and hell can do to stop and to frustrate God's great plan for the world has already been done yet God's plan goes on. The Son of God came into the world in spite of the devil and hell and humanity, and he goes on operating in spite of them, and he will come again in spite of them. So the apostle Paul, looking at it all, says at the very end of Romans 8: 'I am persuaded, that neither death, nor life, nor angels, nor principalities, nor powers, nor things present, nor things to come, nor height, nor depth, nor any other creature, shall be able to separate us from the love of God, which is in Christ Jesus our Lord' (*Rom.* 8:38–39). There it is, my friends. It is in spite of us, in spite of the world, that God's plan is certain and sure. Let the world do what it will, it will make no difference. God's plan will certainly be carried out. Hold on to that.

And let me just say a final word: God's love for his people and his provision for them in a world like this. 'The law was given by Moses, but grace and truth came by Jesus Christ.' Oh, this grace! 'The Word was made flesh . . . (and we beheld his glory, the glory as of the only begotten of the Father,) full of grace and truth . . . And of his fulness have all we received, and grace for [upon] grace.' That is it! That is God's provision for his people. What God has already done in his Son, his beloved Son, is a guarantee of everything else. 'No man hath seen God at any time; the only begotten Son, which is in the bosom of the Father, he hath declared him.' The one who was born at Bethlehem is the everlasting Son of God, the eternal Word, God's own Son, his beloved Son.

And this is my argument: God sent that Son into this world and he was made flesh for us! That is the stupendous and staggering and almost incredible fact! God sent his Son into the world for us, for our benefit, for our blessing, for our ultimate salvation. That was the sole reason for his coming.

Or look at it like this: in this world the Son 'endured such contradiction of sinners against himself' (*Heb.* 12:3) – why? For us! Read the pages of the four Gospels, remind yourselves again of what man did to him: the buffeting, the jeering, the sarcasm, the scorn, the unbelief – oh, look at what he suffered! And then remember this: he endured all that for you, for your sake, for my sake, that he might save us, that he might be a sympathetic high priest for us, that he might be able to have a feeling for our infirmities. Who knows what is going to happen to you? You may be forsaken, you may be buffeted, you may be misunderstood, you may have to endure hardships – you do not know. But whatever happens to you, remember this: the Son of God endured all that kind of thing for you!

And then, on top of it all, as we are reminded by the bread and the wine of this Communion table, the Son of God even went to the death of the cross, and it was God the Father who sent him there. It was God who 'laid on him the iniquity of us all' (*Isa.* 53:6). It was God who smote him. It was God who 'made him to be sin for us, who knew no sin; that we might be made the righteousness of God in him' (*2 Cor.* 5:21). It was God who was 'in Christ, reconciling the world unto himself, not imputing their trespasses unto them' (*2 Cor.* 5:19). My friend, it was God who did all these things – for you!

And so the argument is this – it is the brilliant argument of the mighty apostle Paul, again in the Epistle to the Romans: 'If, when we were enemies, we were reconciled to God by the death of his Son, much more, being reconciled, we shall be saved by his life' (*Rom.* 5:10). Work out this argument. What God has already done for you in his Son in delivering him up unto death and sparing him nothing is an absolute certain proof that he will never withhold anything that is good from his people. The God who has already done the greatest thing that even God can do – abandon his own Son to the punishment and guilt of sin – the God who has already done that for us, can never refuse us any lesser mercy or grace or blessing. The greater includes the lesser. He has done the greatest of all. 'He that spared not his own Son, but delivered him up for us all, how shall he not with him also freely give us all things?' (*Rom.* 8:32) – all things that can ever be necessary for our comfort, our happiness, our peace, our joy, our well-being and our ultimate and final glorification, full salvation in the perfection of heaven and everlasting glory.

So there, in the Prologue to John's Gospel, are these fundamental postulates of our faith. Let us lay hold upon them and never forsake them. Let us remind ourselves of them, whatever may come to meet us. They are verities. They are eternal verities, founded on God himself, and they will never fail us. That is the way to face a new year, that is the Christian way of facing an unknown and uncertain future. Blessed be God who has sent grace and truth to us his people by Jesus Christ. ∾

14

Know . . . Receive . . . Believe

He was in the world, and the world was made by him, and the world knew him not. He came unto his own, and his own received him not. But as many as received him, to them gave he power to become the sons of God, even to them that believe on his name (John 1:10–12).

I should like to turn now to John 1:10–12. It is not my intention this morning to look at the great doctrine found in verse 12 – the doctrine that we are given 'power to become the children of God' – but to consider three words that are to be found in these three verses. The words are: *know* in verse 10, *received* in verse 11 and *believe* in verse 12. Here are three words that are used to describe the relationship of men and women to the Lord Jesus Christ – knowing, receiving and believing on him.

Now let me explain why I am calling attention to these three words. We have been engaged for some time in a consideration of this Prologue to John's Gospel and our reason for looking at it is precisely that which animated John and moved him to write the Gospel at all. He tells us what that is at the end of the twentieth chapter, where he says, 'And many other signs truly did Jesus in the presence of his disciples, which are not written in this book: but these are written, that ye might believe that Jesus is the Christ, the Son of God; and that believing ye might have life through his name' (*John* 20:30–31).

John's primary interest was pastoral. He was not writing merely for the sake of providing a theological disquisition. He was not even concerned primarily with the enlightenment of the minds of these people. He was concerned about that but only in order that it might lead to something deeper and more profound, namely, their enjoyment of the Christian life. In other words, he was concerned with the whole matter of assurance.

Now what I am saying about this Gospel can be said, in a sense, about every single book in the New Testament. We must always bear in mind that in the first instance the gospel was *preached*. It was something that was passed to men and women by word of mouth. Most of the first generation of Christians became Christians in that way. They entirely lacked any documents such as we have in the New Testament. They had only their Old Testament Scriptures. So there is a sense in which it is true to say that the New Testament Scriptures came into being very largely because of situations that arose in the life of the early church. False teachings began to appear, people were troubled by the devil and were tempted to error and to heresy. So all these scriptures were really written in order to establish and to confirm believers in the faith. The Gospels were not primarily written for unbelievers but for believers in order that they might know surely the things they had believed. Luke tells us that in the prologue to his Gospel and so does John and it is the same with Matthew and with Mark.

Now John, as we have seen, is particularly concerned with this matter of certainty and assurance, and that has been our object as we have studied this great Prologue. There is no doubt at all, it seems to me, but that the great question that should be in our minds is this: Why is the Christian church today failing to attract the masses of the people to the message? Why are these people utterly indifferent and outside the church? And I think it is more and more clear that there is only one primary answer to that question and that is that we are failing to give them the impression that we have and believe and hold on to the most marvellous and wonderful truth in the world. If we could but give people outside the church the impression that we have here a source of joy and peace, something that fills us with wonder and amazement and thrills the whole of our being, then they would immediately begin to pay attention, because the world is unhappy and in trouble. In other words, I think it all comes back to the fact that Christian people far too often give the impression to the outsider that they are filled with problems and perplexities. Indeed, they often appear to be much more unhappy than people who are entirely outside the church. The world looks upon the church as a gathering of miserable people. The church claims that it has life and enjoyment and happiness but it seems to those outside that the main effect of being religious is that people are made miserable. Of course, this is appalling, it is extremely sinful and there is nothing to be said for it. So I am arguing that our most urgent task is that of obtaining full assurance of salvation, full assurance of faith, full assurance of hope, absolute certainty in every respect. And as John's object in writing his Gospel was to bring people to that very position, we are studying the Prologue together in order that we too may arrive there. I am anxious that we should bear in mind, above everything else, that we are not studying the Prologue in an academic or theological manner, we are not studying the Scriptures in some remote and detached way simply for the enlightenment of the mind, but in order that we may function more efficiently and more powerfully as Christian people, that we may be lights in the heavens in the midst of the present darkness, and above all that we may be those who show the world that we are filled with 'joy unspeakable and full of glory' (*1 Pet.* 1.8).

So what is John's method? Let me remind you very hurriedly. There are certain principles, he says, that we must be clear about. We must be perfectly clear as to the darkness that is in the world. If we are in any doubt at all about the power of evil, the power of the devil and the power of hell, then it is not a bit surprising that we are the dupes of the devil and are captives, willing captives, able to be used by him at his will whenever he likes and in any circumstances whatsoever. As Christians we must start with the realization that we are set in a world of darkness. As Paul puts it so perfectly in the last chapter of his Epistle to the Ephesians: 'For we wrestle not against flesh and blood, but against principalities, against powers, against the rulers of the darkness of this world, against spiritual wickedness in high places' (*Eph.* 6:12). We must be clear about that.

Then we must also be clear about the law, the law that was given by Moses or through Moses. We have tried to see – and I think we have succeeded – that so many people are lacking in joy and assurance because they have never fully realized what salvation has done to them. They have salvation, we grant that they are Christians, but there is no depth, there is no power, no coherence, there is no joy, because they have never quite realized what they have been saved from, in themselves, in their relationship to the law of God and in relationship to the final judgment of God himself. There is no doubt at all but that a deeper 'law-work' always leads to a corresponding height of joy and of happiness and of glorying in the Lord and in his salvation.

I remember a man once telling me about the first prize that he had obtained for his sweet peas in the horticultural show. I asked him what his secret was. 'Ah,' he said, 'the secret is this – if you want a tall, high stalk and a wonderful bloom, you must have a great depth of root. People never dig deep enough,' he said. 'You must dig a trench – you must go down if you want to go up.' Perfectly right! It is exactly like that in the Christian life, and the law does this digging. It reveals our emptiness and woe and our utter guilt before God.

When our Lord was in the house of Simon the Pharisee, a woman came and washed his feet with her tears and dried them with her hair. The Pharisee was astonished that our Lord allowed such a woman to come so near to him in this way, but our Lord's answer was: 'To whom little is forgiven, the same loveth little' (*Luke* 7:47). That does not mean that we put a premium on sin, but we do say that a realization of the depth of our sin and of our need of forgiveness is always the measure of our love of the Lord and our rejoicing in him. So we need to be clear about the law-work and the whole position of man as he is by nature under the law of God. 'The law was given by Moses, but grace and truth came by Jesus Christ.'

And then last time we went on to show that there are certain great fundamental postulates about which we must always be absolutely certain so that whatever happens in the world, whatever disappointments, whatever may seem to be working against us, we do not immediately begin to question and to query the whole of our faith, and to wonder whether God's Word is true and whether we are Christians. No, no! There are certain things about which Christians never argue. They are certain of them. These truths are axiomatic to them and their whole assurance and confidence are based upon them.

So now we come to this next matter, which is, of course, in many ways the most important of all, and that is our relationship to the Lord Jesus Christ himself. This is what is specifically Christian. A Christian does not merely believe in God. He does believe in God but as our Lord himself puts it later on in this same Gospel, 'Ye believe in God, believe also in me' (*John* 14:1). In other words, the Christian should have a much greater assurance than any Jew could possibly have had under the Old Testament dispensation. The Jews had assurance; they knew. Abraham believed God in spite of everything – he hoped against hope. That was assurance – he believed the word of God. 'He staggered not at the promise of God through unbelief; but was strong in faith, giving glory to God' (*Rom.* 4:20). Those men and women of faith in the Old Testament would leave their country, they would leave everything, and go out like Abraham, who went 'not knowing whither he went' (*Heb.* 11:8), but knowing with whom he went. That was assurance. But the whole argument here is that our assurance ought to be infinitely greater because of what God has done in and through his Son, our blessed Lord and Saviour Jesus Christ.

The first step in this Christian assurance is, therefore, to make absolutely certain of our relationship to the Lord Jesus Christ. Now I am anxious to put this in a pastoral manner. People have often come to me throughout the years to ask about this whole question of happiness and assurance in the Christian life. A man or woman will say, 'I don't seem to be like so and so. This other Christian has got something I don't have.' These people who come to me feel that they are Christians and yet they say they do not have that joy, or that assurance; they do not have that certainty. They have been trying to obtain it and have not been successful. But so often it has seemed to me that they have not started at the right point. They have been starting too far along the road instead of at the beginning.

Now these verses from the Prologue that we have before us compel us to start at the very beginning. There is always the great danger of taking things for granted, and this is particularly true of those of us who have been brought up in the church and in Christian homes or in a Christian tradition. There is the terrible danger of our assuming that we are Christians when perhaps we may not be Christians at all. And, of course, if we are not right at the foundations, we cannot have a right superstructure. It follows that it is no use our spending time on the superstructure if there is no true foundation. Or, to use a different illustration, if there is poison in a stream, the first place to examine is the source because if the pollution is at the source, it is a waste of time and money and energy to put chemicals downstream to purify the water. Similarly, if people who regard themselves as Christians do not know what they really believe and do not understand what faith in Christ means, it is no use attempting to remedy anything else until you have made sure that they are clear about this.

We must not, I repeat, act upon assumption. It is always the duty of Christians to examine themselves. As the apostle Paul puts it to the Corinthians, 'Examine yourselves, whether ye be in the faith; prove your own selves' (2 Cor. 13:5). There was trouble in the church at Corinth, so Paul says, in effect, 'Now, then, let us go right back to the beginning; let us make quite certain that there is no problem there.' In other words, at the beginning of a new year – we are still in the early days of 1963[1] – I am suggesting that it is always very good and right to examine the whole of your position. If there is something wrong, if you are dissatisfied, if you are unhappy, if you have a feeling that the Christian faith that you have espoused does not seem to be giving you what you thought it was going to give you, and not as much as it seems to be giving other people, then you must not take anything at all for granted.

You yourself will be able to think of endless illustrations. Your car suddenly stops and will not start again. What do the experts tell you? They say, 'Examine the petrol system. Is the petrol coming through? Start there. Look at your carburettor – whatever it is. Then check your electrical system. Is everything tightly screwed in? Is there some loose connection? The fault may be something very simple, very trivial. Do not begin to indulge in heroics until you have looked at the obvious first things that may be wrong. Indeed, I myself have made an even

---

[1] This sermon was preached on 13 January 1963.

more basic error. If your car stops, the first thing to make sure of is that you have petrol in your tank! Then you proceed from that point. I am sure that every motorist here knows exactly what I mean. You can spend a lot of your time with the refinements but very often, when you call in the expert and he points out the cause of the problem, you find that it is something simple, fundamental and primary, and you just feel utterly ashamed of yourself because you did not think of it. There are many people like that in the Christian life. So I say again that you must go right back to the beginning. You must make no assumptions. John is compelling us to do that here in the very Prologue of his Gospel. He goes back to the first principles, the fundamental matters.

Do not start with your feelings. You may have to examine them but do not start with them. I have known people spend years trying to work up some feeling when their trouble was that they really did not know what they believed; the fault lay in their beliefs. Feelings are always the result of something else, so if you start with them you will be wasting your time.

Do not even start with an examination of your life in terms of looking for the fruit of the Spirit. That is a very good thing to do; the presence of the fruit of the Spirit is a form of assurance. John expounds all that in his first epistle: 'We know that we have passed from death unto life, because we love the brethren' (*1 John* 3:14); we know we are Christians because 'his commandments are not grievous' (*1 John* 5:3) and so on. But you do not start with tests such as those because if the foundation is not right, they will avail you nothing. So you end with the whole question of the testimony of the Spirit and do not begin with it.

So what is it that you do begin with? You must begin with this person, the Lord Jesus Christ, and your whole relationship to him. You must be absolutely certain that that is right. John helps us to do that in this way: he tells us here, in the very Prologue to his Gospel, that from the very beginning the Lord Jesus Christ always divided humanity into two groups. He himself said that he must inevitably do so. He said: 'Think not that I am come to send peace on earth: I came not to send peace, but a sword' (*Matt.* 10:34). He acted as a sword from the moment he was born. You have your King Herods on one side and your wise men from the east on the other; those who want to get rid of him, those who want to worship him.

And as you go on reading the accounts of the life of the Lord Jesus Christ as they are given in the Gospels, you see that he was always a cause of division. There were those who left everything to go after him and those who turned their backs upon him; those who took up stones to throw at him and those who washed his feet with their tears and wiped them with the hairs of their heads. He causes division! This is an astounding fact, but it is true. And he has continued ever since, right up until today. He divides the world into two groups, Christians and non-Christians. So it is very important that we should examine ourselves in the light of these primary tests that are given by John.

And there is a further reason why it is important for us to examine the foundations of our faith. According to this message, the Lord Jesus Christ is absolutely central. 'No man cometh unto the Father, but by me,' he says (*John* 14:6). Here in the Prologue we are told: 'All things were made by him; and without him was not any thing made that was made.' There is no true knowledge of God except in him. 'No man hath seen God at any time; the only begotten Son, which is in the bosom of the Father, he hath declared him.' It is all dependent upon him. That is why we must take nothing for granted when we are considering our relationship to him. We go to God through him. All the blessings of God come to us through him, by him. All God's treasures of wisdom and of grace and of knowledge are stored up in the Lord Jesus Christ and are mediated to us by the Spirit. Therefore, there is obviously nothing that is so central, so urgent and vital for us than to be quite clear about our relationship to him.

Here, then, are the three things that John says are characteristic of true Christians in their relationship to the Lord Jesus Christ. The first is that they *know* him. It is put here in verse 10 in terms of its opposite: 'He was in the world, and the world was made by him, and the world knew him not.' There is the first step, the lowest step, if you like. He was in the world, his own world, the world he had made, and among his own people, but the world did not know him. Now you can find out what that means by looking at the way the Pharisees, the scribes and the Sadducees treated our Lord. They never knew him. The same was true, says the apostle Paul, of all the 'princes of this world': 'Which none of the princes of this world knew: for had they known it, they would not have crucified the Lord of glory' (*1 Cor.* 2:8).

Now this term 'know' means, in the first place, to recognize, to recognize him for who he is. And that, of course, was the tragic failure that we see in all those Jewish religious authorities. They looked at him and said, 'Who is this fellow?' They saw a person, they were looking at a man, and they said: Who is this fellow, this carpenter? 'How knoweth this man letters, having never learned?' (*John* 7:15). This man is a blasphemer, they said. And the extraordinary thing is that they were looking at the Son of God, the Word who was 'made flesh, and dwelt among us'. But they did not recognize him. John, on the other hand, looked at him – everybody was looking at the same person – and was able to say: 'We beheld his glory, the glory as of the only begotten of the Father, full of grace and truth.'

So in the word 'know' there is the element of recognition and, of course, that is quite basic and fundamental. There are so many people in the world today – and, alas, some of them in the church – who always talk about 'Jesus'. Watch them: they rarely refer to our Lord as 'the Lord Jesus Christ'. It is always 'Jesus', not even 'Christ'. They call him 'the Master', rather than the Saviour. What is the matter? Well, ultimately, they only believe in the human person – Jesus. To them he is just a great teacher. They do not stand in amazement before the Son of God, the Word who was made flesh. No, they are interested primarily in a man who lived in Galilee, Jesus of Nazareth, a teacher. That is their whole attitude towards him; they never go beyond that. And that is all there is to it. They have not known him. They have not known that he is indeed the eternal Son of God. They have not known anything about the real mystery and marvel of the incarnation. They have not recognized him. That is the blindness that afflicts the unbelieving world. Again, the apostle Paul puts this quite explicitly: 'If our gospel be hid,' he says, 'it is hid to them that are lost: in whom the god of this world hath blinded the minds of them which believe not, lest the light of the glorious gospel of Christ, who is the image of God, should shine unto them' (*2 Cor.* 4:3–4). They do not know him.

But to know means not only to recognize, it also means to acknowledge. It means not only to see something of this glory, who he is and the whole mystery of the incarnation, the mystery of godliness – God 'manifest in the flesh' (*1 Tim.* 3:16) – but also to acknowledge it and to be filled with a sense of wonder and amazement at it all. Now this word 'know', as it is used commonly in the Scriptures, always carries that fuller connotation. When God says to the children of Israel, 'You only have I known of all the families of the earth' (*Amos* 3:2), he means not merely that he is aware of their existence, but, oh, that there is an intimacy in his knowledge, an interest and a concern. And this applies to the word 'know' as it is used in the Prologue.

It is not just that, having read, perhaps, the Gospels and certain books about religion, we are aware of specific statements made about 'Jesus of Nazareth' and are familiar with these statements in a kind of detached, intellectual manner. Oh, this word 'know' is much more than that. There is an acknowledgement, a recognition leading to an acknowledgement. We are filled with wonder and astonishment and say, 'This has happened. God has sent forth his only Son, and he has been in this world and he has done certain things.' Those, therefore, who know him are those whose central interest in life is in him, those for whom everything is coloured by the fact that 'the Word was made flesh, and dwelt among us', that the eternal Son of God was in this world of time in the likeness of sinful flesh.

Now as I leave that first word, let me ask a question: Do you know him, my friend? Do you know him in the sense that he is central to all your thinking about everything? Do you know him in the sense that he is pivotal to your whole outlook? Do you know him in the sense that this is not just something that you remember on Sundays but that you are always remembering? Is knowing him the basis and orientation of the whole of your life? 'He was in the world, and the world was made by him, and the world *knew him not*.' It did not realize that he had come, and it did not realize who it was who had come. There are so many people today for whom, if you could somehow or other blot the Lord Jesus Christ out of human history, it would not make any difference at all. They have never really known him, they have never really recognized him. Their lives are not dependent upon the fact that the Son of God has come and has dwelt among us.

Let us, then, leave that first word and go on to the second. It is the word 'receive'. 'He came unto his own' – his own people – 'and his own received him not. But as many as received him . . .' This word is more experiential than the first word. There is an experiential element that comes into 'know', as I have tried to show, but 'receive' takes it further. 'But as many as received him' – to receive him means to welcome him. When you receive a person, you show that you are glad that the person has arrived. There is a knock at your door, you go and open it and you see some great friend. 'Come in,' you say. You not merely know this person in the sense of recognizing and acknowledging him, but you receive him. You are pleased that your friend has come and therefore you welcome him with a willing heart.

So the word 'receive' takes us further. We are told in the Scriptures that 'the devils also believe, and tremble' (*James* 2:19). It is quite clear that many of the demons during our Lord's time on earth recognized him. 'I know thee who thou art; the Holy One of God' (*Luke* 4:34). They recognized him, they knew him, but they did not receive him. And it is very clear, as we read about the Pharisees and these various other people, that not only did they not recognize who he was, but they resented him. That is the opposite of receiving. And they resented his teaching even more. They resented the fact that he was teaching at all. He was not a trained Pharisee, they said. He did not belong to the schools. He was not one of them. Who was this upstart? They were offended by his teaching and were hurt by it. They felt that he was going too far. They felt that he was making them out to be sinners and they bitterly resented that.

Now here is a most important point. There are people who think that they believe in, that they recognize, that they know and receive, the Lord Jesus Christ, but when you show them exactly what he said and the real meaning and essence of his teaching, they resent it. If you go to them and say, 'You must be born again before you can be a Christian', they say, 'But why should I be born again? I've never done any wrong. I've never hurt anybody. I can understand someone who has lived a very sinful life needing some great change, but I . . .!' Now people who say things like that have never received the Lord Jesus Christ. Indeed, they are rejecting him.

When you read that our Lord says, 'The Son of man is come to seek and to save that which was lost' (*Luke* 19:10) and, 'I came not to call the righteous, but sinners to repentance' (*Mark* 2:17), when you see him receiving tax-collectors and sinners, what is your reaction? We assume that we have always recognized him and that we have received him. But have we? This is where this matter becomes subtle. To receive him means to receive everything about him, to receive all his teaching, all the implications of his teaching. It means that you really believe that he died upon that cross because you are so vile and so damned and so hopeless that nothing but that could save you. You believe and say with the apostle Paul: 'This is a faithful saying, and worthy of all acceptation, that Christ Jesus came into the world to save sinners; of whom I am chief' (*1 Tim.* 1:15). That is what it means to receive him.

This is a vital matter. Let me show you how vital. In this Prologue we are told this about John the Baptist: 'There was a man sent from God, whose name was John. The same came for a witness, to bear witness of the Light, that all men through him might believe' – and John says some very wonderful things about him. Later on in this first chapter of John's Gospel we are told of John standing and saying, 'Behold the Lamb of God, which taketh away the sin of the world' (*John* 1:29). Now you deduce from that, do you not, that John had known him and had received him, and yet we read at the beginning of the eleventh chapter of Matthew's Gospel, 'Now when John had heard in the prison the works of Christ, he sent two of his disciples, and said unto him, Art thou he that should come, or do we look for another?' (*Matt.* 11:2–3).

What was the matter? Oh, I can tell you what the trouble was. Poor John had been in prison for about six months, ill, cold, weary, tired . . . but why does he send these two disciples with that question? Well,

John was beginning to be a little bit uncertain about him. Why? The answer was that our Lord was not doing what John had anticipated. John, after all, was a Jew and he had in a measure this Jewish notion that the Messiah would come as a great king, gather a great army, drive out the Romans and set up Israel again as the supreme nation over all the world. He had that materialistic notion of the kingdom of God with the Jews ahead of all, triumphant with their king. But our Lord was not behaving like that at all. Our Lord was spending his time up in Galilee; he had not gone down to Jerusalem to set himself up as a king. He was among a very common lot of people and there he was working these miracles. So Jesus sent back this reply:

Go and shew John again those things which ye do hear and see: the blind receive their sight, and the lame walk, the lepers are cleansed, and the deaf hear, the dead are raised up, and the poor have the gospel preached to them. And blessed is he, whosoever shall not be offended in me (Matt 11:4–6)

– offended by what I am doing; offended by what I am not doing; offended by what I am saying; offended by what I am not saying. You take him as he is! And when you receive him, you not only believe all he says, you rejoice in it.

Now the New Testament tells us about many people to whom the cross of Christ was an offence. '. . . unto the Jews a stumblingblock' (*1 Cor.* 1:23). A crucified Messiah? The thing was mad! The Messiah as the great deliverer, the mighty King, but crucified on a gibbet? Stumbling block! Obviously, at first, the Jews were interested in him. They said, 'This man is speaking in a most remarkable manner and look at the things he's doing! But the cross!'

And to the Greeks his death was nothing but sheer folly, 'foolishness' (*1 Cor.* 1:23). The Greeks said that you were saved by philosophy, by ideas, not by a person dying on a tree! This was rubbish, utter nonsense. And the intelligent philosopher still regards it as rubbish and ridicules it. Philosophers may admire Jesus the teacher but they do not receive him. They do not receive him in his death; they do not receive him in his exposition of his death. They do not receive him in his resurrection. They do not believe the resurrection. They say that these things do not happen.

So to receive means that you not only know him in the sense of recognizing him and acknowledging him, but you also receive everything and you are delighted in the fact that the Son of God has come and has done what he has done. Why do you receive him? There is only one answer. The only ones who receive Christ are those who see their need of him. Those who realize their own weakness, their own emptiness, their own sinfulness, take him as he is. They say, 'He is just what I want. Someone must die for me. Someone must give me strength and power. He gives me all.' They receive him. They do not merely know and recognize him, they go beyond that and welcome him. They say:

> *I am coming, Lord,*
> *Coming now to thee;*
> *Wash me, cleanse me in the blood*
> *That flowed on Calvary.*

Lewis Hartsough

They have received him!

And then that brings me to the last word: 'As many as received him, to them gave he power to become the sons of God, even to them that *believe on* his name.' John does not say this haphazardly. He does not start with 'knowing', and then say 'receiving', and finally go on to 'believing', merely to use different words. He is not interested in style. John is, indeed, a very bad literary stylist. He is concerned about truth, and these terms all mean something different. So to 'believe on his name' takes us yet further. This is the great message that was preached by the apostles from the beginning. There you have Peter preaching on the day of Pentecost and suddenly the people cry out, 'Men and brethren, what shall we do?' And here is Peter's answer: 'Repent, and be baptized every one of you in the name of Jesus Christ for the remission of sins' (*Acts* 2:37–38). That is it!

Similarly in the case of the Ethiopian eunuch, who was met on the road by Philip the evangelist. After Philip had expounded the gospel to

him, the man believed and said, 'See, here is water; what doth hinder
me to be baptized?' When Philip replied, 'If thou believest with all
thine heart, thou mayest', the Ethiopian said, 'I believe that Jesus Christ
is the Son of God' (*Acts* 8:36–37). That is 'believing on his name'. And
it was the same with the Philippian jailor. 'Sirs,' said this man, 'what
must I do to be saved?' And there was only one answer: 'Believe on
the Lord Jesus Christ, and thou shalt be saved, and thy house' (*Acts*
16:30–31) – and he immediately believed.

Let me summarize what this means. The 'name' represents the
power and the ability. So when you believe on the name of the Lord
Jesus Christ, you believe not only in his person, but in all that he has
done. There is a perfect explanation of this in Acts 3. Peter and John
had worked a miracle on the man seated at the Beautiful Gate of the
temple, and the people came crowding together, imagining that Peter
and John had healed the crippled man themselves, but this is what
Peter said to them:

*Ye men of Israel, why marvel ye at this? or why look ye so earnestly
on us, as though by our own power or holiness we had made this man
to walk?*

Now, this is it:

*And his name through faith in his name hath made this man strong,
whom ye see and know: yea, the faith which is by him hath given him
this perfect soundness in the presence of you all* (Acts 3:12, 16).

The 'name' means the power of our Lord himself, the power of his
life. So to believe on the name of the Lord Jesus Christ means to have
trust and confidence in him. Not only to recognize who he is, not only
to welcome his coming into the world as the only way of salvation, but
to trust absolutely in all the glory of his divine Saviourhood, to rest
utterly and completely on him and on what he has done. To believe
on the Lord Jesus Christ, in other words, means this: that we see and
know why he ever came into the world, why God ever sent him. It is to
see that men and women are utterly and hopelessly condemned, lost,
under the law and its bitter condemnation, and that he came into the

world because it was the only way whereby anyone could be delivered from the curse of the law. And those who believe commit themselves to that. They believe it, they accept it, they rest their faith upon it.

> *I rest my faith on him alone*
> *Who died for my transgressions to atone.*
>
> Author unknown

That is the confession of those who believe on the Lord Jesus Christ. They say:

> *Nothing in my hand I bring;*
> *Simply to thy cross I cling;*
> *Naked, come to thee for dress;*
> *Helpless, look to thee for grace;*
> *Foul, I to the fountain fly;*
> *Wash me, Saviour, or I die.*
>
> Augustus M. Toplady

That is the Christian confession.

> *Just as I am, without one plea,*
> *But that thy blood was shed for me,*
> *And that thou bidd'st me come to thee,*
> *O Lamb of God, I come!*
>
> Charlotte Elliott

That is what it means to believe in him: that you cease to believe in yourself, you cease to believe in other people, you cease to believe in the development of the world. You say, 'I believe in nothing and in no one except the Word who was made flesh and who died for me on the cross on Calvary's hill, who rose again, who is seated at the right hand of God, ever living to make intercession for me.' That is it! You renounce yourself and all your goodness, your righteousness and everything else, and you trust only, utterly, absolutely to the fact that the Son of God loves you and has given himself for you.

Let me summarize it in the words of the apostle Paul: '. . . who of God is made unto us wisdom, and righteousness, and sanctification, and redemption' (*1 Cor.* 1:30). He is everything. I know nothing apart from what he teaches me. He is my wisdom. He has borne my guilt. He has taken my punishment. I am given his righteousness. He is my righteousness, my sanctification. I, if left to myself, would still remain hopeless but in him I receive power: 'Of his fulness have all we received, and grace for grace.'

And, ultimately, the Lord Jesus Christ is my redemption, my glorification. I know that as he has risen from the dead so, because I am in him, I will also rise from the dead. The Spirit he has put into me proves that to me. The apostle presses this upon the consideration of the Romans when he puts it like this: 'But if the Spirit of him that raised up Jesus from the dead dwell in you, he that raised up Christ from the dead shall also quicken your mortal bodies by his Spirit that dwelleth in you' (*Rom.* 8:11). It is certain! 'Who of God is made unto us wisdom, and righteousness, and sanctification, and redemption' at this moment! My confidence is that the Son of God came into this world and lived and died and rose again in order to save me. That is my only confidence.

> *I dare not trust the sweetest frame,*
> *But wholly lean on Jesus' name;*
> *On Christ, the solid rock, I stand,*
> *All other ground is sinking sand.*
> Edward Mote

I rely on him alone to cover my past; it is on him alone that I rely in the present; it is on him alone that I rely for the future: 'Christ in you, the hope of glory' (*Col.* 1:27). That is what it means to believe on his name.

There, then, are the three terms that are used by the apostle at the very beginning of his Gospel, the very Prologue. Do not go on to consider anything else until you are absolutely clear about this. Do you know him? Have you received him? Are you believing on the Son of God for everything? If you are, you are on the foundation, there is something to build upon. And in the light of that we shall now be in a position to go on to consider the various other things that – the apostle tells us here – come out of that source, that fount, that origin, which is the Lord Jesus Christ himself, the Word made flesh, who dwelt among us, who 'is in the bosom of the Father', who ever lives and reigns with the Father and the Holy Spirit, one God glorious for ever. ☙

15

How We Become the Children of God

But as many as received him, to them gave he power to become the sons of God, even to them that believe on his name: which were born, not of blood, nor of the will of the flesh, nor of the will of man, but of God (John 1:12–13).

We come here to the next stage in the series of steps that the apostle gives us from this Prologue to his Gospel. These truths are essential to a true and full enjoyment of the Christian life and a full assurance of faith and of salvation. We are concerned to look at these one by one as the apostle puts them before us. He wrote both his Gospel and his first epistle – as I have reminded you repeatedly and must go on reminding you – not only that we may arrive at certainty and assurance, enjoying the Christian life as we were meant to enjoy it, but also, of course, that we may function as we should as Christian people. These always go together. 'The joy of the LORD is your strength' (*Neh.* 8:10). The ultimate need of all Christian people is assurance. That is the way to godliness; it is the way to true activity in the Christian church; it is the key and the secret of everything. It was only after they were given that great assurance as the result of the baptism of the Spirit on the day of Pentecost that the apostles – even the apostles – were able to preach with a holy boldness and could be used of God in the way described in the book of Acts.

We have considered some of these great steps that John puts before us. Central to everything is the realization of the truth concerning our Lord himself. We must then realize our need of him in terms of the law and in terms of the darkness that is round and about us and inside us. In our last study we saw that the apostle brings us to this point – that it is basic and essential that we should *know* the Lord, that we should *receive* him, and that we should *believe on* him. If we do, he tells us, this, of necessity, implies a further step, which we are now going to look at together.

But, first, I must emphasize that the words 'believing on his name' do not mean giving a mere intellectual assent to a number of propositions concerning him but refer to what we may call 'the faith of reliance': the whole element of trust and of reliance must of necessity come in. It is not merely that we believe a number of doctrines that are quite right and true concerning him – that is not truly receiving him and believing in him. No, it is a real looking to him individually and in a known and specific manner, and a reliance upon him for all the things that we so sadly need, which have been revealed to us by the operation of the law that was given through Moses.

John goes on to tell us here that if we do have that true faith of reliance, if we do really believe in him and have truly received him, then we find one of the most wonderful things we can ever know, and that is that we become the children of God. 'As many as received him, to them gave he power to become the sons of God, even to them that believe on his name: which were born, not of blood, nor of the will of the flesh, nor of the will of man, but of God.' With these words the apostle John introduces us to one of the great basic, fundamental doctrines of the Scriptures.

We can look at it like this: salvation does not only mean that our sins are forgiven and that we are justified in the sight of God. It does mean that, of course; that is our first need. The first thing a guilty person in the dock needs is to be set free, and we all, in the first place, need forgiveness. Before anything else, we are guilty people – we are not merely people who are sick. Sin is not just sickness. The first thing that is true of us is that we are under condemnation; we are guilty in the sight of God and need forgiveness, absolution, justification. And all who believe on him are justified by faith in the Lord Jesus Christ. But salvation does not stop at that and the tragedy is that we so often tend to stop there, as if the whole of Christianity just means that we are forgiven, that our past is blotted out and we know we shall go to heaven. Nor does salvation stop at sanctification, at a growth in grace and holiness. Again, of course, this is vital and essential. It is wonderful that we are not only delivered from the guilt of sin, but also from its power. But even that does not exhaust what is offered to us in this great salvation. The most wonderful thing of all is that our whole status and standing before God, our whole relationship to God, is entirely changed and becomes something completely new.

It is possible that we might be forgiven and still remain as we are. We might become better by means of the teaching and the operation of the Holy Spirit, and yet still be essentially the same people. But we are not! The glory of this Christian message is that it tells us that this further fact is true of us – we become the 'children of God'! Now this is, I repeat, the most thrilling fact of all, and John puts it beyond any question here in the very Prologue. And he also puts it here, I believe, because it is one of the leading themes of his Gospel. Everybody is familiar with it as it is elaborated in John chapter 3 in our Lord's conversation with Nicodemus on that famous occasion when Nicodemus came to see him by night. It is also a great theme of John's first epistle – in the third chapter, for instance. It seems to be the doctrine that was given to John in particular to write about. But, of course, this teaching is not confined to John; you find it in all the New Testament writers, though they use different language.

So what exactly does this doctrine mean? Here in the Prologue, John collects together the stupendous truths that he will go on to expound. That is the business of a prologue, as it is of an overture; both hint at the major themes that will be put before us. This is one of John's themes and one of the most important from our subjective standpoint. There are, however, two preliminary matters that seem to me to demand our attention before we come to the details. The first concerns the difference in meaning between 'sons' and 'children'. The Authorized (King James) Version says this: 'As many as received him, to them gave he power to become the sons of God . . . ' It is a pity that the translators put 'sons of God', because what John actually wrote was not 'sons of God' but 'children of God'. John never uses the term 'sons' but always talks of 'children', not only in his Gospel, but also in his epistles. The apostle Paul, by contrast, uses the term 'sons'. It seems to have been his favourite word of the two.

Why do we trouble to pause at that point to draw this distinction? The reason is, of course, that John went out of his way to do so, and therefore we must also. There is a very real significance in John's choice of the word 'children' rather than 'sons'. The difference in the connotation of the two words is something like this: the word 'sons' has a more objective meaning. It suggests position, status, something that, as it were, results from adoption. When you use the term 'son', you are indicating the position that is held by a person or by a child, you are referring to the status of sonship with all its prerogatives and privileges. The emphasis is upon the external, the objective, aspect of the relationship. The word 'children', on the other hand, emphasizes something that is internal, something that partakes of the same nature, and, therefore, the term at once conjures up the whole notion of regeneration. That is the essential difference, from the strictly philological standpoint, between these two words. It is therefore not surprising that John should have chosen the word 'children' rather than 'sons'. It is good that we should realize that what John actually says is, 'To as many as received him, to them gave he power to become the *children* of God.'

The second preliminary point is, again, very important. It is that the Bible, in its teaching about this relationship with God, our relationship as children of God, always presents it to us in terms of our Lord and Saviour Jesus Christ. It never teaches this directly, apart from him.

'But,' someone may say, 'are we not told in the book of Acts that the apostle Paul, preaching in Athens, said, 'For we are also his offspring' (*Acts* 17:28)? Aren't all people the children of God? What right have you to say that this teaching about our being children is always presented in association with our Lord and Saviour Jesus Christ?'

That we are all God's children is a very popular view today. People teach what they call 'the universal Fatherhood of God'. It is believed outside the church, of course, and that is why people no longer trouble to go to a place of worship. They think that they are God's children – if they believe in God at all – and that therefore all is well. But that idea is actually also being taught in the church. It is said that the tragedy of the world is that it does not know that everybody is a child of God, and therefore the real business of preaching, the essence of the proclamation of the gospel, is to let people know this good news. That is what many in the church at this present time regard as the gospel. They say: 'God loves us all, God is the Father of us all, but the trouble is that people have been in ignorance of this, living a life to the flesh and to selfishness and so on. Christians need to go everywhere and tell people that God loves them and that they are his children whether they know it or not. Let them do what they will, they are still his children and all will be well. What a shame, what a tragedy, that they should have missed this knowledge for so many years!'

Now the answer to that view, it seems to me, is in this verse that we are looking at. We need not go any further. The contrast is this: 'He came unto his own, and his own received him not. But as many as received him' – not everybody, but those who did receive him – 'to them gave he power to become the children of God, even to them that believe on his name.' Here is a verse that, in and of itself, is a final and complete answer to that error, to that lie, concerning the universal Fatherhood of God. If it were true that all people were the children of God, then the Son of God need never have come into this world. If all people were already the children of God, if they were already under the love of God, and were all finally to be saved, why the incarnation? Why all this that John tells us so magnificently in this Prologue? And the answer, given not only here but elsewhere, is that it is only in and through the Son that we have any hope of becoming children: 'to as many as received him', and to nobody else.

As to the reference that I quoted from Acts 17 – and there are others that point in the same direction – the term 'Fatherhood' is used simply in the sense that God is the Creator of all. In that sense, there is a unity and a solidarity in the entire human race. We are all creatures who have been made by God. The context always makes the meaning perfectly plain and clear. Scripture never contradicts Scripture. You cannot have, on the one hand, a scripture that says, 'to as many as received him', and to them only, gave he this power, and then, on the other hand, another scripture that teaches that all are already children and all we need to do is to tell them that they are. It is quite clear that running right through the Bible from beginning to end, in the Old Testament and the New, there is a great division between those who are the children of God and those who are not.

The view that every human being is automatically a child of God makes much of the New Testament utterly meaningless. The teaching of the New Testament is that all the benefits we ever get always come to us only in and through our Lord Jesus Christ. Look at our Lord's words in chapter 14 of this Gospel: 'I am the way, the truth, and the life: no man cometh unto the Father, but by me' (*John* 14:6). There is no other way. Indeed, all benefits, whatever they are, come to us through him – justification, sanctification, glorification; yes, and especially this of becoming the children of God. As this Prologue tells us, he is, and always was, the eternal Son of God, and if we are to become children or sons of God, then it must be through him. His is the eternal Sonship, and he has come into this world in order to give us a share and a participation in sonship. Not that we ever become sons in the sense that he is. But we derive this relationship to God from him. You see, it is important to pay attention to everything we are told in a verse like John 1:12. All people are not the children of God. Something has to happen to us first. The good news of salvation is not that we are all, always and already, the children of God; the good news is that we can *become* the children of God. This is the proclamation.

There, then, are those two preliminary matters that strike us on the surface of this statement. That brings us to the teaching itself. Now you notice that John says, 'But as many as received him, to them gave he *power* to become the children of God.' What is the meaning of this 'power'? It is an interesting term and it is vital that we should be clear about it. There are those who say that it means something like this: if you believe on the Lord Jesus Christ, then you have in your hands the possibility of becoming a child of God. The 'power' is that possibility. It is for you to exercise it, for you to decide what you do with it. Only if you lay hold of it do you become a child of God. That has often been taught; it is, indeed, the official Roman Catholic teaching on this particular verse.

But I want to try to show you that that interpretation is completely erroneous. Take the Greek word that is here translated 'power'. It is a most interesting word. It is used 102 times in the New Testament, in several different senses, but never in the sense of physical, moral or spiritual strength to do something. Its meaning is 'authority': 'to them gave he *authority* to become the children of God'. It also means 'right', 'privilege' or 'honour'. Indeed, it seems to me that we cannot improve on what is stated by John Calvin. He says it really means, 'being reckoned worthy of': 'To as many as received him, he gave this right to be reckoned worthy of being children of God, even to as many as believe on his name.' This is an important point. This verse, I repeat, does not mean that power is given to us to decide one way or the other, but that our Lord places those who believe on him in the position of honour in which they really are the children of God. This is not a possibility to be exercised one way or the other. It is something that happens to all who know him and receive him and believe on him.

Now a very interesting point that has often been taken up and debated concerns the order in which these two things happen – which comes first, is it the believing or the honour of becoming children of God? To me, this is not a matter that is essential to salvation, though it is interesting in and of itself. It seems to me that, in a sense, the two are virtually synchronous and that we cannot divide between them. If I were pressed as to which comes first, I would be driven to say that the birth comes first, in view of the many things that we are told about the 'natural man'. For instance, 'The natural man receiveth not the things of the Spirit of God: for they are foolishness unto him' (*1 Cor.* 2:14) and, 'The carnal mind is enmity against God: for it is not subject to the law of God, neither indeed can be' (*Rom.* 8:7). How can such a person believe on the Lord Jesus Christ and then, because of that, become a child of God? No, the natural man cannot believe, we are told. He rejects the gospel, he hates it, he regards it as 'foolishness'. We also have great statements such as this in Paul's epistle to the Ephesians: 'And you hath he quickened, who were dead in trespasses and sins' (*Eph.* 2:1). Even when we were dead in sins, says Paul, he quickened us. So it is all the action of God. While it is a matter of interest intellectually to try to apportion particular times to these matters, it seems to me that the truth we must concentrate on is that it is all of God. Both are given. It is all his action upon us; it is all through the Lord Jesus Christ. It is he who puts us in this position of honour.

That, then, brings me to the next point – the word 'become'. (We must deal with these words because they are so important and so fascinating and they bring us right into the very heart and centre of this great truth.) 'To as many as received him, to them gave he power *to become* the sons of God.' Here, again, is an interesting point. We are never told about the Lord Jesus Christ that he 'became' the Son of God – for the good reason that he always was. There are false teachers going about selling books on your doorstep who will teach you an alternative view. They say they do not believe in the eternal Sonship and the co-equality and the co-eternity of the Son with the Father. They believe that by denying this truth they are Jehovah's Witnesses. But here is the answer: we are never told in the Scriptures that he became the Son of God. All we are told about him is that he 'became flesh'. That is in verse 14: 'The Word was made [became] flesh.' He was the eternal Son of God, everlasting in his deity; he had to become flesh, but he never had to become the Son because he always was. But with regard to us, it is true to say that we *become* the children of God. That is the whole point. It is a further proof of the error of the doctrine of the universal Fatherhood of God. We have to become children of God because by nature we clearly are not. Indeed, we are all by nature 'the children of wrath, even as others' (*Eph.* 2:3).

Now this word 'become', I believe, was used here very deliberately in order to emphasize the fact that a very definite and a very real change does take place in us before we can become the children of God. The apostle does not say, 'To as many as received him, to them gave he the honour of *being called* the children of God.' That would be wonderful in itself but not as wonderful as what we are told. The position of Christians is not that they remain what they were, somewhat better, perhaps, but now called the children of God. No, no! They *become* the children of God. Something happens to them. Indeed, John is very careful to tell us what it is that does happen. That is the meaning of verse 13: 'which were born . . . ' They have to be born before they become. The whole emphasis, in every word that is used, is upon the great change that takes place. It is not that we are given a position and a status. That can happen. You can adopt a child and put that child in the position of your child and give it all the privileges and so on. But there is no change of nature there, whereas here the whole point is that there is a real becoming. As the Word became flesh in a real sense, so those who receive him become, in a real sense, the children of God and it involves, as John says, a very real birth.

Then that brings us to the phrase, 'children of God'. Here, again, is one of these specific definitions – I am taking the trouble to go through this in detail because, as I said, the problem with most of us is that we do not realize these things. We say we are children of God and leave it at that. But we must go down into the depths, we must get at the real fulness of meaning, if we are to begin to appreciate something of what is true of us as Christians. 'Children of God'! In name, yes; but over and above that, I repeat, in nature, too. It is not merely a title that is given me. The world understands that. If a man is given a title it does not make any difference to him; he is the same man. We are foolish enough to regard him in a different way because he has a handle to his name but it does not make any difference at all to the man. But that is not what we have here.

When John says 'children of God', he is not talking of an honorary title that leaves the person unchanged. No, no! There is a real transformation. We are children of God in the sense that children are like their parents, that they have something in them of the nature of their parents, that the relationship is that between children and their natural parents. It means that we have become transformed into the likeness of God! Nothing less than that. It means, therefore, a change in our vital capacities, in our perceptions, in our emotions. There are many statements to this effect in various places in the Scriptures. Take, for instance, Paul's words in the Epistle to the Galatians: 'For ye are all the children of God by faith in Christ Jesus' (*Gal.* 3:26). Or take that magnificent statement in 2 Peter 1:4, where Peter says that we actually and literally become 'partakers of the divine nature'. This is a staggering statement and it is tragic that we do not seem to realize this. Listen:

Grace and peace be multiplied unto you through the knowledge of God, and of Jesus our Lord, according as his divine power hath given unto us all things that pertain unto life and godliness, through the knowledge of him that hath called us to glory and virtue: whereby are given unto us exceeding great and precious promises: that by these ye might be partakers of the divine nature, having escaped the corruption that is in the world through lust (2 Pet. 1:2–4).

That is what is being emphasized here in the Prologue. 'Children of God': it carries all that meaning. We become more and more like God.

Now a very good exposition of the verses we are looking at is to be found in the First Epistle of John, where John works out the implications of being children of God. He tells us, in an extended manner, something of the meaning of the phrase 'children of God', particularly in terms of love. He says that if you do not love your brother, if you are like Cain, then it is no use saying you are a child of God because God is love and the child is like the parent. Therefore, John says, 'We know that we have passed from death unto life' – in other words, we know that we are children of God – 'because we love the brethren' (1 John 3:14), that is, we are like our Father. Similarly with the commandments; they are God's commandments, they are an expression of his character and of what he likes, so if you say you are a child of God but you do not keep his commandments, you are contradicting yourself, you are a 'liar' (1 John 2:4; 4:20). The child loves the commandments because they are the commandments of the Father. The whole point of the exposition is that to be a child of God is to partake of something of the divine nature and manifest it in your life.

Now our Lord himself had already given this very teaching over this same matter of love. 'Love your enemies,' he says, '. . . do good to them that hate you, and pray for them which despitefully use you, and persecute you.' Why? Because your Father does that. 'For he maketh his sun to rise on the evil and on the good, and sendeth rain on the just and on the unjust.' And our Lord says, 'Be ye therefore perfect, even as your Father which is in heaven is perfect' (*Matt.* 5:44, 45, 48). The way we prove that we are children of God is by being loving in our relationships, as he is. This does not mean that ultimate love, as I have already been at pains to point out, but it does refer to our dealings with men and women.

So, then, here in the Prologue we are told that the Son of God came into this world – 'The Word was made flesh' – in order that we might become the children of God, that we might partake of the divine nature. Now I am very ready to agree with those who say that John had the Jews very especially in his mind, because the whole trouble with the Jews was that they thought they alone were the children of God. In reply, John says this in verse 12: 'as many as'. That means 'whosoever', John's great word. To 'as many as', or 'whosoever', receive him he gives the power, to Gentiles as well as Jews. That is a part of the great gospel of the New Testament: 'There is neither Greek nor Jew, circumcision nor uncircumcision, Barbarian, Scythian, bond nor free' (*Col.* 3:11). And here it is announced in this very Prologue.

Another thing that was undoubtedly in John's mind was this: the proud boast of the Jew was that he was a child of Abraham. You will find in chapter 8 of John's Gospel that when our Lord said to people who seemed to have believed on him, 'If ye continue in my word, then are ye my disciples indeed; and ye shall know the truth, and the truth shall make you free', these people stood on their dignity in protest and said, 'We be Abraham's seed, and were never in bondage to any man: how sayest thou, Ye shall be made free?' (*John* 8:31–33). 'Abraham's children'! Listen to me, says John, the glory of this gospel, which announces that 'the Word was made flesh, and dwelt among us' and that '[God] hath visited and redeemed his people' (*Luke* 1:68), is this: that in and through him you are made not 'children of Abraham', wonderful and glorious though that is, but you are actually made the children of God himself. It does not stop at Abraham, it lifts you into the family of God; you become children of Almighty God! And here is the gospel – that the Gentiles, those who were outside, the dogs, the lost, the fallen, the vilest, anybody, can become a child of God if they know and receive and believe in this only begotten Son of God, the Word who was made flesh and dwelt among us. This is what John tells us we must realize about ourselves.

And now we deal with the last aspect, which we may call the mechanics of this great matter. We are not the children of God by nature. We must become the children of God – but how? Here is a vital question. And the answer is given in verse 13: 'which were born'. We read, 'which were born, not of blood, nor of the will of the flesh, nor of the will of man, but of God'. Here, again, unfortunately, there are those who have introduced what seems to me to be a quite wrong interpretation. Is it not extraordinary how with vital matters like this you always find the enemy most active? There are many people who say that the words 'which were born' should be translated in the singular and should read, 'who was born': 'who was born, not of blood, nor of the will of the flesh, nor of the will of man, but of God', and that, therefore, they are nothing but a reference to the virgin birth of our Lord and Saviour Jesus Christ.

Unfortunately, the interpretation 'who was born' was taught by one of the fathers of the early church, Irenaeus. Another early church father, Tertullian, also accepted this idea and argued for it. And there have always been people who have adopted and taught this exegesis. During this present century, the person most responsible for popularizing this view was, perhaps, the late Archbishop William Temple in his devotional commentary on the Gospel of John. And yet let me be quite fair to Archbishop Temple: he admits in his commentary that all the best early manuscripts are against this translation. Not only the best, but the bulk of the manuscripts favour the plural, 'which were born'.

But somehow or other people have been ready to take hold of the singular, 'who was born'. Some of the early fathers, of course, did this solely in the interest of the doctrine of the virgin birth. But it is a shame that they did. They need not have done so; there are other statements that do that adequately. But there have been others since then who have not been happy about the whole doctrine of regeneration, and that has been their interest in preferring 'who was born'. The great consensus of opinion throughout the centuries, however, has been that these words must be taken in the plural and that what we have here is not a reference to the virgin birth of Christ, true though that is, but an explanation by John of his words: 'But as many as received him, to them gave he power to become the sons of God, even to them that believe on his name.'

So how does it happen, how do we become children of God? It happens like this, says the apostle: we are *born*. In other words, here we have the great doctrine of the rebirth, the doctrine of regeneration. As I have said, the business of the Prologue is to gather the leading themes of this Gospel, and this particular theme reappears in the third chapter of John: 'Nicodemus saith unto him, How can a man be born when he is old?' Why does he say that? Because Christ has just said, 'Verily, verily, I say unto thee, Except a man be born again, he cannot see the kingdom of God' (*John* 3:4, 3). And our Lord goes on to elaborate the teaching concerning the rebirth.

The apostle Paul gives exactly the same teaching when he says, 'If any man be in Christ, he is a new creature: old things are passed away; behold, all things are become new' (*2 Cor.* 5:17), and so does James in chapter 1 of his epistle: 'Of his own will begat he us with the word of truth, that we should be a kind of firstfruits of his creatures' (*James* 1:18). Here, again, in the teaching about this wonderful birth, the lie is given to universalism. Peter, also, in his first epistle, says, 'Being born again, not of corruptible seed, but of incorruptible, by the word of God, which liveth and abideth for ever' (*1 Pet.* 1:23). These New Testament writers are all teaching the same doctrine – the doctrine of the rebirth, the second birth, regeneration, the new creation, call it what you will.

But notice the negatives. What is the character of this birth that we undergo? As we have seen, we must be 'born again' before we become the children of God. We are not born the children of God. The gospel does not tell us just to realize that we are. No, no! The message of the gospel is that as we are, we are the children of wrath, we are hell bound and hell deserving, but if we believe in this person and what he has done, and trust to him, then we can become the children of God.

Then notice how this new birth happens – and here again we have negatives. First: 'not of blood'. Actually, the apostle wrote it in the plural: 'not of bloods'. What does that refer to? It is, again, a direct shot, as it were, at the Jews, who believed that everything came by natural descent, through generation after generation after generation until you got right back to Abraham. 'We are children of Abraham,' they said (see *John* 8:39), this superior human descent through many generations. No, says John, it does not come like that: 'not of bloods'.

Second, in order to make it quite plain, John adds: 'nor of the will of the flesh'. What is that? Well, this is a reference to natural procreation, to ordinary human generation, the result of the desires of the flesh. There is nothing wrong in that. It is God who ordained that procreation should take place and that the world should be replenished with people in that way. That is the normal human way in which we are all born. We are born as the result of 'the will of the flesh'. A man falls in love with a woman, they get married, and a child is born. But not here! That does not come in at all. Not only is being the people of God not a matter of national descent, it does not even have anything to do with the individual, physical family into which we are born. In other words, you may have a father and mother who are both Christians but that does not mean that you will be a Christian. It is not the result of natural transmission, natural procreation, human generation.

Third, neither is it 'the will of man'. What does this mean? What is the difference between 'the will of the flesh' and 'the will of man'? It is this. We have excluded the natural process of procreation but somebody may say, 'Well, perhaps it is as the result of human influence, human teaching, human learning, human knowledge, human oratory. Is it not just the influence of one mind upon another, and a matter of upbringing? You train children to be Christians and you make them children of God by human endeavour.' No, that is all excluded. It does not come in at all.

So here John has chosen three negatives that exclude between them the whole of human activity: 'not of bloods, nor of the will of the flesh, nor of the will of man'. In other words, becoming a child of God has nothing at all to do with man! And so John puts it positively by saying, 'but of God'. It is altogether and entirely 'of God'. And, of course, if we have understood the teaching about the law, on which we have spent some time, we will not be in any difficulty about this at all because we saw there that the law makes it abundantly plain and clear to us that as we are we can do nothing. We are not only guilty and lost, we are also helpless and hopeless. There is a law in our members dragging us down (*Rom.* 7:23). Though I may feel that God's way is good, and want it, even when I see things at their best, I am paralysed. 'In me (that is, in my flesh,) dwelleth no good thing' (*Rom.* 7:18). I am sold under sin. I am the slave of sin. I am a 'wretched man' (*Rom.* 7:24)!

Not only that; we have been seeing quite clearly how 'the natural man' is even at enmity with God and not subject to the will of God. 'The natural man receiveth not the things of the Spirit of God: for they are foolishness unto him: neither can he know them, because they are spiritually discerned' (*1 Cor.* 2:14). But it is all right: 'You hath he quickened, who were dead in trespasses and sins' (*Eph.* 2:1). We cannot produce life, and this is a new birth, the coming into being of a new life, a new person, a new nature, a new being. It is only the Creator who can bring this about. So Paul says in Ephesians 2:10: 'We are his workmanship, created in Christ Jesus.' And here it all is, in the Prologue.

What a wonderful Prologue this is! It has all this teaching here, in a nutshell. We shall have to work it out, of course, but here it is in its essence. In its very brief compass it shows us that to become a child of God is all of God. You do not become a Christian because you are born in and belong to a particular nation; you do not become a Christian because you are the child of certain parents; you do not become a Christian as the result of human activity, not even human endeavour at its best and highest. That is all impossible. Becoming a Christian is all of God.

We come back to James: 'Of his own will begat he us with the word of truth' (*James* 1:18). There is the mechanism. John does not go into it here. You would not expect it in the Prologue. But it is done by the Word, and the Spirit on top of the Word. In speaking to Nicodemus, our Lord says, 'born of the Spirit' (*John* 3:6). 'The Spirit', and in James, 'the word of truth'. And Peter says we are born again 'by the word of God' (*1 Pet.*1:23). The Word, and the Spirit using the Word. We are impregnated by the operation and the power of the Spirit using the seed of the Word. And new life comes into being, and a new nature comes into being, and 'a new man' comes into being; and it is this 'new man' alone who is a child of God. He has been born, 'not of bloods, nor of the will of the flesh, nor of the will of man, but of God'. It is only the Father who can beget and as God is our Father, he is our 'begetter'.

That is what it means to be a Christian, my friend. If you and I are not the proudest people, in a spiritual sense, in the world, it means that we do not understand this doctrine. 'Beloved, now are we the sons [children] of God . . .' (*1 John* 3:2). Now! Do you think of yourself like that? Do you behave like that? Do you glory in the fact that you are that? That is why I am writing my Gospel, says John; you do not seem to realize it. 'The Son of God', as John Calvin put it, 'became the Son of man, that we, the sinful sons of men, might become sons of God.' Oh, may God through the Spirit give us a living awareness of the fact that we are indeed the children of God. ∽

16

Our Relationship to the Son and to the Father

But as many as received him, to them gave he power to become the sons of God, even to them that believe on his name: which were born, not of blood, nor of the will of the flesh, nor of the will of man, but of God (John 1:12–13).

e have been looking at these two verses from different angles, and last time we were considering them from the standpoint of the amazing message they bring that those who have believed on the Lord Jesus Christ and who know him and who receive him are given the honour and the privilege of becoming children of God. This is one of the great truths that John puts before us here at the very beginning of this Prologue to his Gospel, and it is vital that we should lay hold upon it. Christians are not merely men and women who have been forgiven. They have been forgiven, and it is terrible that one has to use the word 'merely', but one is driven to do so because there are so many Christians who give the impression that to them the whole of Christianity is about the forgiveness of sins. That is all they are interested in. They have a sense of guilt and they want to get rid of it. Then they hear this message about sins being forgiven in the blood of Christ and they jump at it with avidity, and stop at that. But that is not the essence of Christianity. In a sense, that is merely preparatory, something that must take place before we can have real dealings with God.

The end of Christianity is not forgiveness; it is restoration to God. The apostle Peter tells us that Christ came and suffered 'that he might bring us to God' (*1 Pet.* 3:18). And that is the essence of the Christian faith – that men and women are being restored, and more than restored, to the position they once occupied in Adam. That is the very truth that the apostle puts before us here and it is, I repeat, important for us to consider it because there can be no true joy in salvation, there can be no freeness and abandon and sense of glory in the Christian life, unless we realize this and lay hold upon it. The New Testament puts very great emphasis upon the status, the position, of the Christian, whereas far too often we spend our time with our subjective moods and states and conditions. It is, perhaps, the chief trouble with most of us that, failing to realize what we are and who we are and what we have become in Christ, we are preoccupied with what someone has called, 'the mumps and measles of the soul'.

Now the best antidote to any kind of spiritual depression is the objective realization of who and what we are. This is something that appeals even to people as they are by nature. They take pride in country and in family and these always spur them and stimulate them in times of difficulty and crisis. Elevate all that to the spiritual realm and multiply it, as it were, by infinity, and you see what the New Testament says to the Christian. And here it is before us. According to John, the way to realize what is possible to us as Christians, and what we are meant to be, is to realize, first and foremost, this glorious truth about the incarnation, the coming of the Son of God into this world. So John gives that the chief place in his Prologue.

But salvation does not stop at that. John wants us to realize at once that the result of salvation is that we become the children of God. I ended last time by quoting those words of John Calvin: 'The Son of God became the Son of man, that we, the sinful sons of men, might become sons of God', and here it is before us. So it seems to me that the next step in our consideration of this subject is to ask ourselves: Are we enjoying these benefits of the Christian life? Do we find this a life of joy, a life of freedom? Do we know anything about 'the glorious liberty of the children of God' (*Rom.* 8:21)?

The Christian life was never meant to be a task or just a duty. It was never meant to be something that one drags oneself to, perhaps against one's will, and feels a certain amount of merit for having done so. That is not Christianity! That is religion! That is the typical attitude of the merely religious person. Christianity is filled with joy and glory and triumph and praise. You cannot read the New Testament without seeing that. These people were filled with such a joy that when the world condemned them to death and consigned them to the lions in the arena, they praised God all the more. They praised him that they had been accounted worthy to suffer shame for Christ's sake.

So, Christian people, we must examine ourselves in the light of these words of the apostle John. Is this our position? Are we rejoicing in the Lord? Can we say that the joy of the Lord is our strength? If we cannot, or if there is any doubt or hesitation, it is probably due to the fact that somewhere or another we are defective in our appreciation, our true realization, of what we have been made in Christ Jesus. 'As many as received him, to them gave he power to become the children of God.' So the question before us is this: Do we know that we are the children of God? Do we realize it? It is not enough just to go mechanically through an exposition of Scripture and say he has made this possible. I repeat that we are meant to enjoy it. It is not something that you know only with your mind or intellect. This is something very real, experiential. So it seems to me that if there is any doubt or hesitation in our minds or in our lives and hearts with regard to this matter, the best thing that we can do is examine ourselves.

Now the New Testament provides us with many tests to help us to make sure that we really are the children of God. It is inevitable that it should do so. These New Testament documents were written to Christian people. Let us never forget that. Even the Gospels. The Gospels were not written for the world but for the church. There is a tendency to forget that, it seems to me, at the present time. They were written to strengthen the faith of believers as, inevitably, were the epistles. So it is not surprising that almost everywhere in the New Testament you find that tests were constantly being applied. Some of the New Testament documents do this much more thoroughly than others. The First Epistle of John was written almost entirely for this very purpose. A writer commenting upon that book called his commentary *The Tests of Life* and in that epistle there are many wonderful and profound tests on this very matter.[1] There are several places in the first and second chapters, where the apostle argues like this: If you are doing this or that, or not doing something else, then there is no value in your profession, you are not 'born of God', you are not truly the children of God. That is John's way of putting these tests before us but there are many others.

The apostle Paul gives us an obvious test in Romans 8:14, where he says, 'As many as are led by the Spirit of God, they are the sons of God.' That is a typical New Testament way of dealing with this matter. Similarly, in Ephesians 5:1, the apostle Paul says, 'Be ye therefore followers of God, as dear children', and then he asks us to love one another and to help one another and to refrain from certain things. We have abundant material, therefore, that we can use in our endeavour to make certain that we really are the children of God. Are you in doubt about this matter? Let us approach it along the natural line, along the human analogy that immediately suggests itself. How does one test true sonship? How does one test this relationship of child and parent and child and family? There are certain obvious tests, which we must put in the order given in the New Testament.

The first way of knowing for certain whether you really are a child of God is, as we have already seen, the test of your relationship to the Lord Jesus Christ. We have to start with that. Why? Because God is Spirit, and because, as we are told, 'No man hath seen God at any time' – but our Lord has come – 'the only begotten Son, which is in the bosom of the Father, he hath declared him' (*John* 1:18). 'God was manifest in the flesh' (*1 Tim.* 3:16). And so we start with him.

We also start with the Lord Jesus Christ because we could never have become the children of God if he had not come and done all that he has done. We need not stay with this now because we have already dealt with it but it is an obvious test. Our relationship to the Lord Jesus Christ, in and of itself, proclaims whether we are born of God and are the children of God. In the Prologue of John's Gospel, it is put in terms of those three words to which we have already referred: Do we *know*

[1] Robert Law, *The Tests of Life: A Study of the First Epistle of St John* (Kerr Lectures), first published in 1909 by T. & T. Clark.

him? The princes of this world did not know him. But the Christian knows him for who he is, the Son of God. Do we *receive* him? The Pharisees and scribes did not receive him: 'His own received him not.' And, third: Do we *believe* on his name?

Now in his first epistle, John puts all that in the first verse of the fifth chapter, where he says: 'Whosoever believeth that Jesus is the Christ is born of God.' There it is. Obviously, there is a content in that statement, is there not? John means those who really believe that Jesus is the Christ, the Messiah, the Deliverer. It is not enough just to say, 'Oh yes, of course, I believe on the Lord Jesus Christ, I always have.' If you put it like that, you are telling me that you do not believe in him. To believe that Jesus is the Christ is to know and to confess that you are a hopeless, condemned, vile sinner, that all your righteousness is but as filthy rags, that you have the spirit of poverty in you, that you mourn about your life, that you hunger and thirst after righteousness and know that he alone can fill you. That is the content. It is not just a mechanical statement, not merely something intellectual. No, no! To believe on him means that you are utterly committed to him, that you abandon yourself to him, and that you have no hope apart from him. But it is quite clear: 'Whosoever believeth that Jesus is the Christ', in that way, 'is born of God.'

Self-righteous religious people do not believe that Jesus is the Christ. They may say that they do, but if they are relying upon their own goodness and their own lives and works, they do not believe that Jesus is the Christ. They need no Saviour; they are like the Pharisee who says, 'God, I thank thee, that I am not as other men are' (*Luke* 18:11). They have never seen the need of Christ's death upon the cross; they are not born of God. But as for those who really have seen their own utter helplessness and hopelessness and who rejoice in Christ Jesus – well, let me put it in terms of Philippians 3:3, where the apostle Paul has summarized it all: 'We are the circumcision' – who are we? – 'which worship God in the spirit, and rejoice in Christ Jesus, and have no confidence in the flesh.' That is it! That is what believing that Jesus is the Christ means – 'no confidence in the flesh', rejoicing in Christ Jesus, the Messiah, the Deliverer, the Saviour and trusting ourselves utterly and entirely to him.

We must not stay with this, but it is essential that I should put it there. 'As many as received him' – there it is – 'to them gave he power to become the sons of God.' I say this to comfort you, my friends. If with Edward Mote you can say honestly,

My hope is built on nothing less
Than Jesus' blood and righteousness;
I dare not trust the sweetest frame,
But wholly lean on Jesus' name;
On Christ the solid rock I stand
All other ground is sinking sand

– if you can say that honestly, I pronounce to you that you are a child of God, you are born of God. The two always go together. 'Whosoever believeth that Jesus is the Christ' is 'born of God'. Not, you are going to be, you *are*. By saying that, you are giving proof of the fact that you are born of God. You would never say such things if you were not. So we leave that first test – our relationship to the Son.

Then we come to the second test, which is our relationship to the Father. Here again there are endless tests, and all I want to do now is to put them before you. This is not an occasion for exhortation but for examination. There is nothing that I know of that is more important than just this very subject. Am I a child of God or am I not? For if I am, come what may, I know that I am all right in the end because '[nothing] shall be able to separate us from the love of God, which is in Christ Jesus our Lord' (*Rom.* 8:39). This is the greatest and most powerful thing in the world. How do we test our relationship to the Father? Well, how do you test any sort of sonship? Let me split it up and put it to you in a number of statements. The first, obviously, is this: children of God have a sense of belonging to God. Every child has a sense of belonging – he belongs to his father and mother, he belongs to the family. He does not have to persuade himself. He just feels it, he knows it, it is there. It is not something that you can demonstrate logically to the child, perhaps, but there it is. The child is in a different relationship to this man, his father, from every other relationship to every other man. It is elemental, deep down in the consciousness.

And this is true, therefore, of the children of God; they have a sense that they belong to God. The man of the world does not have that sense. God is an ogre to him, a tyrant. Whenever he thinks of God, his attitude is one of fear and antagonism. But Christian men and women – and, again, they may not be able to put it logically, they may not even be able to analyse it or to understand it – just have this sense, this feeling, this consciousness, that they belong to God and to God's people. There are many expressions of this. There is one, it seems to me, at the end of the seventy-third Psalm, that puts it perfectly. The Psalmist has been in trouble, tempted, unhappy, but then he recovers himself and ends by saying this: 'Whom have I in heaven but thee? and there is none upon earth that I desire beside thee' (*Psa.* 73:25). He has come to that final point. He does not care how successful these godless people are, these people whose 'eyes stand out with fatness' and for whom, 'there are no bands in their death' (*Psa.* 73:7, 4). All that has been troubling him but now, he says, it does not matter. Only one thing matters to him – God!

Do you know that you are a child of God? Do you *know* that you are? Or is God somebody outside you, somebody you are reminded of occasionally in a spirit of fear? Do you feel you must do this, that or the other just to keep in with him, as it were? Which is it? You see, the difference is the difference between the child relationship, the child consciousness, and the external, legal relationship that some ordinary little citizen has with a king or a great emperor. These are the ways in which we test whether we are children of God.

Let me elaborate that a little bit as a second test in connection with our relationship to the Father. Children of God think of the whole of life in terms of God. The child's life is bound up with the father and instinctively children think of everything and look out upon everything in these terms. In its broadest form, this can be put in the words that the apostle Paul used in Athens: 'In him we live, and move, and have our being' (*Acts* 17:28). That is all right, but it is philosophical; children go much farther than that. They may not realize that philosophically but actually, in practice, they do know it. 'Like father, like child.' Children look out upon everything in exactly the same way as their fathers. This seems to me to be one of those very basic and fundamental points that we tend to forget.

Christian men and women, I repeat, always and habitually think about everything and look upon everything in terms of God. They have this basic outlook, as it were, this approach. In the last analysis, there are only two views of life. Either my life is entirely governed and controlled by God and my relationship to him, or else I live a god-less life. It is one or the other. And children of God are God-centred, God-controlled. Our Lord himself, who is *the* Son, said, 'I do nothing of myself; but as my Father has taught me, I speak these things' (*John* 8:28). He is saying, in effect, 'All I know and all I am doing and all I am saying is what is given me of the Father.' His whole life is centred in God the Father. It is obvious. He is entirely controlled by him in every respect. He faces everything in this way. Even when he is facing death upon the cross, and shrinks from that terrible consequence of being the sin-bearer, he adds, 'Nevertheless not my will, but thine, be done' (*Luke* 22:42). And this must of necessity be true of every child of God; it is something that you find in yourself and you are amazed at it.

There are two outlooks. Again, John puts this very clearly in his first epistle: 'Love not the world, neither the things that are in the world. If any man love the world, the love of the Father is not in him' (*1 John* 2:15). What are we to love? 'The things that be of God' (*Mark* 8:33). The Christian is no longer bound by the world. Non-Christians are, of course; they think in worldly terms and categories. That does not mean that they are of necessity vile sinners or reprobates, they may be highly respectable. But they are worldly; they have a worldly outlook. God, this revelation of God, does not come in. They depend upon their own reason and that of others, and on human knowledge and learning.

Christians may lapse, they may fail, but fundamentally their whole life is bounded by God. This world? Ah, they do not see it with that old eye, that old worldly eye – they see through it. 'This is the victory that overcometh the world, even our faith' (*1 John* 5:4). They see 'the lust of the flesh, and the lust of the eyes, and the pride of life' (*1 John* 2:16). The non-Christian has not seen that, only the Christian. Why?

It is this relationship to God. Christians no longer think that the world is wonderful because they know of something that really is wonderful, something that is glorious.

What, then, about our thinking, our general thinking? What about the climate of our thinking? Oh, how important that is! I must not stay with this but I am more and more impressed by the difference between the particular statements that people make and the climate of their thinking. There are people I know, people I listen to, who, if I took their individual statements, I might feel were truly Christian, children of God. But the climate of their thinking tells me that they are not. You can learn the right phrases and repeat them like a parrot but that does not mean that you are thinking as a child of God. It is the fundamental outlook and attitude that reveals whether or not we are. The child may stumble and be very incorrect – even irreligious, in fact, in particular statements – but there is something about the total outlook, there is something about the atmosphere, about the very accent, as it were, that proclaims the child of God. Oh, my dear friends, let us make sure of this: Is our thinking godly thinking? Is it biblical? All our thinking, I do not care what it is dealing with. Christians, I repeat, face everything in terms of their Father.

And then I go on from that. It is very difficult to know the right order in which to place these statements, but clearly the child has love, and the child of God has a sense of love for God. 'The devils also believe, and tremble' (*James* 2:19). The devil believes in God – and hates him. But the child loves. 'The carnal [natural] mind', says the apostle Paul, 'is enmity against God: for it is not subject to the law of God, neither indeed can be' (*Rom.* 8:7). That is the antithesis of being a child. Children love. They know, though they may have temporary lapses, that their father loves them and they have a sense of gratitude to him. And Christians, of necessity, have within them a sense of gratitude to God for who he is and for what he has done for them through his dear Son. If you believe that the Word was made flesh and dwelt among us in order that you might be saved, why, you cannot help thanking God. You must have love for God in your heart, and your relationship to God is not one of habit or of custom or of practice or of law or of fear but is essentially one of gratitude and praise and thanksgiving and love. This is inevitable.

In his epistle, John draws the contrast: 'If we say we have fellowship with him, and walk in darkness . . .' (1 John 1:6). It is all very well to say things, the real test is what we *are*. 'Manners maketh man' – manners proclaim the man, and they very much do so in this Christian sense. So let us ask ourselves that simple yet perhaps most profound of all questions: What is our real feeling with respect to God? Do we love him? My question is not whether we love God with all our heart, and all our soul, and all our mind, and all our strength. I am not asking that because I know the answer. But what I am asking is this: Do we know that we love him? Can we say:

> *Lord, it is my chief complaint*
> *That my love is weak and faint*

but go on to say this:

> *Yet I love thee, and adore:*
> *O for grace to love thee more.*
> William Cowper

That is it! That is the expression of the child. The children of God know that their love is unworthy, that it is weak, it is faint, it is feeble, but it is love, nevertheless. It may be a wayward love but it is nevertheless love. God is their Father.

But now, in the fourth place, I must add another test, lest we mis-interpret that third one, and it is the test of respect. This is infallibly an element in the relationship of a true child, a child worthy of the name of the father. The child loves the father, yes, but at the same time respects the father. The child may at times dislike some of the father's commandments and edicts but nevertheless has a fundamental respect. It is a very poor father, or a very poor child, if there is not this sense of respect.

This is something, perhaps, that the modern generation finds it difficult to understand. I am reminded of the old preacher who, when dealing with the apostle Paul's description of God as 'the God and

Father of our Lord Jesus Christ', said, 'Why does Paul put it like that? Why didn't he just say that God is his Father, or why didn't he just say, "Our God, and our Father"?' And I rather like that old preacher's explanation. He said, 'It is there we see the tenderness and the consideration of the Holy Spirit. He knows that alas there are many people in this world to whom the word "father" does not conjure up a notion of love and of kindness and of goodness and concern and justice and compassion. There are some to whom the word "father" but conjures up a picture of a drunken beast, an object of terror and alarm. If the Scripture had said, "God, who is our Father", it would not help somebody in that position, indeed, it might be a little bit misleading. So the Holy Spirit thus led the apostle to say, "The God and Father of our Lord Jesus Christ." I see him, I have these records of him, and like Son, like Father. If he is like his Father, then I know that God is not like my father.'

We are living in an age that has unworthy notions of fatherhood and of sonship. That is obviously the cause with the breakdown in discipline in this world at this present time. The question is: Do modern children respect their parents, respect their fathers? Let us not be too hard on children and young people. Undoubtedly, the blame for juvenile delinquency and the failure of children and young people must be placed solidly on the shoulders of the parents; they are primarily responsible. One gathers from the papers and the literature that there is very little respect for the modern parent and that a part of this rebellion that we are witnessing is a rebellion against parents who have not been worthy of the name and have not commanded the respect of their children.

When you come into the realm of the relationship of the child of God to the heavenly Father, this element of respect is, of course, absolutely central; it is vital. There are many people who are ready to say, 'I love God', but there is no value in their statement. There is an easy familiarity that causes one to shudder. There is a sloppy sentimentality that one never finds in the New Testament. You never find the expression 'Dear God' in the New Testament but I have known people who have thought that the hallmark of spirituality was to speak to God in that way. You do not get that here. Even the Son prays, 'Holy Father', and what he has taught us to pray is this: 'Our Father' – yes! But – 'who art in heaven, hallowed be thy name.' Love is not incompatible with respect; indeed, they should go together. It is not love unless there is respect, also. Take the sloppy sentimentality of the romantic film. That is not love, that is lust, some silly infatuation. Where there is love, there is respect: supremely, in love to God. Where you get the true father-child relationship, the child not only loves the father, but has respect for the father, looks up to the father and tends to think that the father is omniscient and all powerful and so on. Respect is inevitably a part of this whole relationship.

So let us not just say, 'I have always loved God.' Do you respect God? Is there this element of holy fear? Not a craven fear. 'Fear hath torment' (*1 John* 4:18). That is not what I am talking about. I am, rather, talking about what the author of the Epistle to the Hebrews means when he says, 'Let us . . . serve God acceptably with reverence and godly fear: for our God is a consuming fire' (*Heb.* 12:28–29). That, remember, is written by the man who said, 'Having . . . boldness to enter into the holiest' (*Heb.* 10:19). There is no contradiction between a holy boldness and reverence. There is no contradiction between love and respect, or between adoration and awe – indeed, these go together. And if you separate them, you will always go astray and God will be thought of as a benevolent father who winks at everything, pretending he has not seen it, who loves everybody, who sees to it that everybody goes to heaven whether or not they believe in his Son and however they may have lived. No, no! Love with respect! 'Our Father, who art in heaven, hallowed be thy name; thy kingdom come . . .'

My fifth characteristic, my fifth test – and this is always true, is it not? – is that the child is proud of belonging to the family. There is nothing wrong in that; indeed, there is everything right in it. That is what we can call a good and healthy pride. The child feels that his family is the greatest thing in his life and he glories in it. Of course, this healthy pride is abused, sin comes in and it becomes something evil and selfish. It is the same with pride in country. There is nothing wrong in that. The New Testament does not frown upon or condemn in any way a natural patriotism. It is only when patriotism says, 'My country right or wrong!' that it becomes sinful. God made these units, he ordained them, he brought them into being. We have come into this world in these realms, and we are naturally proud of our position, proud of belonging to our family. So, then, are we proud of the fact that we are the children of God? Is this the greatest thing in our lives? How easy it is to talk about God and about Christianity and about religion, but children, those who are really born anew, 'not of blood, nor of the will of the flesh, nor of the will of man, but of God', oh, they know that has happened to them and they are proud of their position, they glory in it. It is to them the greatest and the most wonderful thing in their lives.

Then my sixth test follows by a logical necessity: it is that there is a desire to know God better. Children like to spend time in the company of their father. They wait for him to come home every night, rush to him, will not leave him, put down their toys, forget all about them, to be with their father. This is instinct; this is nature. And it is true in the spiritual realm. I do not agree with Henry Drummond's argument in his book *Natural Law in the Spiritual World*, but it is true that natural law is to be found in the spiritual realm, and we must apply it to ourselves. Do we desire to know God better? We desire to know great people in this world, do we not? We want this privilege. We talk about it. We boast about it. We spend money in order to get it. We like to be in this 'upper circle', this 'upper ten', or whatever it is. Oh, my dear friends, let us examine ourselves in the light of this law, this natural law. Do we desire to know God better? Do we desire to spend as much time as we can in his presence? Are we prepared to drop other things, and do we forget them, in order to be with him? You know what I mean: you find him in the Bible, you find him in prayer meetings, you find him in the fellowship meetings of Christian people, and you get to know God partly in that way; but then you get to know him on your own and still more directly.

And let me give you one further statement, the seventh test under this heading. We have not exhausted these tests but we will stop at this point. Is there anything that is more thrilling in the life of a child than to have some unusual and special token of love from the parent, to have a word of praise, to have a smile, to have some expression of deep love? There is nothing more thrilling in the experience of a child than just that. There is nothing comparable to it. And there is nothing comparable in the spiritual realm.

Can you say with absolute honesty that the greatest joy in your life, the greatest thrill in your life, if you like, is to have some expression of God's love to you, some manifestation of it, some drawing nearer to God, as it were, some tenderness in the heart, some movement in the spirit, something that tells you that God loves you and you are well pleasing in his sight? Can you say honestly that you would gladly give the whole world and all that it possesses for the smile of God, for some expression of God's tender love to you, telling you that he has loved you with an everlasting love? Is there anything in your experience, anything you have ever heard of or come across or ever known, that is in any way comparable to those moments when God just lets you know that you are one of his children and that he loves you? It is only the child of God who can say that, who is meant to say that and to know it.

God sent his only begotten Son into this world in order that we might no longer have 'the spirit of bondage again to fear', but 'the Spirit of adoption, whereby we cry, Abba, Father' (*Rom.* 8:15)! ∾

17

Our Relationship to the Father:
The Father's Purpose

But as many as received him, to them gave he power to become the sons of God, even to them that believe on his name: which were born, not of blood, nor of the will of the flesh, nor of the will of man, but of God (John 1:12–13).

*H*aving considered how we become the children of God, we are now in the process of examining ourselves to make quite sure that this is true of us. These are not mere theoretical truths, they are not merely matters of interest. God deliver us from any intellectual, mechanical study of the Scriptures. It can be quite useless. It can puff us up with a kind of head knowledge but it will be of no avail to us in our personal experience and in our daily life and living. So it is no use continuing with our study of the Prologue until we are all quite certain that we have this privilege, that we understand what John means when he tells us that God has given us this power, this right, to become the children of God. We have begun to examine ourselves in terms of this great and glorious statement in the Prologue and we are taking it along the lines of the human analogy.

In our last study we saw that first of all we must test ourselves about our relationship to the Son because it is he who gives us this right: you cannot be a child of God until you believe on the name of the only begotten Son of God. Then we went on to consider our relationship to the Father. We looked at this mainly from the subjective standpoint, from the standpoint of our personal relationship with God our Father, our consciousness of this, our love for him, our pride in our position, our desire to know him and our feeling of respect for him. But we have not finished. We start with that because it is the first thing that characterizes the relationship of father and children. But there are other tests that are equally valuable, indeed, that are vital, because there is always the danger of our deluding ourselves. So the larger the number of tests that we can apply to ourselves, the better for us and the safer our position. So now we go on to try out certain consequences that are the inevitable result of our realization of the fact that we are the children of God, and these tests have a more practical nature.

Here, for instance, is a practical test. It is the eighth in our series of tests in connection with our relationship to God our Father. The child always has an interest in the affairs of the parent. That follows logically from the points we were making last time. If we are proud of the relationship and proud of our father, then we will be interested in his affairs. We all know how true this is. And it is equally true in the spiritual realm. So there are certain practical questions that we can ask ourselves – for instance, are we concerned about the name of God and that his name may be made glorious?

We know how proud nations are of their name. We see evidence of that in the world at the present time: the glory of a country, the glory of the name of a country.[1] We want this name to be made glorious. We in this country have known a great deal about this in past centuries, whatever may be the position and the truth today. It is equally true of families. People are proud of the family name and there is nothing that they are not prepared to do for the glory of the name that is theirs, the name of the parent, the name of the founder of a family or of a dynasty.

The Bible makes it plain and clear to us that a longing for the glory of God to be manifest is always a characteristic of the child of God. You find it throughout the Psalms and in many other places in the Old Testament as well as in the New. Take the book of Lamentations, for example. How upset Jeremiah was! But not for himself or his own personal position. What really upset him was that God's name was being

---

[1] Possibly an allusion to President de Gaulle of France's first veto of the U.K.'s application to join the European Economic Community in late January 1963.

blasphemed. The failure of Israel was, in and of itself, something that grieved him but what grieved him above everything else was the fact that God's name had been lowered before the nations of the world; and so he wept. He describes his feelings in a most intimate and yet most powerful and dramatic manner. His eyes were running with tears, he tells us. His heart was melted and broken. And he was in this position, this condition of almost inconsolable grief, because God's name had been besmirched and brought down.

So here is a very good test for us to apply to ourselves in these days. Does it grieve us to see God's name being blasphemed and reviled? Does it hurt us? Christians are not amused by blasphemy; they do not think that that sort of thing is clever. They hate it because it concerns God's most holy name. So they grieve. They cannot help themselves. It is a very good test, therefore, to ask: How do we feel about all this? Are we aware that this is something personal?

Let us go on from that and work it out like this: Do we see that the world and the whole of creation is God's and belongs to him and do we enjoy everything in those terms? What is our view of the world? What is our view of the whole cosmos? The child of God sees it as 'the work of thy [God's] fingers' (*Psa.* 8:3). So when Christians look out upon the world, they look upon it as God's glorious creation, God's handiwork. And as they look at the human race and the whole of history and everything that has ever happened in this world, they see it all in terms of God, and as they consider the human race at the present time, they look out upon it in terms of God. It is God who made man, and not man himself. So man is, as it were, a reflection upon the being and the glory and the majesty of God.

Now all these questions become tests as we apply them to ourselves. What is our view of creation? Are we content to adopt scientific theories that would exclude God and explain it all apart from him? Do we believe it is all the manifestation of some brute force, some inanimate power, or do we see it as something that God has brought into being? Christians, the children of God, see this world as God's estate, God's property, and they delight in it, they glory in it and are interested in it. They do not live for themselves, they do not live selfish lives, but they are concerned about it all because their Father has brought it into being, because it belongs to him and he sustains it.

Then that brings us to something that is still more urgently relevant. What marks out Christian men and women in a particular manner is that they are aware that God has a purpose with respect to this world. And to me, at a time like the present, perhaps one of the most wonderful and delicate tests of all is this awareness of God's purpose with respect to the human race and with respect to the whole world. Now this is something that only the Christian can know. Nobody else believes in it. Even those who may say that they believe in God, if they do not have this particular Christian view, if they do not believe the truth concerning the Son of God, if they are not regenerate, 'born, not of blood, nor of the will of the flesh, nor of the will of man, but of God', then they do not know of God's purpose and do not understand it. And even in the faith, there are many, it seems to me, who are born again and yet have very little knowledge of the purpose of God.

Again, the human analogy will help us to see this quite clearly. The newborn infant does not have much understanding and is not able to think of the affairs of the parent in the way that we are now indicating. When this understanding increases, it is a sign of growth and development. Therefore, I am applying this as a test. Christian men and women – and especially mature Christians – are aware that God has a great purpose with respect to this world and they are concerned about that purpose. They know that they are Christians because of God's purpose. They know that, having made man, and man having fallen, God introduced his great plan and purpose of redemption and of salvation, and they can see this being unfolded in the story of the Scriptures. So they watch the history, and the history that is of real interest to them is not secular history – that is only interesting as it impinges upon and illustrates this other history, which is the history of redemption, the history of salvation, the unfolding purpose of God going on throughout the ages in spite of all opposition and leading to something glorious that is yet to come. And, obviously, God's children cannot help but be tremendously interested in this purpose.

Consider again the human analogy. When a father has some great plan or purpose, he takes the child into his confidence. He knows the child will be interested and will want to know about it, so he speaks of his plan. It is not told to everybody; it is a secret kept within the family. A plan, a purpose, is being put into operation and something wonderful will happen at the end. The child is let into the secret. And that is exactly how the New Testament puts it. It talks about 'the mystery of God', which is this great plan and purpose of redemption. It is a mystery because it is hidden from the world. The apostle puts this perfectly in his first letter to the Corinthians:

But we speak the wisdom of God in a mystery, even the hidden wisdom, which God ordained before the world unto our glory: which none of the princes of this world knew: for had they known it, they would not have crucified the Lord of glory. But as it is written, Eye hath not seen, nor ear heard, neither have entered into the heart of man, the things which God hath prepared for them that love him. But God hath revealed them unto us by his Spirit (1 Cor. 2:7–10).

The wonderful thing is that the secret has been revealed unto us who are children of God. I say again that the world is not aware at all of God's secret purpose, his great plan of recreating the whole cosmos, restoring it to what it was and even something more wonderful than that, peopling it with his own children. That is the purpose, and here it is being unfolded. Now we who are children have had an insight, we know this and we are watching it. That does not mean that we are not interested in any other history, it does not mean that we do not read a newspaper, but it does mean that we are not bound by our newspaper; it means that our hopes are not fixed on what the statesmen are doing.

We know that things may be better for a while and then get worse. It has always been like that. The history of civilization is just up and down, and in the end there is no real advance; back and forth, there it is. We are not surprised at that, nor are we depressed. We do not feel that everything is becoming utterly hopeless. No, no! We see God's independent purpose above all that happens, working in it, through it, influencing it. And, of course, being children and being let into the mystic secret, we are not only fascinated by this, but we are also tremendously concerned about it. So, then, all I am asking is this: Is this something that is thrilling you? Are you a child of God? Well, if you are, you must be very concerned about this great purpose.

Let me divide it up a little – this great teaching in the Bible about the kingdom of God. Our Lord's preaching was mainly about this kingdom. It had been spoken of in the Old Testament, the prophets were concerned about it. Our Lord preaches, the apostles preach, about this kingdom, which 'has come', which 'is coming' and which 'is yet to come'. Or, still more simply, let me put it in terms of the church, for the church is the present form of the kingdom of God. All of us who are children of God are citizens of God's kingdom, the terms are used interchangeably. 'Our conversation [citizenship] is in heaven,' says the apostle Paul (*Phil.* 3:20). Of course! We have been made 'fellowcitizens with the saints, and of the household of God' (*Eph.* 2:19). Both are true. We are children of God but we are also citizens of God's kingdom, and we are members of the church, which is the body of Christ, the present form of the kingdom of God.

The church, then, is the church of the living God, so that we can put this test to ourselves in a very simple and practical way by asking: Are we at all concerned about God's church and God's kingdom? Are we concerned about the state of the church? I do not know a better test of sonship at the present time than just this. Here is God's community, God's people; this kingdom of God is not a visible kingdom but is here in this form at the moment. And, therefore, there is no more sure test of our whole relationship than our interest in, and our concern about, the church of God.

Now you see how this test works itself out. It is a test not only of our relationship, but also of our growth within the relationship. The child, as I say, soon begins to develop a certain interest in the affairs of the father and of the family but as he gets older the concern becomes very much greater and deeper. When still very young, the child is mostly concerned about himself and his own pleasures and happiness and the benefits that he gets from his relationship with his father. There is nothing wrong in that; it is perfectly natural. You do not expect an old head on young shoulders, as we put it. But the point here is that as you grow and mature, then you think less and less about yourself and the benefits that you get and you are more and more concerned about the name, the honour, the glory and the success of God's interests and God's affairs. So the depth of our concern about the Christian church is a very good test of our whole position as children of God. What is our attitude to the church? What is our attitude even to coming here to our services? Is this a place to which you come to get something, or are you interested in the coming, the success, of God's kingdom?

In other words, does it grieve us to see the church of God derided and scorned, ridiculed and blasphemed? That attitude is rampant at the present time. We are in a superior position to Jeremiah. He only looked forward to the coming of Christ and to all these glories. He saw them all in a very distant manner. But you and I are looking back upon them. They have happened, Christ has come, and the Spirit has been poured out in profusion. Jeremiah wept and shed tears and was even ill because he saw Jerusalem reduced to a heap of ruins, sacked by the enemy and the object of ridicule. It grieved this man, he was utterly cast down by it and he wrote his Lamentations. If all that was true of Jeremiah, what about us? Are we grieved about the state of the Christian church? How often do we think about it? How often have we wept for the church? How often have we prayed for her? How often have we prayed for the success of the church because she is the kingdom of God? How often have we asked for God to arise and to pour his blessing upon us?

Now there is no need for me to press the analogy. Children worthy of the name become deeply concerned if they see their father's business affairs going into a kind of decline. They are disturbed and unhappy. They wonder if they can do something. This is an inevitable reaction. And how much greater should be the concern of the children of God. They must be concerned about the success and extension of God's kingdom. They must be interested in every enterprise, therefore, that is calculated to extend this kingdom, to make it known, to make the gospel known. The level of their concern about the church, about the missionary enterprise of the church, the expansion of the church, the spreading of the good news of salvation, is a very good test, always, of their relationship to the Father.

Now what hope is there until you and I are clear about these things? It is all a part of our sonship. The danger is always that we are interested in the benefits of Christianity, the benefits of salvation. Yes, but they are benefits that are given to children and it is only as we really function as children that we have a right to expect these special blessings. It is no use saying that you are a child of God if you are not giving some evidence of it and I know of no better evidence at the present time than real grief because of the state of the Christian church, and a yearning and a pleading with God and a longing for revival, a longing to see the old estate, which is almost in ruins, rehabilitated, set upon its feet again, made mighty and strong and powerful. How easy it is to take a theoretical view of sonship. But sonship is something that is real.

And then, finally under this heading, the children of God always look forward with longing to the final triumph, the final consummation. If we really know anything about the purpose of God, oh, we know that there is a glorious day coming – the whole Bible points to it, looks forward to it. God's plan, God's purpose, God's kingdom, will finally come in a visible, external manner, and Christ shall reign from shore to shore and from pole to pole. It is a glorious day! God will be over all! He will be all and in all! The glory that is coming! Now you cannot be a child of God and be indifferent to that – it would be unnatural. At any rate, it is a very poor child who is simply interested in present enjoyments and has not this great interest in, and concern about, the whole – the plan, the purpose, the affairs of the Father.

So let me give you a final word about this. Our Lord, at the age of twelve, had been taken up to Jerusalem by his mother Mary and by Joseph. When they were on their way back, Mary and Joseph suddenly found that Jesus was not with them. He was missing and they could not find him. So they returned to Jerusalem and they found him in the temple reasoning and arguing and confuting the doctors of the law. Mary upbraided him for not having gone with them, and his reply was: 'Wist ye not that I must be about my Father's business?', which means, 'the things of my Father', his heavenly Father (*Luke* 2:49). He was concerned about the things of the kingdom; at the age of twelve, he was reasoning and arguing about them. We who are the children of God by adoption, by this new birth, must inevitably have the same interest and the same concern.

My dear friends, to what extent are you concerned about the things of your heavenly Father? How often do you think about them? Do you only think about them on Sunday, or do you think about them every day? Do you meditate upon these things? Do you pray about them? Do you read the Bible in order to have greater understanding? These questions are important not merely from the standpoint of your own enjoyment but because this is how you will be judged in eternity. Can there be anything more terrible for a Christian than to arrive in the glory and find that for the whole time he had been here in this life he had never grown but had just been a selfish little child, almost an infant, thinking only of himself and his own pleasures and his own interests and never of the affairs of his Father? This is a very deep test of our whole relationship to God as his children.

We sing:

> *Thy kingdom come, O God,*
> *Thy rule, O Christ, begin.*
>
> Lewis Hensley

But do we sing those words honestly? As you live in this evil world and see the blasphemy and the godlessness and all the arrogance and evil round and about you, do you not sometimes say, 'Oh, that he would come and end it all and destroy his enemies and set up his glorious kingdom of light and truth and beauty and joy and holiness!'? Do you know something about this longing? Do you understand John as he ends the book of Revelation with the words, 'Even so, come, Lord Jesus'? Christians, you see, are not merely disgusted at the evil that is rampant round and about them, they long for this great Day. It will come and the children are filled with anticipations of glory because they know that their Father shall be over all, and all his enemies shall be consigned to a final perdition. They must rejoice in the thought of it. They must look forward to it with eager anticipation.

The next test of our relationship to the Father, the ninth – and all these are linked to one another, of course – is the desire to please him. And, again, here is something that grows as we grow. The desire to please increases as the child grows and develops. That is the mark, is it not, of growth: from pure self-centredness and selfishness and the desire to have things and to have things done to us, to a concern about others. The realization of benefits received immediately leads to the desire to thank our fathers, and we show that by pleasing them. And, of course, in terms of our relationship to God, that becomes a question of keeping his commandments.

Now I indicated last time that there is no better exposition of this whole subject than the First Epistle of John. There these tests of our relationship to God are stated and brought together in a most wonderful manner. They are the tests of life, they are the tests of whether or not we are truly the children of God. And John tells us: 'For this is the love of God, that we keep his commandments: and his commandments are not grievous. For whatsoever is born of God overcometh the world: and this is the victory that overcometh the world, even our faith' (*1 John* 5:3–4). John is emphasizing that God's children rejoice in the commandments of God; they are truly joyful in the performance of them.

Again, here is a very deep and subtle test of our position. There are people who 'admire' the commandments of God, recognizing that they are good social enactments. I have heard Moses described as 'the first minister of health'. There is a great deal of truth in that. The commandments are wonderful looked at even from that standpoint. There are people who admire the morality and the teaching of the Sermon on the Mount. They say it is very good for society and they would like to impose it upon society. Nevertheless, to the natural man, keeping God's law is grievous, a burden to be borne, something that goes against the grain. He feels that God's commandments are prohibitive and restricting and restraining. The law is a collection of vetoes, he says.

But according to the teaching here, the characteristic of the children of God is that they do not find his law grievous. Why not? Well, because Christians are born again; they have a new disposition; they see everything in an entirely new way. To them, keeping God's law is no longer a matter of duty but is now a matter of pleasing their Father. I need not keep you with this. I think the analogy makes the point perfectly. The moment you realize the relationship, the moment the element of love comes in, duty goes out the window. You can be very correct in a matter of duty but that is very different from love. You do not force yourself to do things when love is in control. You delight in doing them, you wish you had more to do. That is the whole relationship of the child to the commandments of God.

I can sum it up very easily. Do you still feel that Christianity is rather narrow? If you do, you are not a child of God. It is inconceivable that the children of God should regard God's law as narrow. Because they are children, they must hate sin. They now see sin as that which entered into God's perfect universe and brought calamity upon it. They see it as rebellion, as hatred of God, and therefore they must hate it. 'Ye that love the LORD, hate evil,' says the Psalmist (*Psa.* 97:10). That is a wonderful bit of logic: if you love the Lord, it follows that you must hate evil. If you still feel that, well, it is probably better to be a Christian, it is probably right to go to church on a Sunday morning – if that is your attitude, and sometimes you really wish that you had never heard of Christianity, but there it is, you are afraid not to keep its commands and you are hoping it is somehow going to help you – then, my dear friends, you are in almost the opposite condition to that of a child. You are being forced by a fear, by some kind of law and legalism. That is not Christianity!

The Christian says, with the Psalmist, 'O how love I thy law!' (*Psa.* 119:97). There is nothing grievous to Christian men and women about the commandments of God. They see that these commandments are absolutely, essentially right, that they are a reflection of God himself, and Christians want to be like God. They do not have to lash themselves into keeping his law; they do not feel that they are making a great sacrifice. Those who feel they are making a sacrifice by worshipping God, or by coming to his house, or reading his Bible, or living the Christian life are not Christians at all. They are deluding themselves. They have a bit of morality, which they talk about in Christian terms. In Christianity there is a liberty. There is an abandon. There is love. There is rejoicing.

Do you enjoy worshipping God, my friends? Do you enjoy doing everything you can to please him? Is it your supreme delight to hear and obey his dictates? These are the tests of a childlike relationship. To Christians, God is no longer just a stern lawgiver. He has become their Father who loves them with an everlasting love and sent his only begotten Son into the world to die for them and to make them his children. John has put it all for us: 'There is no fear in love; but perfect love casteth out fear: because fear hath torment. He that feareth is not made perfect in love' (1 John 4:18). And again: 'If a man say, I love God, and hateth his brother, he is a liar: for he that loveth not his brother whom he hath seen, how can he love God whom he hath not seen?' (1 John 4:20). What is our attitude, therefore, and our relationship to the commandments of God at this moment? Are we striving to keep them because we are afraid of what will happen to us if we do not? Oh, that is that craven fear, the fear that has torment, of which John speaks, which perfect love casts out. That is not 'reverence and godly fear'! I will put it all in a question: Are you enjoying your Christianity? Are you enjoying your Christian life? Are you enjoying your strivings after holiness? This enjoyment is inevitable in the child who is anxious to please the Father and to promote his interests.

Let me put the negative side of that as my tenth test – and, again, John does this in his first epistle. The Christian is someone who does not continue in sin. Now here is very profound teaching. We are told today that people do not like sloppy sentiment, that they like plain speaking. Well, here it is: 'If we say that we have fellowship with him' – who John has just described as 'light', 'God is light, and in him is no darkness at all' (1 John 1:5) – 'and walk in darkness' – well, there is only one thing to say about us – 'we lie, and do not the truth' (1 John 1:6). You cannot mix light and darkness, you cannot mix God and Belial, and if you say that you are a believer in Christ, that you are rejoicing in being a child of God, when your life is still that old life of darkness, then there is only one thing to say about you: not only are you not a Christian, but you are a liar!

You notice how the New Testament writers keep on emphasizing the teaching that they give. They know us so well! It is not enough to tell us a thing once, we will soon forget it. So in chapter 2 of his first epistle, John repeats the point he has just made: 'He that saith, I know him, and keepeth not his commandments, is a liar, and the truth is not in him' (*1 John* 2:4). This does not need any demonstration. A man who claims that he is a Christian, that he is changed and is born of God and knows God, yet, at the same time, is not keeping God's commandments, is just a barefaced liar. There is no truth in him at all. The devil is clever and he sometimes persuades people that they are Christians. He can give you a bogus experience, he can create feelings within you, he can make you say the right things, but the test is: Have you got a new nature? Have you got a new disposition? Are you like the Father? Do you love the Father? Are you concerned about the Father's interests? Is it your supreme delight to please the Father? If it is, you cannot go on walking in darkness; it is impossible.

Well, I have anticipated what John says. Listen to this: 'Little children, let no man deceive you . . .' (*1 John* 3:7). There were false teachers deceiving the early Christians. There have always been people who have a scaled-down kind of Christianity, which gives you everything for nothing and makes no demands at all upon you, which is all very nice and happy and comfortable. 'Let no man deceive you'! There is a false representation of Christianity that has always troubled the church – the short cuts. The cults are experts at it, of course, and it tends to come into the Christian church: everything made easy.

Let no man deceive you: he that doeth righteousness is righteous, even as he is righteous. He that committeth sin is of the devil; for the devil sinneth from the beginning. For this purpose the Son of God was manifested, that he might destroy the works of the devil. Whosoever is born of God doth not commit sin; for his seed remaineth in him: and he cannot sin, because he is born of God. In this the children of God are manifest, and the children of the devil: whosoever doeth not righteousness is not of God . . . (1 John 3:7–10).

Now, then, what does that mean? 'He that doeth righteousness', John says, does it because he is righteous, because he has this righteous nature, even as God is righteous. 'He that committeth sin' – well, he is proving that he is of the devil, 'for the devil sinneth from the beginning'. Now, John says, 'For this purpose the Son of God was manifested' – here it is, we are back again in the Prologue. Here is the great announcement. 'In the beginning was the Word, and the Word was with God, and the Word was God . . . And the Word was made flesh, and dwelt among us' – what for? Here is the answer: 'that he might destroy the works of the devil'. Undo them, get rid of them. Therefore, John says, 'Whosoever is born of God doth not commit sin; for his seed remaineth in him: and he cannot sin, because he is born of God.' Now what does that mean?

It is quite obvious, is it not, that John is not saying that if we sin at all or at any time, we are not Christians. If he were saying that, there would not be a single Christian and there would never have been a Christian. There has never yet been a man or woman who has not sinned. John has already told us that in verse 8 of the first chapter of this epistle: 'If we say that we have no sin, we deceive ourselves, and the truth is not in us.' No, in these verses, the present continuous tense of the Greek verbs makes the meaning perfectly clear. John is saying that Christians are men and women who do not go on committing sin or living a life of sin, whereas anyone who goes on living a life of sin is 'of the devil' (verse 8). Before people become Christians, before they are born of God, they live in sin, they are immersed in sin and they never get out of it. They may extricate themselves up to a certain point but they are still in the bog, they abide in sin. But when they become Christians, they are taken right out of that and are put into a new realm, into the kingdom of God. Now they may fall in that kingdom of God, they may fall into sin, yes, but it does not mean that they go back into the kingdom of sin, they do not lie down in sin, they are not immersed in sin – that is what John is saying.

I remember once trying to illustrate this point by putting it in terms of two graphs. Imagine two lines. Here is the moral man, here is his line, which is his basic life. Sometimes, as the result of a great effort, or of an illness, or somebody dying, he tries to pull himself together and instead of continuing on his basic line he rises a little bit above it for a while, but then back he goes again. His whole life is something like that. A little bit better at times, but back he falls; the basic line is down here. What of Christian men and women? What are their lives? Their basic line is up there. Sometimes they fall but then they repent and go back and continue. It is the difference between a low basic line trying to elevate itself, and a line that has been elevated by the Son of God but occasionally falls. That is the interpretation of 1 John 3:7–10.

If you want to know whether you are a Christian or just a moral person trying to make yourself a Christian, here it is. Someone who is not a Christian has spasms of being good and of trying to be good; the Christian is a man or woman who occasionally does wrong. The whole question is: What is the tenor of your life? What is your basic position? Is your life fundamentally a life of holiness? That is the question. These statements by the apostle John make the issue abundantly plain. Because we are children of God, we cannot go on living that life of sin; it is impossible. 'For his seed remaineth in him: and he cannot sin, because he is born of God. In this the children of God are manifest, and the children of the devil.' The Christian simply cannot go on living a sinful, evil life.

Now, then, let me end by putting it like this. You say, 'But I've known Christians who at times have lived sinful lives.' I agree. Such people are what we call backsliders, are they not? How do you tell the difference between a Christian backslider and a man who is merely trying to make himself a Christian? Well, here is the essential test. A backslider must come back. If you tell me you know a man who was born again and seemed to be a bright Christian but lived the remainder of his life after a given point in unrelieved sin, scoffed at the things of God, never came near a church and died like that – I say that that man was never a Christian at all! The backslider, by contrast, however grievously he may fall into sin, never stays in it. He may stay in it for some time but he never ends his life in it. He must come out of it; he cannot help himself. The backslider is a miserable sinner, in this sense – that he does not enjoy sin as he did. He enjoys it in one sense but in another he hates it. He is a man in conflict, he is a man in confusion, and he hates himself for it. He is miserable even when he is apparently enjoying his sin. The 'seed remains in him' and it never fails to bring him back. That must be true, of necessity. Because he is born of God, he will come back, he will be brought back. He cannot 'abide' in a life of sin, whatever may be true of him temporarily.

My friends, I still have not finished our tests but we must leave it at that for now. Oh, may God give us grace to examine ourselves! 'Little children, let no man deceive you'! There is nothing more urgent for every one of us at this moment than to know that we are the children of God. It is urgent not only because of the present, but because of the fact that we are going to die and the glory of eternity is there ahead of us. Let us make certain. Let us not be content merely with words and with statements or anything superficial. Let us *know* beyond any mistake that we are the children of God. Let us, therefore, apply to ourselves the tests that we have been looking at together in this study and prepare ourselves for that which is yet to come. ❧

18

Our Relationship to the Father and to the Spirit

But as many as received him, to them gave he power to become the sons of God, even to them that believe on his name: which were born, not of blood, nor of the will of the flesh, nor of the will of man, but of God (John 1:12–13).

As we continue to consider the great subject of what it means to be children of God, the next step, it seems to me, in this logical and inevitable sequence – and it is a very practical step – is to ask: What do we feel like when we fall into sin? That may strike you as being a strange test but I want to try to show you that it is one of the most valuable and subtle of all the tests. What is our reaction when, very wrongly and inexcusably, we fall into sin? If you again work this out in terms of the human analogy, I think you will find that the following spiritual principles emerge.

First of all, the child of God, when he falls into sin, does not feel that therefore he is lost. That is one of the best tests for differentiating between the true and the false in this matter of our relationship to God as his children. We have seen that the child of God does fall into sin. You remember that John himself says that this happens: 'My little children,' he says, 'these things write I unto you, that ye sin not. And if any man [inadvertently] sin, we have an advocate with the Father, Jesus Christ the righteous' (*1 John* 2:1).Now here is a Christian, here is a man who has fallen into sin. If he is a true child of God, he will not feel that, because he has fallen into sin, he is lost, he is not a Christian at all. If he does feel that he is lost, then it is obvious that he is still trying to justify himself by works, and has not really 'believed in the name of the only begotten Son of God' (*John* 3:18). He is really believing that it is what *he* does that makes him a Christian. So, in a very wonderful way, this test works negatively.

Second, the true child of God is not filled with a mere sense of fear – fear of punishment – because he has sinned. John brings that out towards the end of the fourth chapter of his epistle, where he says, 'Herein is our love made perfect, that we may have boldness in the Day of Judgment: because as he is, so are we in this world.' Then he continues: 'There is no fear in love; but perfect love casteth out fear: because fear hath torment. He that feareth is not made perfect in love' (*1 John* 4:17–18). Now all that follows in a sequence from this: 'And we have known and believed the love that God hath to us. God is love; and he that dwelleth in love dwelleth in God, and God in him' (*1 John* 4:16). John is saying: If you have fear that leads to torment, then you are not a child of God because perfect love casts out that kind of fear. If our main feeling when we fall into sin is fear of judgment, if we feel terror and alarm that we are under the law of God, then it is good presumptive evidence that we are not truly the children of God.

Third, another negative principle that I feel is valuable is this: If your main feeling when you fall into sin is that you have let down your own standard, or spoiled your record, that is again indicative of a wrong relationship. It implies self-centredness, self-concern, and you are back in the position of justifying yourself by your works; and according to the Prologue of John's Gospel, that is to deny everything. The whole of salvation, as we have seen, depends entirely upon the fact that the Word was made flesh and dwelt among us, was crucified, died and was buried, rose again and returned to heaven and is there making intercession for us – salvation is 'believing on the name of the only begotten Son of God'.

But let me put this test in a more positive way. What do children worthy of the name really feel when they have sinned against their father? The feeling is not so much that they have broken a law as that they have sinned against their father. This is a quite different matter, a quite different sensation. The man who is under the law is all along watching himself and what he does. He is trying to accumulate merit. He gives a tick when he has done the right thing and puts a mark against himself when he has not. That is legalism. But the moment one becomes a child of God, one is in a relationship that is personal – a relationship between persons – and no longer in a relationship to a mechanical law. So, immediately, true children of God feel, not that they are lost and that the law is thundering against them and they are once more in condemnation, but that they have interrupted and upset a very personal and intimate relationship with their Father.

That can work itself out like this: they are aware of the fact that they have hurt *love*. It is no longer a matter of transgressing law, but of wounding love, hurting someone who loves us and whom we love – an interruption, a breaking of this wonderful relationship that has been experienced and enjoyed. And that, in turn, leads them to feel, not so much that they are failures, as that they are cads. They feel ashamed of themselves because they have wounded and grieved the one who loved them to such an extent that he sent his only begotten Son into the world for them. They feel ashamed because they have hurt the one who has loved them with an everlasting love. I put it to your own consciousness, your own awareness of human relationships. What a world of difference there is between breaking the law of England and doing something that you know has hurt and grieved someone who loves you and whom you love. The whole realm is different.

Let me sum this up by putting it in the words of David. David had committed terrible sin – murder and adultery – and yet that was not what troubled him or really grieved him, that was not what was breaking his heart. In Psalm 51 we hear him crying out, 'Against thee, thee only, have I sinned, and done this evil in thy sight' (*Psa.* 51:4). That was what David could not get over. That was what, for the moment, he could not forgive himself for. The things David had done were terrible, they were vile, they were inexcusable. But, oh, the most terrible thing was that he had sinned against and wounded the God who had lifted him up and exalted him and made him king. He had sinned against the one who had showered his blessings down upon him and had singled him out in such an amazing manner. That was what David was feeling in the bitterness of his heart as he was repenting. That was why he wrote Psalm 51. This is a very valuable test. What do we really feel like when we fall into sin? Is it this sense – something that we feel at once – of having hurt and wounded and grieved the heart of God our heavenly Father?

But something further emerges at this point and this, again, is wonderful. If you fall into sin, apart from what you feel, what do you do? Do you stop praying? Do you just go out and try to rehabilitate yourself, pull yourself up and try to live a better life, make amends for what you have done – is that what you do? Well, if it is, then you are again under works, you are again under law and you again have an entirely wrong conception of the whole of salvation; you are again not really believing on the name of the Son of God.

What does the child do when he thus transgresses and fails and disobeys and falls into sin against his father and mother? This, to me, is a wonderful thing about this relationship, whether with our parents or with our heavenly Father. There is absolutely no question as to what the child does. This is the mystery of love. What the child does is the exact opposite of what philosophers would expect him to do. The child who has sinned against the parent rushes to the very parent whom he has offended. You would have thought that that would be the last thing he would do, but it is actually the first. Why is this? It is because of this relationship. The child cannot work it out in philosophical terms but he knows that though he has offended that parent who loves him more than anybody else does, that parent who has done more for him than anybody else has, in spite of that, the parent is still prepared to do more for him than anybody else. So the child is in this position: he cannot forgive himself, as it were, but he knows his parent will forgive him, and he returns to that parent.

The classical illustration, of course, is the one our Lord himself painted for us in the parable of the prodigal son. The son has offended against his father, he has wounded and grieved him, and yet when he is in terrible trouble in the 'far country', the thought that comes to him is this: 'I will arise and go to my father' (*Luke* 15:18). The one whom he has offended and grieved above everybody else is the one he goes to. When we sin against God, if we are his children, this is what we know: 'But there is forgiveness with thee, that thou mayest be feared' (*Psa.* 130:4). We do not know that about anybody else but we do know that about God.

There is a great statement of this in the Old Testament, once more in the case of David. David, as the result of the great military success that had come to him, lost his head and was lifted up in pride. So he gave a command to his people to number Israel and Judah. He should not have done that, but he did, and by doing so he grieved and wounded God and sinned against him. So God reprimanded him. God sent his prophet Gad, his servant, to David with the message: 'Thus saith the LORD, I offer thee three things; choose thee one of them, that I may do it unto thee.' David was being given the choice of three different forms of punishment. And Gad said, 'Shall seven years of famine come unto thee in thy land?' That was number one. Or, second and third: 'Wilt thou flee three months before thine enemies, while they pursue thee? or that there be three days' pestilence in thy land?' And David answered, giving proof that he was a child of God, 'I am in a great strait' – which of the three was he going to choose? – 'let us fall now into the hand of the LORD; for his mercies are great: and let me not fall into the hand of man' (2 *Sam.* 24:12–14).

Now there it is, there is no more to be said. David would sooner be in the hands of the almighty God to be punished than in the hands of a man, 'for his mercies are great'. And the child of God instinctively does what David did. Though he knows he is going to suffer, though he knows he will be punished, he nevertheless knows that he is more likely to get love and mercy and compassion and pity at the hands of the God whom he has offended than from anybody else. So he says, 'Let me fall into the hands of God.'

Now I can drive this home by giving you the contrast. The tragedy of Judas was that he did not respond as David did, and that is the final proof that Judas was 'the son of perdition' (*John* 17:12). Judas betrayed his Lord and he sold him, thinking that thereby he would ingratiate himself with the authorities. But he soon discovered that the authorities were only using him to serve their own base ends. They were not interested in Judas. They had got what they wanted out of him. So when he was feeling unhappy, they said, in effect, 'Don't talk to us about that, don't come crying to us, that's your business.' And there he was, left to himself. And Judas went out and hanged himself; and he did that because he was the son of perdition. Do you know what he would have done had he been a child? He would have gone to the one whom he had betrayed, he would have rushed to the Lord Jesus Christ and fallen at his feet and said, 'Oh, I cannot understand what made me do this but I've done it; have mercy on me!' And all would have been well. But he did not act with the instinct of the child, proving that he did not have the heart of the child. He dealt with his grief by himself and he went out and hanged himself.

Now when people who think they are Christians fall into sin, they go out and metaphorically hang themselves, thereby proving that they are not children. And it is as certain as we are here that this is one of the most thorough and subtle tests there is as to whether or not we are children of God. What do you do, what do you feel like, how do you react, when you have sinned against God? I say, if you have the child instinct in you, you will go back to him, you will rush to him and put yourself in his hands. The child always does this and finds strange comfort and peace as he does so.

And that is therefore my last test in connection with our relationship to the Father. The true child is aware, even in and through the rebuke, that there is reconciliation. He recognizes the justice of the rebuke and does not want to defend himself. All he wants is for the relationship to be put right. That is all he is interested in, not his little record! Ah, people who keep records are not Christians. Christians are not interested in records. They are interested in relationships and all they want to know is that everything is all right again. They have felt the rebuke, and may have been punished severely, but they feel the pressure of love surrounding them and they know they are back in the relationship and that even the rebuke and punishment are an expression of love. 'Whom the Lord loveth he chasteneth, and scourgeth every son whom he receiveth' (*Heb.* 12:6).

My dear friends, are you the children of God? Your reaction to your own sin will help you to know whether or not you are; it will tell you at once whether you are under the law or in the love of God. 'The law was given by Moses, but grace and truth came by Jesus Christ.' Are you in this realm of grace? What is your chief concern? Is it your own morality and rectitude and godliness, or is it to enjoy his love, to know he is well pleased with you, to make sure that nothing comes between you and that love, to allow no break in the relationship? This is the ultimate test of love. It is the ultimate test of the relationship of the child to the father.

So we move on to our next main test. We have considered our relationship to the Son, and our relationship to the Father, and so, of course, inevitably, we now come to our relationship to the Holy Spirit, because our relationship to God is a relationship to the three Persons. Christianity is Trinitarian – God the Father, God the Son, God the Holy Spirit – and you cannot be related to one without being related to the others also. 'He that honoureth not the Son honoureth not the Father which hath sent him,' says our Lord (*John* 5:23). There is one sin that is never forgiven and that is blasphemy against the Holy Spirit (*Matt.* 12:31). So our relationship to the Holy Spirit must be one of our tests of whether or not we are truly the children of God. And, of course, the New Testament is full of this. 'As many as are led by the Spirit of God, they are the sons of God', is the apostle Paul's statement of this principle (*Rom.* 8:14).

Are you led by the Spirit of God? That is the question. So you must determine what that means, must you not? There is nothing more comforting, more reassuring, than to know exactly what it means to be led by the Spirit of God! If you are, then you know you are a child of God. You will never have assurance if you do not know your Bible, if you do not understand its meaning, if you do not dig into the depths and get out the treasures. All this builds up assurance and confidence and enables one to rejoice and to function truly as a Christian.

A very good test of whether or not you are a child of God is whether or not you are aware that the Spirit of God is within you. Again, I quote the apostle Paul: 'You are not in the flesh, but in the Spirit, if so be that the Spirit of God dwell in you. Now if any man have not the Spirit of Christ, he is none of his' (*Rom.* 8:9). Or take it in the way in which John puts it in his first epistle. He says in 1 John 3:24: 'And hereby we know that he abideth in us, by the Spirit which he hath given us.' That is the answer and there is no need to say any more. It is there also in 1 John 4:13: 'Hereby know we that we dwell in him, and he in us, because he hath given us of his Spirit.' Has he given you his Spirit?

'But,' you say, 'I believe in the Lord Jesus Christ, I've always believed.'

Yes, but, 'the devils also believe, and tremble' (*James* 2:19). There is such a thing as giving an intellectual assent to a number of propositions. There is such a thing as 'believism', as 'fideism'. This has troubled the life of the Christian church from the very beginning. John says in that first epistle that there were certain people who used to be among the believers and, he says, 'They went out from us, but they were not of us; for if they had been of us, they would no doubt have continued with us: but they went out, that it might be made manifest that they were not all of us' (*1 John* 2:19). They had been accepted in the Christian church, they had subscribed to the right statements – you could not belong to the early church without making a verbal confession of faith – but they had not really belonged, says John, for if they had, they would have stayed. In reality, they belonged to the antichrists, these false teachers. But the point is that they had, at one time, said the right things. So what you say is not a sufficient test. It is the test with which you begin but it is not enough, you must go deeper. Because of the false spirits, because of the antichrists, you need to test and to prove the spirits. Not every spirit is of God, John says. 'Believe not every spirit, but try the spirits, whether they are of God' (*1 John* 4:1). There must be a way of testing and of proving the spirits.

Here is a test to apply to ourselves: Do we know that God has given us his Spirit? Is the Spirit of Christ in us? For if the Spirit of Christ is not in us, we are none of his. What does this mean? I can put it like this. At its minimum, it is an awareness of something in us that is not ourselves; it is the awareness of Another. It is a consciousness that we are what we are not because of our effort, not because of our will, not because of our determination – oh, but because of this Other! I put it at its lowest. I am going to borrow those words of Wordsworth again. I know he did not mean this, but I am going to adapt his words:

> *And I have felt*
> *A presence that disturbs me with the joy*
> *Of elevated thought . . .*

> From 'Lines composed a few miles
> above Tintern Abbey', 1798.

That is it! The Christian is aware that there is always Another – a 'Presence'!

But let me take it to a higher level. The apostle Paul puts it like this: 'I live; yet not I, but Christ liveth in me: and the life which I now live in the flesh I live by the faith of the Son of God, who loved me, and gave himself for me' (*Gal.* 2:20). 'I, yet not I' – that is it! It is inevitable in the Christian. You know the presence of the Spirit in you, in other words, partly by knowing, by being aware, that there is a new nature in you. I must not call it a dualism, that is not right, but you are aware that there are these two elements in you. There are the manifestations of that old nature, which is still there, but there is something else – and Someone else. And you are aware that your life is being controlled, that you are what you are by the grace of God! You cannot account for all you are and all you do, you are not in control of yourself, you are not managing the business, as it were. Somebody else is over you and you are aware of him constantly.

Now I want to put that in a way that I find very helpful, and that the writers on the depths of the spiritual life have always emphasized, but about which we have heard so little during the present century – I am referring to what the fathers called 'desertions'. Do you know what I mean by this term? Its meaning is this: at times, Christians have the feeling that they are just left to themselves, that they are alone. They knew this other blessed experience when they were born again 'not of blood, nor of the will of the flesh, nor of the will of man, but of God'; then they knew this Other, this Presence. The Spirit had been given to them, the Spirit of Christ was in them. But they now feel that they are alone, that the Other seems to have left them. The Puritan writers used to write a great deal about desertions because they were pastors and because they were physicians of the soul and people came to them and said, 'Where is the blessedness I knew when first I saw the Lord?'[1] They said, 'I've no longer got it. I feel bereft, left to myself. I knew – I no longer know. I'm uncertain, unhappy.'

Now all I am trying to say is that it is only the child of God who can ever go through the experience of desertion. Non-Christians, obviously, cannot speak like this because the Spirit has never been in them. They have always been themselves; they have always been self-contained. They have always been in control and have never known this Other. Anybody who knows anything about desertion is a child of God. It is a strange sort of comfort, is it not, but it is a very wonderful one. It is inevitable in this relationship of love. The slightest cloud interrupts the relationship of love, and it is only true lovers who can know the heartache of something coming between them and the one they love. Someone who has never been in love does not know what it means to be lovesick!

Desertions! You are aware of a kind of interruption; you are aware that you have been left. Look at that little child. There is nothing that so breaks his heart as that his father or mother will not look at him. You have seen the child – you have done it yourself – clinging to his father or mother, trying to pull his parent's face round. There is nothing more terrible than the averted face, it is a kind of desertion, and the child feels that more than anything. It is the worst form of punishment. Physical punishment is nothing, it is almost an enjoyment by contrast with that! It is this refusal of your parent to look at you, your parent's determination to have nothing to do with you, as it were – that is what kills love. So the consciousness and feeling of desertion is in and of itself a proof of the fact that you are a child of God.

I will put it like this: if you are troubled about your relationship, if you are querying in a bitterness of soul whether you really are a child of God, I say that that in itself is very powerful presumptive evidence that you are. The self-righteous person never worries about it. He is all

[1] From the hymn, 'O for a closer walk with God' by William Cowper.

right; he is paying his twenty shillings in the pound. He has done no wrong and does not need anything. He is like the Pharisee who says, 'God, I thank thee that I am as I am, and I'm not like this tax-collector.' He does not know anything about desertions.

Let us go on to another test: the presence of the Holy Spirit in a life always leads to an understanding. John puts this clearly, once and for ever and twice over, in the second chapter of his first epistle: 'But ye have an unction from the Holy One, and ye know all things' (*1 John* 2:20). He has just been talking about the antichrists and has said:

Little children, it is the last time: and as ye have heard that antichrist shall come, even now are there many antichrists; whereby we know that it is the last time. They went out from us, but they were not of us; for if they had been of us, they would no doubt have continued with us: but they went out, that they might be made manifest that they were not all of us (1 John 2:18–19).

Would to God they went out of the Christian church today! But, alas, they stay in, and are allowed to stay in. The early church made it intolerable for them to stay. 'But', John says, 'ye have an unction from the Holy One, and ye know all things.' And he repeats this point:

But the anointing which ye have received of him abideth in you, and ye need not that any man teach you: but as the same anointing teacheth you of all things, and is truth, and is no lie, and even as it hath taught you, ye shall abide in him (1 John 2:27).

The 'unction'! The 'anointing' of the Holy One! Here is the test: the child of God understands the truth of God. Let me give you the contrast, the opposite to that. We go to the apostle Paul in 1 Corinthians 2, where it is once and for ever put before us:

The natural man receiveth not the things of the Spirit of God: for they are foolishness unto him: neither can he know them, because they are spiritually discerned (1 Cor. 2:14).

Listen to him!

Which none of the princes of this world knew: for had they known it, they would not have crucified the Lord of glory.

They do not know, they have not seen.

But as it is written, Eye hath not seen, nor ear heard, neither have entered into the heart of man, the things which God hath prepared for them that love him (1 Cor. 2:8–9).

People as they are by nature cannot see them, they do not understand them and say they are rubbish. To them, Christianity just means recognizing the excellence of the teaching of Christ and doing your best to carry it out. No atonement, no Saviour, no need of a rebirth, no need of the coming of the Spirit. They do not believe that. That is doctrine; that is definition. That is what they say, though such people may call themselves Christians. But, you see, says Paul:

God hath revealed them unto us by his Spirit: for the Spirit searcheth all things, yea, the deep things of God . . . Now we have received, not the spirit of the world, but the spirit which is of God; that we might know the things that are freely given to us of God (1 Cor. 2:10, 12).

'Ye have an unction,' says John – you have an anointing. Let me remind you that when John the apostle said that, he was not writing to philosophers, he was not even writing to church leaders. He was writing to very ordinary Christians, most of whom were slaves and serfs, and here he was, handling these great matters – 'That which was from the beginning, which we have heard, which we have seen with our eyes, which we have looked upon, and our hands have handled, of the Word of life' (*1 John* 1:1) – these great Christian doctrines. He is saying: You have the anointing from the Holy One and you know them. These others have gone out, revealing what they were; you are staying in. Why? Well, because you know, you understand, you know the doctrines concerning the incarnation and the virgin birth, this teaching that the antichrists deny while still calling themselves Christians! You know them, says John, the Spirit has revealed them.

What I am trying to say, my dear friends, is this: Do you delight in Christian truth? Do you delight in the doctrines of the Christian faith? Or is 'Jesus', as people call him, only a man to you, only a great teacher and a wonderful example, a man who lived such a good life that he 'achieved divinity', as it is put? Is that your view? Or do you really believe that 'in the beginning was the Word, and the Word was with God, and the Word was God', and that 'the Word was made flesh, and dwelt among us'? Do you delight in these truths? Are these the things by which you live? Do you believe in his miracles, that they are inevitable because he is who and what he is? Do you believe this Word and rest on its authority? The people who have this anointing do not have trouble with the Bible, with either the Old Testament or the New Testament. They see it as one great piece, one pattern, one truth. They rejoice in both the Old and the New Testaments– the unction enables them to see and understand.

Do you have this anointing? It is only the children of God who have it. A man may get up and say pompously, 'Of course, at one time I was a Christian in the accepted sense, but nowadays I no longer accept the doctrines. I've shed all that. I just cling to the ethic.' And the world says, 'A great man'! That was what was said when one such man died not long ago. Such people are utterly inconsistent. You cannot practise the Christian ethic unless you have the Spirit in you; it is impossible.

What I am asking, however, is: Are these Christian doctrines your doctrines? Do you delight in them? Or do you stumble at the virgin birth? Do you stumble at the miracles? Do you stumble at the substitutionary atonement? Do you stumble at the doctrine of the wrath of God upon sin? If you do, well, I do not see that you have any right to regard yourself as a Christian at all. Your idea is probably that Christians are nice, good, moral people who follow Christ by their own will-power and get a certain amount of help from God. But that is antichrist! That is the teaching that ought to be out! The unction, the anointing of the Holy One, leads one into an understanding of this blessed truth. Do you have it? Can you give a reason for the hope that is in you? Can you explain the way of salvation to your neighbour next door who may be dying and does not know what to do nor where to turn? The Christian can; he has the anointing.

Oh, let me put it like this: Do you recognize these antichrists? Do you have discrimination, my friends? These questions have to be asked in days like these. There is a spirit abroad today that says, 'Let a man believe what he likes as long as he calls himself a Christian. Let the Church of Rome preach what she likes, let her call Mary the Co-Redemptrix – what does it matter? We're all Christians together.' Are we? Have we any discrimination? Have we any tests these days? Christians had to have them in the early church; we need them today. Not everything that masquerades under the name of Christian is Christian; it never has been. There are certain things that are specific and definite, and the unction, the anointing, of the Holy One, reveals them to us. Do you believe every spirit? Do you say, 'Well, I know the man says things, perhaps, that he shouldn't say, but, after all, he's a very nice man, look at his spirit. I've never known a kinder man.' Do you say that sort of thing? If you do, you have not received the anointing. There are many nice people in the world who are bitter opponents of Christianity. So do you have this anointing, this unction? The child of God has it, and if we do not, then we had better examine our foundations.

And then, to finish with this particular subject, Christians not only have this general unction that gives them an understanding of the truth and the way of salvation – this is not boasting, *they* have not brought it about; there was a time when they could not see it – not only do they have this general, constant anointing, but – and this is a much greater proof, obviously – they have the special illumination that sometimes comes, that most thrilling and wonderful experience that any Christian can ever have. Certainly, every preacher knows this. Suddenly you come to a word that you have read, perhaps, many times, but the Spirit seems to lift it right off the page and there it opens out before you, and you are given your sermon, or whatever it is. It is all there – given; you have done nothing, you have just been a passive receiver, as it were. The Spirit has illuminated the subject or verse in a special manner, with an unusual clarity. It is only the Spirit who can do that.

I am not talking now of the ordinary unction but of the special anointing, an occasional one, when the Spirit comes and underlines something and says: That is for you! And if ever you have had that, well, go home happily, you are a child of God! You may be distressed at the moment, you may be ill, you may be lacking in growth, you may be taking the wrong food, you may have been slack and indolent – I do not know. But if you have ever had that special illumination, you are a child of God. And if you have ever been a child of God, you are still a child of God and you will always be a child of God. This 'abides', says John. Of course it does! It is inconceivable that God should put his own life into you and then that anybody or anything should take it out of you. It just cannot happen. The child can be temporarily unhappy and disturbed about the relationship but if any of these proofs prove to you that you have ever been a child of God, you are still a child of God.

Rush back to him, thank him, fall at his feet, hold on to him, and he will turn his face back to you and you will be lifted up again and filled with rejoicing as you look into the smile of his holy face. ❧

19

The Leading of the Holy Spirit

But as many as received him, to them gave he power to become the sons of God, even to them that believe on his name: which were born, not of blood, nor of the will of the flesh, nor of the will of man, but of God (John 1:12–13).

As we have been seeing, most of the New Testament is given in order that those who have already believed might have assurance. This is necessary because the devil, our adversary, is always trying to rob us of this joy, always making us look at ourselves instead of the Lord, turning us inwards, keeping us under the law. But, as John has reminded us, 'The law was given by Moses, but grace and truth came by Jesus Christ.' We are no longer under the law, which 'worketh wrath' (*Rom.* 4:15). Or, as the apostle Paul puts it in Romans 8:15: 'Ye have not received the spirit of bondage again to fear' – and that is what we have under the law – 'but ye have received the Spirit of adoption, whereby we cry, Abba, Father.'

So we are trying to show how we can tell for certain whether or not we are the children of God. We began with our relationship to the Lord Jesus Christ. This is the first thing we must be sure of. Do we really believe on the name of the Son of God? Next, we considered our relationship to the Father, and now we have moved on to the third test, which is our relationship to the Holy Spirit, because if we are children of God, we are in a relationship not only to the Son and to the Father, but also to the Holy Spirit.

Now let me explain exactly what I am doing, lest there be any confusion here. My whole case – and we see it unfolded in profusion in the pages of the New Testament – is that there are many, many signs of our being children of God. We have taken the human analogy and have seen that a child has many grounds for knowing that he is the child of his parents, and it is exactly the same in the Christian life. I am therefore giving you a large number of signs or tests so that you may, of necessity, be able to find all these signs in yourself. I am far from suggesting that you should find all these signs and tests present in you in all their fulness, because you will not find that. None of us is perfect. No, I am giving the picture, as it were, of the ideal child. But, thank God, though we may not have reached full maturity, and though we may not be aware of all these things in ourselves in all their fulness, if we are aware of any one of them definitely and certainly, if we are aware of all of them in some degree, however small, then that is enough in and of itself to prove that we are children because an imperfect child is still a child.

Now I am saying all this because I know how ready the devil is to come along and to trip us. These tests that I am putting before you have a double object. The first is that we may examine ourselves because, as we know, it is possible for the devil to delude us into thinking that we are children when we are not. So I am giving you the tests in order that you may know for certain. Yes, but I realize that while I am doing that, the devil may come along, as he does, and twist it to his own advantage. While I am trying to show to those who are not children but think they are, that they have never been children, the devil may use that to shake the faith and confidence of those who truly are children. He will take the picture at its maximum and say, 'You are not like that and therefore you are not a child at all.' I emphasize that the answer is that you need not be perfect to be a child of God, but the vital question is: Are there any evidences in you of the fact that you are a child – however incomplete, inchoate, undeveloped, unworthy in many respects?

Indeed, let me put it like this. You may be very dissatisfied with yourself; that in itself is a good sign. The Pharisee is never dissatisfied; he is the man who steps forward and says, 'God, I thank thee, that I am not as other men are . . . or even as this publican' (*Luke* 18:11). My dear friend, the fact that you are dissatisfied is in itself indicative of the fact that you are a child. Any feeling of unworthiness and dissatisfaction is a very good and healthy sign. So if the devil comes to you and says, 'Ah, well, there are the signs of a child but you have not got them perfectly', you say, 'No, I haven't got them perfectly, that's what worries me, and because I'm worried about it, I'm a child.'

I am giving, I repeat, the largest possible number of tests in order that we may examine ourselves against them. My principle is that these essential characteristics of the child are only found in the child and not in anybody else: this relationship is a particular one. So if you have characteristics of this relationship, however incompletely, you are a child of God. You may be very small, you may be very young, nevertheless, you are a child as certainly and as definitely as the mature, developed, grown-up child.

Now, then, let us proceed. The next test of the relationship of the child to the Holy Spirit is that he or she is aware of being led by the Spirit. 'As many as are led by the Spirit of God, they are the sons of God' (*Rom.* 8:14). That is quite specific, is it not? Notice that in much of the first half of that eighth chapter, the apostle draws a contrast between those who are 'in the Spirit' and those who are 'in the flesh'. That is another way of showing the difference between those who are children of God and those who are not. It is the great distinction. 'The law of the Spirit of life in Christ Jesus hath made me free from the law of sin and death' (*Rom.* 8:2). That is true of every Christian, not merely of some. Every Christian is finished with the law; every Christian has died with Christ to the law. Christians are now in the realm of the Spirit. And so the apostle gives us some of the characteristics of life in the flesh and life in the Spirit, and here is one of them: 'As many as are led by the Spirit of God, they are the sons of God.' Are you led by the Spirit of God? If you are, you can be certain that you are a child of God.

Now it is easy to read these phrases, but we must work them out, we must know that we are led by the Spirit of God. What does this mean? Let me suggest some of the answers. The word 'led' is a strong word; everybody is agreed that it means 'a constraining influence'. That is very important. To be led by the Spirit of God does not just mean that your hand is taken hold of loosely and in a more or less detached manner. No, there is a sense of constraint about this word. So this verse means:

'As many as are aware of the constraining influence of the Spirit, they are the sons of God.'

Again, what do I mean by this 'constraining influence'? I mean a pressure. There is a firmness there. You are aware that the hand is upon your shoulder, as it were. Or take it in terms of someone riding a horse. The horse knows when the master is holding the reins and not some frightened child or servant. There is power in the grip, a constraining influence, a sense of control. So this means, obviously, that we are aware of the companionship and the fellowship of the Holy Spirit. I do not want to stay with this now, I really dealt with it, in passing, last time when I said that Christians are aware, however incompletely, that there is an influence in their lives, a Presence. The New Testament talks a lot about the fellowship, the companionship, of the Holy Spirit. 'The grace of the Lord Jesus Christ, and the love of God, and the communion [the companionship] of the Holy Ghost, be with you all,' says Paul (*2 Cor.* 13:14). So you cannot be led by the Spirit without being aware that he is there, that he is with you and that he is guiding you and leading you.

Now how does the Spirit lead us? It is like this – and do hold in your minds this matter of degree. The pressure can be so slight that you are almost not aware of it, or it can be tremendous and overwhelming, and it can be anything in between. If you are aware of the slightest constraint, the Spirit is there and you are a child of God. But how does this constraint manifest itself? Well, I have divided it up into two main groups: general and particular.

First, there is the general constraint and pressure of the Spirit. We see this in his upbraiding us, in his convicting us. In other words, Christians are aware of the fact that they are not left alone. They are tempted to backslide, they are living in a world that is against them, they are always up against the world and the flesh and the devil. Oh, in this modern world with its newspapers and television and a thousand and one things, how easy it is to fall away, as it were, in mind and in thought! We are all tempted to that, and we may yield to the temptation though we are children of God. But if you are a child of God, you will not be allowed to go on like that. You will be disturbed, you will be upbraided and convicted. You will be annoyed at the conviction, as a child always is. The misbehaving child is having a wonderful time and when suddenly a parent comes in, the child is furious. Of course! But it does not matter, the parent, because he or she is the parent, comes in and disturbs that child.

If you and I are the children of God, the Holy Spirit will come and upset us and spoil the enjoyment and convict us and upbraid us. We may feel recalcitrant, we may feel rebellious, but it does not matter, he will not leave us alone. Why not? Because if you are a child of God, God has chosen you. What has he chosen you for? That you might be 'conformed to the image of his Son' (*Rom.* 8:29). And whether or not you want it at the moment, if you are a child of God, he will bring you there; he will bring you to the place he has designed for you. He has predestinated you to be conformed to the image of his dear Son and if you will not come willingly, then he will make you come. He will chastise you; he will whip you. Sometimes there may be illness and sometimes accident, misfortune, loss of money. He has a thousand and one ways. If you are a child of his, then the Spirit will constrain you. Do you know anything about that?

Now the good moral person knows nothing at all about the Spirit's constraint – there is an absolute division here. Moral people may feel a twinge of conscience now and again, they may feel they are not living up to God's standard, but there is an essential difference. Christians have the sense that this Other, the companion, the Holy Spirit, is dealing with them, convicting them, making them see what they are doing, making them feel ashamed, urging them to repent and to go back to God. He is always doing that.

There, then, is one part of the constraint of the Spirit. And another aspect – and this is very general – is that the Holy Spirit disturbs our lethargy. I suppose the greatest trouble for most of us is lethargy, laziness. The church is full of lazy Christians. Compare the activity of men and women in the business and professional realms or in connection with their enjoyments – contrast all that with the life of the church! Look at the enthusiasm and zeal of people for football and various other sports. They are not put off by the snow. They are not frightened by a little frost. They do not jump at the slightest excuse to remain indoors. Of course not! But look at God's people – lethargic, lazy, indolent. And, thank God, the Holy Spirit disturbs us and shakes us.

Oh, it is a fearful thing to fall into the hands of the living God, my friends. If you are a child of God, believe me, you will not be allowed to get away with your lethargy and your laziness. You are not only depriving yourself of something of the riches of God's grace, you will have to pay in other ways also. Here is all this glorious fulness – how much do we know about it? How ignorant we are! It is because we do not apply ourselves. Thank God that the Spirit does not allow us to remain in that condition; thank God that he disturbs us and rouses us to action. And he will go on disturbing us because he is in us to bring us to the place for which he has designed us. Now I must not stay with the ways in which the Holy Spirit disturbs us; work them out for yourselves. All I am asking is this: Do you know something about this?

But let us come to something a little more specific – the guidance and the companionship of the Holy Spirit. I think this still belongs under the heading of the general constraint of the Spirit.

'But what do you mean by guidance?' asks somebody.

Well, let me give it to you at its maximum, as it were, and then we can see the kind of thing I am talking about and work it out for ourselves on a lower level. We read in Acts:

Now there were in the church that was at Antioch certain prophets and teachers; as Barnabas, and Simeon that was called Niger, and Lucius of Cyrene, and Manaen, which had been brought up with Herod the tetrarch, and Saul. As they ministered to the Lord, and fasted, the Holy Ghost said, Separate me Barnabas and Saul for the work whereunto I have called them (Acts 13:1–2).

Then let us look at another passage in Acts – Acts 15:28. Here is the Council at Jerusalem sending out a message and they do not hesitate to say this: 'For *it seemed good to the Holy Ghost, and to us*, to lay upon you no greater burden than these necessary things.'

What does all this mean? It is, I maintain, a great example of the Spirit guiding and leading. How do you think he did that in those two instances in Acts? There can be no question, it seems to me, that this was not a matter of an audible voice. This is the way the Spirit guides: he puts a pressure upon the mind and upon the heart. He raises an idea and puts it in the centre of the mind and then he arranges that circumstances should be such that everything points in that direction. Do you know anything about that? Are you aware of this pressure of the Spirit in your life? Looking back, can you see it? The non-Christian is not guided like this, he is not aware of being brought to a specific place and position.

Look at the Spirit's guidance in terms of a review of your past life. Look at yourself as you are at this moment. What are you doing here in this church? How have you ever come here? Why are you what you are and not something else that you might so well have been? Why is it? Is it something that *you* have decided? Are you not standing in amazement as you look at your life? And are you not saying to yourself, 'This is God! I've been brought to this!'?

Yes, let me help that still further by putting it in the negative form – the Spirit guides negatively as well as positively. We see an example of that in Acts 16:6–7: 'Now when they had gone' – that is to say, the apostle Paul and his companions, and, remember, it is the *apostle Paul* we are dealing with here – 'throughout Phrygia and the region of Galatia, and were forbidden of the Holy Ghost to preach the word in Asia, after they were come to Mysia, they assayed to go into Bithynia: but the Spirit suffered them not.' Now that is most interesting and, to me, most helpful and most valuable in this matter that is before us. The apostle Paul, as far as he, as a man, was concerned, was obviously anxious to preach the word in Asia. He was on the verge of leaving when the Holy Spirit forbade him. The Spirit not only presses forward, sometimes he holds back.

Oh, I know of nothing that is more wonderful in experience than the restraints of the Holy Spirit, the forbidding of the Holy Spirit, when a man with his mind and his reason, having taken all the factors into consideration, says, 'Well, now, this is the obvious thing to do', but he is not allowed. This may happen in many ways. Here is one of them. Sometimes, with your mind you seem to see the way forward quite clearly and have taken your decision, but then you are aware of some-thing wrong: your heart is not convinced, your heart is not happy. That is the Holy Spirit. And if you are a child of God, you will know it is the Holy Spirit and you will not dare go against him; you will be afraid to do so. When God guides us, he makes us unanimous; when the Spirit is leading, it must be unanimous. And we read in Acts 16 that there was some restraint. The Holy Spirit may also manipulate factors and circumstances so that you cannot do the thing you had planned to do – the two work together.

Then Paul and his company thought they would go and preach in Bithynia: 'They assayed to go into Bithynia' – they made every effort – 'but the Spirit suffered them not' (Acts 16:7). And the Spirit does act in this way. You are aware, therefore, of this conflict. Intellectually, you may be perfectly convinced about something, but your spirit is not – and that is the constraint of the Holy Spirit. So he works both positively and negatively. He puts his pressure upon the mind, he puts his pressure upon the spirit, the feelings, as it were, and in this way he leads us on or he restricts us.

The whole time we are conscious that the Spirit is there, that the Companion is with us, that we are enjoying the fellowship and the companionship of the Holy Spirit, and that we are not living our lives independently, that he has got hold of us. If we are lagging and slack and slow, he just puts that pressure on the shoulder and he braces us up and pushes us on. Or if we are rushing ahead in self-confidence and in a carnal zeal, the hand comes and holds us back and stops us and asks us to think what we are doing. The Spirit does both, but only to the children, because he has been sent to the children. 'The world', said our Lord himself in his last sermon, 'cannot receive [him], because it seeth him not, neither knoweth him' (*John* 14:17). It is only the children who know him.

Are you aware of these things to any extent? Looking at your life, the past and the present, do you see this? Do you say, 'By the grace of God I am what I am' (*1 Cor.* 15:10)? That is another way of saying, 'I am what I am because I am led of the Spirit.' He led me to conviction, he led me to conversion, he led me to belief, he has been leading me ever

since. Here I am at this moment. I am what I am because by the grace
of God the Spirit of God is in me and he is leading me and guiding me;
he is constraining me. I am not my own; I am not living an independent life: 'The life I now live in the flesh I live by the faith of the Son of
God, who loved me, and gave himself for me' (*Gal.* 2:20).

Very well, there it is. I must not wait – I could, but I must go on.
Let me come to the next heading. We have dealt with the constraint
and leading of the Spirit in general, and now I turn to consider this
subject in its particular manifestations because I want to be still more
helpful and practical.

You may say to me, 'Ah, that's all right, this general pressure and
constraint, but I want to be quite sure about this.' So let me give you
some more details. What does the Spirit lead us to, apart from the
great decisions in our lives? There are other things, and here is one
of them. The Spirit of God always leads us to the Bible. It is his book,
and he always leads people to it. He always urges them to go to it
and he gives them a delight in it. If you do not enjoy the Bible at all,
then I make free to suggest that you are not a child of God. Watch
the extremes again – watch the extremes! 'As newborn babes, desire
the sincere milk of the word, that ye may grow thereby' (*1 Pet.* 2:2).
The babe does like the milk but, remember, the child can also be
wayward: the child would like to eat nothing but sweets. Do not pay
too much attention to the judgment of the child. All I am asking is
this: Have you got any taste for the Bible? Do you get enjoyment out
of reading the Bible?

Now let us be still more particular. I am not asking primarily about
intellectual enjoyment because it is possible to have an intellectual
enjoyment of the Bible. I have known people who have had that. It has
simply been their way of doing crossword puzzles. The unregenerate
can take up the Bible as a hobby. It is a wonderful book. There is no
greater intellectual treat than reading and studying the Scriptures
and there are people who hop about the pages of the Bible with their
concordances and their working out of different subjects, while others
get interested in figures, in prophecy and things like that. In contrast
to that, I am talking about spiritual enjoyment.

'What do you mean by spiritual enjoyment?' asks someone. 'How can I tell whether my enjoyment is intellectual or spiritual?'

Well, here is one of the best tests I know. Ask yourself what effect your study of the Bible has had upon you. If it just puffs you up in pride because of your great knowledge and understanding, then you had better examine yourself again. But if it humbles you, if it makes you doubt whether you are a Christian at all, then you have very good evidence that you are a child of God. In other words, when the Spirit leads us to the Bible and when the Spirit is illuminating the page and our minds at the same time, as he does with the child of God, the first thing we are conscious of is that the Bible, after all, is speaking to us.

When we read about the Pharisees, we are not reading about people who lived two thousand years ago, we feel we are reading about ourselves; and when we read about some of these characters in the Old Testament, David and so on, we are not reading a history book, we are reading about ourselves. We say, 'That's me! It's terrible to see that in David but I have that sort of thing in me!' When the Bible speaks to us like that, we are children of God. God never does that with a hypocrite, he never does that with a man or woman who has only an intellectual interest in the Bible. If we feel, therefore, that the Bible is speaking to us about ourselves, speaking to us directly, that it is not merely some general truth or collection of doctrines, but is a living word that is upbraiding us, condemning us, increasing our hunger and thirst – then that is a living, spiritual relationship, which the Holy Spirit alone can produce.

The tragedy of non-Christians is that they can read their Bibles all their lives and be the same at the end as they were at the beginning. I am almost afraid to say something like this, but there is an awful danger in mechanical schemes of Bible study – the danger that you just rush through a set reading in order to say that you have done your portion. My friend, does the Bible speak to you every day? If it does not, I am inclined to suggest that you drop your schemes for a while and just take a verse and begin to think about it and work it out and ask what it is saying to you. We are not meant just to rush through the Bible a given number of times in a year, or however often a reading plan suggests. The Bible is the Word of God. It is the food of the soul. It is the Spirit's message to you. Make certain that it is speaking to you, and if you are aware that it is, then you can be quite sure that you are a child of God.

Another aspect of the Spirit's specific leading is that the Holy Spirit always leads to prayer. It is a part of the work of the Companion. Look at our Lord himself, here in the days of his flesh. The Spirit was not given by measure unto him (*John* 3:34); he had the Spirit in all his fulness – and what was the great characteristic of our Lord's life? It was his prayer life, the time he spent in prayer – though he was the Son of God! The Spirit always urges us, moves us, to prayer. If you read the lives of the saints of God throughout the centuries, you will find that they always testified to the fact that they suddenly felt a desire to pray. They did not know why, they may have been thinking of something quite different, and yet, suddenly, they were disturbed and there was an urge to pray.

Oh, let me put it at its very lowest: if you have this feeling within you that you are not praying enough, that you want to pray more and want to be in more immediate contact with God, that you long to be able to speak to him, almost, as it were, as with a man face to face – that is the work of the Spirit, always. In other words, I am using this test: the more we grow in grace, the more spiritual we become, then the more we enjoy prayer, the more we depend upon it, the more we realize what a privilege it is. But I repeat that any first beginnings of a true, a real desire, are indicative, in and of themselves, of the fact that we are the children of God and that we are being led by the Spirit.

But let me go on and take this a bit further. In Romans 8 Paul makes a wonderful statement: 'Likewise the Spirit also helpeth our infirmities: for we know not what we should pray for as we ought: but the Spirit itself maketh intercession for us with groanings which cannot be uttered' (*Rom.* 8:26). Then Paul tells us the value of this: 'He that searcheth the hearts knoweth what is the mind of the Spirit, because he maketh intercession for the saints according to the will of God' (verse 27). But it is verse 26 that helps us from the particular angle that we are considering: 'The Spirit also helpeth our infirmities'. Now it is children of God Paul is talking about; children of God have infirmities. Do not let the devil make you think that because you have infirmities, you are not a child of God; do not let him make you think that you are not a child at all because you are not a full-grown, fully developed adult child. Not at all! The Spirit helps our *infirmities*.

These New Testament Christians seemed to be very weak Christians, hence their need of the Gospels and the epistles. It was to help and strengthen them, groaning under their trials, that Paul says that 'the Spirit also helpeth our infirmities', and that 'we know not what we should pray for as we ought'. There are circumstances and conditions in which we are so perplexed that we do not know what to do or what to say, and even on our knees before God we feel helpless and do not know what to ask him for. The apostle says: Right, just at that point, because you are a child of God, the Spirit takes charge of the situation and he begins to make intercessions for you. What are these intercessions? In a sense, you do not know, all you can do is groan – 'with groanings which cannot be uttered'. But this, again, is one of the most glorious things about the Christian life, and one of the most wonderful tests as to whether or not we are the children of God.

The little child is in terrible trouble, his little world has collapsed, everything has gone wrong and he is breaking his heart. Suddenly he rushes to his father and his mother and he is so overwrought with his troubles and with his pain and sorrow that he can do nothing but sob and sigh. And he finds tremendous relief in doing so. He knows he is expressing to his father and his mother the depth of his grief; he is not using words – he cannot – he is simply sobbing and groaning. And the children of God know something about this. They still cannot formulate their prayer but sometimes they utter an 'Oh . . !' from the very depths of their beings and there is more meaning in that than in all the words they have ever uttered in all their prayers. This 'Oh . . !' that sighs for God and longs for him and just rushes to him and abandons itself in his arms. This longing, as if to say, 'You know all about me because you are my Father. I cannot tell you, but you know!' 'Groanings which cannot be uttered.' And it is all right. 'He that searcheth the hearts knoweth what is the mind of the Spirit, because he maketh intercession for the saints according to the will of God.'

In other words, though, as it were, you are intellectually in a state of complete confusion, and cannot explain and cannot give your reasons, you are suddenly aware that everything is all right; you are speaking to God, though you cannot express it, and you know that God is hearing you. And that is an absolute proof that you are a child of God. The child next door does not do that with your father or mother. Of course not! That is something that the child only does with his father and mother, nobody else; it belongs to this relationship. And if you know what it is just to sigh and to sob and to long to express your longings, I say that you are a child of God and the Spirit of God is in you. In the depth of your misery you have found more joy in that occasional 'Oh . . . !' than the whole world has ever been able to give you.

Now we must leave it, I am afraid, at that point. We have other things to consider under this heading. The next aspect, God willing, that we will come on to deal with, is the way the Holy Spirit leads us and guides us and constrains us in the matter of our daily life and living. But I have said enough, and more than enough, to convince you of whether or not you are a child of God. Any one of these things that you know to be true should give you certain, absolute knowledge that you are a child of God. Hold on to that one thing. Go to him, thank him, praise his name, and just ask him to give you grace to love him more, and he will hear you. ∾

20

The Spirit and the Word

But as many as received him, to them gave he power to become the sons of God, even to them that believe on his name; which were born, not of blood, nor of the will of the flesh, nor of the will of man, but of God (John 1:12–13).

As I am trying to show, it is most important that we should be certain of the fact that we are the children of God, and we are applying tests in order that we may be clear about this. We have reached the point at which we are considering our relationship to the Holy Spirit. The Christian is related immediately to the three Persons in the blessed Holy Trinity because the three are one. So we are in a very special relationship to the Holy Spirit as well as to the Father and to the Son.

Last time we considered the great theme of the leading of the Spirit, and we divided this subject up into the general and particular ways in which the Spirit leads us. We are now in the process of looking at the particular ways and have seen that the Holy Spirit always leads us to the Bible – to a spiritual rather than an intellectual interest in it. He makes us know that it is the Word of God, the word of life and the food of the soul, the heavenly manna. We saw, too, that the Holy Spirit likewise leads us to prayer and we considered the various ways in which he teaches us to pray.

But now we must move on to yet another particular way in which the Spirit leads us, and that is in the matter of life and living, of practice and behaviour. This is a most important subject. What is perhaps most important of all is that we should realize its connection with everything that we have been saying hitherto. We all like to think of and dwell in the realm of experience; we all like this idea of the Spirit living within us and giving us experiences and feelings and sensations as we read the Bible and pray. But the teaching of the New Testament about the leading of the Spirit does not stop there. The Scripture goes on to tell us that the Spirit equally leads us in the matter of our behaviour, the way in which we actually live.

Our business is to follow the Scripture and to allow it to lead us in all things, and here I want to emphasize the amazing balance in Scripture. We are all prone to pick and choose from the Bible but that is always fatal. We all like to be able to say, 'Lord, Lord', but we must remember that our Lord himself has taught us that it is no use saying, 'Lord, Lord', if we do not do what he tells us, if we do not keep his commandments. We all remember our Lord's picture of the two houses, the one on the rock and the one on the sand, which depicts two types of people. There are those who say, 'Of course we're Christians. We delight in our faith and always enjoy it.' And they build their houses quickly upon the sand, not taking trouble about the foundations. But when the test comes, there is nothing left; all is entirely demolished.

So the teaching of the New Testament about the Holy Spirit leads us on to this most practical and ordinary matter. It says: Yes, the Holy Spirit can give you wonderful experiences, so wonderful that you can scarcely put them into words, but what is your daily life like? How are you actually living? It is all very well to recite your experiences, but what kind of a person are you to live with? What are you like in the mundane affairs of life?

And there, I repeat, we see the extraordinary *balance* of Scripture. It has both these aspects and it stresses the two with equal force. I want now to try to show you the all importance of this balance. In a most extraordinary way, we are provided with a perfect illustration of this very principle by something that is happening in the contemporary world. It is not my practice to preach topical sermons from this pulpit but when something that is happening at the moment does help to illustrate the truth, well, I take advantage of it. I trust that as I do, I may in passing be of some little help to those who may be in considerable perplexity with regard to what they have been reading recently. I refer to the whole question of the Quakers and the report that some of them have produced, since last we met together, with regard to the whole question of morals.

Now this report, which is called, *Toward a Quaker View of Sex*, has astonished many people. They are surprised, for instance, at the things that are said about premarital sex, and sex in the marriage relationship, and also at its stance on sexual perversions, at the way in which these are obviously condoned by the report. It asserts that these are not of necessity wrong and says that if we had a true view of love, our opinion would be very different from the view we now hold. And it is just here that we have a very practical illustration of this great New Testament teaching about the Holy Spirit.

Now let us be clear about this. The Quakers, the members of the Society of Friends, have always been regarded as exceptionally good and moral people – and so they are, so they have been. Quakers do not believe in preaching and teaching in their meetings. They just sit in the quietness and the severity of their buildings and wait for the movement of the Spirit. You may gather together and not a word may be said because nobody has been moved to speak. Quakers say, 'What right have you to speak unless you have had this direct and definite moving and leading of the Spirit?' There has consequently been an idea that they are of all people the most spiritual and enlightened, though they have not encouraged that thought, and, as I said, in the realm of morals and ethics and behaviour they have always been exceptionally honest. It is no wonder, then, that a report like this, coming from such people, has caused great surprise.

But I want to try to show you that we should not be a bit surprised, because this kind of teaching is the inevitable result of the whole position and outlook of Quakers. Let me explain what I mean. What is the essence of their teaching? Well, Quakerism began three hundred years ago, in the seventeenth century. It was started by George Fox, who was without any doubt a most remarkable man, an unusually fine Christian man, and a man, I would not hesitate to say, who was filled with the Spirit. But in his original teaching there were certain wrong tendencies and these very soon became exaggerated and aggravated. In the next century, the problem became quite obvious and continues to this day.

So what is Quaker teaching? In its essence, it is this: Quakers put their emphasis upon what they call 'the inner light', 'the inner witness', or 'the Christ within you'. That is where the Quakers differed from the other Puritans of the seventeenth century and that is how they have differed from everybody else ever since. As well as not believing in preaching or in the exposition of truth, they do not have sacraments, either the Lord's Supper or baptism. Why not? Well, they say that all this does not matter and, indeed, can be very misleading. They say, 'Look at all those people going to their churches and chapels, they are just traditionalists. They have been taught certain things and they repeat them like parrots – but what does it mean to them? Has it entered into their lives? Is it a power in their lives? Of course it isn't. Those people have the letter of the law but nothing else. It's a dead letter and they know nothing about the life of the Spirit. The essence of Christianity is that it's a life, it's spirit, and this is what has been missed by the church throughout the centuries.' And Quakers claim that this is what they rediscovered and recaptured.

So, you see, the teaching of Quakers is really very germane to this matter that we are considering together. But – and this is a serious point – while George Fox and some of the other originators of the Quaker movement believed in the Bible and read it, the tendency soon came in – and it is incipient in George Fox himself – to say that the Bible, after all, was not really very necessary. If you have this inner light, this inner illumination, and if God through the Spirit, the Christ within, speaks to you, then what need is there of a Bible? You are getting a direct revelation, a direct leading, and you do not need this external, this objective, treatment of the truth.

Over the years less and less emphasis was placed upon the Word of God and its teaching, and more and more upon direct illumination. Individual Quakers would argue with Christians who expounded the Scripture and would say: 'I do not care what you say, I *know*. It has been revealed to me, it has come to me, the light has dawned upon me.' So this inner experience was emphasized over and against the Word. And as time passed and you came to the eighteenth and nineteenth centuries, there were those who said that the Bible was not necessary at all. But while not all have gone to that extreme, their essential position today is just this – that the Bible is not really necessary; its chief value is that you have a portrait of 'Jesus', who, they say, had more of the inner light than anybody else. The result is that the Quakers have become increasingly philosophical and today are in a position that we must not hesitate to say is far removed from that of the Christian.

Now let us see what this means, therefore. It shows that the moment you separate the Spirit from the Word, the teaching of his own Word, you are courting disaster and eventually will certainly land up in trouble. (I know that there are people who, by contrast, put all their emphasis upon the Word and do not like any talk about the Spirit. They are equally wrong; but we are dealing at the moment with this particular error that characterizes the Quakers.) The beliefs of the Quakers have led to certain inevitable results. One is that they have gone hopelessly astray in their doctrine. Most of them, by now, are nothing but Unitarians: that is, they no longer believe in the deity of Christ. They say that he was just a great man, a great religious and moral teacher, one who was exceptionally endowed with this inner light and illumination, and, therefore, we can benefit from reading about him and trying to follow him.

Then, having gone wrong on the person of Christ, Quakers have obviously gone wrong in their understanding of his work, his atoning death upon the cross. They do not believe in it, they do not even see any need of it. Believing, as they do, that this inner light is in everybody if people but realized it, they see no need of a rebirth; and because they do not recognize sin as such, there is no need for Christ to bear the punishment of their sins and to die upon the cross. God is love, Quakers say. He has put the spark of spiritual life in everybody and all that is needed is to kindle it into a flame. You do that by becoming passive and stopping all thought, and listening, and the light will come and the voice, as it were, will begin to speak and you will be led out into the truth. All that is needed is to give this spark that is in us, the light that is already there, an opportunity to do its own work within us.

Judged from the standpoint of biblical teaching and orthodox Christianity, Quakers are complete deniers of the truth. And that is what people do not realize in these evil days in which we find ourselves. The argument is: 'But Quakers are such good people! Look at the way they suffer, look at all that they've organized during wars, their ambulance units and the work they've done with refugees and people who are starving. Look at their good works!' Of course, when you say that, you are revealing that you are not a Christian either, because you are suggesting that what makes someone a Christian is good works. So you have no atonement and you do not need the new birth. That is the whole fallacy! But I am trying to show you that the moment you say that the Spirit alone is enough and you do not need the Word and its teaching, inevitably you must go astray in your doctrine. For years that has been the truth concerning Quakers. They are nothing, I repeat, but Unitarians.

But we must go further, and this is what is now becoming so interesting and so obvious. The next step is that you begin to go wrong in your practice. You cannot separate doctrine and practice. 'Evil communications corrupt good manners,' says the apostle Paul (*1 Cor.* 15:33). That is why he was fighting with the Corinthians over the doctrine of the literal, physical resurrection of the Lord Jesus Christ. They were beginning to listen to teachers who said, 'It does not matter whether he rose literally from the grave or not. We have the Spirit still, we have his teaching – so what does the doctrine of the resurrection matter?'

The doctrine does matter, says Paul. 'If Christ be not risen, then is our preaching vain, and your faith is also vain . . . ye are yet in your sins' (*1 Cor.* 15:14, 17). Paul says: No! The resurrection is absolutely necessary! Do not say that doctrine does not matter. 'Evil communications corrupt good manners.' Ungodliness always leads to unrighteousness – as the whole world is showing at the present time. And – and this is what is most interesting – Quakers, who have always been praised for their ethical, moral living, are at last beginning to show the truth of Paul's words to the Corinthians, for now they are telling us, in this teaching, that they have gone wrong in their practice. They are definitely allowing and condoning premarital experiences of sex; they are trying to justify adultery in certain circumstances; and they are putting up a defence of homosexuality. I know that it is not true of all Quakers, but those who have issued this report are considered to be among their best leaders. I do not apologize for mentioning these things from the pulpit. You are reading about them in your newspapers, you are hearing about them on the television. It is time the Christian church spoke about these matters.

'What is wrong with this report?' you ask.

Well, in the first instance, on the three issues I have just mentioned, the writers are plainly and blatantly and openly denying biblical teaching. The Bible is perfectly clear on these points; it condemns all three. Where does the biblical teaching come from? It comes from God. 'All scripture is given by inspiration of God, and is profitable for doctrine, for reproof, for correction, for instruction in righteousness,' says the apostle Paul to Timothy (*2 Tim.* 3:16), and that is the view that all the apostles took of the Old Testament. It is the view that our Lord himself took. He describes it as 'the word of God', and he says 'the scripture cannot be broken' (*John* 10:35) – and it is that very teaching that condemns fornication, adultery and homosexual perversions. In the Old Testament, adultery and sexual perversions were punished by death, and nothing short of death. But these people, with their modern ideas, modern thinking and modern understanding, do not hesitate to say that the biblical teaching is wrong, that it is antiquated, behind the times, and we must be delivered from it. It is legalism, they say, and not love; it puts chastity in place of love, and so on.

Now the first answer to that is, as we have seen, that these views are a blank, blatant denial of explicit, oft-repeated, biblical teaching. I do trust that you are following me in the principle. The Quakers have arrived at their position for this one reason: they are going only on what they call 'the inner light', and are not checking it by the Word. They are putting all the emphasis upon one and not keeping the balance by putting an equal emphasis upon the other. You trust your own feeling, your own understanding, your own enlightenment more than the objective Word of God.

It is not our business at this point to go into any defence of the Bible and its teaching on these matters, although that would not be at all difficult. Why does the Bible teach that these things are wrong? It does so because its view of man is that he is not just an animal but is made in the image of God and has a mind and is meant to govern and discipline and restrain himself. He is not some creature living in the farmyard, still less the jungle. The thing that differentiates a human being from an animal is that a human being can exercise control and restraint. The biblical teaching is based upon the dignity of man's being. It says that marriage, man and woman, is ordained by God: 'They twain shall be one flesh' (*Matt.* 19:5). Marriage is the fundamental unit, it is the only thing that safeguards the sanctity of the family and the interests of children. Then, with regard to homosexual perversion, surely no argument is necessary. Nature itself cries out in protest that the thing is wrong, that it is a violation of what is seen right through the whole realm of nature. And yet these people are justifying it.

But, to us, the serious matter is that Quakers are brushing aside the Word of God so that there is no objective standard. A committee of enlightened people sit together and they wait for the leading – and there it is, and therefore it must be right. You cannot check it by anything. They do not know that there are evil spirits and that you must prove and try and test the spirits 'whether they are of God' (*1 John* 4:1). Modern enlightenment, modern understanding! So there we find these people violating, in this arrogant manner, the plain, unvarnished teaching of Scripture.

But it does not stop at that. These unbalanced views lead to an entirely wrong view of love. The report puts it all in terms of love, of course, this wonderful feeling that the ordinary person among us does not understand. You have to be one of these perverts to understand love, you have to be one of these esoteric, literary people, and then you will have a beautiful notion of love, which allows you to trample upon all the sanctities. The rest of us are not aware of the beauty of all these relationships.

But there is a very simple answer to all this. The Bible talks about three kinds of 'love'. One of them it calls *eros*, which is animal, physical. It is in all of us, of course; God put it there. There is nothing wrong in it, in and of itself. But then there is another kind of love, which rises to a higher level, the kind of love that we normally denote as friendship.

The Greek word for this love is *philia*. This love is not as physical and primitive and elemental as *eros*; it is a kind of soulish attachment and understanding of one another.

Then the New Testament uses the word *agape* to describe God's love to man and the love that man becomes capable of in return. This love is in a different realm altogether from *eros* and *philia*. It is not physical but is the love of God himself, full of benignity, full of purity, full of holiness – God's holy love to human beings. You will find this contrast in the last chapter of John's Gospel. You remember the questions that our Lord put to Peter after his betrayal, when he was with the Lord by the lakeside: 'Lovest thou me more than these?' Peter replies, 'I am very fond of you.' But the question was not whether he was 'fond' but whether he loved (*John* 21:15).

The great apostle Paul, when he is dealing with *agape*, has to write the whole of that thirteenth chapter of the First Epistle to the Corinthians to describe it. He wants to convey to his readers the notion of God's love, so he says, in effect, 'Look here, when I talk about love, I am not thinking of that *eros* of yours, nor even of this other love, *philia*. I am telling you of this great love of God, which must be in your hearts because if you do not have this, it does not matter what you are. You may speak with the tongues of men and of angels, you may do good works and you may have faith powerful enough to remove mountains, but it is all of no value unless you have this love. So what is this *agape*? Well, Paul says, it does not boast, it is not self-centred. So what is it like? Then he begins to tell you something about it. And he has to do all that because of the inadequacy of language.

And it is just there, it seems to me, that we have the whole tragedy of the Quaker report. The writers are taking that lowest form, that *eros*, and are trying to elevate it into the supreme position. They really do not understand the biblical teaching about love. That is another consequence of turning your back upon the Bible and trusting to some inner illumination. You are trying to justify everything in terms of your own understanding instead of bringing it into the light of this great and glorious biblical teaching about love. And so in the end the writers of this report have become wrong even about chastity. It is not true to say that the Christian church has put chastity before love! Oh, I know that there have been individual people who have done that. There have been people in the Christian church who, falsely imagining themselves to be true Puritans, have been sheer legalists; I do not think they were Christians at all. They were just moralists. But, generally speaking, the church has never done this.

The church has, however, emphasized the importance of chastity. Why? Well, for this reason – that it is a *test* of love. Ultimately, you tell the difference between *eros* and *agape* by the test of chastity. It is these foolish people who contrast law and love and say they are opposites. I must not go back over this; we dealt with it at great length in connection with verse 17: 'The law was given by Moses, but grace and truth came by Jesus Christ.' As I am trying to show, it is fatal to put them as opposites. They are not! They go together. And the New Testament says this: if the love you talk about is not chaste, then it is not love but is *eros*.

Let me give you my authority for saying this. It is in Romans 13, where the apostle Paul is dealing with this whole matter. He has been handling high doctrine but has now come down to the practicalities of daily life and living. He is telling these people in Rome to obey the powers that be and he says, 'Ye must needs be subject, not only for wrath, but also for conscience sake. For for this cause pay ye tribute also' (*Rom.* 13:5–6). He is saying, in effect, 'You must not say, "We are enlightened people, Christians. We are no longer subject to the law of the land. We need not pay our taxes. We need not be subservient to the powers that be." That is quite wrong. Christianity is not law-lessness. Christianity is not every man a law unto himself.' What is it, then? Well, listen:

Render therefore to all their dues: tribute to whom tribute is due; custom to whom custom; fear to whom fear; honour to whom honour. Owe no man any thing, but to love one another: for he that loveth another hath fulfilled the law (Rom. 13:7–8).

Do not put law and love as contrasts, says Paul. You must not talk about love unless you are keeping the law.

He that loveth another hath fulfilled the law. For this, Thou shalt not commit adultery, Thou shalt not kill, Thou shalt not steal, Thou shalt not bear false witness, Thou shalt not covet; and if there be any other commandment, it is briefly comprehended in this saying, namely, Thou shalt love thy neighbour as thyself. Love worketh no ill to his neighbour: therefore love is the fulfilling of the law (Rom. 13:8–10).

And yet these foolish people say, 'Ah, you mustn't put chastity in the supreme position; love must go there.' Love and law have now become opposites. But, I repeat, the answer is that 'love is the fulfilling of the law'. And if what people today call 'love' does not fulfil the law, it is not love but lust, and they have lost the distinction between *eros* and *agape*. And, of course, this becomes perfectly obvious the moment you work it out in practice.

'Love worketh no ill to his neighbour.' Never! It is always concerned about the good of the neighbour. And that must be worked out in detail. When the love of God is shed abroad in our hearts, we love ourselves truly, and we love others truly. 'The first of all the commandments is . . . Thou shalt love the Lord thy God with all thy heart, and with all thy soul, and with all thy mind, and with all thy strength . . . the second is like, namely this, Thou shalt love thy neighbour as thyself' (*Mark* 12:29–31). That is a good test. You love yourself – you love yourself as a creature of God, not as what you are but as a child of God – and you love your neighbour as yourself. You never work any ill to your neighbour, therefore. You do not consider your own desire only, you do not consider your own lust and its gratification, but you consider the consequences to your neighbour. You respect your neighbour, and whatever you may desire, you will curb it and crush it rather than do any harm to your neighbour. But that is the very attitude that, it seems to me, is being denied at the present time, and it is all being denied in the name of love.

Well, my friends, I have taken you through all this, much as I dislike doing so, in order that I might illustrate this great theme that is before us. Nothing is more fatal than to separate the Spirit from the Word. That has been the whole tragedy of the Quakers from beginning to end. It led to certain excesses at the very beginning; it has continued to do so. And now we have it in this most refined, intellectual, sophisticated manner, which, nevertheless, has revealed the cloven hoof. The Quakers' position, I repeat, is nothing but the logical and inevitable outcome of the fatal dichotomy that they have introduced between the Spirit and the Word of God.

Where did the Word of God come from? It was the Spirit who indited it. 'Prophecy', says Peter in his second epistle, 'came not in old time by the will of man' – it is not of any private interpretation; it is not what a man thinks. Not at all! Scripture was not a man allowing his mind to be led, somehow, vaguely. But – 'holy men of God spake as they were moved by the Holy Ghost' (2 *Pet.* 1:21). The Holy Spirit gave them the revelation, he guided them in the recording and in the writing of it, and here we have it in an objective manner before our eyes. So the apostle Paul says to Timothy: Pay careful attention to this, check everything by the Scriptures, '. . . which are able to make thee wise unto salvation through faith which is in Christ Jesus. All scripture is given by inspiration of God [God breathed], and is profitable for doctrine, for reproof . . .' (2 *Tim.* 3:15–16). It is not what you and I think about the Lord Jesus Christ that matters, but what has been revealed about him. But silly people today are saying, 'I admire Jesus. I like his teaching. I'm going to follow him, and that makes me a Christian.' Well, all right, let them say so, but that is not what the Bible says.

You will never get hold of doctrine unless you submit yourself to this book. Here is the repository of doctrine. We know nothing about doctrine apart from this. Here alone are we given the truth. I may get wonderful ideas – yes, but I know something of church history. I see how the heretics have gone astray. I see how people have fallen into error, even good people, because they began to listen to some inner light instead of checking their ideas by the Word of God. Why did God ever give us the Scriptures? It was in order that we might be safeguarded against the wiles of the devil, that we might be safeguarded against our own 'beautiful thoughts'. Oh, the whole of church history is strewn with the tragedies that followed when men and women divided the Word from the Spirit and ignored that Word and said it did not matter. 'I have had this light. I have had this illumination.'

About twenty-five years ago a book was written on this whole theme. Its original title was *Group Movements of the Past and Experiments in Guidance* and its author is Ray Strachey, who, incidentally, was one of the family of Mrs Hannah Whitall Smith and her husband, who started the Keswick movement.[1] This book gives a factual and strictly historical account of what may be called freak religious movements in America in the nineteenth century. The author writes that various groups arose during this century. How did they come about? Well, a man would simply stand up and say that he had been given some extraordinary light. Let me show you the ridiculous extremes to which these things can go. There was a community known as the Oneida Community, founded and run by a man who had quite a considerable following. This man eventually claimed that he was so filled with the light and with the Spirit that it actually radiated from his body, and the end of his teaching was that if you found difficulty in obtaining this blessing and entering into the same experience, you could get your experience by making physical contact with him. The final result was that men and women would lie in the same bed with this man to receive the blessing that emanated and radiated from his physical body.

'Well,' you may say, 'that's quite fantastic.'

Yes, but that man started as quite an orthodox believer, as the Quakers did, but he departed further and further from the Word until he was not led by the Word at all but by this direct illumination. And so you land up in a position that, to anybody who knows the elements of the Bible, is patently not only wrong and sinful but is even ridiculous.

I have given you one example, but there are many others. There have been movements like this throughout the centuries, including all the cults. They arise and flourish but end in disaster and scandal simply because the whole emphasis is put upon some inner experience. The result is that whatever light they claim to have, is not of God but is of the devil. And here you have this most intellectual and ethical and moral Society, the Quakers, now, at long last, showing the inevitable end at which you arrive when you make an artificial division between

---

[1] This book was published in 1934 by Faber (London). Chapter 7 deals with the Oneida Community.

the Word and the Spirit. So we have them in this appalling position of encouraging people to disobey the Word of God, to break God's holy commandments. And the end of all that will be not only the demoralization of society, it will be the collapse of society in every respect, even politically. But if you keep true to the Word, you cannot follow such teachings. The Word will pull you up. It will condemn you. It will say, 'Thou shalt do this; thou shalt not do that.'

Now, my friends, this was not meant to be an attack upon the Quakers. They are only an illustration. They have stated their views themselves, in public, so I am entitled to reply in public. But I am not interested in Quakerism. What I am interested in is this: that anyone should put all the emphasis on the teaching I have given about the leading of the Spirit, and should begin to object and retract and dislike it when I go on to say that the Spirit also guides us in our morals, in our practical daily life and living. I emphasize again that the Scriptures teach us that it does not matter how well you may know your Scriptures, nor what wonderful light you may have, if you are living a life of sin. 'If we say that we have fellowship with him, and walk in darkness, we lie, and do not the truth' (*1 John* 1:6). Thank God for the balance of the Scriptures, the Spirit and the Word, the Spirit on the Word, the Spirit through the Word. Let us keep our minds and hearts open to it as a whole, omitting nothing. ❧

21

Practical Holiness

But as many as received him, to them gave he power to become the sons of God, even to them that believe on his name; which were born, not of blood, nor of the will of the flesh, nor of the will of man, but of God (John 1:12–13).

We are examining the particular evidence that we can have within ourselves that we are being led by the Spirit of God. We have seen that when the Spirit does lead, certain things inevitably happen. We have found that he leads to the Bible and to prayer – and to certain types of prayer. Then we moved on and said that he also leads us in our conduct and behaviour, and that is the matter we are dealing with at the moment.

Now we had to give the whole of our last study to a general principle with regard to the danger of separating between the Spirit and the Word – a danger that arises the moment we begin to talk about the leading of the Spirit. To illustrate this, we considered the Quakers, who have recently called attention to themselves in a report entitled *Toward a Quaker View of Sex*, and we saw that it is fatal to put a wedge between the Spirit and the Word and to say that you do not need the Word because you are now directly guided and motivated and moved by the Holy Spirit himself. That is a very grievous danger as this striking modern example clearly shows.

And, of course, this danger is not confined to the Quakers. All people in the church today who do not recognize the authority of the Word are in exactly the same position. Unitarians are not confined to that particular body that calls itself the Unitarian Church. Alas, there are Unitarians in every section of the church and they fall into precisely that same error of judging everything by their own reason, or their own intuition, or their own insights, rather than by the plain, objective teaching of the Word of God.

So having established that all-important principle that we are to be guided in conduct and behaviour, in our view of morals and of everything, by the illumination of the Spirit upon the Word and not by modern developments or modern theories, we now come to the more practical aspect of this great subject. There are three general points, it seems to me, that we must further note before we come to the actual details. The first is that this test of our being guided in conduct and behaviour by the Spirit through the Word is one of the most practical tests of all and that is why it is one of the most important. A great danger to the Christian, as we have seen, is antinomianism, which is the belief that it does not matter what I do because when I am saved, I am eternally safe. Antinomianism says that, because I am born again, because I am no longer in Adam, because I am no longer under the law, I am free to live as I like.

Now that is a terrible danger, a danger that is often dealt with in the Scriptures themselves. The apostle Paul was always being accused by his adversaries of being a teacher of antinomianism because he taught so powerfully about the Christian being dead to the law and dead to sin. 'What shall we say then?' he writes. 'Shall we continue in sin, that grace may abound?' (*Rom.* 6:1). He has just said, 'Where sin abounded, grace did much more abound' (*Rom.* 5:20), and people responded by saying that this means that conduct does not matter because the more we sin, the more we shall experience grace. 'God forbid,' replies the apostle (*Rom.* 6:2). It is unthinkable! That is indeed to misunderstand the whole of the teaching of justification by faith only and our incorporation into Christ and the Spirit coming to dwell within us. 'Reckon ye also yourselves to be dead indeed unto sin' (*Rom.* 6:11); 'Being then made free from sin, ye became the servants of righteousness' (*Rom.* 6:18).

So our conduct is a most important test, which is why we do not like it. We would rather dwell in the realm of feelings and experiences. We are like the people depicted by our Lord who said, 'Lord, Lord, have we not prophesied in thy name . . . and in thy name done many wonderful works?' (*Matt.* 7:22). But, my dear friends, I do not care what experiences you have had, if they have not affected your daily life and living, your ethics, your morals, they are not experiences produced by the Holy Spirit. You are not born of God unless there is a change in your whole outlook and attitude towards conduct and behaviour; and unless it is manifesting itself practically, you are not being led by the Spirit but by some false spirit, some evil spirit masquerading as a spirit of light and as the Spirit of God. No, no! As the Spirit and the Word are indissolubly linked and bound together, so are the new birth and new conduct. This test of conduct and of behaviour is therefore, I say again, very practical.

You may say, 'I've never had these exalted feelings that people talk about, I don't know these thrilling experiences of the Spirit, so how can I tell whether or not I'm a Christian?'

You can tell in this way: Has your whole outlook upon life and living changed? If it has, you have good presumptive evidence of the fact that you are a Christian. But we will be looking at that in detail. For now, I am simply laying down this principle that antinomianism is a grievous error. The Christian life is essentially a practical life. It is not *only* a practical life – that is the error of today – but it is a practical life. It is a life that starts in the realm of the Spirit, this 'new birth', but it manifests itself in all the practical details of everyday living.

Our second general point is this: the practical outworking of the life of the Spirit, or life in the Spirit, is meant to be constant in the life and experience of the Christian. 'As many as are led by the Spirit of God, they are the sons of God' (*Rom.* 8:14). Now Paul says here, 'As many as are constantly being led', 'As many as go on being led': he is using the continuous tense. And I do want to emphasize this continuous aspect. Christians are not to be good by fits and starts, they are not to be good only at certain times of the year. There is not a scrap of evidence in the whole of Scripture, for example, for the observance of Lent – none at all! Indeed, I could very easily demonstrate to you that this is diametrically opposed to the teaching of Scripture and is nothing but a human, carnal tradition. There is no need to go any further on this than to read the end of Colossians 2, which puts it all perfectly:

Let no man beguile you of your reward in a voluntary humility and worshipping of angels . . .

But still more specifically:

Wherefore if ye be dead with Christ from the rudiments of the world, why, as though living in the world, are ye subject to ordinances, (Touch not; taste not; handle not; which all are to perish with the using;) after the commandments and doctrines of men? Which things have indeed a shew of wisdom in will worship

– exercising your will power and your discipline –

and humility, and neglecting of the body; not in any honour to the satisfying of the flesh (Col. 2:18, 20–23).

There it is; that is how Paul deals with the whole subject. It looks very wonderful – 'show of wisdom', 'will worship'. During this period of Lent I do not smoke, or I do not drink, or I do not do this, that or the other, and it is marvellous, this period of denying myself. But the answer of the New Testament is this: you are always to do what the Spirit leads you to do. Always! Not only at certain times of the year, not only for certain periods in the calendar of some human-made organization. No, no! This is to be constant; you are always to be led by the Spirit. If it is right to deny yourself during Lent, it is right to deny yourself always.

Here, again, is something that is very subtle. Lent, of course, is a relic of Roman Catholicism. One can easily understand it in such an organization – it gives power to the priest, and so on – but there is, I repeat, no evidence whatsoever in favour of it in the New Testament, and it simply leads to this show of wisdom and human will power. It is people adding their works to the grace of God, and this is essentially Roman Catholic teaching. Well, my friends, let us get rid of this, let us not waste our time with it. We are to be led by the Spirit *always*.

The third general principle is that the leading of the Spirit in this matter of conduct and of behaviour is never mechanical – and this, of course, is a continuation of the previous point. It does not mean conformity to an imposed number of rules and regulations. This, again, is quite a subtle point and is a trap that has often ensnared many

Christian people. It is always easier to live under a rigid law than in the freedom of the Holy Spirit, under his guidance. What we all pray is this: 'Now we have become Christians, what are we to do? What are we not to do?' And we would like to have everything worked out for us – one, two, three! Drill-sergeant Christianity, you might call it. Of course, it is much easier that way. You do not have to think; there are no tensions. But that is not the New Testament. That is typical of the false asceticism that the apostle denounces at the end of the second chapter of the Epistle to the Colossians.

No, the Spirit leads us in the more general manner that Paul goes on to put before us in Colossians chapter 3: 'If ye then be risen with Christ, seek those things which are above, where Christ sitteth on the right hand of God. Set your affection on things above, not on things on the earth' (*Col.* 3:1–2). Now there is your principle. In other words, Paul is saying: Realize what you are and who you are as the children of God. Realize that you now belong to that heavenly realm. Our citizenship is in heaven, not upon earth – very well, set your affections there. You do not just say, 'Now what am I supposed to do here? What am I not to do there?' That is a ready-reckoner view of Christianity and not the Christianity of the New Testament.

No; instead, you say to yourself: 'What am I? I am born "not of blood, nor of the will of the flesh, nor of the will of man, but of God". I belong to Christ and I am a co-heir with him. My home is there!' So you begin in that way. And then you carry out the implications: 'For ye are dead,' Paul says, 'and your life is hid with Christ in God' (*Col.* 3:3). It is theological! You see yourself in Christ! Not a matter of rules and regulations and stipulations – never do this, never do that. No, no! That is all wrong. That is mechanical, that is human, that is an imposed morality. Again, of course, it is the delight of institutional Christianity but it knows nothing about the freedom of the Spirit, nothing about the position of the early Christians.

So instead of telling us thus to conform to a pattern and obey these mechanical notions of morality and ethics and conduct and behaviour, Paul speaks in more general terms: 'When Christ, who is our life, shall appear, then shall ye also appear with him in glory' (*Col.* 3:4). That is the difference in outlook. Not, 'What am I to do now that I'm a Christian?' but, 'I'm a Christian and he is going to appear and I'll see him and will be like him! Very well, what do I do? "Mortify therefore your members which are upon the earth . . ."' (*Col.* 3:5). Paul gives the details in order that we may see how the principle will inevitably work itself out.

Let me summarize that third general principle by putting it like this: If our conduct is not the outcome of our doctrine, if our behaviour is not dictated to us by the fact that we realize who and what we are as the children of God and in Christ, then it is not New Testament ethics and morality but is philosophical morality, human morality. Here is the analysis of every New Testament epistle: you start with your great doctrine and then the writer says, 'Therefore' – and if your conduct and behaviour are not determined by this 'Therefore', by this deduction from the doctrine, you have fallen into a false asceticism. That is not the way the Holy Spirit leads the children of God in their daily conduct and behaviour.

There, then, are the general points that govern this all-important matter of our conduct. But now let us go on to the details, and we do so mainly because in this whole series of sermons we are trying to give comfort to God's people. In the forefront of my mind is not merely the desire to inculcate a certain way of living but to give assurance of salvation. So, as we come to the details, I am concerned that we should examine ourselves in their light and say, 'Well, that's true of me and therefore I'm being led by the Spirit of God. I may not have known great experiences – alas! – but I do know this . . .' Now that is not a criticism of the great experiences. We all ought to have them and we all ought to seek them. It is possible to know God and to know Christ more fully. Do not stop short of that. But you can be a Christian though you are short of that. So I am putting this before you, not that I may fall into the error I have been denouncing, but rather that I may encourage you, as you examine yourself, to find full assurance.

What, then, are these details? How may I know that the Holy Spirit is indeed leading me in this very practical way? Here is my first answer, from the second chapter of the Epistle to the Philippians: 'Wherefore, my beloved, as ye have always obeyed, not as in my presence only, but now much more in my absence, work out your own salvation with fear and trembling. For it is God which worketh in you both to will and to do of his good pleasure' (*Phil.* 2:12–13). Christians are conscious of this fact that God is working in them 'both to will and to do'. It is the Holy Spirit who does that. God works in us, in and through and by the Holy Spirit, and he works in us both to will, to desire, and to do.

To be conscious of the Holy Spirit working within us is, to me, a very wonderful and a very consoling test, and I would add that it is also a very subtle and profound test. We are conscious not only that he is working in us, but often that it is against our own desire. He will not leave us alone. If I may adapt the words of George Matheson here: 'O Love, that wilt not let me go'! There you are as a Christian but you have been enticed by the world and its attractions, its way of living and of thinking and, quite unconsciously, you have been backsliding. You have been going back into that old life. You did not do anything very deliberately but you have just been slipping and sliding. You are beginning to enjoy that life again and you think it is rather wonderful and clever.

But then you are suddenly disturbed, you are pulled up, and begin to feel that this worldly life is wrong. You do not like being disturbed like this – you want to go on enjoying that life. You say, 'Of course I'm a Christian. I believed in Christ and I became a member of a church.' But the Spirit says, 'No, be careful! How can you, as a true Christian, go on doing the things you are now doing?' That is God working within you both to will and to do. The Spirit addresses you and disturbs you. He pulls you up. He upbraids you. He condemns you. He makes you feel guilty. He says, 'This is what you ought to be doing.' And he reminds you of your Christian duties, which you have been neglecting. You have stopped reading the Word. You have stopped praying. You have stopped attending the house of God. 'It is God which worketh in you both to will and to do', and you are rebelling and fighting. And, my dear friend, in all that, you have an absolute proof that you are a Christian! You are not 'dead in trespasses and sins' if that is true of you.

Those who are not believers, who are not born again, do not know this pressure of the Spirit within. They may get what is called 'twinges of conscience' but that is entirely different – they are just looking at their own standard. But here it is, the very definite activity of the Spirit, and you try to get away from him – you go out with your friends, you close your Christian books and you try to listen to this or that in the world. But the Spirit will not let you: it is God working in you, pulling you back, disturbing you, sending some sort of Nathan the prophet to you, as he sent him to David, to put questions to you.

Do you know the working of God in you? Do you now find that you are not allowed to sin with impunity? Do you find that you are not allowed to enjoy a sinful and unworthy life? Are you constantly being pulled up and upbraided and condemned and convicted? That is a sign that you are being led by the Spirit. He does it in the matter of willing and of desiring; he does it in the matter of doing. He provides the desire; he gives the energy. It is all from him. He works in us. That is why we are able to work it out. We could not otherwise, we would have no strength. But being 'born, not of blood, nor of the will of the flesh, nor of the will of man, but of God', we have the Spirit in us. There is energy, and he works within us 'both to will and to do of his good pleasure' (*Phil.* 2:13).

But come to a second point, which is this: the Spirit always leads to self-examination. Self-examination! And throughout the whole year, not only during Lent, not because we have arrived at a certain day – you cannot reconcile that kind of thing with the freedom and liberty of the Spirit that we see in the New Testament. That is how we fool ourselves. And we who set aside the first day of January for self-examination are equally guilty, remember. This is altogether out of the realm of calendars. This is the operation of the Spirit, the work of the Spirit, who always leads us to self-examination.

What does self-examination mean? It means that whoever is led by the Spirit is never glib, never feels that he or she is complete because they say, 'I've believed in Christ.' They never feel that everything has been done and that all they should do now is rest on their oars and they need have no troubles. That is inconceivable under the leading of the Spirit. Why? Because the Spirit's function is to bring us into conformity to the Lord Jesus Christ, the Son of God. The Spirit's work is to carry out the injunction, 'Ye shall be holy: for I the LORD your God am holy' (*Lev.* 19:2). It is at this point that the Spirit safeguards us from an easy believism and the notion that as long as we say we believe in the Lord Jesus Christ we are Christians. But we are not! 'The devils also believe, and tremble' (*James* 2:19). Many people have said that they believe, but their lives have denied it. 'Having a form of godliness, but denying the power thereof' (2 *Tim.* 3:5). The New Testament is full of warnings against what were once called 'false professors' – men and women who make a profession of Christianity and who clearly are not Christians. Our Lord constantly warned against that. The New Testament epistles are equally full of these same solemn warnings. Anyone who is led by the Spirit is afraid of that danger and therefore is never self-satisfied and, above all, is never superficial.

Now here is the great dividing line between the cults, along with a kind of cultic Christianity, and New Testament Christianity. The cults give you all in one act. 'So simple,' they say. 'Nothing to it! Do this and there you are!' Put your coin in the slot, have your fill – everything you want! That is always characteristic of the cults and of a so-called Christianity that is cultic rather than New Testament. New Testament Christianity is always based upon the leading of the Spirit. He is a person, he is the *Holy* Spirit and in his presence the best people feel that they are vile and unworthy and sinful. Those who join the cults feel that as long as they have signed on the dotted line, it is all done, they are all right, they are in. 'No, no,' says the true Christian. 'This is a new birth. I have new life.

Am I aware of this new life? Am I sure of it? 'Examine yourselves, whether ye be in the faith; prove your own selves,' writes the apostle Paul to the church at Corinth (2 *Cor.* 13:5). Peter has exactly the same teaching: 'Make your calling and election sure' (2 *Pet.* 1:10). Do not live on assumptions. Do not be glib. Do not be superficial. Do not feel it is all finished. Oh, just realize what you are as a child of God – and the moment you do that, and begin to examine yourself, you will be dissatisfied, you will feel that you are not right, that what you have done is not enough, that it is unworthy. The Spirit always leads us along that line. You will find, if you trouble to read the literature, that the greatest saints have always spent time in self-examination. Indeed, we can say that their greatest danger was to overdo that and to become introspective and morbid. But that is a much better danger, if I may so put it, than the danger of glibness and superficiality, the danger of not even realizing the possibility of being false. 'Make your calling and election sure': therefore, examine yourself, 'prove your own selves'. It is in the Word. It is exemplified in the lives and practice of the saints.

Let us look at it like this: If you do not know what it is to be afraid that you may be a Laodicean, I do not think you are a Christian. No one with the Spirit leading and guiding can read that letter to the church of the Laodiceans, recorded in Revelation chapter 3, without having a certain amount of fear.

These things saith the Amen, the faithful and true witness, the beginning of the creation of God; I know thy works, that thou art neither cold nor hot

– in other words, you are just respectable and nothing else; you do not like being hot or cold, you like being balanced and dignified and decent and polite –

I would that thou wert cold or hot. So then because thou art lukewarm, and neither cold nor hot, I will spue thee out of my mouth. Because thou sayest, I am rich, and increased with goods, and have need of nothing; and knowest not that thou art wretched, and miserable, and poor, and blind, and naked (Rev. 3:14–17).

This is all spiritual and those who do not realize that this is their condition are in a bad way.

'But,' you say, 'we're all in that condition.'

All I am asking is this: Are you never afraid that you *are* in that condition? Are you one of these people who says, 'I am rich, and increased with goods'? 'I've never had a doubt since I became a Christian. I've never had any trouble at all. I know!' Do you not have any fear about yourself? Listen: 'He that hath an ear, let him hear what the Spirit saith unto the churches' (*Rev.* 3:22). And the Spirit comes to you and says: Look here, are you a Laodicean? Are you quite sure you are not resting on your oars and are not self-satisfied in this bad sense?

It is a very good test, my friend. The Spirit searches! He searches the deep things of God, and he searches the depths of our being and personality. And those who are led by him are those who give him time to do that. He will hold these things before you and there may be times when he will almost make you feel that you are not a Christian at all. But you will know that you are because when you feel utter uncleanness and condemnation, you know that the blood of Jesus Christ his Son still cleanses from all sin and unrighteousness and you do not lie down in final despair and hopelessness. He does lead to self-examination, and this is an unmistakable sign of his leading. So, I repeat, if you have never been disturbed about yourself and have never had a fear, examine yourself very carefully lest you be a Laodicean.

But let me go on. Over and above leading us to self-examination, the Spirit leads to this – and this is the positive side – 'breathings after holiness'! 'It is God which worketh in you both to will and to do'; 'Work out your own salvation with fear and trembling' (*Phil.* 2:13, 12). Do not forget that 'fear and trembling', that is where self-examination comes in; it will lead to fear and trembling. Do you have 'breathings after holiness'? Or let me use other terminology – a longing for heart purity! A longing to be pure in heart! Now this is inevitable if we are led by the Holy Spirit. David knew something about it. 'Create in me a clean heart, O God; and renew a right spirit within me' (*Psa.* 51:10). He is no longer stopping with his particular sins. The Christian does not. The moral man says, 'I was a fool, I shouldn't have done that.' But he stops there. 'I'm going to be better,' he says, and no more. But Christians do not stop there. Those who know the Spirit of God say, with David, 'Create in me a clean heart, O God; and renew a right spirit within me.' Or, in the language of the apostle Paul in Romans: 'O wretched man that I am! who shall deliver me from the body of this death?' (*Rom.* 7:24).

Someone who has never known that longing is not a Christian. It is impossible! The Holy Spirit must make us feel like that at some time or another. That is all I am saying. I do not say you should feel like that always; I do not believe that is a true interpretation of Romans 7. But what I do know is that if you have never felt that to some degree, some time or another, if you have not known that final despair about yourself and have not said, 'In me (that is, in my flesh,) dwelleth no good thing . . . O wretched man that I am! who shall deliver me . . ?' (*Rom.* 7:18, 24), then you are not a Christian. Breathings and longings after holiness!

Oh, our Lord has said it all. Who are the people who are blessed? 'Blessed are they which do hunger and thirst after righteousness: for they shall be filled' (*Matt.* 5:6). Yes, that is it! The hungering and the thirsting, not after happiness, but after righteousness. The feeling that though you are a member of a church, though you have believed in Christ, though you are born again, it is not enough. You want to be righteous; you want to be holy. The Holy Spirit leads ever to that desire. He never allows us to rest upon our oars and to feel that that decision was everything, or that since I *said* I believed . . . No, no! But when he works within us – and he works in every Christian – he creates a great hunger after holiness. Oh, that I were more like him! Oh, that I were more like the Lord Jesus Christ! Oh, that I were righteous through and through. He makes you hunger, he makes you thirst after this righteousness.

> O for a heart to praise my God,
> A heart from sin set free!
> A heart that always feels thy blood
> So freely shed for me.
>
> Charles Wesley

So I will sum up this test by putting it like this: if you have a greater desire to be holy than to be happy, you, my friend, are being led by the Spirit of God. That is a wonderful test. Can you say that your desire for holiness is greater than your desire for happiness? Can you say, 'I don't care what happens to me as long as it makes me more holy'? The moment you can say that, you know that you are a child of God and are being led by the Spirit, because 'whom the Lord loveth he chasteneth' (*Heb.* 12:6). And you will even thank God for chastisement, whatever form it may take, because, in looking back upon it, you will say with the psalmist, 'It is good for me that I have been afflicted', because, 'Before

I was afflicted I went astray' (*Psa.* 119:71, 67). It was good for me that I suffered – illness, accident, loss – it has made a better person of me, and I would sooner be holy than happy.

> *E'en though it be a cross*
> *That raiseth me . . .*
> *Nearer, my God, to thee.*
>
> Sarah Flower Adams

Very well, my friends. Let us apply these truths.

And the last word I say on this subject for now is this – and it follows, of course, each one of these points leads to the next – there is an increasing sensitivity to temptation, the cry for that heart that trembles at the very approach of sin. You are not only grieved by sin when you have committed it, but you are grieved because of its very approach. 'Ye that love the LORD, hate evil' (*Psa.* 97:10). Does it not worry you that you do not hate evil as you should? Does it not worry you that you still like things that you should not, and that you can still be attracted by things that are unclean? Does it not worry you? If it does, it is the Spirit. If it does not, then you do not have the Spirit. The Spirit is sensitive and he, above all, detects sin at its merest suggestion, at its first glimmering. Those who can say that they are increasingly sensitive to the enticements, the attractions, the approach, the first moves, of sin, are those who are filled by the Spirit. It is they who are being led by the Spirit.

I am trying to show and to say that what we should be concerned about is not so much the details as our whole approach and attitude. But we will leave it there for now and, God willing, will continue next time. ∾

22

The Mortification of Sin: The Negative Approach

But as many as received him, to them gave he power to become the sons of God, even to them that believe on his name: which were born, not of blood, nor of the will of the flesh, nor of the will of man, but of God (John 1:12–13).

We are told by the apostle Paul in Romans 8:14, 'For as many as are [being] led by the Spirit of God, they are the sons of God.' It is an absolute proof. Anyone who is led by the Spirit of God is a child of God, while anyone who is not a Christian is not led by the Spirit. So we are examining the question: How do we know that we are being led by the Spirit of God? We have seen that he leads to the Scriptures and to prayer and we are now looking in particular at his leading in this matter of daily life, of conduct and behaviour. He causes us to examine ourselves and he creates within us breathings and longings and a hungering and thirsting after righteousness. I said that a very good test is this: If you are more concerned about being holy than you are about being happy, then you are a Christian beyond any doubt. That is only true of a Christian. But if you are more concerned about being happy than being holy, there is doubt. Then at the end of our last study we went on to consider the increasing sensitivity of the Christian to the very approach of sin.

Now we have not quite finished this matter of the leading of the Spirit. There is one big subject that we must still deal with and that is none other than what is called 'the mortification of sin' or 'the mortification of the flesh'. Let me give you my authority for saying that. The first is again in the Epistle to the Romans, and notice the terms Paul uses: 'Therefore, brethren, we are debtors, not to the flesh, to live after the flesh. For if ye live after the flesh, ye shall die: but if ye through [by] the Spirit do *mortify the deeds of the body*, ye shall live' (*Rom.* 8:12–13). The parallel statement of the same doctrine is to be found in Colossians 3: '*Mortify therefore your members which are upon the earth*; fornication, uncleanness, inordinate affection, evil concupiscence, and covetousness, which is idolatry: for which things' sake the wrath of God cometh on the children of disobedience: in the which ye also walked some time, when ye lived in them' (*Col.* 3:5–7).

Now here is a vital and essential part of the work of the leading of the Spirit. As we have seen, the Spirit is the *Holy* Spirit. He is the exact opposite of sin in every respect. And, therefore, it follows, without need of demonstration, that those who are under the control and leading of the Spirit will develop an increasing hatred of sin, which will, in turn, lead to their doing something about it. You cannot hate sin only theoretically. You begin to do something about it if you really hate it. 'Ye that love the LORD,' says the psalmist, 'hate evil' (*Psa.* 97:10). Hate it! And this is, of course, emphasized everywhere in the New Testament.

Now as we approach this subject, we must emphasize that mortification of the flesh is something that you and I are called upon to do. It is a command. It is not done for us. I put it like that because there is a well-known and popular teaching that tells us that the way to sanctification is to do nothing, that it has all been done for us: 'Look to the Lord, he will do it for you, he will fight your battles for you.' But here is a definite instruction: 'If ye through the Spirit do mortify the deeds of the body, ye shall live.' I repeat, *you* must do it. 'Mortify therefore your members which are upon the earth.' This is absolutely vital and essential. The Scriptures do not say, 'Hand yourself over, and it will be done for you.'

The whole doctrine of the mortification of the body, the mortification of sin and of the flesh, is a doctrine that one very rarely hears these days; it has almost gone right out. And yet there were times when it was one of the most prominent doctrines in Christian preaching and in the life of the church. And here it is before us in Scripture, in various shapes and forms. It is everywhere in these New Testament epistles. Passivity is not taught in the New Testament. We can put it like this: the Spirit leads us to mortify the flesh and at the same time he gives us the power to do it. 'If ye *through the Spirit* do mortify the deeds of the body.' That is the perfect balance. I cannot do it myself. That is where the whole notion of monasticism breaks down.

Let us say this for monasticism: the fundamental idea behind it was in many ways right; at least, it was right in its origin. These were people who realized that as Christians they must no longer go on living the life in the world that they had lived before. They realized that holiness is taken very seriously in the New Testament, that you do not just say, 'Thank God I'm a Christian and now it doesn't matter what I do.' They found that in the world were the flesh and the devil. These people were failing and they said that they must do something about this failure. So they decided to segregate themselves, to go out of the world and to live in communities or sometimes as hermits entirely on their own. They would fast in a rigorous manner and clothe themselves with camel-hair shirts and do violence to their bodies. That was their idea of obeying Paul's injunction to 'mortify therefore your members [your body] that are upon the earth'.

But these people were mortifying their bodies in their own strength; they were doing it by taking this drastic action. And that seems to me to be almost the opposite of Paul's words, 'If ye through the Spirit do mortify the deeds of the body.' Let us pay tribute, I repeat, to their desire. They were prepared to forego all worldly pleasures and worldly prospects, to forsake all that the world has to give, and in that way to become what they called 'religious'. But the truth was, of course, that it did not work, it did not succeed. You do not get rid of the world by taking yourself physically out of it. You can take the world with you in your mind, and in their lonely cells and caves on the tops of mountains they found that the imagination, the desires, were still there. That is not the way to mortify the deeds of the body. No, the right way is through the Spirit. He has been given to us because in and of ourselves we are incapable. He gives us the power, he gives us the enabling, and then it is for us, by the power provided, to put this command into practice.

I cannot think of a better illustration than the man with the withered hand who was healed by our Lord. This man had been incapable of moving that hand, it was lying helpless at his side, and at first our Lord's method of healing him sounds quite ridiculous. Our Lord said to a man who had a paralysed hand, 'Stretch forth thine hand' (*Mark* 3:5). How could a man whose essential trouble was paralysis stretch forth his hand? But when our Lord said those words to him, that is what the man did. In other words, as the Lord gave the command, he gave the power, but the man had to take the action. The man stretched forth his hand but the power to do so was given to him by our blessed Lord and Saviour. And so it is here: 'If ye through the Spirit . . .' You do not just become passive and leave it all to him. No, no! You must do something, you must 'mortify the deeds of the body'.

So how is this done? And, again, we are given an abundance of teaching. Indeed, it is astounding to notice the wealth of the teaching. How can people apparently be blind to it and say, 'Let go, let God – you have nothing to do at all; he does it all for you', when here is the New Testament full of instructions as to what we are to do with the enabling that is given to us by the Holy Spirit?

Let us take the teaching negatively first. 'Therefore, brethren, we are debtors, not to the flesh, to live after the flesh,' says the apostle Paul. 'For if ye live after the flesh, ye shall die: but if ye through the Spirit do mortify the deeds of the body, ye shall live' (*Rom.* 8:12–13). What does that mean? Paul is saying that though we are Christians, we are still in the body, and sin makes use of the body and tends to reside in it. And that is the trouble that we all find. Spiritually, I am in heaven, seated in the heavenly places in Christ Jesus. Yes, but my members are still on the earth. I am still living a life 'in the flesh': 'The life which I now live in the flesh I live by the faith of the Son of God, who loved me, and gave himself for me' (*Gal.* 2:20).

What am I to do about all this? Well, the teaching seems to me to be this: it is absolutely essential to realize the true nature and character of sin. Now I say 'sin' and not 'sins'. Of course, we must deal with particular sins but I feel more and more that if we concentrate only on particular sins instead of looking at sin as a whole, we will go astray. I say again that we must realize the character of sin. The Bible is full of teaching on this subject, beginning in the book of Genesis and continuing right the way through. The moment we realize the exceeding sinfulness of sin, we are on the highway to mortifying the deeds of the body. That is a most important truth. Sin and God are eternal opposites. God hates sin, and you and I are meant to hate it with all our being. But how do we put this into practice? Well, there are many instructions that are given and I have tried to classify them.

I begin with the apostle Paul's words: 'Have no fellowship with the unfruitful works of darkness' (*Eph.* 5:11). You start by realizing that the works of darkness are utterly unfruitful. There is no value, no profit, in them. If only we could see that, my friends! Why do Christian people live as near as they can to the world? Why do they want to play with sin? It is because they do not realize that it is 'unfruitful', that it is useless, a waste of energy, that there is nothing in it. These unfruitful works belong to the realm of 'darkness' and, 'God is light, and in him is no darkness at all' (*1 John* 1:5). So do not touch them. Have no fellowship with them.

The first Psalm begins: 'Blessed is the man' – here is the happy man – 'that walketh not in the counsel of the ungodly, nor standeth in the way of sinners, nor sitteth in the seat of the scornful.' Where are you walking, my friends? If you are led by the Spirit, you are not walking in the counsel of the ungodly. If you are led by the Spirit, you are not standing in the way of sinners. You do not frequent the places where they go and where you know sin is taking place. You do not stand about there. Nor do you sit in the seat of the scornful. Where do you spend your time? If we are led of the Spirit, we are the opposite of that ungodly person. So the apostle says, 'Have no fellowship.' Have nothing to do with it; keep as far away as you can.

Let me also give this teaching in the words of the apostle Peter: 'He that will love life, and see good days' – what must he do? Let go and let God? No – 'let him refrain his tongue from evil, and his lips that they speak no guile: let him eschew evil . . .' (*1 Pet.* 3:10–11). Now the word 'eschew' is a very picturesque word. The image is of a horse being driven or ridden along a country lane – and if you know anything about nervous horses, you will know what I am saying – when suddenly he sees just a sheet of paper, and he shies, jumps aside and nearly throws the rider. 'Eschew'! The moment you see sin you shy away from it. 'Let him eschew evil, and do good; let him seek peace, and ensue it' – let him pursue it (1 *Pet*. 3:11). So the apostle Peter is equally plain and clear. He gives this teaching right the way through his first epistle. In chapter 4, for instance, he says:

Forasmuch then as Christ hath suffered for us in the flesh, arm your-
selves likewise with the same mind: for he that hath suffered in the flesh
hath ceased from sin; that he no longer should live the rest of his life in
the flesh to the lusts of men, but to the will of God. For the time past of
our life may suffice us to have wrought the will of the Gentiles, when we
walked in lasciviousness, lusts, excess of wine, revellings, banquetings, and
abominable idolatries: wherein they think it strange that ye run not with
them to the same excess of riot, speaking evil of you' (1 Pet. 4:1–4).

What a contemporary document the New Testament is! People are still doing these things, are they not? But the point is that we are not to do them. Peter says: You have spent enough time doing that sort of thing, do not go wasting your time any longer. Keep clear of it. Have no fellowship with it at all.

There is a great statement of this teaching in 1 Thessalonians 5: 'Abstain from all appearance of evil' (verse 22), which means that we are to avoid evil in every shape and form, that we are not to make any exception, that we are to have nothing to do with it. Could anything be clearer? And if you do that, you are already on the road to mortifying your body. Obviously! If you put yourself in the way of sin, it will not be surprising if you find yourself sinning. This is pure common sense. The New Testament is a book that appeals to our common sense. It says: You are proud of the fact that you are in the light whereas you were in the dark. Very well, have nothing to do with 'the unfruitful works of darkness', keep clear of them, do not walk in the way of the ungodly, you know where it will lead you. And if you are led by the Spirit, then you are aware of all this, and if you feel an inclination to go the way of the ungodly, the Spirit pulls you up and you begin to see it all. That is a sign that you are being led of the Spirit.

Then there is the great passage in Ephesians 4: 'Put off . . . the old man' (verse 22). 'Ye have not so learned Christ,' Paul says, as to go on living in the way you used to live (verse 20). 'This I say therefore, and testify in the Lord, that ye henceforth walk not as other Gentiles walk' – how do they walk? Oh – 'in the vanity of their mind' (verse 17). And if ever a generation ought to know anything about 'vanity of the mind', it is this one. We are seeing it at its very zenith – the vapid, empty entertainments that people gloat over today 'in the vanity of their mind'!

And Paul continues in verses 18 to 22: 'Having the understanding darkened, being alienated from the life of God through the ignorance that is in them, because of the blindness of their heart: who being past feeling' – and they obviously are – 'have given themselves over unto lasciviousness' – and that is what they have done, they have 'given themselves over'; all restraints have gone, they are boasting and gloat-ing over it, even in public – 'to work all uncleanness with greediness.' And people are defending it; it is almost the most beautiful thing in the world now, this 'uncleanness with greediness'. 'But', says the apostle, 'ye have not so learned Christ; if so be that ye have heard him' – Paul asks: Have you heard him? If you are doing that sort of thing, he says, you are not being led by the Spirit, and I am beginning to doubt whether you have ever heard him at all. You cannot say that you have heard Christ, and find your pleasure in that sort of thing – 'and have been taught by him, as the truth is in Jesus' – and what is this truth? It is – 'that ye put off concerning the former conversation [way of living] the old man, which is corrupt according to the deceitful lusts.'

'Put off the old man'! What does this mean? Well, there's no time to go into this in detail, so let me summarize it by putting it to you like this. It means that you must talk to yourself. I think that half our trouble as Christians is that we do not talk to ourselves sufficiently. You must preach to yourself. You must take yourself in hand and say, 'Now, realize what you were. There you were, and the end of that was not only misery and loss in this world but, at the end, hell.' It is foul. It is evil. And you were like that once in your whole mind and outlook. That was natural and instinctive to you. But something has happened to you. You are a 'new man', a new person. So, then, if you are, *put off* everything to do with 'the old man'. It is as if you had an old cloak that you always wore; it was something you were very proud of and people recognized you when you came. 'But now,' you say, 'I want them to know that I'm different. The very first sight of me will tell them that something has happened to me. I take off that old cloak with its gaudy colours that I was so proud of and put on a different cloak so that when they look at me, they'll say, "What's happened to you?"'

We put off altogether that whole worldly outlook, that whole way of thinking, everything that belonged to it. We say, 'That's who I once was. I'm no longer that person.' Do that thoroughly, says the apostle, not only in your speech and thinking, but also in your practice. 'Put off the old man'! You see how much more thoroughgoing the New Testament is than any superficial teaching about a little temporary denial of self during Lent.[1] No, no! Permanent Lent! Put off that old self for ever. Disassociate yourself entirely from it. Do not say, 'I'm going to do it for a few weeks, then I can look forward to going back to where I was.' No, no! You have finished with that once and for ever.

Then let us go on to another word that one finds so often in the New Testament: *abstain*! This word has become unpopular because it has been narrowed down a bit too much, perhaps, and when people hear it, they think of alcoholic drinks. But the word 'abstain' covers a much wider field than that. Let me quote to you the words of the apostle Peter. From out of his pastoral heart, he says, 'Dearly beloved . . . abstain from fleshly lusts, which war against the soul; having your conversation honest among the Gentiles: that, whereas they speak against you as evildoers, they may by your good works, which they shall behold, glorify God in the day of visitation (*1 Pet.* 2:11–12). Peter is writing to Christians, remember. He is not saying: 'Now that you are a Christian and have been converted, take the next step and hand yourself over for sanctification as you did for justification. You have nothing to do;

---

[1] This sermon was preached during Lent, 1963.

sin will all be taken out of you.' No, no! You must 'abstain from fleshly lusts'. Why? Because '[they] war against the soul'.

As a Christian, you have come to see that the most important thing is your soul. It is much more important than anything else, more important than the body, more important than your appearance, more important than success. The soul! This immortal thing, my relationship to God! 'Fleshly lusts', says Peter, are inimical to the soul's highest interests. It does not matter what form these 'fleshly lusts' take. By 'fleshly lusts', let me remind you, Peter does not only mean sex and drink, but also feelings such as ambition, jealousy and envy. In writing to the Ephesians, the apostle Paul divides 'the lusts of the flesh' into 'the desires of the flesh and of the mind' (*Eph.* 2:3). There are lusts of the mind as well as of the body. 'Abstain from them,' says the apostle Peter.

Or let me again give this teaching in the words of the apostle Paul – I am so anxious that we should all be clear that we ourselves must mortify the flesh:

This I say then, Walk in the Spirit, and ye shall not fulfil the lust of the flesh. For the flesh lusteth against the Spirit, and the Spirit against the flesh: and these are contrary the one to the other: so that ye cannot do the things that ye would. But if ye be led of the Spirit, ye are not under the law. Now the works of the flesh are manifest, which are these; Adultery, fornication, uncleanness, lasciviousness, idolatry, witchcraft, hatred, variance, emulations, wrath, strife, seditions, heresies, envyings, murders, drunkenness, revellings, and such like: of the which I tell you before, as I have also told you in time past, that they which do such things shall not inherit the kingdom of God (Gal. 5:16–21).

Abstain from them, my dear friends!

The same exhortation is addressed to the individual. Listen to the apostle Paul pleading with his own disciple and follower, Timothy: 'But thou, O man of God, flee these things' – *flee* them, get as far away from them as you can – 'and follow after righteousness, godliness, faith, love, patience, meekness. Fight the good fight of faith' – activity, you see, all along, telling us what to do – 'lay hold on eternal life' (*1 Tim.* 6:11–12). *You* must do it. Do not wait to be laid hold of, that has happened to you;

'lay hold on' now! You must 'apprehend' that which has apprehended you, to use the language of the apostle Paul in Philippians 3:12.

There, then, is the teaching about abstaining from things that are inimical to the best and the highest interests of the soul, and it is to be found in many places. But let me take you to another heading. So far we have been looking at these things as they are outside us, as it were, and we have seen the injunction to keep as far away as we can, to finish with them in our minds and then rigidly to put this into practice. But now the teaching goes a bit further and it becomes a little more subjective and personal. I now find a word that says this: 'But I keep under my body' (1 Cor. 9:27). This is the apostle Paul's illustration. 'Know ye not that they which run in a race run all, but one receiveth the prize? So run, that ye may obtain. And every man that striveth for the mastery is temperate in all things' (1 Cor. 9:24–25).

Olympic Games! Test matches! For a number of days before a great contest the team members do not drink. They do not smoke. Wonderful! Everybody applauds! Have you ever heard anybody saying that cricketers and athletes are narrow because they do not drink and smoke before their great event? Never! But when a Christian does not drink or smoke, then it is 'narrow Christianity', 'miserable Christianity'! And yet we are running in a race infinitely greater than Olympic races; we are in a match that is more crucial than any test match that has ever been known. So the apostle uses the illustration, 'So run, that ye may obtain.' You see the contrast. The Games last only for a few days or weeks, so those taking part abstain for a limited period. Then the event is over – celebrate! But in this life there is no end to the Christian race, the contest is always on.

So run, that ye may obtain. And every man that striveth for the mastery is temperate in all things. Now they do it to obtain a corruptible crown

– oh, yes, but the world does not think so. The Ashes! The Cup! Marvellous! And we admire sportsmen and women for their abstinence –

but we an incorruptible

– a crown that will never fade away!

I therefore so run, not as uncertainly; so fight I, not as one that beateth the air: But I keep under my body, and bring it into subjection: lest that by any means, when I have preached to others, I myself should be a castaway (1 Cor. 9:24–27).

Now that last phrase does not for a moment refer to salvation but to the apostle Paul's work as a preacher. Here is the prize, the crown, that he is going for. Do not miss the whole point of that injunction by thinking that Paul is teaching a falling away from grace. That has nothing to do with it. That is how the devil turns the point and the thrust of the Scriptures. No, listen to what the apostle is really saying – 'I keep under my body' – and yet the popular teaching tells us, 'You must not do that, that's legalism. Hand yourself over and it's all done for you.' It is not! 'I keep under my body,' says the apostle Paul. 'I therefore so run, not as uncertainly; so fight I, not as one that beateth the air.' He says, in effect, 'I am concentrating on this with all my might and main. I realize that the body can be a danger to me and a temptation. I have found that I must keep it under and I am keeping it under.' And you and I, my friends, must do the same.

You find the same teaching in Romans 8:13: 'If ye through the Spirit do mortify the deeds of the body . . .' This is a great mystery, we cannot understand it. But God has made us, body, soul and spirit, in such a way that we are responsible for the body, and the body interacts upon the soul, and the soul upon the body. It is only the Spirit of God that can separate, 'piercing even to the dividing asunder of soul and spirit, and of the joints and marrow' (*Heb.* 4:12). We cannot! Therefore, we must recognize these things. If there is anything in your life that you find tends to get you down, or to stand between you and thoughts of God and of Christ and of being who you know you are meant to be in Christ, get rid of it; keep it down. The body must be dealt with.

You see, before man fell and became a sinner, all the powers that God originally gave us worked together harmoniously. The effect of sin has been that the greatest powers can become our greatest enemies. Some people are gifted with great imagination. It is a wonderful gift. It makes poets and dramatists and they produce their glorious classics, their masterpieces. But is there anything that can be a greater problem to

Christian people than the imagination? Very well, says the apostle, keep it under. Imagination is wonderful, yes, but when wrongly directed, sin comes in. The devil will try to turn every power you have to his own ends, so you must keep these powers under control.

I have already referred to the illustration of a rider on horseback. Think of that spirited and powerful horse. Now the one thing the rider must do is hold the reins firmly. It is thrilling to be riding such a glorious animal, filled with power, but he has to be watched. He will bolt. He will run away with you. He may kill you. Keep a firm hold upon him. Hold him in. Put a bearing rein upon him, perhaps. That is the illustration – 'I keep under my body.' And the original Greek is most interesting. What Paul is really saying is, 'I beat my body until it is black and blue; I pummel it.' The body is a good thing, yes, but it can be so full of vigour and power that it becomes a positive danger to me. So I must keep it down. Why? Because we are after a crown that is not corruptible and, therefore, for the sake of the soul and for the sake of that great 'crowning day', keep the body under control.

Let me give you the words of our Lord, who put it in a most extra-ordinary statement:

If thy hand or thy foot offend thee, cut them off, and cast them from thee: it is better for thee to enter into life halt or maimed, rather than having two hands or two feet to be cast into everlasting fire. And if thine eye offend thee, pluck it out, and cast it from thee: it is better for thee to enter into life with one eye, rather than having two eyes to be cast into hell fire (Matt. 18:8–9).

Those words are to be taken metaphorically. Those poor hermits, anchorites, monks and so on often took them literally. That is where they went wrong and became legalistic. This injunction is spiritual. Metaphorically cut off hands and feet, pluck out eyes! It is better to be blind and yet holy and pleasing to God than to see the whole universe and sin.

And then, to complete this section, here is another wonderful word that is most essential in mortifying the flesh. The apostle Paul writes: 'Make not provision for the flesh' (*Rom.* 13:14). Let me read this extraordinary passage to you, the one that the great St Augustine came upon when he was in an agony and the moment of conversion had arrived. '*Tolle lege*: Take up and read', came the voice. And this is what he read:

The night is far spent, the day is at hand: let us therefore cast off the works of darkness, and let us put on the armour of light. Let us walk honestly, as in the day; not in rioting and drunkenness, not in chambering and wantonness, not in strife and envying. But put ye on the Lord Jesus Christ, and make not provision for the flesh, to fulfil the lusts thereof (Rom. 13:12–14).

Be careful about what you read in newspapers, in books, be careful what you watch on the television and listen to on the radio: 'Make not provision for the flesh'! You need not give it any encouragement, it does not need any, it is bad enough as it is. Starve it! Do not give it any food!

And, finally, it comes to this: nip everything in the bud. When you see the approach, the first suggestion, do not play with it, do not reason, do not argue – reject sin *in toto*, at the first appearance. It is easier then than later. At first it is not so strong. The more you play with it, the stronger it becomes. Have nothing at all to do with it. Mortification of sin, mortification of the deeds of the body, mortification of the members that are upon the earth. And that is how you do it negatively. God give us grace to do so! God give us grace to see the race on which he has set us! God give us a glimpse of the crown, the incorruptible crown, that is awaiting us! ❧

23

The Mortification of Sin:
The Positive Approach

But as many as received him, to them gave he power to become the sons of God, even to them that believe on his name: which were born, not of blood, nor of the will of the flesh, nor of the will of man, but of God (John 1:12–13).

We are concerned that we who claim to be Christian should really know that we are the children of God. The New Testament provides many tests with regard to this very matter, and the one we are considering at the moment is from Romans 8:14, where the apostle Paul says, 'As many as are led by the Spirit of God, they are the sons [children] of God.' We are therefore trying to discover whether we can say honestly that we are being led by the Spirit. Again, here is a very great subject and we have had to subdivide it. We are now dealing with this aspect of it: that the Spirit, when he leads us, invariably leads us to 'mortify the deeds of the body'. Having looked at this subject negatively, we can now turn to consider it positively, and this, of course, is equally essential.

There is always a balance in the New Testament. You get the positive and the negative. The tendency today is to ignore negatives and, therefore, in order to put extra stress upon them, we started with the negative aspect. But you must not merely seek to mortify the deeds of the flesh in a negative manner because if you do, you just become a moralist or an ethical person and cease to be a Christian. This is important because there is no doubt at all but that a great deal of the licence and the appalling, flagrant sinfulness that is so evident in the world at the present time is partly – only partly, but it is certainly that – a reaction against a false kind of Christianity that was to be found during the Victorian era.

It is very important that we should be able to draw a distinction between Christianity and Victorianism. Victorianism was very often not only not Christianity, but almost its exact opposite. It had largely degenerated into a kind of legalism in which people were only aware of the negative side of Christianity. They did not know why they should carry out its precepts and they had no joy as they did so. It was repressive and made people miserable rather than joyful. That is not Christianity, and that is why we do not stop at the negative but go on to the positive aspect, which is in many ways the more important of the two.

Let me put it to you in terms of an analogy. Whenever there is an infection around – I mean a physical infection such as influenza, typhoid fever or smallpox – there are two good rules that should always be put into practice. The first is to avoid exposing yourself to infection. That is common sense, is it not? That is why, when there are epidemics, it is good not to go into overheated, crowded places. You avoid infection. But that is the negative aspect. There is a second rule, and this is more important. You must build up your resistance. Then, if you have done this as you should, you will be able to walk into the midst of the infection – though common sense would, of course, prevent you – with very much less danger to yourself.

We have looked at the negative aspect of the teaching concerning mortification of the flesh – we avoid every appearance of evil. Yes, but we still have to live in the world; we do not become monks or nuns. As we saw in the last study, the error of monasticism was the emphasis only on the negative, on the avoidance of infection. You avoid it by becoming a monk or an anchorite. You build a great wall around yourself, you do not mix with the world, and you think that by doing this you are not subject to the temptation, to the infection, of sin, and you will therefore be a holy person. But it did not work. The positive aspect is therefore much more important. However careful you are to avoid infection, you cannot get right away from it, you cannot live in a glasshouse. So the thing to do is to build up your resistance, not by going out of the world, but by making yourself strong, so that as the germs attack you and try to infect you, you can throw them back. If all your spiritual antibodies are present in large numbers, then the infecting agent stands no chance when it comes along in your direction. That is the kind of approach that we find put before us so constantly in the New Testament teaching.

I will put it like this: How do we mortify the flesh positively? Again, let me divide it up into the general and the particular. I divide it like that because the New Testament teaching does so and it is a good classification. First, then, the general – and if you want a text, it is this: 'Put on the new man' (*Eph.* 4:24). We have been told, negatively, to 'put off the old man'; we must now 'put on the new man'. You do not remain naked, as it were, you are not just a negative person who has got rid of the old nature and there you are, naked. Not at all!

But what does it mean to 'put on the new man'? There are two points, it seems to me, that are stressed in the New Testament teaching and the first is this: I build myself up. I build up my resistance. I 'put on the new man' by making certain that my thinking is spiritual thinking. Now you see why I make this division into general and particular. Before you consider doing anything at all, you must think correctly. Half the battle in the Christian life is to learn how to think, and how to think in a spiritual manner. Let me give you the two great New Testament statements of that. The first is in the Epistle to the Romans: 'Be not conformed to this world: but be ye transformed by the renewing of your mind, that ye may prove what is that good, and acceptable, and perfect, will of God' (*Rom.* 12:2). What a statement! 'Be not *conformed* to this world' – what then? – 'but be ye *transformed* – how? – 'by the renewing of your mind' – why? – 'that ye may prove what is that good, and acceptable, and perfect, will of God.'

The second statement is to be found in Ephesians 4: 'That ye put off concerning the former conversation the old man, which is corrupt according to the deceitful lusts; and be renewed in the spirit of your mind' (*Eph.* 4:22–23). Then Paul goes on to say: 'And that ye put on the new man.' And the point of transition is the being 'renewed in the spirit of your mind'. What a wonderful phrase that is! There is a great deal of talk today about psychology, but it is all very pathetic. If you really want psychology, come to the Bible. Here is analysis! The Bible draws a distinction between the mind and the spirit of the mind, and there is nothing more important than the spirit of the mind.

What does Paul mean? Let me put it like this – the phrase, 'the spirit of your mind', refers to the *way* in which you think. The brain is an instrument, it is an organ of the body, and a very wonderful one. Now the thing that really differentiates one person from another is not so much the size of the brain or even its consistency, its constitution. What really differentiates between people is 'the spirit of the mind', that controlling power that organizes the activity. That is what makes one person great and greater than others. When people become Christians, they still have the same brain as before. They have the same powers and faculties. A dull person who becomes a Christian does not become clever. When someone who is a poor thinker becomes a Christian, that person does not become a great thinker. The instrument is not changed. What is changed, then? Oh, it is 'the spirit of the mind', the direction that is given to the mind, the organizing ability. The central control is changed and renewed and now uses all the powers of the brain in a different way from before.

The apostle Paul's injunction not to be conformed to this world is another way of saying: Do not be governed by the way of the world, by the mind of the world, the outlook of the world; do not allow your thinking to be determined by newspapers and television. That is it in its modern form. Do not be governed by 'the thing to do', and by those few men and women who control the means of propaganda and determine life and fashion. The apostle is very fond of making this point. Take Ephesians 2:1–2: 'You hath he quickened, who were dead in trespasses and sins; wherein in time past ye walked according to the course of this world' – the merry-go-round of life, doing what everybody else does. People live like sheep, dictated to by these 'powers that be' who are in control of the mechanisms that determine the outlook of the world. Oh, says Paul, be transformed in the spirit of your mind. That is the first thing.

Now the interesting thing that is before us is that Paul puts all this in the form of a command. He does not say, 'Because you are Christians you are of necessity completely changed and transformed in the spirit of your mind.' There is a sense in which that is true, as we have seen, but it is not a complete process. What happens in the rebirth, the regeneration, is that the *principle* is put there, but then you and I must develop it and apply it. It is not done for us automatically. We do not just let go and let it happen to us. It is obviously something that you and I control, otherwise this would not be addressed to us as a command. There is nothing more pathetic than the people who believe in a sort of passivity, who think that all you have to do is stop thinking, stop doing anything at all, because it will all be done for you. It is not true. We must take ourselves in hand in this whole matter of thinking. That is the purpose of reading the Bible. It teaches us how to think; we learn to think in a biblical manner. It is wonderful that we are ever called upon to do such a thing at all. But that is what the New Testament holds out to us.

Take another way in which the apostle puts this teaching. In writing to the Corinthians, he points out that the princes of this world did not know our Lord. There he was before them but they did not know him: 'Which none of the princes of this world knew: for had they known it, they would not have crucified the Lord of glory' (*1 Cor.* 2:8). What was the matter with them? Well, their whole trouble was that they did not know how to think. 'The natural man receiveth not the things of the Spirit of God: for they are foolishness unto him: neither can he know them, because they are spiritually discerned [spiritually understood, spiritually apprehended]. But', Paul says, 'he that is spiritual judgeth all things' – he has a way of estimating, a way of understanding – 'yet he himself is judged of no man' (*1 Cor.* 2:14-15). In other words, the man of the world looks at Christians and says, 'What's gone wrong with them? They've developed a religious complex, they've gone soft!' And he does not understand; it seems the height of folly. Ah, says the apostle Paul, 'For who hath known the mind of the Lord, that he may instruct him?' And then this astounding statement: 'But we have the mind of Christ' (*1 Cor.* 2:16). Now that is it!

Paul is exhorting us to make certain that all our thinking is Christian and spiritual. Do not live in compartments, he says. Do not think as a Christian only when you are in chapel, and live an entirely different life when you go out into the world. Here you are, you come to chapel, you are unlike your colleagues whom you will be with tomorrow. But then on Monday you are one of them; there is no difference. But there must be, says Paul. That does not mean you must be awkward or angular or anything like that, but it does mean that you must look at everything from a different standpoint. You do not conform to the world's pattern, and this is because you have been made conformable unto the Lord Jesus Christ and your desire is to be made more and more like him. Our thinking must be spiritual thinking. If only we would put that into practice, it would save us from many troubles and pitfalls. As Christians, we are not simply people who try to remember what we must and must not do next. No, no! That is being under the law. What you do is this: you say, 'I'm a Christian – therefore . . .' and you begin to think as a Christian, 'renewed in the spirit of your mind'.

But let me go on to show you that principle more clearly in my second heading under this general division of the positive aspect of the mortification of the body. Having put it in general by saying that we must be renewed in the spirit of our mind, I will put it like this: we are always to be aware of the ultimate end and aim of salvation. That is the presupposition from which we must always start. Why are we saved? What is the object and purpose of salvation? Now this is what is put before us in the New Testament. It is not merely that we are forgiven. We are all concerned about forgiveness, and rightly so. There is nothing more terrible than not to know that your sins are forgiven. But salvation is not only forgiveness. That is negative. Nor are we saved merely to be happy. Salvation does make us happy but that is not the end, that is not the ultimate objective. Many people turn Christianity into a cult, and that is why it is so often seen as competing with the cults. They offer happiness; they offer immediate deliverance from all our problems: 'You will never worry again if you take this up, you will never be ill', and so on. That is the cults, but it is not Christianity.

So what is the ultimate end and object of Christianity? Let the New Testament answer that question for itself. We find the answer in the very first chapter of Matthew's Gospel. Here is the angel speaking to Joseph: 'Joseph, thou son of David, fear not to take unto thee Mary thy wife: for that which is conceived in her is of the Holy Ghost. And she shall bring forth a son, and thou shalt call his name JESUS: for he shall save his people from their sins' (*Matt.* 1:20–21). Now that is more than delivering them from the condemnation of their sins. That is more than delivering them from the guilt of their sins. 'He shall save his people *from their sins.*'

Then turn to the First Epistle of John, where there is a wonderful commentary on that statement. John puts it so clearly: 'For this purpose the Son of God was manifested, that he might destroy the works of the devil' (1 *John* 3:8). Now that is the comprehensive statement. If our Lord had stopped at forgiveness, he would not have destroyed the works of the devil. Man was made perfect and it is the devil who has made him sinful and imperfect and brought about all the other consequences of the fall. If our Lord came to undo, to destroy and nullify the works of the devil, then he must restore man to a position of perfection, and that is the ultimate end of salvation. The object of salvation is not to save us from hell and then just leave us outside the gate that goes to hell. Not at all! It is to put us into heaven! We must look at these things positively.

Listen to the apostle writing to the Thessalonians about the end of our salvation: 'For this is the will of God, even your sanctification' (1 *Thess.* 4:3). Or, again, in 1 Thessalonians 4:7: 'God hath not called us unto uncleanness, but unto holiness.' Of course! Or take that glorious statement in the Epistle to Titus:

For the grace of God that bringeth salvation hath appeared to all men, teaching us that, denying ungodliness and worldly lusts, we should live soberly, righteously, and godly, in this present world; looking for that blessed hope, and the glorious appearing of our great God and our Saviour Jesus Christ; who gave himself for us

– why? Why did he die on the cross?

that he might redeem us from all iniquity, and purify unto himself a peculiar people, zealous of good works (Titus 2:11–14).

Now that is the end and object of salvation. Or listen to it in what is perhaps the most glorious statement of all in this respect. It is in Ephesians 5, where the apostle Paul is dealing with the relationship between husband and wife, and this is how he puts it:

Husbands, love your wives, even as Christ also loved the church, and gave himself for it; that he might sanctify and cleanse it with the washing of water by the word

– why? Not simply that we might not be punished, that is negative. His real object is –

that he might present it to himself a glorious church, not having spot, or wrinkle, or any such thing; but that it should be holy and without blemish (Eph. 5:25–27).

That is why our Lord gave himself for the church. And all I am arguing is that those who have been renewed in the spirit of the mind should always realize that and keep it in the forefront of their minds. They are not painfully trying to remember what they must do and what they are not to do; they keep this in their minds. That is what Paul means by saying, 'Put on the new man'; that is what he means when he says, 'Be renewed in the spirit of your mind.'

Now let me go on to show you how this great general principle is worked out in detail. The first heading under the particular division is this: I must, therefore, in the first instance, understand my position, realize who I am, in a spiritual sense. What does this mean? It means that I am now to talk to myself. And this is what I say: 'You are a Christian. You are entirely different. You are a new creature, a new creation. You are not simply someone who is trying to live a better life, but you have been *made* a child of God: "But as many as received him, to them gave he power to become the children of God." You are a joint-heir with Christ.' This is the positive way of looking at the mortification of the flesh. I am not painfully trying to discover how much and how near I can go to the world. I dismiss all that kind of thinking. That is carnal, worldly thinking, that is being conformed to this world. I say, 'Look here, you are an entirely new being. You have been born "not of blood, nor of the will of the flesh, nor of the will of man" – that is what you were before – "but of God".'

So what does this tell me about myself? In the light of this, how am I to live? Let the great apostle answer, again in the Epistle to the Romans. Oh, says Paul, you are as you are because 'where sin abounded, grace did much more abound' (*Rom.* 5:20). Does that mean, therefore, that you can say, 'Well, I'm saved. I'm all right. I can never be separated from the love of God so it doesn't matter what I do. I can do anything I like. I'm free!' No! says the apostle, that is the lie of the devil. 'What shall we say then? Shall we continue in sin, that grace may abound? God forbid' (*Rom.* 6:1–2). Listen, here is an appeal to your reason, to your logic:

How shall we [how can we], that are dead to sin, live any longer therein? Know ye not, that so many of us as were baptized into Jesus Christ were baptized into his death? Therefore we are buried with him by baptism into death: that like as Christ was raised up from the dead by the glory of the Father, even so we also should walk in newness of life. For if we have been planted together in the likeness of his death, we shall be also in the likeness of his resurrection: knowing this, that our old man is crucified with him, that the body of sin might be destroyed, that henceforth we should not serve sin (Rom. 6:2–6).

Now that is a little bit of instruction to those who are told to renew themselves in the spirit of the mind. Say things like that to yourself. Say, 'I am a new person.'

What does that mean?

It means that I am 'dead' to sin.

How am I dead to sin?

I am dead to sin in that I am now 'in Christ'. I am not merely forgiven and then left to myself. No, no! I am given a new nature and, more than that, I am a part of the Lord Jesus Christ. He is the Head and I am a member of the body. There is a unity prevailing here and I am in him. Very well, because I am in Christ, it is true to say that I have been crucified with Christ. When he was crucified, I was crucified, I died with him. He died; I died. He was buried; I was buried. He has risen; I am risen. He is with the Father; I am with the Father. That is the argument. Now this is spiritual thinking, and if only we all persistently thought like that, our problems would be largely solved.

You and I must do this talking to ourselves. We do not wait for some experience suddenly to deliver us. No, no! We work it out. We think this out for ourselves. We listen to the logic and see the reasonableness of it and agree that it is true. This is the great, profound teaching of the New Testament. I am dead to sin in the sense that I no longer belong to the territory and the dominion of sin. The apostle puts it specifically in that sixth chapter of Romans: 'Sin shall not have dominion over you: for ye are not under the law, but under grace (*Rom.* 6:14). This means that we, with Christ, have died to the law. He was 'made of a woman, made under the law' (*Gal.* 4:4) and by dying on Calvary's hill he fulfilled the law in every respect. He had already fulfilled it positively in his obedience and there he bears its ultimate penalty. And all who have died with him, and in him, have finished with the law as a means of condemnation. It cannot condemn us any longer. We are absolutely free. 'There is therefore now no condemnation to them which are in Christ Jesus' (*Rom.* 8:1).

Yes, and because we are dead to the law, we are dead to the whole power of sin. That does not mean that we cannot sin again, but it does mean that we are taken out of that realm. Christ came into the realm of sin. He is no longer there. He has gone out of it and in him we are out of it. Now this is what we must say to ourselves. The whole world is still in the realm of sin. It belongs to it and do what it will, it still belongs there. People who are not Christians can be highly moral but they are still under the law, under the dominion of sin and Satan. It does not matter what they do, that is their realm and they remain there until they become Christians. But then they are in the realm of sin no longer; they are in the realm of God and of Christ and of light.

Not only that, but, because of this new position, Christians are destined to be conformed to the image of God's Son. That is God's purpose – nothing less – as we have been seeing. Again, let the apostle Paul put it to us: 'We know that all things work together for good to them that love God, to them who are the called according to his purpose. For whom he did foreknow, he also did predestinate to be conformed to the image of his Son' (*Rom.* 8:28–29). We are destined for God; we are destined for glory. Nothing less! This is what it means to be a Christian.

Now someone who is conformed to this world thinks like this: 'I'm going to work for a certain number of years and then I'll retire. After that, I'll relax and enjoy myself.' That is the outlook of people in the world and they never get beyond it. Everything they do is determined and governed by that. They save a certain amount of money and are careful in this and that respect. They play their cards well, as we put it, because that is their plan for themselves. But if you say to them, 'Of course, you will die some time', they will retort, 'Ah, that's being morbid. I don't consider things like that. "Sufficient unto the day is the evil thereof!"' That is their worldly thinking.

And, of course, within that godless view there are any number of positions. People all want to 'live the good life' from their own standpoint. One man is highly moral – he does not drink, he does not smoke and so on. But to another man the good life is, well, as was said recently on the television, 'The basis of real culture and of the good life is good food and good drink.' And he was a highly intelligent man who said that and said it very seriously. He meant it. And if you read the more intelligent weekly journals, you will notice that increasing space is given to food and drink. This is the basis of culture, we are told, of the real, good, full, cultured life. Then with your food and your drink there is, of course, art, and so on. This way of thinking encompasses all gradations, from highly moral living to loose and dissolute lifestyles, but they are all conformed to this world.

But Christians are altogether different in their thinking. They are not conformed to this world but are transformed by the renewing of their minds. As a Christian, you say, 'I'm only a pilgrim in this world. I'm only a stranger here. This is not all there is. This is an evil world, which I pass through. I'm a child of God. Heaven is my home; I'm moving in the direction of heaven. My ambition is not just to plan the life I would like to live in this world. I'm meant to be conformable to the image of

God's Son. The Son of God came into this world to deliver me from this world, even at its best, and to prepare me for this other world.'

'Now are we the sons of God.' That is how John puts it in his first epistle (*1 John* 3:2). This is Christian thinking, this is being renewed in the spirit of our minds:

Behold, what manner of love the Father hath bestowed upon us, that we should be called the sons of God: therefore the world knoweth us not, because it knew him not.

It did not understand him and it should not understand us.

Beloved, now are we the sons of God, and it doth not yet appear what we shall be: but we know that, when he shall appear, we shall be like him; for we shall see him as he is.

And there is only one conclusion to draw from that:

And every man that hath this hope in him purifieth himself, even as he is pure (1 John 3:1–3).

That is what spiritual thinking means. Not sitting down in passivity waiting for things to be taken out of your life. No, no! It is saying to yourself, 'I am a child of God.' Start your day like this. Address yourself. Pull yourself together. Remind yourself of who you are.

We are looking at the positive approach to mortification of the flesh, and are thinking of the particular ways in which we do this. The first is that we must understand and *realize* who we are. We are to tell ourselves that we are 'in Christ'. That brings us to the second particular way, which is that we must *reckon*, as Paul says in Romans 6:11: 'Reckon ye also yourselves to be dead indeed unto sin, but alive unto God through Jesus Christ our Lord.' What does this 'reckoning' mean? Some people turn it into a kind of Couéism.[1] They tell you to say to yourself, 'I am dead to sin. I am never going to sin any more. Sin has no more power over me.' You are to try to work up your courage by saying that as a kind of incantation. But Paul's words do not mean anything of the sort! Paul means that you are to count on the fact that

[1] See p. 190.

you are actually dead to the realm of sin and its power because you have died with Christ. It is not that you try to persuade yourself that sin has no power over you. No, it is a fact! And because you know this about yourself, well, you live accordingly.

I close by putting it in some famous words, which we all can understand. Lord Nelson was a profound psychologist and on the morning of the Battle of Trafalgar he did not send up a long list of rules and regulations telling his men what to do and what not to do. He knew that there was only one thing to say to them, and it was this: 'England expects that every man this day will do his duty.' 'England expects'! That was enough! And that is what the New Testament says to us: Realize who you are! God expects! Heaven expects! The country you belong to expects that you this day will do your duty, that you will not be conformed to this world. The world is your enemy. You do not belong to this world, or to the devil and hell: all that is going to corruption and destruction. Very well: Heaven expects! 'Every man that hath this hope in him purifieth himself, even as he is pure' (*1 John* 3:3).

How do you start your day, my friend? How do you walk along the street? Do you say, 'Now I must not let myself down, I must not fall into sin'? If you do that, you are already defeated. You are looking at things negatively and are interested in your own little bit of morality. No, no! Start by saying, 'I am a child of God! I am one for whom Christ died in order that I might be made conformable to his image. I belong to the family of heaven. I am going to stand before my Father, and I am his representative while I am here. Because of that – therefore! I am going to walk down that street as a child who is worthy of my Father.'

'Let your light so shine before men, that they may see your good works, and glorify your Father which is in heaven' (*Matt.* 5:16). 'Be not conformed to this world, but be ye transformed by the renewing of your mind.' ॐ

24

The Mortification of Sin: The Surrender of the Body

As many as received him, to them gave he power to become the sons of God, even to them that believe on his name: which were born, not of blood, nor of the will of the flesh, nor of the will of man, but of God (John 1:12–13).

The New Testament pays great attention to the question of assurance. God does not merely make us his children, he has provided ways whereby we can know that we are his children in order that we may enjoy the benefits and the blessings of this relationship. We are considering together the various tests suggested by the New Testament itself, and the one we have arrived at is the leading of the Spirit: 'As many as are led by the Spirit of God, they are the sons of God' (*Rom.* 8:14). Here is a very valuable test. If we know that we are being led by the Spirit of God, then we can be certain that we are the children of God.

But how do we know that we are being led by the Spirit of God? We have considered various aspects of this question and have arrived at the all-important teaching that is called 'the mortification of sin', or, if you prefer, 'the mortification of the deeds of the body', or 'the mortification of the flesh', which, as I have been showing, is dealt with in many places in Scripture. We have seen that this process of mortification can be divided up into a negative and a positive approach. Having dealt with the negative, we are looking now at the positive, which we have divided into the general and the particular. By 'general' we mean that we must learn to think in a spiritual manner, and we do this, first, by being 'renewed in the spirit of [our] mind', and, second, by keeping in mind the great object and purpose of our salvation.

Now we have come to the particular, or the application, of all this and we have seen that the first great principle is that we must *realize* our position, we must realize that we are 'in Christ', that we are 'new creatures', that we are indeed children of God. We do not live unto ourselves. The whole reputation of the family is in our hands, as it were, and God is being judged by what people see in us. The way in which you mortify the deeds of the body is by starting every day by reminding yourself of who you are and what you are and what is expected of you: 'For this is the will of God, even your sanctification' (*1 Thess.* 4:3).

At the end of the last study we touched on the second principle under this heading, which is that we must *reckon* this, as Paul says in Romans 6:11: 'Likewise reckon ye also yourselves to be dead indeed unto sin, but alive unto God through Jesus Christ our Lord.' As I said last time, there is a great deal of confusion about this verse. It is often handled as if it were a form of Couéism – as if Paul were telling us to say to ourselves, 'There is no sin in us and therefore we will not sin.' It does not mean that at all. It cannot. No, it means that we are dead to sin in the sense that we no longer belong to the realm and dominion of sin. That must be true, for this reason: Paul says of the Lord Jesus Christ, 'For in that he died, he died unto sin once: but in that he liveth, he liveth unto God. Likewise reckon ye . . .' (*Rom.* 6:10–11). The Lord Jesus Christ died unto sin once and we have died unto sin with him. That is the argument and that surely settles the matter.

There never was any sin in the Lord Jesus Christ. He did not have to persuade himself or say to himself that there was no sin in him. We are told that 'he died unto sin *once*'. He came from heaven into this world. He was 'made of a woman, made under the law' (*Gal.* 4:4). He came into the realm and the domain of sin – this world, which is governed by the god of this world, the devil, 'the prince of the power of the air' (*Eph.* 2:2). Not only that, by taking our sins upon himself, he put himself into the position where sin, as it were, had a claim upon him, and the law had a claim upon him, but he dealt with it once and for ever by his death upon the cross: 'In that he died, he died unto sin once

... Likewise reckon ye also yourselves to be dead indeed unto sin.' So to be 'dead unto sin' is something positional. Paul's words in Romans 6 refer to the fact that we must say to ourselves, 'We no longer belong to the dominion of sin or of Satan.'

Paul puts this truth explicitly a few verses later, in Romans 6:14: 'Sin shall not have dominion over you: for ye are not under the law, but under grace.' It is clear, therefore, that Paul is not telling us to indulge in some sort of auto-suggestion. We do not have to persuade ourselves that there is no longer any sin in us. That is not true – there is sin in us. Sin remains in us as long as we are in this life. There is nothing to the contrary taught in the whole of Scripture. But though there is a remnant of sin remaining in us, we are no longer in the domain, the dominion, under the rule, of sin.

Then we go on from there. This sixth chapter of the Epistle to the Romans is a most vital chapter in this whole question of the mortification of the deeds of the body, this aspect of the process of sanctification. You notice that the outstanding characteristic of this chapter is the way in which it reasons with us. It is an extended argument. The apostle starts off by saying:

Shall we continue in sin, that grace may abound? (Rom. 6:1)

And his answer is not, 'Oh, there's no need for that, all you have to do is to surrender yourself to Christ and he will do it for you. Let go, let God.' No, no! Paul's response is to reason. He says:

God forbid. How shall we, that are dead [that died] to sin, live any longer therein? (verse 2)

The thing is contradictory. It is unreasonable. It means that you have not grasped your position, and you are not working it out.

Know ye not, that so many of us as were baptized into Jesus Christ were baptized into his death? (verse 3)

So that when he died to sin once, we died to sin once and so on. And Paul goes on with his great argument, putting it like this:

Knowing this, that our old man is crucified with him, that the body of sin might be destroyed, that henceforth we should not serve sin (verse 6).

That is the point. We must not 'serve' sin any longer, we are not under its dominion. But, you notice, this is put to us as an argument. It is something that we must reason through. It is because so many fail to do this that they are in trouble. I know many people who have spent a lifetime waiting for something to happen to them, for sin to be taken out of them. It does not happen.

There is, of course, always the possibility of various psychological experiences. There are people who tell you that suddenly something was taken out of them. Well, that can happen. That can happen apart from Christianity. There are people who have undergone a profound psychological change quite suddenly; they have finished with something they had been doing and they have never done it again. We must not dispute that. That is a real fact. All I am saying is that that is not the teaching of the New Testament. The New Testament goes on appealing to us to work, to reason it out. And so Paul says:

Likewise reckon ye also yourselves to be dead indeed unto sin, but alive unto God through Jesus Christ our Lord (verse 11).

Then:

Let not sin therefore reign in your mortal body, that ye should obey it in the lusts thereof (verse 12).

It is an argument and we must follow it through.

What then? shall we sin, because we are not under the law, but under grace? God forbid (verse 15).

And then there is this bit of argument:

Know ye not, that to whom ye yield yourselves servants to obey, his servants ye are to whom ye obey; whether of sin unto death, or of obedience unto righteousness? But God be thanked, that ye were [once] the servants [slaves] of sin

– you are no longer that –

but ye have obeyed from the heart that form of doctrine which was delivered you. Being then made free from sin

– that is the term, *made free*, and, as we have seen, it means that we are no longer under the dominion of sin and Satan. Sin no longer has coercive power, it does not have the right over us that it formerly had; we are now translated into the kingdom of God. We are free from sin in that sense, and that sense only. We must look at this objectively. This is, all along, a matter of our position –

ye became the servants of righteousness (verses 16–18).

You and I, my friends, are now in the kingdom of righteousness. We are in a world of evil, yes, but we do not belong to the kingdom of evil, we are not 'of the world' any longer. 'Ye are of God, little children,' says John (*1 John* 4:4). 'The whole world lieth in wickedness (*1 John* 5:19). That is what we are told here. So we must understand all this and work it out.

Then Paul continues:

I speak after the manner of men because of the infirmity of your flesh (verse 19).

In other words, he says that because they find it difficult to follow the argument, he is going to use an illustration in order to help them work it out. Now could there be a more conclusive proof of the fact that the New Testament method of sanctification and mortification of the flesh is a process of reasoning and application of the doctrine, and a realization of our position? It is not just a surrender in order that everything may be done for us. This is the illustration:

For as ye have yielded your members servants to uncleanness and to iniquity unto iniquity; even so now yield your members servants to righteousness unto holiness.

And he adds:

For when ye were the servants [slaves] of sin, ye were free from righteousness (verses 19–20).

In other words, when you were in the kingdom of evil, you were the slaves of that kingdom and you had nothing to do with the kingdom of righteousness. Oh, yes, you may have pulled yourself up now and again. Sometimes you may have been a little better than you were at other times. You may, indeed, have been a very moral person. But you belonged to that kingdom and you had nothing to do with the kingdom of righteousness. You were 'free from righteousness'. That cannot mean that there was no good at all in you. It is not subjective. It is describing positions in kingdoms. You were free from righteousness in that you had nothing to do with that realm.

And then Paul puts a great question – and this is the sort of question that you and I must put to ourselves if we are being led by the Spirit to mortify the deeds of the body:

What fruit had ye then in those things whereof ye are now ashamed? for the end of those things is death (verse 21).

Tell me, says the apostle, can you not see this? What return, what benefit, what fruit, did you have in the things that you used to do, even while you did them? Look back across your lives, he says, and you are ashamed of some things that you see. But go further: What did they really give you even while you were doing them? The answer is: Nothing! They just took from you:

For the end of those things is death. But now being [having been] made free from sin

– by being put into a new dominion –

and become servants to God, ye have your fruit unto holiness, and the end everlasting life (verses 21–22).

And then the final conclusion:

For the wages of sin is death; but the gift of God is eternal life through Jesus Christ our Lord (verse 23).

All I am concerned to do for now is to say this: patently what you and I must do, and what we will do if we are led of the Spirit, is to work out that kind of argument. In other words, you are not governed by your feelings; you are not governed by whether or not something appeals to you, by whether or not you like it. You are not governed by whether or not other people are doing it. You put it all into the light of this truth about yourself and you say: Is that compatible with where I am now? Is that compatible with my being a citizen of the kingdom of righteousness? Is that compatible with the fact that I am 'freed from sin'? You put that crucial question to yourself, or, in the light of this, that command of the apostle: 'Let not sin therefore reign in your mortal body' (*Rom.* 6:12). It is inconsistent. You are being a fool.

Paul repeats the same injunction in chapter 8:

Therefore, brethren, we are debtors, not to the flesh, to live after the flesh. For if ye live after the flesh, ye shall die (Rom. 8:12–13).

Now why does he say 'therefore'? It is because he has just been saying:

If Christ be in you, the body is dead because of sin; but the Spirit is life because of righteousness. But if the Spirit of him that raised up Jesus from the dead dwell in you, he that raised up Christ from the dead shall also quicken your mortal bodies by his Spirit that dwelleth in you (Rom. 8:10–11).

What Paul means is this: As Christians you are already saved in your spirits but the body is not yet saved; sin still remains in the body. One day, however, the body also will be saved. In the light of that, 'We are debtors, not to the flesh, to live after the flesh' (*Rom.* 8:12). If you say you are a child of God and are looking forward to going to heaven, you are contradicting yourself if you go on living as if you still belonged to time and to the earth and to the kingdom of unrighteousness and of Satan. Do not do that, he says, it is monstrous. We are not debtors to the flesh; we have finished with that. This is a great principle that we must keep ever in the forefront of our minds, and we will, if we are being led by the Spirit.

Christians go on through life always working these principles out, following the argument. They do not say, 'No, I mustn't do that, somebody might see me.' To argue like that is worldly and carnal. They say, 'I can't do that because I am what I am. It is incompatible with my whole position, with my relationship to God.' They do not hesitate and wonder and feel troubled or rather annoyed at having to do this and not do that. No, no! They have reasons, which follow inevitably, for what they do and for what they do not do.

But if that is the great principle, we must apply it in detail, and the New Testament gives us details. You see, *we* must do it; *we* must work out the argument and then apply it in detail. This is stated many times in the Epistle to the Romans. Take, for instance, the first verse in the twelfth chapter: 'I beseech you therefore, brethren, by the mercies of God, that ye present your bodies a living sacrifice, holy, acceptable unto God, which is your reasonable service.' (Do not worry about that last bit. The important thing is that you 'present your bodies a living sacrifice, holy, acceptable unto God'.) And Paul means that literally – 'present your *bodies*'. Here again, I am convinced, is the point at which so many of us break down and fail. We will persist in thinking that this is a matter of some general decision. I make my great act of surrender. Hand over! Crisis! Then the process goes on in me and is worked out in me. That is not true! I must go on presenting and surrendering my body, and in detail.

Let me show you the details. Come back again to Romans 6:12–13. Paul does not say, 'Let not sin therefore reign in you', but, 'Let not sin therefore reign in your mortal body.' This is a profound statement.[1] In a sense, in this practical matter, it is the profoundest doctrine of the whole of the New Testament. 'Your mortal body', that is what the apostle is talking about. Do not think of yourself purely spiritually. You have a body, after all, and most of your troubles in life are going to arise because of this. You will have your body as long as you are here. So Paul says, 'Let not sin therefore reign in your mortal body.' It cannot reign in your spirit because you are dead to it in that respect, you have died with Christ. But there is a danger of it reigning in your mortal body, and it will reign there unless you stop it. It is for you to do this. *You* must 'let not sin therefore reign in your mortal body, that ye should obey it in the lusts thereof'.

So what do you do? Now here are the details – you do not even take the body in general – 'Neither yield ye your members as instruments of unrighteousness unto sin: but yield yourselves unto God, as those that are alive from the dead, and' – the details – 'your members as instruments of righteousness unto God' (*Rom.* 6:13). Now by 'members', Paul does not simply mean the various parts of the body, though he includes that. He means all the faculties of the soul, which normally

---

[1] Dr Lloyd-Jones added here, 'Those of us who come here on Friday nights have spent weeks, not to say months, on all this.' These sermons were published in *Romans Chapter 6: The New Man* (Edinburgh: Banner of Truth Trust, 1973).

manifest themselves through the body. So you must come to details. Paul does not merely say: Surrender yourself unto God. No, he says: Surrender your body also unto God. Not only that: Surrender every part and portion of your body unto God. This means, for instance: Surrender your eyes unto God. Say to yourself: 'I am a child of God and my eyes, therefore, are no longer my own, they belong to God.' There are certain things you do not look at because they are evil. And you must do that in detail. You do not just take one great decision. No, no! You must go on. There will be things on all sides of you acting as magnets to draw your eyes, and you do not let them. You do what Job says: 'I made a covenant with mine eyes' (*Job* 31:1). He says, in effect, 'I looked straight forward always.' If we only did that, my friends, we would avoid a lot of trouble. 'Yield [surrender] your members' – your eyes, your hands, your feet, the whole of your body.

But it does not stop there. You must surrender your mind and your thinking. Obviously! As a child of God, you must. 'Let this mind be in you . . .' (*Phil.* 2:5). 'We have the mind of Christ' (*1 Cor.* 2:16). I have no right to use my mind in the old way. I must use it in the new way. I must surrender it and keep on doing so. What else? My imagination! How terrible is the power of the imagination! How many sin in imagination who do not sin in act! But that is quite as bad in the sight of God. You remember our Lord's words: 'Whosoever looketh . . . hath committed adultery with her . . .' (*Matt.* 5:28). Surrender your members, your imagination (that is one of them), 'as instruments of righteousness unto God'.

Notice how Paul constantly repeats this principle. 'As ye have [in the past] yielded your members servants [slaves] to uncleanness and to iniquity unto iniquity; even so now yield your members' – one by one, take every one of them – 'servants to righteousness unto holiness' (*Rom.* 6:19). That is the way to mortify the deeds of the body. It is to realize that every part of the body is always capable of doing that which belongs to the old life and to the realm of unrighteousness. Therefore, you take the members of your body one by one and you say, 'I give them all. I must constantly be exercising them all in this new way, which is the exact opposite of what I used to do in the past.'

But why all this? The answer can be found at the end of 1 Corinthians 6, where the apostle Paul puts it like this: 'What? know ye not that your body is the temple of the Holy Ghost which is in you, which ye have of God, and ye are not your own? For ye are bought with a price: therefore glorify God in your body, and in your spirit, which are God's' (*1 Cor.* 6:19–20). The body is as much God's as is the spirit. And the Spirit will lead us to live in this way if we are led of him and allow him to remind us. That is New Testament holiness. You must just go on reminding yourself that this body of yours is the temple in which the Holy Spirit is living. As the Lord Jesus Christ, the Son, when he came to earth, tabernacled in the body that he received from his mother Mary, so the Holy Spirit tabernacles in our bodies. That is the way to deal with the body. Not having a number of rules and regulations and ticking them off as you do or do not do them; not having some mechanical legalism put upon you. No, no! You just go on reminding yourself that he, the Spirit of holiness and of truth and of beauty, is in you; he is actually in you. If you are a Christian, that is a fact.

The Holy Spirit has been given to you. He always dwells in you, and you are not your own because you have been bought with a price. So, then, if the Holy Spirit is dwelling in my body, I must remember that everything my body does, every part, every instrument, every member, involves him. Do you see the eternal difference between morality and Christian holiness? The moral person knows nothing at all about this. But this is Christianity, this is essential Christianity, that having realized the truth concerning ourselves, our relationship and our position, we then apply it and argue and reason it out and go on doing so, constantly and in detail.

There is something we can add even to that because in the Epistle to the Galatians the apostle makes this categorical statement: 'They that are Christ's have crucified the flesh with the affections and lusts' (*Gal.* 5:24). What does this mean? It is a most important point and we must be careful in our interpretation. There are many who have interpreted this in a way that has brought them into terrible bondage. I am referring to a false asceticism. Let me show you what I mean by again listening to the apostle as he puts this before us:

Now the Spirit speaketh expressly, that in the latter times some shall depart from the faith, giving heed to seducing spirits, and doctrines of devils; speaking lies in hypocrisy; having their conscience seared with a hot iron

– then –

forbidding to marry, and commanding to abstain from meats, which God hath created [ordained] to be received with thanksgiving of them which believe and know the truth. For every creature of God is good, and nothing to be refused, if it be received with thanksgiving: for it is sanctified by the word of God and prayer (1 Tim. 4:1–5).

Now that is a reference to what I am calling 'false asceticism'. It is perpetrated by people who say, 'They that are Christ's have crucified the flesh with the affections and lusts', therefore sex is evil and the true Christian never gets married. But that is the opposite of what the Scripture teaches. Sex is a gift of God; he has made us male and female and there is to be an attraction between male and female. There is nothing wrong in that. It is right; it is ordained of God.

So what does Paul mean when he says, 'crucified the flesh'? Well, 'the flesh' there carries the connotation of a false and wrong use of the gift of God. And what an important distinction that is! Every gift of God is good and every gift is meant to be used. But there is a wrong use of God's gifts, a selfish use. Every gift of God should ultimately be used to the glory of God. If we do not do that, there is something wrong. Christianity never calls us to be unnatural, Christianity never asks us literally to chop off hands or feet. That is false teaching, that is to go back under legalism. Christianity tells us to do that metaphorically but never literally. It teaches the right use of the body. As I have been showing you, you are to surrender your members as instruments, every single one of them. Anything that has been given to you by God is *ipso facto* right and good as long as it is used in the right way. I must not continue with this but there is a right way for the use of the particular gift I have mentioned, and that is in marriage and what leads to marriage, and it is anything outside that which is condemned in the Scripture.

To crucify the flesh with its affections and lusts does not mean, I repeat, that the true Christian never gets married. That is the charge people bring against the apostle Paul. It is a lie! The apostle himself, as I have shown you, contradicts this idea in his teaching in 1 Timothy 4 and also in many other places. He was always denouncing that false asceticism. No, no! That is the whole error of the Roman Catholic Church with its celibacy and so on – utterly unscriptural. What we are taught in Scripture is that we crucify everything that is based upon self and selfishness, or the use for our own ends of the gifts that God has given us as human beings for the purpose of glorifying him. So what Paul means is this: the Christian says, 'Right! Hitherto I've used the gifts of God to serve and to suit my own selfish ends. I'll do that no more' – and the moment you have said that, and for as long as you hold this fundamental attitude, you have crucified the flesh with the affections and lusts. You may fail at times but that does not mean that you are no longer a Christian.

We must, therefore, be very careful about this false asceticism. I repeat that it was ordained that man and woman should love one another, should fall in love. There is nothing wrong in that; there is everything right about it. The Bible never condemns the natural. And, therefore, to feel that you are crucifying the flesh or that you are mortifying the deeds of the body by, as it were, going out of life and becoming some kind of monk or hermit or anchorite – which many people can do without actually going into a monastery – is a terrible misinterpretation of the Scripture. I am emphasizing this because I know that there are many who keep themselves in a perpetual torment at this point. They have come to regard the natural as sinful. But it is the misuse of the natural for selfish ends that alone is condemned in the Bible.

So let me close this whole matter by putting it like this: the next thing we must realize is that we have the power to do all this.

'Where do you find that?' asks someone.

Well, here it is: 'If ye through the Spirit do mortify the deeds of the body, ye shall live' (*Rom.* 8:13). We are being given the power; the Holy Spirit within us is the power that enables us to do this. That is why it seems to me that that other teaching that comes to us and says, 'Have you got troubles and problems? Very well, do not struggle any more but hand it over to the Lord and he will do it', is a denial of the doctrine of the indwelling Spirit. The Spirit is within us to enable us to mortify the deeds of the flesh.

Now let me give you one statement that puts this in particularly blunt, plain and explicit terms:

Furthermore then we beseech you, brethren, and exhort you by the Lord Jesus, that as ye have received of us how ye ought to walk and to please God, so ye would abound more and more. For ye know what commandments we gave you by the Lord Jesus.

You notice he gave them 'commandments'. He did not just say to them, 'You have been saved, now very well, take step number two, let go and let God. No, no!

For this is the will of God, even your sanctification, that ye should abstain from fornication: that every one of you should know how to possess his vessel in sanctification and honour; not in the lust of concupiscence, even as the Gentiles which know not God.

There it is quite plainly.

That no man go beyond and defraud his brother in any matter: because that the Lord is the avenger of all such, as we also have forewarned you and testified.

Then:

For God hath not called us unto uncleanness, but unto holiness. He therefore that despiseth, despiseth not man, but God, who hath also given unto us his holy Spirit (1 Thess. 4:1–8).

Now could anything be plainer? Paul is saying, in effect, 'God has not called us to uncleanness – that is what the Gentiles did, that is what you were doing before you became Christians – but unto holiness. Very well, then, you are not disobeying men, you are not disobeying me, you are disobeying God. And on top of that, you are disobeying the God who has also given us his Holy Spirit in order that we might have the strength to crucify the flesh and to mortify our bodies. So you have no excuse at all. You do not say, "I cannot do anything . . ." God has given you his Holy Spirit and in the Holy Spirit, who is in you, there is power, more than sufficient power, to carry out all the commandments and do everything to which we are exhorted.'

Very well, we must leave it at that for now. All I have been trying to say to you is this: if that is the way in which you normally and habitually face life and think about these things, then it is my privilege to tell you that you are a child of God; but if all I have been trying to say means nothing to you and is a sort of gibberish, then I say to you that you are not a child of God. If you see this and say 'Amen!' to it, you are being led of the Spirit and therefore you are a child of God. Go on your way rejoicing and yield yourselves unto God as those who are alive from the dead. ✢

25

The Mortification of Sin: Work out Your Faith; Walk in the Spirit

But as many as received him, to them gave he power to become the sons of God, even to them that believe on his name: which were born, not of blood, nor of the will of the flesh, nor of the will of man, but of God (John 1:12–13).

We are still considering this great statement in which we are reminded that the Son of God came from heaven to earth, the Word was made flesh, the incarnation, and all that followed it, took place, in order that you and I might be made and become the sons, the children, of God. There is nothing we can ever hear that rises above this wonderful statement. As Christians, we are not merely forgiven, we are not only reconciled to God, but we are adopted into the family of God and we are destined to enter into a great and a glorious inheritance of which we are now the fellow-heirs with our blessed Lord and Saviour Jesus Christ. We are meant to know it. We are meant to believe it. We are meant to be assured of it. We are meant to rejoice in it. And that is why we are taking all this time to try to bring this truth home. And it seems to me that it still needs to be brought home to us. We do not sing as if we believe it.

Do you really know that you have been taken up from a horrible pit and the miry clay? If we do know and believe this, we are bound to express it. If you had had some narrow escape in a car accident, if you had been desperately ill and your life had just been saved, then you would let everybody know it, would you not? You would speak with emotion. There would be a thrill in your voice. We are not meant to mourn as Christians; we are meant to be a rejoicing people. 'Rejoice in the Lord alway', says the great apostle: 'and again I say, Rejoice' (*Phil.* 4:4).

But it is not my business to make you rejoice. If our rejoicing were only something that I or anybody else could produce, it would not be true rejoicing. What produces rejoicing is the realization of this most wonderful truth, and our spiritual state is a measure of our realization of this truth. A languishing and mourning church is a travesty, it is an insult to the name of God. It is not surprising that the masses of the people are outside the church. They seem to have all the excitement and the laughter. Listen to them at football matches and races. How keen they are, how excited, how animated! And look at us! The church gives the impression that she is uncertain of her truth, uncertain of her faith. We give the impression that we are a burdened people who are looking for something, not people who have been given the gift of eternal life and sonship and heirship of the eternal bliss. All this makes it very necessary that we should be spending time in making sure of this teaching.

That we are the children of God is not just a phrase, a statement. We are to *know* it. And we are to let everybody else know it. We are, all of us, always ready to boast, are we not? We boast of our birth, we boast of our family, we boast of our brains, we boast of our achievements, we boast of what we call good luck, or of something wonderful that has happened to us, yet here is the greatest thing of all and we seem to be doubtful and hesitant and almost apologetic. I am concerned about all this not merely that you and I may enter into the riches that are put at our disposal by God in Christ, but that the grievous state of the church and of the world should rouse every one of us to a sense of our responsibility in this evil day in which we find ourselves.

We have reached the point at which we are trying to know for certain whether or not we are being led by the Spirit of God. If we are sure that we are, then there is no doubt about it, we are the children of God. So this is a very good way of examining ourselves. We have been considering the various ways in which the Spirit does lead us, and we are now looking at the work of the Spirit in what the Scriptures call 'the mortification of the deeds of the body'. Having looked at this great subject negatively, we are now looking at it positively. There are certain things that we must do in practice and in detail. In our last study, we were looking at the whole question of the surrender of the body: 'Present your bodies a living sacrifice' (*Rom.* 12:1) – every faculty, every part. Every propensity that you have is to be given to the glory of God and for his service.

The next great principle, it seems to me, is the importance of realizing and emphasizing that we must constantly practise these things, that this is something that we must go on doing. Now I can most conveniently show this by opening to you two portions of Scripture. Let us first of all look at what we are told by the apostle Peter in the first chapter of his second epistle. Here is the exact doctrine that we have in Romans 6, but with Peter's own characteristic emphasis. In the first four verses, he starts off by telling the people who and what they are and what is possible to them. He says he is writing:

To them that have obtained like precious faith with us through the righteousness of God and our Saviour Jesus Christ (2 Pet. 1:1).

What else? Well:

According as his divine power hath given unto us all things that pertain unto life and godliness, through the knowledge of him that hath called us to glory and virtue

– now we are told here that everything that is necessary for our life and godliness is already available for us in and through the Lord Jesus Christ. That was our final point last time – that the power is already given us, the power of the Holy Spirit and the indwelling Christ. That is true of all Christians. We have power –

whereby are given unto us exceeding great and precious promises: that by these ye might be partakers of the divine nature, having escaped the corruption that is in the world through lust (verses 3–4).

Now there it is, always the first thing. We have already escaped 'the corruption that is in the world through lust'. The world is corrupt and it is corrupt as the result of lust. Is there anybody who doubts that any longer? Is there anybody who thinks that this life is wonderful and this world is wonderful? No, it is corrupt as the result of lust – and there it is shouting at us. But, says the apostle, you have escaped all that, you have been taken out of it by the power and excellency of God and you are now in this new realm, this new kingdom. That is our position, and that is where Paul, too, starts: 'Reckon ye also yourselves to be dead indeed unto sin' – you are no longer there in that mass of corruption – 'but alive unto God' (*Rom.* 6:11). And here it is in the words of Peter: 'partakers of the divine nature'. Here is the point that we have constantly been making – that we start with the realization that that is true of us. That is our spiritual condition, our spiritual position.

What about it? Now, then, continues Peter in verse 5, 'And beside this' – because of all this, in the light of all this. This is only the beginning. It is an essential beginning, but you do not stop at that. Peter is saying, 'Because this is true, what are you to do?'

'Well,' says someone, 'having received Christ for justification by faith, all we have to do now is take the second step, take our sanctification by faith in exactly the same way. As we did not struggle for our justification, we must not struggle for our sanctification. We must not do anything, but just let go and let God do it all, hand it all over.'

Is that it? Listen:

And beside this, giving all diligence

– concentrating all your powers, taking yourself in hand and making yourself do it – *you –*

add to your faith virtue; and to virtue knowledge; and to knowledge temperance; and to temperance patience; and to patience godliness; and to godliness brotherly kindness; and to brotherly kindness charity (verses 5–7).

That is what you and I must do. We do not just go to meetings and wait for 'it' to come to us, or for something to happen to us. No, 'giving all diligence, add' – and that means, of course, 'furnish with', 'supplement with'. The Greek word translated here by 'add' is an interesting word. It was used in connection with the Greek drama. When it was felt that the action on stage needed to be furnished, as it were, or elaborated, then the chorus was introduced. That was the origin of the Greek chorus. Its purpose was to 'furnish' the play, to fill it out, as it were, to make it more artistic, more presentable, not so bald. So you must furnish your faith with the qualities that Peter enumerates.

For now, I am concerned not so much with looking at these qualities that we are to add to our faith, or work out our faith in respect of, as with showing the importance of realizing that we must *do* this. In effect, the apostle Peter is saying: 'Here you are. You are a Christian. You have received this "like precious faith with us through the righteousness of God and our Saviour Jesus Christ". You are no longer in the world. You are no longer in that corruption. You are "a new man" in Christ Jesus and you are in this new life, which is a life of faith from beginning to end. Very well, then, do not stop at that.'

So what do you do? Well, Peter says, work that out. You must work your faith out with diligence, and it does need diligence. You must pay attention to it. It does not just happen to you. Nobody can do it for you. The preacher cannot give you the experience. The business of preaching is to stimulate you and to urge you but it cannot do it for you.

Now our faith must be worked out, Peter says, in terms of 'virtue', and in terms of 'knowledge'. How little we know! How little we know of the Scriptures! So study them; get books that will help you to study them. Read them, digest them, grapple with them. Do not say you have not got time. Do not think that because you have read five or six verses and a little comment on them you have done everything. That does not take much diligence, does it? No, no! Diligence means application. It means thoroughness. It means real hard work. You must take yourself in hand and discipline yourself. You must curb yourself. You must do anything you like that wakes you up. Put a wet towel round your head, if necessary, read your Bible standing rather than sitting – do anything. Give all diligence to ensure that you add to your faith virtue, and then knowledge, temperance (control), patience, godliness, brotherly kindness and charity (love). Peter means that all along we must be *exercising* this faith of ours, working it out along various lines and constantly practising it. So let us go further and follow Peter's argument because he knew the people to whom he was writing.

For if these things be in you and abound

– if you do this, if you show this great diligence and furnish your faith with these other qualities –

they make you that ye shall neither be barren nor unfruitful in the knowledge of our Lord Jesus Christ (verse 8).

What does that mean? Well, Peter says: You know, it is possible for you to be a Christian but rather a useless one; you can be an unfruitful Christian. It has to be granted that you are a Christian, you are in God's orchard, as it were. You are no longer in that wilderness where you were. You have been transplanted. But you are a very poor specimen, without much fruit, and of not much help or use to anybody else. You are barren. Yes, you are a Christian but nobody else derives very much benefit or encouragement from that. You are a miserable looking tree in an orchard where many of the trees bear wonderful crops of fruit, of great value and help to others.

So Peter says: Look here, if you are a barren Christian, there is only one explanation – you are not giving all diligence to furnish your faith as you should. You are sitting down and waiting for something to happen to you. You have been waiting all your life and you are as bad now as you were twenty or thirty years ago. Your trouble is that you think you need a new experience. That is not what you need. What you need is to shake yourself, to pull yourself together, to begin to apply yourself, to begin to be diligent in the furnishing of your faith. 'If you do these things', he says, 'ye shall neither be barren nor unfruitful in the knowledge of our Lord Jesus Christ.'

This is most wonderful. The more you know and practise these qualities, the greater the blessings you receive. It is inevitable, is it not? If that old tree there is not bearing much fruit, then you begin to examine it. You say, 'What's the matter? The other trees are fruitful, what's wrong with this one?' And then you look and you see, perhaps, that the earth around the base of the tree is too hard. 'Well,' you say, 'I must get hold of my fork and loosen the soil a bit.' That is what you do – you are 'giving diligence'. It will take effort; you may perspire. It does not matter. You want the tree to bear fruit, so you do that. And if there is anything wrong with the tree itself, then you apply the appropriate remedies. It may need a little compost or some fertilizer. And as you deal with it, you begin to find the old tree lifting up its head, as it were, and it will bear fruit in the following season.

That is precisely what the apostle Peter is saying. The whole emphasis of the New Testament is that you and I must do this work; it is not done for us. Of course, unbelievers cannot justify themselves. They are dead and you do not ask them to do these things. But here are men and women who have been given life through the 'exceeding great and precious promises', who are 'partakers of the divine nature', and to whom 'all things that pertain unto life and godliness' have been given.

Yet there they sit, waiting for something to happen! It is a denial of the New Testament teaching! No, no! Go on and do this, says Peter, and you will no longer be 'barren nor unfruitful in the knowledge of our Lord Jesus Christ'. The more you do, the more you will get; and the more you know him, the more you will manifest that knowledge in your life and the greater will be your benefit to others.

But then Peter goes on. It is not enough to leave it like that.

But he that lacketh these things

– that is to say, the person who does not show diligence and furnish the faith –

is blind, and cannot see afar off, and hath forgotten that he was purged from his old sins (verse 9).

Not only has he forgotten, he does not realize where he is going! He is content with the fact that he is now what he calls a believer. He believes his sins are forgiven, and there he stops. He has not realized the full meaning of salvation. Salvation includes being purged from your old sins, being taken from the corruption that is in the world through lust. That is translation from the kingdom of Satan into the kingdom of God's dear Son. Salvation includes all that. But this man is living, as it were, just outside the realm of corruption. He does not want to be in it, of course; he does not want to go to hell. No, but he stays as near as he can to that realm. He does not realize that he has been taken right away from it. He does not see afar off. He does not see what he is in Christ. He does not see the glory of the kingdom of God and the wonderful things that are being prepared for him in salvation. He is blind and 'hath forgotten that he was purged from his old sins'. To see all this is the whole secret.

We will persist in living from day to day and from hour to hour, and we consult our feelings and our moods and our states, and they govern us. So we spend our days in shallows and in miseries. We must pull ourselves up and say to ourselves, 'Look here, you've been delivered from the corruption that's in the world through lust. You've been purged from your old sins. You are dead to sins.' Not only that, do you not see where you are going? Do not just think of today. Do not think in terms of time. In a sense, you are out of that. You are now a citizen of the kingdom of God – heaven is your home and your citizenship is there. Very well, then, live with your eye on that. Open your eyes! Do not be blind, do not look into some perpetual mist, but see the eternal glories gleaming afar. Look at that!

'Set your affection on things above, not on things on the earth,' says Paul (*Col.* 3:2), and that is what Peter is saying. Make yourself see them, because they are there, and they are there for you. Do not be blind! Do not be like somebody who is short-sighted. Realize that in Christ there is this power to cleanse your eye, to give power, as it were, to your optic nerve and enable you to see the things that are invisible. Be like Moses! 'He endured, as seeing him who is invisible' (*Heb.* 11:27). That is it! The paradox! The glorious paradox of Christian living! Peter is trying to show his readers the utter reasonableness of all this. It is an argument. Peter can argue as well as Paul and in the same way. It is a much simpler argument, always, with Peter, but the argument is essentially the same. Let us go on. What else does Peter say?

Wherefore the rather

– do not be blind, do not be short-sighted, and back comes the same word, 'give diligence' –

give diligence to make your calling and election sure

– and that does not mean that you must work to save yourself. Peter means that you have been called by God, you are elect of God, and if you do the things he is telling you to do, you will know that, you will make it sure to yourself. *You* do not bring about your calling and election! If our eternal destiny depended upon us, then not a single one of us would ever reach salvation. Is it likely that we ever would? Thank God, what guarantees my salvation is that I am called and elected of God. But I am meant to enjoy that knowledge, I am meant to know it. So I make my calling and election sure to myself by giving this diligence, adding to my faith virtue and knowledge and so on. It is the only way –

for if ye do these things, ye shall never fall

– but not only that –

for so an entrance shall be ministered unto you abundantly into the everlasting kingdom of our Lord and Saviour Jesus Christ.

Peter is making the same point. When you come to lie on your deathbed, you will not be filled with doubts and uncertainty. You will not say, 'I wonder where I'm going? Am I truly a Christian?' You will not die in an agony of doubt and uncertainty, just hoping. No, no! Peter says that if you do these things, there will be an abundant entry. The flags will be flying, the hooters will be sounding. It will be a glorious, triumphant entrance into the everlasting glory.

'Our people die well,' said John Wesley. And he was right! The great doctrine of all sections of Methodism was the doctrine of assurance. That was the keynote two hundred years ago in the great Evangelical Awakening. Whitefield and Wesley, and all the others who worked with them, were always preaching 'assurance', 'certainty'. And the result was that when their people came to die, they did not die in fear and terror and doubt and alarm, hoping that they were saved. They knew! 'I know whom I have believed, and am persuaded that he is able to keep that which I have committed unto him against that day,' said Paul (2 *Tim.* 1:12). 'An entrance shall be ministered unto you abundantly into the everlasting kingdom of our Lord and Saviour Jesus Christ.' Now, then, my friends, that is the argument of the great apostle Peter. We must realize these truths and then put them into practice.

Let us look at the argument as it is presented by the apostle Paul in Galatians chapter 5. It is almost exactly the same teaching but put in different language. And, I say again, the important thing for us to grasp here is the principle. Work out the details at your leisure, but get hold of the principle. Here it is. Paul starts off with a general exhortation:

This I say then

– here it is, here is your principle –

Walk in the Spirit, and ye shall not fulfil the lust of the flesh. (Gal. 5:16).

Now that is a categorical statement. The whole secret, Paul says, is this: 'Walk in the Spirit', which means, live in the Spirit; be occupied with the Spirit; spend your life in the Spirit; live your life in the Spirit. That is another way of saying, 'Reckon ye also yourselves to be dead indeed unto sin, but alive unto God' (*Rom.* 6:11); 'Ye are not in the flesh, but in the Spirit' (*Rom.* 8:9). This is a great principle, says Paul, and he works it out in a very interesting way. He says that it is inevitably true for this reason:

For the flesh lusteth against the Spirit, and the Spirit against the flesh: and these are contrary the one to the other: so that ye cannot do the things that ye would (verse 17).

Realize, Paul says, that you are now a Christian, in this position. This is how you are, as it were, constituted. You are 'a new man', a new person! You are dead to sin. You are dead to the law. You have received newness of life with Christ and are indeed seated 'in heavenly places in Christ Jesus' at this moment (*Eph.* 2:6). Nevertheless, you are still in the body, you are still in this world, and, therefore, 'the flesh' is still left. By 'the flesh' Paul means the wrong use of the body – that is a good definition of the flesh. We were dealing with that last time and we said that all we have in the body, all our instincts, are given to us by God. They are not sinful; sex is not sinful. It is the wrong use of them that is sinful – and, I repeat, that is the flesh.

Now, says Paul, there is still flesh remaining in you, and that will always militate against the life of the Spirit, who is also in you, and these two are contrary, the one to the other. They fight against one another. The Spirit is there to uplift you and to bring you to God; the flesh tends to hold you to earth and reminds you of the corruption out of which you have been delivered. Now, then, says the apostle, you must realize that these two are opposites but that in some strange sort of way they are connected. And, he says, it works like this: if you give way to the flesh, the flesh will be prominent and the Spirit will be out of sight; but if you walk in the Spirit, the flesh will go back and be out of sight.

Now the obvious illustration is the little weather indicators that you can buy in the shops at the seaside. They have a little cottage, and a little man and a little woman made of wood, and they are on the same piece of wood. The woman comes out when there is fine weather, the man comes out when there is bad weather, and they are never out at the same time. It is impossible. They are on a pivot and when the one is out the other must be in. It is like that in your life. If you walk in the Spirit, then you will not fulfil the lust of the flesh. But if you fulfil the lust of the flesh, the life of the Spirit in you will be correspondingly out of sight. These two are opposites and cannot go together. 'The flesh lusteth against the Spirit, and the Spirit against the flesh'; it is a question of warfare. That is always true of the Christian. The New Testament never tells you anywhere that there will be an end to that warfare while you are in this world. What the New Testament tells you is how to deal with it. And the way to deal with it is to walk in the Spirit and then you will not fulfil the lust of the flesh.

'Ah,' you say, 'but I've been waiting for an experience that will take the flesh right out of me.'

My friend, you will go on waiting. You may get some psychological experience that will relieve you in one or two respects, perhaps, but you will never get rid of the flesh. The body will not be delivered until the end, the resurrection – then there will be glory for the body. But while we are here, the body is here and we have this struggle, and we overcome by walking in the Spirit. So Paul says that you must realize that this is the position, and the moment you realize it, you then 'walk' in the Spirit, and so you will not be fulfilling the lust of the flesh. And do we not all know this to be perfectly true? When you are walking in the Spirit and giving diligence to do the things that Peter tells us to do, you do not get worried so much by the flesh, do you? When you are in a spiritual atmosphere, when you are reading your Bible and reading good books about the Bible and are uplifted, these things of the flesh seem abhorrent; but if you neglect the things of the Spirit, the flesh seems attractive again. This is just simple experience; it is inevitable. It works on this pivot, this swivel, and there it is as long as we are here, flesh and spirit. Very well, says Paul, 'Walk in the Spirit, and ye shall not fulfil the lust of the flesh.' Realize that, but realize the opposite also. And then Paul goes on to make a very interesting statement:

But if ye be led of the Spirit

– this is the fundamental text, the leading of the Spirit –

ye are not under the law (verse 18).

That is a very profound statement and I can only give you the essence of its meaning, but whoever has gone thoroughly through the seventh chapter of the Epistle to the Romans knows exactly what it means. It is saying that when you are under the law – and you are only under the law as long as you are not a Christian – you are very much under the domination of the flesh; and the law, as the apostle points out, even seems to aggravate the whole problem. 'For when we were in the flesh, the motions of sins' – that were in us – 'which were by the law' – stimulated by the law – 'did work in our members to bring forth fruit unto death' (*Rom.*7:5). In other words, while you are under the law, it is a hopeless contest because the flesh always wins. That is why mere morality is finally always defeated. In this country, for the last fifty years there has been an attempt to teach morality without Christianity. The gospel and the doctrines of the gospel have been dropped, and people say they want the ethics and the moral teaching of Jesus. It cannot be done! You are under the law, and in that position you will always fail because the law stimulates the flesh.

But, Paul says, you are no longer under the law: 'If ye be led of the Spirit, ye are not under the law.' You are in a new condition, and therefore there is no inevitable failure. You have been taken out of that realm where you are under the law. Not only that, the power of the Spirit is in you, and the power of the Spirit will give you strength. Paul puts this in an interesting way in Galatians 5:23. Giving there the list of the fruit of the Spirit, he says, 'against such there is no law', which is wonderful. Do this, he says, and there will never be any condemnation, there will be joy and abandon and release and fulness. Paul is saying: You are not under the law; realize that you are out of the realm of the flesh. To be under the law is to be in the flesh; to be in the Spirit means that you are no longer under the law. Realize this, and realize the power of the Spirit who is in you. And then, in order to drive this principle right home, Paul puts it like this: If this argument about the flesh and the Spirit is too much for you, and if you say you cannot follow this doctrine about being under the law and so on, then let me come right down to your level and put it very simply and plainly and bluntly to you. Do not live that life in the flesh. Why not? For this reason:

The works of the flesh are manifest, which are these

– look at them –

Adultery, fornication, uncleanness, lasciviousness, idolatry, witchcraft, hatred, variance, emulations, wrath, strife, seditions, heresies

– and we are beginning to learn something about heresies, are we not? Look at the ugliness of heresies. 'Mathematics is God'! –

envyings, murders, drunkenness, revellings, and such like

– they all belong to the same family. Have a look at them. And then Paul says: Having looked at the works of the flesh, can you go on doing things like that, you who are born of God and who are heirs of eternal bliss and citizens of the kingdom of heaven? Look at the ugliness, the vileness of every single one of them! And they are all the same; they have the family mark upon them; they are of the devil; they are of the flesh. 'Works of the flesh'! See them for what they are, says the apostle, and you will not be able to go on doing them. Oh, let me finish my quotation –

of the which I tell you before, as I have also told you in time past, that they which do such things shall not inherit the kingdom of God (verses 19–21).

And people are guilty of those things – and do not forget that 'heresies' is here among them; heresy is as bad as adultery. A man who says that God is not a person is a heretic! He does not belong to the kingdom of God, whatever his position in the Christian church. He is a liar! He is a heretic! 'They which do such things shall not inherit the kingdom of God.' How can they?

But, Paul says, have a look at the other side:

But the fruit of the Spirit is love, joy, peace, longsuffering, gentleness, goodness, faith, meekness, temperance: against such there is no law (verses 22–23).

The Christian who is in any doubt as to how he should live must be terribly blind. There is no law against the fruit of the Spirit. There is nothing here but the approbation of God. Very well, then, Paul says, winding it all up:

They that are Christ's have crucified the flesh with the affections and lusts (verse 24).

Then here is the final word, and it is so typical of Paul. He starts with a general statement, works out his argument and ends with a general statement and inevitable logic.

If we live in the Spirit

– and we who are Christians do –

let us also walk in the Spirit (verse 25).

It really is as simple as that, but we do not seem to realize it, do we? Now let me bring this right home by showing you an interesting point. You notice that in Galatians 5:16, Paul says, '*Walk* in the Spirit', and verse 25 reads, 'If we live in the Spirit, let us also *walk* in the Spirit.' In the Authorized [King James] Version, the word 'walk' is the translation in both verses, but that is not quite right. In a most interesting way, the apostle uses a different Greek word when he comes to verse 25. It is very difficult to get a better translation, I agree, but let me tell you the difference in the meaning of the two Greek words. The word translated 'walk' in verse 16, as I have said, is a very general word. It means 'live in', 'be occupied with', 'do that'. But in verse 25 it is more specific. The word the apostle uses here means 'march in military rank', 'keep in step', 'conform', 'walk in an orderly manner'. It is a military term. You see the analogy? Walk in step: do not be ahead of, or behind, the man marching next to you, keep the line, keep the column, march in military rank, conform to the pattern. In other words, it is the whole question of discipline and of application.

Verse 16 tells you to live your life in general in the Spirit. You will not then fulfil the lust of the flesh. That is right. That is the general exhortation. But then, having taken us through all the details, Paul says, in effect, 'Now, then, in the light of that, keep your eye to the right and to the left; this man, that man. Keep the line. Keep the rank. Be orderly. Watch and march with a steadfast, firm step, knowing what you are doing, with the band of heaven accompanying you and thrilling you as you go along. You are marching to Zion – very well, keep the line, do not look in the wrong direction, do not flag, do not be slack, brace yourself.' All that is implied by these words, 'If we live in the Spirit, let us also walk in the Spirit', and let anybody who happens to look on, standing on the pavement as we pass along, say, 'Look at him, he's one of them! Look at all of them, how wonderful it is to see them! Who are these people?' Well, these are the Christians. There they are, marching with heads erect, with a bright step, with a glory on their faces. They are the children of God, and they are marching to Zion!'

> *Children of the heavenly King,*
> *As ye journey, sweetly sing.*
> John Cennick

That is it! Let it be known who you are! And in order to do that, you must exercise this discipline. You must show this diligence. You must furnish your faith. You must realize the nature of evil. You must realize the glory of the fruit of the Spirit. You must know who you are. You must keep your eye on the recompense of the reward and ever keep that as your first and your chief interest.

'Walk in the Spirit, and ye shall not fulfil the lust of the flesh.' May God enable us to grasp and to implement this inevitable logic of the kingdom of God. ❧

26

'He Shall Glorify Me'

But as many as received him, to them gave he power to become the sons of God, even to them that believe on his name: which were born, not of blood, nor of the will of the flesh, nor of the will of man, but of God (John 1:12–13).

W e have considered quite a number of ways in which we can be quite sure that we are being led by the Spirit, finishing, last time, with what is called 'the mortification of the flesh' or 'the mortification of the deeds of the body'. It is through the Spirit that we are able to do that, and it is the Spirit who ever leads us and gives us the desire.

But now, on this particular Sunday morning before Good Friday,[1] I am anxious that we should look at the subject of the leading of the Spirit from yet another standpoint. And the particular way in which we can do this is by looking at two statements, the first of which is in John 16:14: 'He shall glorify me.' Our Lord is speaking about the Spirit of truth and is telling the disciples about some of the things that the Spirit will do when he comes. Our Lord says, 'He shall glorify me: for he shall receive of mine, and shall shew it unto you.' I want to take with those words a verse that seems to me to be their inevitable corollary as far as our experience is concerned. It is Galatians 6:14: 'God forbid that I should glory, save in the cross of our Lord Jesus Christ, by whom the world is crucified unto me, and I unto the world.'

Now the glory of the Lord Jesus Christ is another very important aspect of the leading of the Spirit. It is also particularly important from the standpoint of experience, from the standpoint of our testing

---

[1] This sermon was preached on 7 April 1963.

ourselves to make sure whether we are in fact the children of God. The terrible thing is that it is possible for us to pay lip service to the Scriptures, and even to make certain statements, without being children of God. It is possible to have an intellectual assent to truth. It is possible to be a formal Christian, hearing these truths and saying, 'Yes', without ever having known or experienced them. They are not true of us; they are not vital to us. So we are concerned about that danger in particular and here we have one of the most thorough tests of all as to whether or not we are in reality the children of God.

Our Lord's statement, 'He shall glorify me', is particularly important, perhaps, at this present time. There are movements in the church in certain parts of the world that – out of a genuine desire to revive the work and to deal with the parlous condition into which the Christian church seems to have entered – emphasize the work of the Holy Spirit and certain gifts of the Spirit. So it is right that we should examine these issues, indeed, that we should examine all things in the light of the teaching of Scripture. There is always the danger of rushing after something new. That has ever been a tendency in mankind, and since Christians are not saved from such tendencies, that is how heresies have arisen from time to time. At one and the same time, therefore, we can be examining and testing ourselves and also discovering the scriptural teaching with respect to certain views that are being offered in these days, especially to those who are anxious to have something deeper in the realm of experience.

So let us take this great statement of our Lord – 'He shall glorify me.' Here is a central and foundational principle. Notice that, in telling the disciples about the Holy Spirit whom he will send to them, our Lord makes it quite clear that the Spirit will not be sent in order to glorify himself. 'He shall glorify *me*,' our Lord says. 'He shall not speak of himself' (*John* 16:14, 13). This means, not that the Spirit will not speak *about* himself, but that he will not speak *from* himself, he will not merely express his own ideas. Our Lord is saying that the Holy Spirit will take of the things of the Lord and manifest them and expound them to the disciples. Our Lord's whole teaching is that the Holy Spirit, in his work, does not primarily lead us to himself or call attention to himself but always to the Lord Jesus Christ. This, I repeat, is a basic and a foundational principle. Throughout the centuries it has always been the case that when men and women have gone astray into some false fanaticism and have become guilty of error, it has usually been because they have forgotten this particular statement, 'He shall glorify me.'

We must grasp the fact that that there is always an extraordinary balance in the Scriptures, and it is when people forget the balance that they always get into trouble. Notice how Scripture puts it. The Lord Jesus Christ constantly said that he had come not to glorify himself but his Father, and the Holy Spirit does not glorify himself but the Son. The conclusion we draw from that is the great and blessed doctrine of the Holy Trinity, that the Father and the Son and the Holy Spirit are co-equal and co-eternal and each ministers to the glory of the other. It is always wrong to put the whole of your emphasis upon one of the Persons to the exclusion of the others. This is an error into which the church herself has sometimes fallen. There are certain epochs and eras in her history when she has been guilty of putting excessive emphasis upon one or the other Person of the Trinity.

Sometimes the whole focus is put upon God the Father, and there are people who talk about believing in God and worshipping God and serving God and never mention the Lord Jesus Christ. There are those who say that whenever you like you can start listening to God and be blessed of God and they do not mention the Lord Jesus Christ at all. If you read their books, you will find that his name does not even appear. God only! The Father! Then there are others who put their whole emphasis upon the Son. I sometimes get the impression that there are many people who forget the Father and the Holy Spirit. They pray to the Lord Jesus Christ only, never to the Father. All their activity and devotion are centred upon the Son – 'the Lord' – Jesus Christ. That is equally wrong. But then there are others who put their exclusive emphasis upon the Spirit and to them nothing matters but the Spirit, and the power and the feelings and the sensibilities and so on. So they always talk about the Spirit and the various activities and works of the Spirit.

It is vitally important that we should always read the whole of Scripture and always maintain the balance of Scripture. We must never be guilty of putting all the emphasis on one member of the Trinity; there must be a perfect proportion. Now the Holy Spirit does wonderful works. This strikes one forcibly as one reads the New Testament. It was after the Spirit had come upon him that our Lord set out on his public ministry. Then, who can forget what happened on the day of Pentecost and in the subsequent history of the early church, told in the Acts of the Apostles? Yes, the Spirit does wonderful works but they are never meant to direct attention to him. 'He shall glorify *me*'! There is our starting point in these matters.

But I draw a second deduction or principle and this is more practical and experiential. As the Spirit does not lead us to glory in him and does not glorify himself, so he does not lead us to glory in experiences – and this is where still more of the element of subtlety comes in. The Holy Spirit does give great and glorious and wonderful experiences – thank God for them. It is his special task to mediate the finished work of Christ. It is he who brings to us the results of the atonement. It is he who produces the new birth, and all that follows out of that.

And the Spirit is not only able to, but has throughout the centuries done extraordinary and wonderful and amazing things in men and women. He produces and distributes graces in us. He is the Lord in these great matters. There is that mighty chapter 12 of 1 Corinthians in which the lordship of the Spirit in the dispensation of his various gifts is expounded with such clarity. And, therefore, the work of the Spirit in these respects is something glorious, something wonderful, something for which we should praise God.

But it is equally important that we should remember that when we are led of the Spirit, we are not led to concentrate upon or to glory in the gifts and the graces of the Spirit, nor in any of his works. Now this has always been a tendency in the church, as I have indicated. The church at Corinth was in a very pathetic condition because the Christians there were dividing up not only in terms of leaders but still more, perhaps, in terms of spiritual gifts. Various gifts had been given, some very dramatic – miracles, for example – and other gifts that were more ordinary, such as administration and wisdom. And it is quite clear that havoc was being wrought in the church because people were glorying in the gifts. They would boast of their great and flashy gifts and tend to despise people with more ordinary gifts.

Now the apostle points out that such behaviour is nothing but schism (*1 Cor.* 12:25), nothing but a rending of the body of Christ; it is dividing Christ. The Corinthians had forgotten the important fact that they were all in the body; they had forgotten their relationship to Christ. He himself had been forgotten. They were glorying in themselves and in the gifts that the Spirit had given to them instead of glorying in the fact that the church is the body of Christ, that they were 'members in particular' (*1 Cor.* 12:27) and that, therefore, the particular gift that someone has is not the important thing at all. You may be an unimportant member of the body, Paul says, one of the less comely parts, but you are as much in the body as is that person with the very flashy and wonderful gift. 'The eye cannot say unto the hand, I have no need of thee', and so on (*1 Cor.* 12:21); all are essential. The Corinthians had gone astray because they were concentrating on the gifts of the Spirit, and were worshipping them and glorying in them.

We must remember that gifts are never to be regarded as ends in themselves. We are never to seek any gifts in and of themselves, for their own sakes, and the gifts of the Spirit should not be the most prominent thing in our testimony and in our experience. But you will find that very often they are and that some people will talk about nothing but 'tongues', for example. Nothing matters but whether or not you have spoken with tongues – this is everything. All the emphasis and all the glory is upon tongues. Now the thing that people talk about most is the thing in which they glory. That is the test. Where is their emphasis? What do they stress most of all? What do they keep on talking about? And it is, to me, nothing less than tragic that there are people who, genuinely, I believe, are concerned about receiving the Spirit but glory in certain gifts only. That seems to me to be violating this most essential principle that our Lord himself laid down and that, as I will try to show you, is laid down equally clearly by the blessed Spirit himself.

There, then, are the two negatives: the Spirit does not glorify himself and the Spirit does not glorify particular gifts – indeed, he does not glorify gifts as such. He is not sent to do that. These are incidental, but means and ends to something else. What is that? It is that the Spirit always glorifies the Lord Jesus Christ – always! 'He shall glorify me.' He was sent for that purpose. That is his place in the great economy of salvation, the division of this great work. The Father plans, the Son comes to execute, to work it out, the Spirit comes and he applies it. So we can safely say that the Holy Spirit always points to the Lord Jesus Christ.

Let me give you some proof of this fact that the Spirit's primary work is to glorify the Lord Jesus Christ. There are the disciples in the upper room on the morning of the day of Pentecost. Suddenly the sound of 'a rushing mighty wind' is heard; the Spirit comes upon them, they are baptized and filled with the Holy Spirit and he begins to lead them. He leads the apostle Peter to deliver a sermon to the assembled company at Jerusalem, these people who have come from all parts of the world. There they are, listening to the apostle Peter, who has been filled with the Spirit and who is speaking with strange tongues. But what does he preach about? Well, you need only read the account of the sermon in that second chapter of the Acts of the Apostles to find exactly what he preaches. His sermon is about Jesus Christ.

Peter reminds the people of how the Holy Spirit himself through the prophets had been foretelling our Lord's coming. He quotes the prophet Joel, finishing with Joel's words: 'And it shall come to pass, that whosoever shall call on the name of the Lord shall be saved' (*Acts* 2:21). Then Peter begins to apply that prophecy. He says, 'Ye men of Israel, hear these words . . .' Now here is a man led of the Spirit, here is a man filled with the Holy Spirit – what does he preach about? Not the Holy Spirit! Not the gifts that he has received! Not certain visions and ecstasies. No, no! He says:

Jesus of Nazareth, a man approved of God among you by miracles and wonders and signs, which God did by him in the midst of you, as ye yourselves also know: him, being delivered by the determinate counsel and foreknowledge of God, ye have taken, and by wicked hands have crucified and slain: whom God hath raised up (Acts 2:22–24).

Peter preaches Jesus Christ. 'He shall glorify me,' says our Lord. And when the Spirit came, he did that immediately through the mouth of his servant Peter. And if you go on to the next chapter, you will find exactly the same thing. One afternoon, at the hour of prayer, Peter and John are going up to the temple to pray when they see a lame man at the Beautiful Gate of the temple and, after a conversation, they heal him. The man leaps up and goes 'walking, and leaping, and praising God' into the temple and the crowd gathers from everywhere in wonder and amazement (*Acts* 3:8–9).

Then Peter begins to address the people – and what does he say? Does he tell them about how he has spoken with tongues and now has this wonderful gift, the ability to work miracles? Does he talk about himself, or about his gifts, or about his marvellous experience? No, no! Listen – this is how Peter puts it:

Ye men of Israel, why marvel ye at this? or why look ye so earnestly on us, as though by our own power or holiness we had made this man to walk? The God of Abraham, and of Isaac, and of Jacob, the God of our fathers, hath glorified his Son Jesus; whom ye delivered up, and denied him in the presence of Pilate, when he was determined to let him go. But ye denied the Holy One and the Just, and desired a murderer to be granted unto you; and killed the Prince of life, whom God hath raised from the dead; whereof we are witnesses. And his name through faith in his name hath made this man strong, whom ye see and know: yea, the faith which is by him hath given him this perfect soundness in the presence of you all (Acts 3:12–16).

Then Peter goes on to preach Christ further to them, and says, 'Brethren, I wot that through ignorance ye did it, as did also your rulers' (*Acts* 3:17). You notice, he is not preaching about the Holy Spirit, though he is filled with the Spirit and the power of the Spirit, and he is not preaching about himself, his experiences, his gifts. He is preaching Christ – 'He shall glorify me' – the Lord Jesus Christ. The Spirit has been sent to glorify him and the moment he comes and leads men in this manner, that is what he leads them to do. That is very valuable evidence and it goes on right through the book of Acts.

But there is something else, which we often tend to forget. Who is the real author of the four Gospels? The answer is, the Holy Spirit. It was the Holy Spirit who filled these men and led them and guided them as they wrote their Gospels. And what are the Gospels? Oh, they are accounts of the Lord Jesus Christ. The Gospels are glorying in him and glorifying him.

The Spirit keeps out of sight, as it were. He puts the Lord to the forefront; he wants us to look at him. Why? Because the Lord is the centre. He leads us to the Father; he sends the Spirit. So if we are right about him, we shall be right about the Father and about the Holy Spirit. The Spirit, in inditing the four Gospels, is doing the very thing that our Lord prophesied.

Then when you turn to the New Testament epistles, it is exactly the same: the Lord is the real theme, the centre, of all the epistles, every one of them. The authors of the epistles are all writing about him. Then look at the last book in the Bible, the book of Revelation, this great prophetic utterance. What is it? Oh, it is 'the Revelation of Jesus Christ' (*Rev.* 1:1). It is simply telling us what he is yet going to do and how he is going to come. It is always glorifying him. He is the one the Spirit always holds before us.

Are we children of God? Well, I ask the other question: Are we led by the Spirit of God? You see how important these questions are to us. How do I know whether I am led by the Spirit of God? Here is the best answer: he will always lead me to the Lord Jesus Christ. Always! Not to himself, not to his gifts, not to his powers, not to experiences. Thank God for all these. God forbid that anybody should misunderstand me. I am saying nothing against experiences. What I am speaking against is glorying in experiences instead of glorying in the Lord.

So the Holy Spirit always leads to the Lord Jesus Christ, and he leads in particular to his death upon the cross. When Peter was preaching on the day of Pentecost, he did not spend his time preaching about the *teaching* of the Lord Jesus Christ. He could have. He had heard him, he had been with him, he was quite an authority on the teaching.

But instead, both here and again in Acts chapter 3, Peter came straight to the *death*. Have you ever noticed, as you look at the four Gospels, that a remarkable amount of space and attention is given to the death of our Lord? Work it out in proportion. He was teaching and ministering for three years; his death did not take very long. But look at the space given to it, look at the attention. Why? Because it is the big, the crucial, thing! It is exactly the same throughout the book of Acts, in the epistles, even in the book of Revelation: 'Unto him that loved us, and washed us from our sins in his own blood' (*Rev.* 1:5). It is the introduction; it is everything.

The pre-eminence of our Lord's death on the cross is confirmed to the very hilt by the history of the Reformation and of the great revivals. No feature is more characteristic of the great revivals in the church than the way in which the death of Christ becomes prominent. Look at it in your hymn books; look at the great hymns, the hymns that were written in the times of revival. I mean the hymns that were written in the eighteenth rather than in the nineteenth century – those are the great hymns, together with those of the Reformation. Those great hymns are always about our Lord and about his death. It is invariable. The movements of the Spirit have always led to him and have particularly gloried in his death upon the cross.

So my last principle is that the proof of the leading of the Holy Spirit in our individual lives is that we glory in the Lord Jesus Christ and especially in his death upon the cross. Listen to the apostle Paul:

God forbid that I should glory, save in the cross of our Lord Jesus Christ, by whom the world is crucified unto me, and I unto the world. For in Christ Jesus neither circumcision availeth any thing, nor uncircumcision, but a new creature. And as many as walk according to this rule, peace be on them, and mercy, and upon the Israel of God. From henceforth let no man trouble me: for I bear in my body the marks of the Lord Jesus (Gal. 6:14–17).

Paul means that here in Galatia the church was bothering and worrying and arguing about circumcision. Could you be a real Christian without being circumcised? Oh, the fuss and the bother! These people had believed in Christ, and had received the Spirit, but then somebody had come along and said, 'That's all right, of course, but if you want to be a real Christian, you must submit to circumcision.' And throughout the centuries people have always made such demands. They have said that you must have this or that, you must be baptized in a given way, you must speak in tongues. 'From henceforth', says the apostle, 'let no man trouble me.' I do not want to hear any more about it. I am not going to waste any more time on it. Circumcision and uncircumcision do not matter at all. 'In Christ Jesus neither circumcision availeth any thing, nor uncircumcision, but a new creature.' He is saying: What is the matter with you? You are glorying in circumcision, you are glorying in the law, you are glorying in this and that. 'God forbid that I should glory, save in the cross of our Lord Jesus Christ.' That is the Christian position. That is the man or woman who is filled with the Spirit, who is led by the Holy Spirit.

And I am simply asking, my dear friends, whether we are led by the Holy Spirit. Is this true of us? I am not asking what experiences you may or may not have had. I am not asking what gifts you may or may not have been given.

What I am asking is this: Where does the Lord Jesus Christ come? Where does he come in your thinking? Where does he come in your life? I am not interested in all the good you are doing; I am not interested in all the gifts you may have;

I am not interested in all your excellencies: those are not the test. The Jews who crucified Christ were very zealous for God. They were a highly religious people. There was never a more zealous people. But they crucified the Lord. They rejected him. They despised him.

So here is the test: Where does the Lord Jesus Christ come? Is he the centre of all our thinking, all our acting, all our life? You cannot be led by the Spirit truly and fully without being led to Christ; and you talk about him, not about yourself, not about your activities, not about your experiences. You talk about him! Thank God, I say again, for the experiences, but do not stop at that. They are simply God dealing with us as children in order to encourage us to come to him. These are but signs, helps. You do not stop with them.

Object of my first desire,
Jesus, crucified for me.

Augustus M. Toplady

My dear friends, Christian people, there is nothing more important than just this. A man once described a Christian as 'a Christ-intoxicated person'. That is a good description. And I believe it is because many of us are not Christ-intoxicated that the Christian church is as she is and the majority are outside. We talk about good deeds and works, we talk about resisting philosophy, we talk about everything except about him and about his 'wondrous cross', about his death. But the Spirit always leads to that. So, you see, those who are truly led of the Spirit are Christ-centred. Not only that, they are people who have an increasing desire to know him and to love him. Read the apostles and you will see their love for Christ, you will see their knowledge of him, the intimate knowledge that they had, and you will see that they were burning with a great love for him so that nothing else mattered to them.

'Leave me alone,' says Paul, in effect. 'I'm sick and tired of your arguments and disputations and the exalting of these secondary and third-rate matters to the prominence of the first position. Leave me alone. I'm not interested. "God forbid that I should glory . . ."' With all his brilliance, with his wonderful experiences, with all the gifts with which he had been endowed, he could have gloried. If ever a man had a right to glory, it was this man. But he did not. He did when he was a Pharisee, of course. But now he is a new man and he glories in Christ and in him alone. And this is his greatest desire – 'That I may know him, and the power of his resurrection, and the fellowship of his sufferings, being made conformable unto his death; if by any means I might attain unto the resurrection of the dead' (*Phil.* 3:10–11). With all his visions, all his activities, churches founded . . . No, no! I want to know him. Oh, that I might know him in a deeper and greater manner!

These are the ways to test ourselves. Let me put it still more simply and plainly. Those who are truly led of the Spirit know that Christ died for *them* personally. The apostle Paul puts it in these memorable words in the Epistle to the Galatians:

I through the law am dead to the law, that I might live unto God. I am crucified with Christ: nevertheless I live; yet not I, but Christ liveth in me: and the life which I now live in the flesh I live by the faith of the Son of God, who loved me, and gave himself for me (Gal. 2:19–20).

Now that is personal. Paul does not say, 'I subscribe to the doctrine of the atonement: I believe that Christ died for the sins of the world' – that is not what he says. That is not enough. It is right, we must believe that. We must believe the doctrine of the cross, the doctrine of the atonement. We must believe it by faith. But when the Spirit leads us, and we are filled with the Spirit, it is no longer only a general belief. We say, 'The Son of God, who loved *me*, and gave himself for *me*.' You know that he died for you.

Was not that the very thing that happened to John Wesley in Aldersgate Street on 24 May 1738? He had believed this doctrine – he had always believed it – he had been brought up to believe it. But he wrote that that night, as a man was reading from the Preface of Luther's commentary on the Epistle to the Romans, he discovered that Christ 'had taken away my sins, even mine, and saved me from the law of sin and death'. And it was from that moment that John Wesley became a witness. That is what the Spirit does. He translates the general into the particular. The truth that we know is true in my particular case, and I know it beyond any argument or disputation. Oh, yes, when you are led of the Spirit, you know that Christ has died for you in particular, and you are amazed and astonished at it. 'And can it be?' The Son of God died for me! Is it possible?

> *And can it be, that I should gain*
> *An interest in the Saviour's blood?*
> *Died he for me, who caused his pain:*
> *For me, who him to death pursued?*
> *Amazing love! How can it be*
> *That thou, my God, shouldst die for me!*
>
> Charles Wesley

Have you ever said that? Have you ever felt that? My friend, if you have, you are a child of God – there is no question about it. I assure you in the name of God that if you have ever felt that or said that, you are a child of God. If you have not felt it, I am not saying you are not a child of God but, oh, you are lacking assurance! Do not stay there! You should know that as a living experience. And the Spirit will lead you to it. We must know this in our own experience and know something of the amazement and astonishment.

And a further good test, again from Galatians 6:14, is this: 'God forbid that I should glory, save in the cross of our Lord Jesus Christ, *by whom the world is crucified unto me, and I unto the world*.' Has the world been crucified unto you? Have you been crucified unto the world? That is the thing to examine yourself about. Can you say quite honestly, 'That cross of Christ has cut me off from the world'? 'I used to be in it. I belonged to it. I was indissolubly linked with it. He severed me from it and I am no longer there. I am in his kingdom. Crucified is the world unto me, crucified am I unto the world. I am no longer *of* the world. I belong to the kingdom of God.' Has the cross done that for you? Do you know and can you say that you have died with Christ, that when he died on that cross, you died with him, that you are in him and you have partaken in his experiences, and therefore you are seated with him in the heavenly places at this moment?

If all these things are true, it follows inevitably, does it not, that we shall also glory in him and in his cross? We shall say: 'God forbid that I should glory in anything else – tongues or no tongues, gifts or no gifts, experiences or no experiences. Oh, no, no! What matters is the cross of our Lord Jesus Christ! Because I would never have had a gift but for that. I would still be in my sins but for that. I would still be under the law, I would have no knowledge of God, I would have no hope of heaven, I would have nothing, were it not that the Son of God loved me, and gave himself on that cross, took my sins upon him, bore my punishment, died my death, was buried in my grave, rose again . . . all for me!'

The one who is led of the Spirit of God is the one, therefore, who glories in nothing but in the cross of the Lord Jesus Christ. 'Let every man examine himself.' ❧

27

Grieving the Spirit;
the Fruit of the Spirit–1

But as many as received him, to them gave he power to become the sons of God, even to them that believe on his name: which were born, not of blood, nor of the will of the flesh, nor of the will of man, but of God (John 1:12–13).

I n these mighty statements in the first eighteen verses of John's Gospel, the apostle puts before us some of the most astounding ideas that we can ever consider. The Word! The Word who was with God, and who was God, was made flesh and tabernacled among us. Why did he do that? Why did he ever leave the courts of glory and humble himself and come 'in fashion as a man' and 'in the likeness of sinful flesh'? Why did he endure 'such contradiction of sinners against himself'? Why did he endure the shame and the agony of the cross? Why was he laid in a tomb? Why did he rise again? The answer is this: that he might give unto us who believe in him the right, the authority, to become the children of God, 'born, not of blood, nor of the will of the flesh, nor of the will of man, but of God'.

In order that we may be sure that we really are the children of God, and that we may enjoy the largesse, the munificence and the unsearchable riches that God has for us, we have considered our relationship to the Son, the Lord Jesus Christ, and then our relationship to the Father himself. And now we are thinking about our relationship to the Holy Spirit. We have been testing the various ways in which the Spirit deals with us, looking in particular at the leading of the Spirit.

We come now to another aspect of our relationship to the Spirit of God. The next test I put before you is this: fear of grieving the Spirit of God. 'Grieve not the holy Spirit of God, whereby ye are sealed unto the day of redemption,' says the apostle Paul in Ephesians 4:30. Here is a particularly delicate and sensitive test. We grieve the Spirit by not listening to him, by sinning, by lacking in diligence and in many other ways. But that is not what I want to direct your attention to in this study. I am not concerned at the moment about the *ways* in which we can grieve the Spirit. I am concerned, rather, with our feeling about it, our attitude towards causing this grief.

The Christian is someone who has an increasing concern about this question of grieving the Spirit. The Holy Spirit is represented by the emblem of a dove – sensitive and delicate – and the teaching of the Scripture is that the Holy Spirit can indeed be grieved, can be caused to mourn and will withdraw. Christians are aware of the fact that the Spirit of God has come to dwell in them; everything about him brings them to that awareness. The epistles constantly put this before us. Take, for instance, 1 Corinthians 6:19: 'What? know ye not that your body is the temple of the Holy Ghost which is in you?' You know that, says Paul. As he was in Christ, so he is in you. Now Christians are aware of this, and become more and more aware of it as they grow, so that they develop an increasing 'anxiety', as it were, or a fear, lest in anything or in any respect they should offend or grieve the Spirit or cause him to mourn. As William Cowper wrote:

> *I hate the sins that made thee mourn,*
> *And drove thee from my breast.*

I would put this test that we are now considering in this way: Christians are more afraid of grieving the Spirit than they are of anything else. Their fear is not so much that they may fall into sin, though, of course, they do fear that, not so much that they may be guilty of failure, as that they may grieve this blessed Spirit who has humbled himself and deigned to dwell in them and to inhabit their very body! It is this that marks them out and should give them assurance. I am stressing this point because it is one of the most searching tests that I am aware of in the matter of differentiating between the Christian and a good moral person.

There are very good, upright, moral men and women in the world, people who seem to be paragons of all the virtues. You cannot point a finger at them. They never seem to do any wrong, they have a high moral code, a high ethical standard, and they believe in living up to this. There are many such who deny the whole of the Christian faith, never darken the doors of a place of worship and are not at all interested in the Lord Jesus Christ. So someone may say to me, 'How do I know whether I'm not just living a good, moral, ethical life myself? How may I know that I'm a Christian?' And it is just here that this test comes in.

When your good moral men and women fall into sin, what troubles them, of course, is that they have failed, that they have fallen from their standard. They may even feel, perhaps, that they have let down the whole human race. But they never go beyond that. By contrast, what worries Christians is that they behaved as they did though this blessed Spirit of God is in them, in their very bodies. He is grieved, he is wounded, he is hurt – they have caused the Spirit of God to mourn. But your good moral people know nothing at all about that. They cannot know it because the Spirit is not in them, because they do not know the Holy Spirit. The argument is inevitable.

'If any man have not the Spirit of Christ, he is none of his' (*Rom.* 8:9). Everyone who is a Christian has the Spirit of Christ, of necessity; he is in all Christians and, I repeat, in some way or another they are aware of that. Now let me again make this quite clear – I am doing this to help those who may be in trouble about this whole question of assurance, those who tend to become morbid and introspective. I am saying it for their comfort. I am not setting up a standard of perfection but am simply demanding and postulating some awareness of the Spirit of God and of Christ within you, some awareness that over and above yourself there is another, some awareness that you are being led and guided, that there is a power working in you greater than yourself. I am not postulating any more than that.

What I am saying is this: those who know anything about that awareness are grieved, when they fall into sin, because they have hurt the Spirit. How could they have been capable of it? How could they have forgotten his presence? How could they for one moment have forgotten the fact that their very bodies are the tabernacle in which the Spirit of God dwells? That is what gets them down and causes them acute distress. It is, in a measure, what David says in Psalm 51: 'Take not thy holy spirit from me' (verse 11). That was what was worrying David. He had committed adultery, he had committed murder – oh, they are terrible things in themselves, and of course he was grieved about that. But that was not what was breaking David's heart. He said: My heart must be unclean! 'Create in me a clean heart, O God; and renew a right spirit within me . . . Take not thy holy spirit from me' (verses 10–11). I deserve any punishment that you may mete out to me, says David, but do not do that. Well, if a man under the Old Testament dispensation could say and feel that, how much more must every Christian, when the Spirit is given in a profusion that the saints of the Old Testament never knew. We are on the other side of Pentecost. Therefore, I say that Christians are sensitive to the presence of the Spirit. And therefore the more they fear to grieve or to wound the Spirit, the more certain they can be that they are indeed children of God.

At this point, let me once more bring in the whole question of what the fathers used to call 'desertions' because it is very germane to the subject of grieving the Spirit. As we have seen, one of the themes in the writings of the Puritan fathers in particular is a concern about 'desertions'.

It occasionally happened that they would be living the Christian life, aware of the blessing of God and the leading of the Spirit, with everything seeming to be clear, the sun shining and light upon the road that was leading them to the Lamb, when suddenly everything would change. The clouds would gather, the sun go out of sight and a kind of darkness, a dullness, a heaviness, would come down upon the soul. They would find they could not pray as they used to, they could not get the same pleasure out of reading the Word of God, and they would feel they had been left to themselves. That is the most terrible feeling – every preacher in this congregation will know exactly what I mean. I know of nothing more terrible in this world than to be alone in this pulpit. By that, I mean that *I* am doing everything, *I* am preaching.

What a terrible thing, to feel that I am left to myself! It happens to me sometimes, God have mercy upon me!

Now I say that those who are Christians know something about this, about desertion, being left to themselves. And it is generally because they have grieved the Spirit, because they have done something they should not have done. It is not always that, but it is most commonly that. And this is the most miserable experience the Christian can ever know. To the Christian, this is much more important than moral, ethical behaviour.

'Ah,' says somebody, 'there it is, that is a typical evangelical statement inciting people to antinomianism.'

No, no! I am saying that while Christians do grieve and mourn about failures in practice, this awareness of desertion means much more to them. Nothing is more wonderful to the Christian than a lively spirit. Nothing is more wonderful than ease and facility in reading the Word, in prayer, in preaching, in any work for God that they have to do. And, oh, when that spirit is not there, how bereft they feel, how abandoned! So turn this into a test. If you, my dear friend, know anything at all about this experience, if you know, in any measure or to any extent, this feeling of desertion, of being left, if you feel that there is a difference, that the Spirit does not seem to be with you as he once was – if you know anything about that, you can take it from me that you are a child of God. You may be a very small, a very unworthy, child but you are a child of God. The 'natural man', the good, moral, ethical person, is a stranger to that experience; he cannot know anything about it. He is self-contained. The Spirit has never been with him. He has never been aware of this Other, this 'presence that disturbs me with the joys of elevated thought',[1] the presence of the Spirit of God, the sense of the holy – call it what you will – but the smallest Christian, the merest tyro in the Christian life, knows it.

The awareness of the presence of the Spirit of God is the most priceless blessing a Christian can know. And, therefore, it follows of necessity that the greatest fear is the fear of grieving the Spirit of God. He dwells in us, my friends! Let us never forget that. I say once more, start your

[1] William Wordsworth, from 'Lines composed a few miles above Tintern Abbey'.

day by reminding yourself of what is true of you – start your day by saying, 'I am a child of God. The Spirit of God dwells within me.' Say that to yourself! Say it to yourself many times during the day and it will help you and prevent you from grieving the Holy Spirit of God.

But let me move on to another group of tests – again important, and more positive, perhaps – the tests of evidences of the growth of the fruit of the Spirit within us. This, again, is inevitable, is it not? The Spirit of God is within us and the Spirit of God works within us, and what he does is produce 'fruit'. Let me give you the relevant and classic passage with respect to this. It is from the fifth chapter of Paul's Epistle to the Galatians, where Paul contrasts what he calls 'the works of the flesh' and 'the fruit of the Spirit':

Now the works of the flesh are manifest, which are these; Adultery, fornication, uncleanness, lasciviousness, idolatry, witchcraft, hatred, variance, emulations, wrath, strife, seditions, heresies, envying, murders, drunkenness, revellings, and such like: of the which I tell you before, as I have also told you in time past, that they which do such things shall not inherit the kingdom of God.

That is a categorical statement. But listen:

But the fruit of the Spirit is love, joy, peace, longsuffering, gentleness, goodness, faith, meekness, temperance: against such there is no law (Gal. 5:19–23).

Here, obviously, is a wonderful test that we can apply to ourselves in order to prove that we are the children of God. If I am a child of God, the Spirit of God dwells in me and the Spirit dwelling in me produces fruit. If I find the fruit in myself, I am of necessity a child of God. That is the way it works.

Now the test of the fruit of the Spirit is, again, a wonderful and also a searching test, a much more delicate test than the test of knowledge. Knowledge is a test – 'Grow in grace, and in the knowledge of our Lord and Saviour Jesus Christ' (2 Pet. 3:18). Those who do not know more about the Scriptures now than they did a year ago are in a bad state. As you go on in the Christian life, your knowledge must of necessity increase and develop, if you are indeed living the Christian life as you should. The knowledge that is before us in the Bible is endless. How little we know! We are but beginners, children paddling at the edge of the ocean. Oh, look at it, this great knowledge! It is wonderful to increase in one's knowledge of the Scriptures, knowledge of theology, knowledge of doctrine. But such knowledge is not sufficiently searching as a test. Unfortunately, you can grow in a kind of head knowledge of the truth, in a kind of intellectual, academic knowledge, but that does not necessarily prove that you are a Christian. This is an amazing fact, but it is quite true. You can, through listening to the preaching of the Word and by reading books, be very interested in scriptural knowledge, but it does not prove you are a Christian. You can do that with your head alone. But what you can never do is produce the fruit of the Spirit – never!

Not only can we of ourselves never produce the fruit of the Spirit but, as the apostle Paul puts it in 1 Corinthians 8:1, 'We know that we all have knowledge'. These people in Corinth were intellectuals and they were very knowledgeable; some of them had been dabbling in philosophy and so on, and many, these 'stronger brethren', were boasting about their knowledge. Paul says: That is all right. We know that we all have knowledge. But, 'Knowledge puffeth up, but charity [love] edifieth [builds up].' You see the difference between being 'puffed up' and being 'built up' solidly, securely, safely? So this is again a very delicate and a very sensitive test. We must grow in grace as well as in knowledge. This is a vital matter. What an important distinction it is!

Now there is a preliminary difficulty about testing ourselves in terms of the presence of the fruit of the Spirit in us because it seems to be self-contradictory. The more of the fruit of the Spirit people have, the more humble they are, the more meek, the more lowly, the more delicate and sensitive in their spirits. And, therefore, the more aware they are of indwelling sin. So at first sight you might say, 'Well, the more saintly people become, the more aware they are of their own deficiencies. Raw, new-born converts think they have become perfect in one stroke; that is because they are ignorant. They have to learn that they are not perfect. That applies to all of us. Infants, children, are always in that position. The older we get, the more we know our own ignorance. And, similarly, the more we grow in the Christian life and the more we experience the work of the Spirit within us, the more we see all this blackness and darkness, the plague of our own hearts, and, therefore, the more hopeless we feel about ourselves.' All that is true in a sense, but it is not the whole truth, thank God, and to argue in that way is quite wrong.

There is another side to the truth, and this is very important. We are told in the New Testament, 'Examine yourselves, whether ye be in the faith; prove your own selves' (2 *Cor.* 13:5). We are constantly exhorted to do that. And there is that great thirteenth chapter of the First Epistle to the Corinthians, which was written in order that the people of Corinth might examine themselves. There they were, boasting about their intellectual knowledge, boasting about their spiritual gifts. 'Yet shew I unto you a more excellent way,' says Paul (*1 Cor.* 12:31). This is the way in which you examine yourselves:

Though I speak with the tongues of men and of angels, and have not charity

– it is no good, of no value at all to me –

I am become as sounding brass, or a tinkling symbol. And though I have the gift of prophecy, and understand all mysteries, and all knowledge; and though I have all faith, so that I could remove mountains

– what a wonderful person! No, no! Wait a minute –

and have not charity [love], I am nothing. And though I bestow all my goods to feed the poor

– what a sacrifice! And the world will laud you and you will get prominence in the newspapers. 'Look what he's done! Look at his sacrifice!' No, no! –

though I [even] give my body to be burned, and have not charity, it profiteth me nothing (1 Cor. 13:1–3).

It is a terrible fact but it is possible for people to be able to 'speak with the tongues of men and of angels', prophesy, possess all knowledge and understanding, have faith that can remove mountains and make tremendous sacrifices, and yet be as hard as a stone. Then all they have is no good, it is of no value. That is what Paul is saying, and it is of necessity true. It is amazing to notice what people can do in their own strength. There are many people in the world today doing a great deal of good and making great sacrifices. Why? In their ignorance they think that thereby they are going to make themselves Christians. *They* are doing it! They are zealous. They are keen. There is nothing they will not do in order to earn salvation and to please God. But it is all wrong. It has not got this principle of *love* in it. So, you see, this teaching is of vital importance.

Christians are always an enigma, are they not? There is nothing enigmatic about the person who is not a Christian. It is very simple to analyse the 'natural man', but the Christian is a problem. Why? Well, because there is this duality, as it were – new nature, old nature. And because each Christian has both a new nature and an old nature, because the Christian is 'a new man' and is aware of once having been 'an old man', Christians feel a double surprise at themselves. I know of no better test that you can apply to yourself at this very moment to know whether or not you are a Christian than to ask whether you are surprised at yourself in two ways.

First, are you amazed that you are as bad as you are? Are you amazed at the fact that your heart is as black as it is? Are you amazed at yourself for having certain thoughts and imaginings? Are you astonished at yourself? Do you say to yourself, 'Is it possible that I'm capable of this sort of thing?' That is one side. But, at the same time, are you amazed at the fact that you are as good as you are? Are you amazed to find that, like the apostle Paul, you say, 'I live; yet not I' (*Gal.* 2:20). Do you say, 'Is it possible that I really am interested in the Bible – I? Is it possible that I really do enjoy prayer? I find this astounding but it's true of me.' Christians can look at themselves and see these two aspects at the same time. That is why their growth in grace does not leave them in a morbid, introspective condition in which they are just grovelling in the dust. This other side is also there, and they are equally amazed at both.

Another way of putting this whole matter is to say that the fruit of the Spirit is a wonderful test of our sanctification. And the reason why it is such a wonderful test is that it is not *our* fruit; it is not anything that we do. That is where the contrast that we have just been looking at in Galatians 5 is so important. 'Now the works of the flesh', says the apostle Paul, 'are manifest, which are these; Adultery, fornication . . .' (*Gal.* 5:19). But he does not go on to say, 'Now the works of the Christian are these . . .' because they are not 'the works of the Christian', they are 'the fruit of the Spirit' (*Gal.* 5:22). And that is why Christian men and women can be aware of this fruit in themselves without being proud, without being puffed up. They know that it is the fruit of the Spirit, not their works but something that has been done in them and through them. They do have a part to play, of course, in their response, but this fruit is fundamentally the work of the Spirit.

No one can produce the fruit of the Spirit except the Spirit himself. You cannot produce fruit. Good moral people can simulate things – they can produce very good artificial flowers, but these have no life, and if you examine them, you see the difference. That is the difference between morality and the fruit of the Spirit. The work of the Spirit, the 'fruit' of the Spirit, comes almost unconsciously and Christians see this fruit and are amazed at themselves. That is the test: that you find within yourself something of the fruit of the Spirit. It is not difficult to see the works of the flesh, and it is not difficult to see something of the fruit of the Spirit. But notice that when Paul talks about the fruit of the Spirit, he is not talking about the gifts of the Spirit. That is the great contrast between 1 Corinthians 12 and 1 Corinthians 13. In 1 Corinthians 12, the apostle is talking about the gifts – miracles, healings, tongues, knowledge, wisdom, understanding, these wonderful gifts. Then he says, 'I now want to show you a more excellent way.' No longer gifts but graces, the inward state and condition. This is the test. The gifts, again, can be misleading. Gifts are sometimes given to people who are not Christians at all. It is quite clear that Judas Iscariot, with the other disciples, had been given power to cast out devils. You will find in revivals that people are given temporary gifts. It does not prove that they are Christians. It is the fruit of the Spirit that proves that we are Christians.

Notice, too, that Paul says 'the fruit', not 'the fruits'. It is singular, not plural. That is significant because it indicates that these are variations of the one fruit of the Spirit. We must differentiate between them, as we are going to do, but they all belong to the same genus, as it were, they are the same kind of fruit, they all belong to the same family. What, then, are they? Notice that Paul mentions nine things. We can classify them into three groups of three. I am merely going to make a comment in passing – there is no need to do any more. Those who have the Spirit in them will know exactly what I mean.

The first three constitute a group that describes our essential state or condition. What is this? 'The fruit of the Spirit is love' – *love*! That is what Paul puts first here, as he does everywhere. Here in Galatians 5 we have the same sort of analysis as we have in 1 Corinthians 13 – you start with love. What does Paul mean by love? Well, here it is: the fruit of the Spirit in men and women means that the love of God is shed abroad in their hearts, and that means that they begin to love God. This is the great characteristic of the Christian. Oh, not some flabby sentiment! Sentimentality, I sometimes think, is the greatest enemy of love. You find it in some of the maudlin hymns in our hymn books. That is not love. No, no! Love is strong. It is noble. There are many people who believe in God but they do not love him, they only fear him. The Christian both fears God and loves God. Christians know that God is their Father. They know something of what God has done for them. They know this new relationship, that they are children of God! They may be bad children, fractious, disobedient and rebellious, but fundamentally, beneath it all, there is this love for God and the desire to know him better.

But the love Paul is talking about is not only love for God, it is love for our fellow-Christians. It goes even further than that, it means that you are able to love your enemies. 'Love your enemies,' says our Lord in the Sermon on the Mount (*Matt.* 5:44). He says that if you only love your friends, you are doing no more than other people do: 'For sinners also love those that love them' (*Luke* 6:32); they are kind to those who are kind to them. It does not take a Christian to do that. But it does take a Christian to love his enemies, to do good to those who hate him, and to pray for those who use him despitefully and malign him. The fruit of the Spirit is love! It means that there is this new element in Christian men and women that governs the whole of their outlook. Now it is not perfect love yet. We do not believe that we can have perfect love in this life. There are people who teach that but I find no evidence for it in the New Testament. No, no! But it does mean that the principle of love is there. The apostle Paul puts it perfectly once and for ever in the third chapter of his Epistle to Titus:

We ourselves also were sometimes foolish, disobedient, deceived, serving divers lusts and pleasures, living in malice and envy, hateful, and hating one another. But after that the kindness and love of God our Saviour toward man appeared, not by works of righteousness which we have done, but according to his mercy he saved us, by the washing of regeneration, and renewing of the Holy Ghost; which he shed on us abundantly through Jesus Christ our Saviour; that being justified by his grace, we should be made heirs according to the hope of eternal life (Titus 3:3–7).

That is it! By nature we live 'in malice and envy', we are 'hateful, and hating one another'. Does that shock you? It should not because it is true of every person in the world today who is not a Christian. Of course, we can be very polite in a party, and we seem to love everybody. But do we? What about our thoughts? What a hateful lot we are as a fallen human race! As the biographies come out and the autobiographies of the so-called great leaders and statesmen, you see it more and more. Loving colleagues, standing together? Rather, people scheming to bring one another down behind the scenes, muttering against one another! Read the books and there you see it. But, says Paul, we are no longer like that. We are not perfect as Christians but it is no longer true to say of us that we are living in malice and envy, that we are hateful and hate one another. My friend, if that is true of you, you are not a Christian. I do not care what you have done. It is no use saying to me that you have never committed adultery. If you are living in malice and envy, if you are full of hate and hate other people, you are not a Christian, you are not born again, the Spirit of God is not in you. The fruit of the Spirit is love, and love even for your enemies!

Let us go on to the second – *joy*. What does joy mean? It does not mean happiness, of course. What a difference there is between joy and happiness! So often, happiness is a sort of artefact. God means his people, his children, to be happy in the Christian, spiritual sense, which is the joy of the Lord, the joy of salvation. Whatever my deficiencies, whatever my faults, I know that I am a child of God, and I cannot know that without rejoicing in it: and you must rejoice in it. The fruit of the Spirit is joy. A certain kind of Christian seems to be developing of whom the supreme proof that he or she is a Christian is the fact of being miserable. But the Christian is meant to be full of joy. 'Rejoice in the Lord alway: and again I say, Rejoice' (*Phil.* 4:4). If you are not a joyful Christian, there is not much evidence of the fruit of the Spirit in you.

Do not forget the two aspects that I have been emphasizing. If the main work of the Spirit in you is only to cast you down, it is probably not the work of the Spirit. If you spend the whole of your time just looking into yourself, then you are not obeying Scripture. You must also look to the Lord. You do not look at yourself and stop there. You do not shake your head and mourn and always want something for yourself. Some Christians at the present time are so concerned about themselves that they do not even believe in any sort of evangelism, they do not believe in evangelistic services. They say, 'I got nothing in that service to help me to live.' They are always wanting something for themselves and have no thought for the unbeliever. They are just miserable Christians turning round in a vortex of morbidity and introspection and self-concern.

No, no! The fruit of the Spirit is joy! Christians delight in God. They delight in their salvation. They know in whom they have believed. And the more the Spirit works in us, the greater will be the joy that we shall manifest. My friends, do we know about this joy? Are you rejoicing in the Lord? Are you always rejoicing in the Lord? That must be as true of you as your awareness of the plague of your own heart. There is no contradiction, the two go together. You see the plague, you see the Lord, and you rejoice in him. Even your sin makes you rejoice in him because it reminds you again of what he has done for you.

And last in this first group of three – *peace*. There is an essential peace in the heart of the Christian. It is said that in the very centre of a hurricane there is absolute quiet and peace. That is a good parable of the Christian, it seems to me. You may be involved in conflict, there may be all sorts of things happening to you – 'without were fightings, within were fears' (*2 Cor.* 7:5) – yet at the centre there is a fundamental peace. As Christians, not one of us is satisfied with ourselves or with our achievements. We are aware of all the deficiencies and the failures and the faults and the sins. Yet at the centre we are able to say this: 'Being justified by faith, we have peace with God through our Lord Jesus Christ' (*Rom.* 5:1). Before, I was not at peace with God and dwelt in fear. I was afraid of God, I was afraid of death, I was afraid of the law, I was afraid of everything, but now, in spite of all that, I know I have peace with God.

And because Christians have peace with God, they have peace with their fellow men and women. Paul says that Christ, by dying on the cross, has made peace – 'for to make in himself of twain one new man, so making peace' (*Eph.* 2:15). I am reconciled to other people. Jew and Gentile have come together and become one. It is the miracle of the Christian church. And so it is with all people – peace with God; peace with others.

And perhaps most wonderful of all, peace with oneself, what the writer of one of our hymns calls, 'a heart at leisure from itself'.[1] The quiet heart! The restlessness has gone. One has found satisfaction in God, in Christ, by the Spirit. There is a fundamental peace within. Before, oh, there was a restlessness, a perpetual dissatisfaction. The heart was heaving like the waves of a sea that could never find rest. 'The wicked are like the troubled sea, when it cannot rest, whose waters cast up mire and dirt', as Isaiah puts it (*Isa.* 57:20). And how true that is. But when people become Christians, the fruit of the Spirit develops and they are fundamentally at rest in the depths and profundities of the personality.

My dear friends, have you been examining yourselves? Have you found some evidence of this blessed fruit of the Spirit – love, joy, peace?

---

[1] From the hymn, 'Father, I know that all my life', by Anna Laetitia Waring.

It does not matter what happens to you: 'Be careful for nothing; but in every thing by prayer and supplication with thanksgiving let your requests be made known unto God. And the peace of God, which passeth all understanding, shall keep your hearts and minds through Christ Jesus' (*Phil.* 4:6–7). Do you know anything about that? Do you know this fundamental, central peace, whatever may be happening round and about you? Can you face the possibility of death with a real sense of peace within – the death of a dear one, your own death, anything that may happen? God grant that we, every one of us, may know that we are the children of God, and that the marks of the Spirit may be discernible even to us, and even more so to others. ∞

28

The Fruit of the Spirit—2

But as many as received him, to them gave he power to become the sons of God, even to them that believe on his name: which were born, not of blood, nor of the will of the flesh, nor of the will of man, but of God (John 1:12–13).

We have looked at the danger of grieving the Spirit, and our fear lest we should ever do so, and have come to a more positive way of testing whether or not we are truly the children of God. This, we have said, is a very searching test. The Holy Spirit dwelling within us produces certain fruit, and we are looking at the description of this fruit given by the apostle Paul in Galatians 5:22–23 – 'love, joy, peace, longsuffering, gentleness, goodness, faith, meekness, temperance' – to see whether there is any evidence of this fruit in our lives.

Let me remind you that Paul speaks of the 'fruit' of the Spirit, not the 'fruits'. These are all different aspects of the same thing. They are all interrelated and it is difficult to have one without at the same time having the others in some measure. I have also emphasized the fact that we are not dealing here with the so-called 'gifts' of the Spirit but with the 'graces'. Furthermore, I have indicated that this is a much more delicate test than the test of knowledge. It is, in other words, one of the most thorough tests that we can ever face. We have suggested that the list given by Paul in Galatians 5 might be classified into three main groups. The first group describes our essential nature as Christians, what we are in ourselves – love, joy, peace – and we considered these in our last study. And now we must go on to our second group, which consists of longsuffering, gentleness and goodness – that is, what we are in our relationship to others.

The second group, of course, follows directly from the first. What we are, we manifest. So we must start with ourselves, and then we will test whether or not this is true of us by the way in which we react to our surroundings and our circumstances. With this second group we are also carrying the test a step further. 'None of us liveth to himself,' said the apostle Paul (*Rom.* 14:7). 'No man is an island', no man lives in isolation. We live in a world of people and we live with others, and it is at this point that the test emerges. It is one thing to be alone in our study, or in a room, or way on top of a mountain, or in a cell in a monastery, and there to feel that we know something about this love of God and Christ, this love, which passes knowledge, and to say that we have a joy in our heart that nothing can disturb, and that we have a settled peace, 'a heart at leisure from itself', but it is very different suddenly to be confronted by people, life, difficulties and problems.

You see, the test goes on. The apostle does not leave it at love, joy, peace, but brings us to this second group. So in the end it comes to this: that you and I can tell best of all, perhaps, whether or not we are Christians, not when we are alone, but when we are with other people, when we are surrounded by problems and difficulties, when we are in the world as it is and with people as they are. And immediately we see the whole error behind monasticism. Patently, that is not the way. The test is whether we have love, joy and peace in the midst of this life. That is the grand discovery that was made by, or rather, that came to Martin Luther. It was the whole origin of the Reformation.

You do not divide people into religious and laity. No, no! We are all religious, we are all saints: the saints who belong to the church at Corinth, or in Rome, or wherever else it is. Our saintliness is of no value at all unless it is a saintliness that shines out brightly in the midst of life. It is not a hothouse plant, it is not a delicate flower cultivated in artificial conditions where no breath of air is ever allowed to disturb it. That is of no value. John Milton in his *Areopagitica* puts that very rightly when he says, 'I cannot praise a fugitive and cloistered virtue.' That is no good. The virtue that he praises is the one that 'sallies out and sees her adversary'. When you are on your own cultivating your soul, you may come to the conclusion that all is well. But now you must emerge.

The business of life calls upon you, there are things to be attended to and there are other people – and here is the test.

Let us look at what Paul tells us about the second group of the fruit of the Spirit. How do we face this group? You say, 'Oh, I thank God for this love that's in my heart!' Then you are suddenly confronted by very difficult people, very stupid people, people who do not understand what you are talking about, people who are selfish, self-centred. Indeed, people who may even be offensive, who may attack you, who may persecute you. And the question is: How do you react to them? What about your 'love, joy, peace' now? Because people can be difficult. We are all very difficult people, every one of us. We do not think that, of course, in the isolation of the solitude; then we are wonderful! But that is of no value unless it can stand up to this test: What is our behaviour with respect to other people? The purpose of the first group is to enable us to fulfil the second.

The apostle says that our first great characteristic with respect to other people, if we are indeed bearing the fruit of the Spirit, is *longsuffering*. What a rare grace this is! All the fruit of the Spirit is rare, alas. In 1 Corinthians 13, the apostle Paul gives us a very wonderful account of what he means by longsuffering. Let me just give you the salient points. 'Charity suffereth long . . . is not easily provoked, thinketh no evil' (verses 4, 5). He tells us, furthermore, that it 'beareth all things, believeth all things, hopeth all things, endureth all things. Charity never faileth' (verses 7–8). So there it is, that is part of the fruit of the Spirit.

You see the contrast, do you not? First, the private cultivation of the soul, but then the coming out into the midst of life with all the pinpricks, the irritations and problems of men and women in their folly, their stupidity and wrong behaviour. How does one react to it all? Well, the apostle is saying that those who have the Spirit of God in them, and in whom the Spirit of God is bearing fruit, are not disturbed, and that is because of the love and the joy and the peace that are in them. The settled condition of their souls and their spirits is such that they cannot be upset easily; they can bear with people and they can take all that comes without losing this fundamental characteristic. That is what it really comes to. The way they live in the world is the test of the depth of the love and the joy and the peace that are in them. The deeper the peace, the less easily will it be disturbed and upset by other people and their ways.

Perhaps the best thing to do is to look at some examples and illustrations of longsuffering. The supreme example, of course, is our blessed Lord himself. Look at his treatment of Judas Iscariot. Though he knew exactly what was going to happen, how patient he was, how longsuffering! Consider how he bore 'the contradiction of sinners against himself', as Hebrews 12:3 puts it and as we see so clearly in the pages of the four Gospels. The apostle Peter sums it up very well in his first epistle, where he puts it like this:

Servants, be subject to your masters with all fear; not only to the good and gentle, but also to the forward.

That is the test.

For this is thankworthy, if a man for conscience toward God endure grief, suffering wrongfully. For what glory is it, if when ye be buffeted for your faults, ye shall take it patiently?

– we all ought to do that – there is no credit in doing that –

but if, when ye do well and suffer for it, ye take it patiently, this is acceptable with God.

When you are suffering grievous injustice. You have done your work, you have done what you were supposed to do, but you are even punished for doing that. Everything is wrong, yet you take it patiently.

For even hereunto were ye called: because Christ also suffered for us, leaving us an example, that ye should follow his steps: who did no sin, neither was guile found in his mouth: who, when he was reviled, reviled not again; when he suffered, he threatened not; but committed himself to him that judgeth righteously (1 Pet. 2:18–23).

Now that is it. And the apostle Paul, in Romans 12, makes exactly the same point. He says: Don't take vengeance; be longsuffering. Remember that God has said, 'Vengeance is mine; I will repay' (*Rom.* 12:19). And when the Spirit is bearing fruit in the lives of believers, whatever may happen to them, they act on that principle. They say, 'It's all right, this isn't my business.' So they are longsuffering! It is only the Spirit who can enable us to be like that – nothing else. You yourself can resolve and decide as much as you like but the moment you are confronted by a trial, you forget all your resolutions. Your native spirit takes charge and you lose all your patience. You are no longer longsuffering. You are irritable. You fall. But the Spirit can enable us. Thank God, it is possible for all of us to show this fruit of the Spirit.

We see longsuffering in the life of the apostle Paul himself. I imagine that by nature he could have been a very irritable man. He was a passionate man, a man of profound feeling, who felt things very strongly, and yet there is nothing more remarkable about him than the way in which he manifested this longsuffering with respect to his own fellow-countrymen, the Jews. From the moment he became a Christian and an apostle, they reviled and persecuted him. They abused him and heaped every insult they could think of upon him – never was a man treated as shamefully as the apostle Paul was by his own fellow-countrymen. But listen to what he says in Romans 9:1–3: 'I say the truth in Christ, I lie not, my conscience also bearing me witness in the Holy Ghost, that I have great heaviness and continual sorrow in my heart. For I could wish that myself were accursed from Christ for my brethren, my kinsmen according to the flesh.' Listen to him again in chapter 10:1–2: 'Brethren, my heart's desire and prayer to God for Israel is, that they might be saved. For I bear them record that they have a zeal of God, but not according to knowledge.' Oh, yes, it is possible for the disciple to follow his Master! The Spirit can produce this spirit of longsuffering within us.

Do you find longsuffering in yourself? Do you find it in yourself when you are concerned, perhaps, with relatives who are not Christians and who are irritable because you have become a Christian and Christ has come before them in your esteem? They hate you because of it, as they hate everything you do with respect to our Lord. How do you bear with them? Are you longsuffering? Are you patient? The fruit of the Spirit is longsuffering.

Let us go on to the next fruit, which is *gentleness*. Now it is generally agreed that while there is a sense in which the word 'gentleness' conveys the right meaning, a better translation here would be the word 'kindness'. Ultimately, there is something negative about longsuffering, but here is something positive: kindness, gentleness. In other words, as Christians, we have to bear with people, to put up with them and to put up with a lot of wrong and injustice and misunderstanding and persecution, but we do not stop there. Not only do we not hit back, but we handle people gently, we are not harsh with respect to them but are ready to forgive. Our whole attitude towards them is one of kindness. And this applies, of course, as the New Testament makes quite plain and clear, even to our handling of our enemies; and this is where 'gentleness' is such a thorough test.

Now I want to make this point clear because it is of great importance for the Christian church today. I sometimes think that at the present time there is a very great danger that many Christian people may misunderstand what is meant by this gentleness and kindness. There are many who seem to interpret it as meaning that we should be tolerant of everything and agree with everything, that we should say that it does not matter what is said and all is well. Kindness is mistaken for a general affability. But it is very, very different.

Let me put it like this. In Galatians 5:22–23, the apostle Paul is dealing with the fruit of the Spirit from the standpoint of our relationships with other people. So we must never interpret gentleness as meaning merely a lack of character. Gentleness and kindness do not mean spinelessness, they do not just mean 'niceness', or the absence of any strong, firm characteristics. One must make this point in order to reconcile the Scriptures with themselves. Remember that the apostle who writes in Galatians 5 about 'gentleness' is exactly the same apostle who writes in the same Epistle to the Galatians: 'Though we, or an angel from heaven, preach any other gospel unto you than that which we have preached unto you, let him be accursed' (*Gal.* 1:8). And he repeats those words in verse 9. Now that is very strong language. Similarly, later on, where he is dealing with the whole question of circumcision and the people who were troubling and bothering the members of the churches in Galatia, he says, 'I would they were even cut off which trouble you' (*Gal.* 5:12).

Now the way we reconcile that strong language with the fruit of gentleness is perfectly simple. You see it in our Lord himself. We are told of him, 'A bruised reed shall he not break, and smoking flax shall he not quench' (*Matt.* 12:20) – the meek and lowly Jesus! Oh, the gentleness and kindness of our blessed Lord! But, remember, he is the one who turns finally upon the Pharisees and says, 'Woe unto you, scribes and Pharisees, hypocrites!' One of the most terrible denunciations in the whole of the Bible is to be found there in Matthew 23. So how do we reconcile this with gentleness and kindness? Well, in this way: by seeing that there is all the difference in the world between contending for the truth with strength, with vigour, with clarity and with power, and our personal handling of, and dealings with, people. This is a very difficult point and some people never seem to grasp it.

There are some people who cannot defend the truth without attacking persons. But that seems to me to be a denial of the New Testament teaching. Paul says, 'Be ye angry, and sin not' (*Eph.* 4:26). That is it. You are to be angry. There is such a thing as righteous indignation. A Christian who can listen to people denying the deity of our Lord, even perhaps denying the very being and Person of God, denying the miracles and the atonement and the resurrection and the Person of the Holy Spirit – someone who just smiles at all that and says, 'Well, of course, I must always be kind and manifest love, and therefore I say nothing', is denying the whole of the New Testament. No, no! Error and sin are to be denounced, and to be denounced strongly. But that is not incompatible with being gentle and kind in your personal relationships. We have to differentiate between error and the people who are the innocent or the deluded victims of the error, blinded by the god of this world.

Now I am emphasizing this because the climate of opinion in which we find ourselves today is one in which anything is smiled at, nothing matters. We are all one and we must all be kind and nice, let people say what they will. But that is not what the apostle means when he talks about one of the manifestations of the fruit of the Spirit being 'kindness' or 'gentleness'. We are to learn how to oppose error without bearing malice, without being unkind to people, without being boorish and offensive. We are to draw a vital distinction between the error and those who are the dupes and the victims of the error. Do we find any evidence of this gentleness, this kindness, in us? With respect to those whom we know to be deniers of the truth, are we as the apostle Paul was to his fellow-countrymen, the Jews?

But then we come to *goodness*, and this again carries us just a step further. Not only are we kind towards others, but we must even manifest this spirit of goodness with respect to them. By this, Paul means that we must desire their good, we must be well disposed towards them, in spite of what they are, in spite of what they are doing, and in spite of what they may be doing to us. He means that our greatest desire with respect to them is to help them and if we get an opportunity of doing them a good turn, we are to jump at it. He means that we must always be ready to do a kind action. Now there is no need for me to keep you with this because in the Sermon on the Mount we have a perfect exposition of this very matter from the lips of our blessed Lord himself:

Ye have heard that it hath been said, Thou shalt love thy neighbour, and hate thine enemy. But I say unto you, Love your enemies, bless them that curse you, do good to them that hate you, and pray for them which despitefully use you, and persecute you; that ye may be the children of your Father which is in heaven: for he maketh his sun to rise on the evil and on the good, and sendeth rain on the just and on the unjust. For if ye love them which love you, what reward have ye? do not even the publicans the same? and if ye salute your brethren only, what do ye more than others? do not even the publicans so? Be ye therefore perfect, even as your Father which is in heaven is perfect (Matt. 5:43–48).

Notice the emphasis: 'Love your enemies, bless them that curse you, do good to them that hate you, and pray for them which despitefully use you, and persecute you.' Now that is what the apostle means when he talks about goodness being one of the manifestations of the fruit of the Spirit. He means that with regard to these people who are acting as your enemies and doing everything they can to upset you and perhaps to ruin your character and your life and your everything, you are ready to do good to them, even as God sends the rain and the sun upon the bad as well as the good, upon the evil as well as the righteous. And so, our Lord says, you are to be perfect even as your Father in heaven is perfect.

We are to be like God in this matter of goodness. It is only those who have the Holy Spirit in them who can do this. Your good moral person may refrain from doing someone harm, perhaps, but will never go beyond that and do good. It is the Christian alone who does this. Why? Because Christians understand other people: they know that they really are the slaves of the devil and of sin and of the evil fallen nature that is in them. Christians differentiate between the man and his own evil nature; they want the man to be delivered, so they delight in doing him good. This is much more difficult, is it not, than being alone in your study with the Scriptures and praying and feeling how wonderful everything is? But oh, my dear friends, these are the tests of life.

And now let us go on and look at the third and last group that the apostle puts before us: faith, meekness, temperance. Here we are back to our general character, especially as it manifests itself in the sight of and before God. First, *faith*. Although the word in the Greek is the ordinary word for faith, the meaning is not so much faith as *faithfulness*. Paul is not writing about faith in the sense of one of the gifts of the Spirit. The gift of faith, which Paul refers to in 1 Corinthians 12, is the special gift that is given to some people, to George Müller and Hudson Taylor, for instance. This gift of faith is not, of course, the faith whereby one believes in Christ, because every Christian has that faith: 'By grace are ye saved through faith; and that not of yourselves: it is the gift of God' (*Eph.* 2:8). That is common to all.

But faith is not what Paul is talking about in Galatians 5. He is not talking about gifts there, but about graces, these manifestations of the life of the Spirit in us and through us. And, therefore, Paul undoubtedly means *faithfulness*, which is one of the wonderful manifestations of the fruit of the Spirit. I suppose faithfulness is what a pastor, a minister of a church, looks for more than anything else in the members of his flock. By 'faithfulness' the apostle means dependability, reliability. He means loyalty. A faithful Christian is the exact opposite of someone who is a Christian, as it were, by fits and starts, someone who manifests this fruit of the Spirit in spasms. Such a person seems, at first, to be the most wonderful Christian you have ever met, but, the next time you meet, he or she is right down. Then you never know what to expect. Fitful, always changing, these Christians are unstable characters. You cannot rely on them. The apostle is saying that the Spirit produces such depths in the character that there is a settled condition, something solid and durable, stable, dependable and reliable. You know where you are going to find such people; you know what they will be like; you can always be certain about them.

Now, again, let us bear in mind that faithfulness is very positive. There is a type of person who is by nature more or less always the same, but such people are like that because there is not very much in them, there is not much in them that can vary. If we were discussing this from the natural standpoint, we would have to defend the person who does change a good deal. The great people of the world, the great leaders, have been people of passion, and sometimes they have been in a rage and at other times they have been gentle. That is because they are big, and where you have bigness, you have variation. But we tend today to glorify the person who is just an aggregate of negatives. So many of these highly paid 'personalities', so called, are just that, it seems to me. We are told they are so good because they are inoffensive and so on. In other words, they lack character; there is an absence of quality. God forbid that we should confuse that with what the apostle is talking about here.

No, Paul is saying that though by nature a man or woman may be explosive and have a big personality, with variations of temperament, what the Spirit does is harness them all. And so you have these mighty forces and powers channelled by the Holy Spirit, and how wonderful that is! They are all brought under the control of the Spirit and then you have a really powerful character. Look again at the apostle Paul and you will see all that I mean; you will see all the strength and the passion and the power mastered, directed and channelled. So such a person is reliable, dependable, faithful.

The next manifestation of the Spirit is *meekness*, which means that Christian people are humble – and, especially, they are humble before God. They are the exact opposite of the Pharisee in the temple who went right forward to the front and said, 'God, I thank thee, that I am not as other men are' (*Luke* 18:11). That is the antithesis of meekness. You see meekness in the tax-collector, also in the temple, smiting his breast and saying, 'God be merciful to me a sinner' (*Luke* 18:13). Meekness! 'Blessed are the meek: for they shall inherit the earth' (*Matt.* 5:5). People who are bearing the fruit of the Spirit are those who are humble before God, who walk humbly with God. They have heard the exhortation, 'Humble yourselves therefore under the mighty hand of God' (*1 Pet.* 5:6) and they are always doing so. Oh, there is a terrible absence of this characteristic, I fear, in the modern church. We are aggressive; we are self-contained; we do things in a businesslike manner. Read the biographies of the saints, read about Robert Murray McCheyne, David Brainerd, Jonathan Edwards, and you will find this meekness and humility.

But not only are Christians meek before God, they are equally meek in themselves and in their own view of themselves. Those who have the fruit of the Spirit know best their own smallness, their own lack of gifts. They have a very poor opinion of themselves. Now this is not mock modesty; they really see it, they really know it. They abominate, they hate, themselves. Charles Haddon Spurgeon said he would not cross the road to listen to himself preaching. That is true meekness. He meant it, he really meant it from the depths of his heart. Here is a very good test: the more meek we become, the less resentful we are of the criticism of others because we know that it is true and we know more about it even than they do; we could say even worse things about ourselves.

And this meekness is also a meekness that shows itself before others and with respect to others. Here, again, the simplest thing for me to do is to read a great statement of this by the apostle Paul:

Let nothing be done through strife or vainglory; but in lowliness of mind let each esteem other better than themselves. Look not every man on his own things, but every man also on the things of others. Let this mind be in you, which was also in Christ Jesus: who, being in the form of God, thought it not robbery to be equal with God: but made himself of no reputation, and took upon him the form of a servant, and was made in the likeness of men: and being found in fashion as a man, he humbled himself, and became obedient unto death, even the death of the cross (Phil. 2:3–8).

That is it, my friends! Be like Moses, the meekest man in all the earth (*Num.* 12:3). Be like our Lord himself! There you see it all. So the apostle is able to appeal to the believers in Corinth in this way: 'Now I Paul myself beseech you by the meekness and gentleness of Christ, who in presence am base among you, but being absent am bold toward you' (*2 Cor.* 10:1).

But listen to some other things that Paul says about himself – how salutary it is, and how we should thank God that he gives us these occasional insights. Whenever the apostle does talk about himself, it is not to say what a wonderful man he is, how great an evangelist and so on. No, this is what he says: 'I am the least of the apostles, that am not meet to be called an apostle, because I persecuted the church of God. But by the grace of God I am what I am' (*1 Cor.* 15:9–10). Then listen to him saying this again – he could never get over it: 'Unto me, who am less than the least of all saints, is this grace given, that I should preach among the Gentiles the unsearchable riches of Christ' (*Eph.* 3:8). The apostle was amazed at the fact that he was ever an apostle, that he was ever in the ministry at all. He was less than the least of all the saints. That is not mock modesty, that is not your type of man who says, 'Of course, I'm nobody in the church, I'm just an ordinary man', and wants you to know how wonderful he is! It is the opposite of that. Paul really believed what he was writing. He was astounded that the grace of God had ever come to him.

So I come to a last word, which is the word *temperance*. This means self-control, discipline. It means behaving like an athlete. You read about players before their test matches or games of football. They do not smoke; they do not drink; they discipline themselves in order to be fit for the great contest. Well, Christians are always like that, not only on special occasions. Temperance – avoidance of evil, keeping away from all that is harmful, the exercise of strength and power and ability to enable me to manifest forth his glory and his praise. Temperance! A disciplined, regulated and ordered life.

Let us listen to the apostle once more. Writing to Timothy, he says: 'God hath not given us the spirit of fear; but of power, and of love' – notice again that power and love are not incompatible; love is not weak and flabby and sentimental and sickly but is powerful! – 'and of a sound mind', which means discipline (2 *Tim.* 1:7). The Spirit always leads to discipline. The more disciplined our lives, the more certain we can be that we are the children of God. In other words, the Spirit enables true Christians to control themselves, to control their temperaments. The temperament is not changed, our temperaments are not taken away from us. We do not become a series of identical postage stamps. No, no! Your temperament, your personality, is left to you but the Spirit enables you to control it and then it can be used to the glory of God. It is under control; it is under discipline. It is controlled by the Spirit, controlled by the truth.

Christians are not wayward. They are not carried away. They are not the victims of circumstances and of other people. They are always under the control of the Spirit and are able to control themselves. That was the trouble with Timothy. He was having difficulties in his churches and he was being persecuted. He had heard rumours that Paul, who was in prison, was to be put to death. So Timothy got alarmed and excited. He said: What's going to happen? Christianity is finished.

'Man,' writes the apostle Paul, in effect, 'where is your discipline? Where is your sound mind? Where is your self-control? Don't you have sufficient grasp of the truth to see what God's purpose is and to know that these things mustn't upset you?' That is it. Temperance, self-control, discipline, orderliness in your life, not constantly losing your balance, but always with a mind that is under that final control of the Spirit.

The teaching about the fruit of the Spirit tells us that everything about us is working to one and the same great end. Everything about the person and the personality proclaims the fact that we are different. That is what you must do, says our Lord: 'Let your light so shine before men, that they may see your good works, and glorify your Father which is in heaven' (*Matt.* 5:16). Oh, he says, be like your Father! And we are like our Father who is in heaven when we are manifesting love, joy, peace, longsuffering, gentleness, goodness, faithfulness, meekness and temperance, which is self-control, orderliness in the life, with everything directed to the glory of God.

My dear friends, have I strengthened you? Have I given you assurance that you are a child of God? God grant that I have! But if I have not, if I have disturbed you, if I have made you feel that you are not a Christian – then do something about it. Go to him, acknowledge and confess it. It is the Spirit who produces the fruit. Ask him to fill you with his Spirit. Ask him so to shed his love abroad in your heart by the Spirit that the fruit of the Spirit will inevitably begin to manifest itself. If you do not find the fruit, what you need is not a decision to do this or that, you need the Spirit in all his fulness. So go and ask God to shed his love abroad in your heart, in great profusion, in overwhelming power, and you will be amazed at yourself as you begin to see more and more of the fruit of the Spirit in your life. ∞

29

Our Relationship to Other Christians

But as many as received him, to them gave he power to become the sons of God, even to them that believe on his name: which were born, not of blood, nor of the will of the flesh, nor of the will of man, but of God (John 1:12–13).

We have been working our way steadily through three relationships – our relationship to the Father, to the Son and to the Holy Spirit – and we have been testing ourselves in terms of what the Bible tells us about that triple relationship. In dealing with the Spirit, we came eventually to consider the manifestation of the fruit of the Spirit in our lives. If the Spirit of God dwells in us, then we show something of the fruit of the Spirit. And so we apply this test to ourselves: Are we manifesting the various aspects of the fruit of the Spirit – love, joy, peace, longsuffering, gentleness, goodness, faith, meekness, temperance? Now in applying that particular test, we were driven, of course, to consider ourselves in our relationship to other people and from that, it seems to me, there follows the next big test, which is none other than our relationship to the family of the church.

You see how it works out: our relationship to the Father, the Son and the Holy Spirit and then, at the earthly, human level, we look at others who are with us in this relationship – in other words, the Christian family to which we belong. The concept of childhood immediately implies the whole notion of a family and a family relationship. So having considered our vertical relationships, we are now going to look at our horizontal relationships and, as I think I shall be able to show you, this is, again, a very practical, a very thorough and a very searching test.

Now our relationship to the family arises, of necessity, and that is why it is dealt with extensively in the pages of the New Testament. In the epistles, in particular, one is constantly finding references to the church. Written as they are to the members of the church, the epistles are concerned, every one of them somewhere or another, with the relationships of church members to one another. It is quite inevitable. One of the last things our Lord prayed for in his high-priestly prayer was that his people might be one, and might be kept as one, because the world is looking on and it is only thus that it can know who these people are, and who he is, and why God ever sent him into this world.

Now we must look at it like this – and this is why I say this subject is inevitable – though we are saved individually, one by one – and that is a fundamental doctrine of the New Testament – we are all, nevertheless, saved in the same way. I do not mean that all the details will be identical in every case, but I do mean that there is only one way whereby anyone can become a Christian, and that is through being 'born again'. The new birth, of course, leads to repentance and faith and so on and these are the manifestations of new life and the new outlook. That, I repeat, is essential. 'Except a man be born again,' said our Lord to Nicodemus, 'he cannot see the kingdom of God . . . Except a man be born of water and of the Spirit, he cannot enter into the kingdom of God' (*John* 3:3, 5). And it is in that way, and only in that way, that we become Christians. It happens to us separately and individually. We are not saved as nations, we are not saved as families: 'not of blood, nor of the will of the flesh, nor of the will of man, but of God'. It is a separate action in the case of every single one of us. But because it happens to all of us, we are at once brought into a common position.

Now the New Testament talks a great deal about our fundamental solidarity. It points out our solidarity in sin and shame and failure and need. It says, 'For all have sinned, and come short of the glory of God' (*Rom.* 3:23). Not only some – all. 'There is none righteous, no, not one' (*Rom.* 3:10). There is no difference between the Jew and the Greek, all are the same; there is this 'oneness'.

The Bible also has a great deal to say about 'the common salvation' (*Jude* 3). There is only one salvation. That is the whole miracle of redeeming grace, says the apostle Paul in writing to the Ephesians, especially in chapter 2. Christ, he says, 'hath broken down the middle wall of partition between us . . . to make in himself of twain one new man' (*Eph.* 2:14–15). Jew and Gentile together, one in sin, one in salvation, believing in the same Saviour, having received the same birth. Therefore I say again that though we are saved individually – and it is a separate experience, God has personal dealings with each of us, one by one, and we cannot be Christians without that – yet, because it is, nevertheless, the same essential action, we are immediately brought together as a company of people.

But Scripture goes even further than that. It has this great doctrine that we are looking at, which teaches us that we are all made 'the children of God'. We are all adopted into the family of God. The apostle Paul, pre-eminently, teaches this particular doctrine. He points out in the eighth chapter of the Epistle to the Romans that 'as many as are led by the Spirit of God, they are the sons [children] of God' (*Rom.* 8:14). 'Ye have not received,' he says, 'the spirit of bondage again to fear; but ye have received the Spirit of adoption, whereby we cry, Abba, Father' (*Rom.* 8:15). That is the position. This adoption! The 'Spirit of adoption'! Or, as Paul puts it still more clearly in Galatians 4: 'Because ye are sons, God hath sent forth the Spirit of his Son into your hearts, crying, Abba, Father' (*Gal.* 4:6). This is just indicative of the fact that over and above being forgiven and saved in the same way, and brought together as a company of people, we have all been adopted in the same way into the family of God. So the apostle is able to say at the end of Ephesians 2: 'Now therefore ye are no more strangers and foreigners, but fellow-citizens with the saints, and of the household of God' (*Eph.* 2:19).

That is it! We are more than just citizens in the same kingdom, though that is a wonderful thing; beyond that, God has adopted us right into his family. Whether or not we are by nature Jews does not matter, together we have become 'members of the household of God', the family of God himself. And all the New Testament teaching with regard to the church as the body of Christ emphasizes that same fact. The apostle says in 1 Corinthians 12:13: 'For by one Spirit [in one Spirit] are we all baptized into one body, whether we be Jews or Gentiles.'

Thus the whole of the teaching of the New Testament emphasizes this particular relationship that we have to the members of the family, stating it in various pictures and analogies.

But Scripture goes even beyond analogies, and makes explicit and perfectly plain statements. The most notable of all is in the First Epistle of John: 'We know that we have passed from death unto life, because we love the brethren' (*1 John* 3:14). Nothing could be plainer. That is what we want to know. How can I know that I am a child of God? Here is the test: I love the brethren. If I love the brethren, I must be a child of God. We know it in that way. Then John puts this negatively to make it quite sure: 'He that loveth not his brother abideth in death.' He makes an equally explicit statement in the first verse of the fifth chapter: 'Whosoever believeth that Jesus is the Christ is born of God: and every one that loveth him that begat loveth him also that is begotten of him.' John's whole argument is that these are indissolubly linked together. If you love the one who has begotten us, you must love the ones who are begotten.

Now there it is in its positive form, but John is also very careful to put that teaching in its negative form. I have given you one reference already, but take another. In the second chapter of his first epistle, he says: 'He that saith he is in the light, and hateth his brother, is in darkness even until now' (*1 John* 2:9). It does not matter what we say, it does not matter what theories we may propound, it does not matter though we know our Bibles from cover to cover, it does not matter though we be expert theologians, if we hate our brother, we are not in the light; we are liars. We are still spiritually dead. Or take it again in verse 20 of chapter 4: 'If a man say, I love God, and hateth his brother, he is a liar: for he that loveth not his brother whom he hath seen, how can he love God whom he hath not seen?' And this is found in other places also.

There, then, is the New Testament setting for this particular test, and I would again emphasize its practical nature. The Christian life is not a theoretical life; the Christian life is not for the head only. The Christian life, thank God, is something so big and glorious that it takes up the whole person. It takes up the intellect and the understanding; it takes up the heart, the feelings, the emotions; it takes up the will. And if the whole person is not involved, there is something radically wrong; it can be just an intellectual assent. So our relationship to the family, our relationship to the brethren, those with whom we come into intimate contact, is, in many ways, the most thorough test of all.

The human analogy reminds us of the searching nature of this test, does it not? 'Blood,' we say, 'is thicker than water.' Of course it is! There is something in a family relationship that makes it deeper than all others. And that is equally true in the spiritual realm. It is equally true of the members of the family of God. And that is why we know, and can know beyond any doubt or peradventure, that because we love the brethren, we are the children of God. So let us test ourselves by this particular test. How does it work itself out? Here, I think, are some of the obvious ways.

How do I know that I love the brethren? First, I must be able to recognize them. When I meet a number of people, how do I know who among them is a child of God? Now this is almost instinctive, something that one can scarcely put into words at all, but it is something that one knows. There are certain marks about the children of God, and a child of God always knows them, always recognizes them. There are many human analogies that show us the truth of this and by which we can work it out. There are certain signs that people give to one another, sometimes deliberately, sometimes unconsciously. People who have been brought up in the same atmosphere tend to do things in the same way; they have certain recognizable characteristics, or marks, in common. You can recognize people by speech, accent, dress, for example. So we say that people 'give themselves away' in certain respects. And this is very true of the family of God. There are certain special and particular things about us that those who belong to the family recognize. They do not have to be told, they know at once and instinctively.

The apostle Paul has a statement that partially, at any rate, includes this very point that we are dealing with. In describing the difference between 'the natural man' and 'the spiritual man', he says this: 'He that is spiritual judgeth all things, yet he himself is judged of no man' (*1 Cor.*

2:15). Paul means that the spiritual person has a faculty of discernment and of understanding that the natural person lacks. He has an extra understanding that is not comprehended by those who do not belong to the same family. There is a differentiation.

This power of discernment is very wonderful. I used to feel it during the war, and since then I have recognized it when young men belonging to this church and to other churches have told me how, on going into the army and finding themselves among men whom they had never met before, they were able to tell fairly quickly who the Christians were in their hut, their regiment and so on. By this kind of instinctive something that is implanted in us with the new life, we are able to recognize fellow-believers. 'Birds of a feather flock together', as we say. There is a kind of mutual attraction. You cannot always define it but you know and you are drawn to other Christians, and you approach them and you find that you were right. The question we ask ourselves, therefore, is: Do we have this ability? Do we find in practice that we do this when among strangers?

Then the second way, of course, is the sense of belonging. The moment you meet other Christians, the moment you come into contact with them, you feel that they belong to you and you belong to them; there is an immediate sense of unity. There is a very beautiful expression of this in the Old Testament, in the book of Ruth. In chapter 1 we read about Naomi and her two daughters-in-law, Ruth and Orpah. Naomi's husband and her two sons, the husbands of Ruth and Orpah, have died. The daughters-in-law are related only by marriage – and look at the difference between them! Unlike Naomi, Ruth and Orpah are Moabite by birth, but something has happened that makes Ruth feel that she belongs to her mother-in-law. When Naomi decides to go back to her old home in Bethlehem in Judaea, Ruth feels that she must leave her own country and go with her. She says: 'Intreat me not to leave thee, or to return from following after thee: for whither thou goest, I will go; and where thou lodgest, I will lodge: thy people shall be my people, and thy God my God' (*Ruth* 1:15–16). That is it. Ruth just knows that she belongs to this woman and she must go with her, and she pleads with Naomi not to prevent her. Now this is something that is deeper than a mere sense of attraction. It includes a sense of attraction but it is stronger than that. This is a very deep bond. In the same way, we are just aware of the fact that we now belong to these Christians and that they have become our people.

But let me analyse this second test and put it still more plainly by proceeding to the third test, which is a very vital point. We know that as the children of God we are in this relationship to the members of the family in a double sense: that we have been *separated from* others and have been *joined to* this new family. This is not a natural family: '[we] are born, not of blood, nor of the will of the flesh, nor of the will of man' – that is natural – 'but of God'. Here, then, is the new family, a family that has been brought into being by the life, death and resurrection of the Lord Jesus Christ and the sending down of the Holy Spirit. A new creation! A new family of God!

The biblical teaching is that you cannot belong to the new family without being separated and cut off from something else. Now this is not only a delicate test, it can also be very painful. But it was our Lord himself who said, when dealing with Christians who were tending to be frightened of persecution and opposition: 'Fear ye not therefore, ye are of more value than many sparrows.' That is because 'the very hairs of your head are all numbered' (*Matt.* 10:31, 30). Then he goes on to say:

Whosoever therefore shall confess me before men, him will I confess also before my Father which is in heaven. But whosoever shall deny me before men, him will I also deny before my Father which is in heaven.

Then, listen:

Think not that I am come to send peace on earth: I came not to send peace, but a sword. For I am come to set a man at variance against his father, and the daughter against her mother, and the daughter in law against her mother in law. And a man's foes shall be they of his own household. He that loveth father or mother more than me is not worthy of me: and he that loveth son or daughter more than me is not worthy of me. And he that taketh not his cross, and followeth after me, is not worthy of me. He that findeth his life shall lose it: and he that loseth his life for my sake shall find it (Matt. 10:33–39).

Our Lord is saying, in effect, 'Now the effect of my coming is not just going to make you and everybody else feel happy. No, no! You know that what I am doing, and what I am going to do to you, is so radical that it becomes a sword, it becomes a rock of offence, something that causes men to hate you and to hate me. It is a sword that is going to divide and cut you off at the most sensitive and delicate parts of the whole of your life.' In the parallel passage at the end of Luke chapter 14, our Lord even talks about husband and wife in this respect. But here it is and the teaching is quite inevitable. There is a new relationship, a spiritual relationship, and you cannot enter into it without coming out of something else.

So the gospel, and the Holy Spirit applying the gospel, becomes a sword and we are divided from old attachments, old relationships – relationships that we had regarded as sacred, as the highest and the greatest and the most wonderful of all. If those to whom we are thus attached are not also Christians, we are of necessity separated from them. That is our Lord's teaching, and it is, I repeat, inevitably true. All those relationships belong to 'blood', to 'the will of the flesh' and 'the will of man'. Our Lord is not depreciating them. The Bible never depreciates the natural relationships, indeed, it enforces them. It is God who ordained the family; it is God who ordained that children should thus be born in wedlock, as a result of wedlock, and should be brought up in the family. This is God's own ordinance. But this new kingdom transcends the natural, and in order to belong to it we have to undergo a new birth. And that new birth changes all our relationships: 'If any man be in Christ, he is a new creature: old things are passed away; behold, all things are become new' (*2 Cor.* 5:17). This is a literal, actual fact.

So the first part of the process is that we must be separated, cut off, set free. But alongside that we put the other side. In this new birth that we share with all other Christians, we come into the new family; we are all together 'partakers of the divine nature' (*2 Pet.* 1:4). The new blood, as it were, is in us all. There is a new outlook, a new orientation, a new everything. We have been given new life, and it is life from God, and because it is in us all, we are one. We are not what we were, we are different and in an entirely new relationship.

That separation from the old is why it was prophesied of our Lord that he would be 'for a stone of stumbling and for a rock of offence' (*Isa.* 8:14). And this was made painfully evident in practice. There are examples in the Bible and many more examples in subsequent church history. Try to understand these first Jews who became converts to Christianity. You may know something about the family life of the Jews. It was and still is one of their most notable and best characteristics – the solidarity of the family. And it meant so much to them. They were so careful and punctilious about this. But then, suddenly, one of them would become a Christian and they would be aware that there was a difference, that something had come between the family members. This Christ had come in and they hated him, and, in turn, would soon hate the one who had come to believe in him. They would erase his or her name out of the book. The new Christian would be ostracized and regarded as dead. How painful it was for the early Christians. And yet they were ready to face it and go through with it.

Now this separation was worked out not only in terms of a family, but also in terms of the state. So many of those early Roman Christians were in an awful predicament. The state, in which they had formerly believed and to which they had given a totalitarian allegiance, was urging them to say, 'Caesar is Lord.' But they could not say it any longer. They said, 'No, there is only one Lord, and that is Jesus. Caesar is not Lord. Caesar is not a god.' And they were threatened with extermination, massacre, in the arena. But it did not matter. They were so certain of this new relationship that they were gladly ready to endure any consequence, even to the laying down of their very lives.

This is a very delicate matter. It is still true today and some of you may find it the most searching test that I have yet put before you. Have you become aware that your most natural, tender relationships have been changed? Has it happened to you that the Christ of God and the new life in him has been a sword that has separated you from someone whom you love more dearly than life itself? My dear friend, if you know that experience, you need have no doubt. You are a child of God beyond any question. If the Lord Jesus Christ comes first to you, and if for his sake your heart is bleeding and breaking because of the severing of ties, you are a child of God. You will have a sense of pity and of sorrow for these people you love, but you know that you no longer belong to them in the sense that you once did, that you are no longer a natural person bound by natural ties only. You know that you have become a spiritual person, tied by the bonds of the love of God, cemented by the love of Christ.

Now this new life is in many ways terrible as well as tremendous. One of the most poignant and, at the time, one of the saddest things I had ever had to witness illustrates this. A man got married and he and his wife were happy, but after a few months of married life this man was born again and became a child of God. He did not love his wife any less, rather, he loved her more and was a better husband, but because he had become a child of God, he was anxious to have fellowship with the people of God. He came to the church not only on Sundays but to the prayer meeting on Monday nights, the fellowship meeting on Wednesday nights and the men's meeting on Saturday nights.

I shall never forget that man coming to me one day and telling me in tears, with his heart breaking, that the previous Monday night he had gone home from the prayer meeting – it had been a wonderful prayer meeting – to be met by his wife at the door. She was looking at him with hatred and bitterness and she said, 'I would sooner see you carried in dead drunk from the working men's club than coming home from this prayer meeting.' That is the work of the sword.

That man just had to go on; he could not give up. Though he loved his wife, Christ came first. He did not love her less, but he loved Christ more, and she knew that. She had detected it. Love is very sensitive. She realized that though her husband's love to her was greater than ever, somebody else had come in, somebody else took priority over her. It was this Christ who came first and she hated him with all her being and with great bitterness. That is the kind of thing I am talking about. The sword had been operating, and there was a new attachment and a new relationship. Thank God, the end of the story was that the wife came to see the horror of her old position and she herself was converted. How they rejoiced as man and wife, both giving Christ the pre-eminence and worshipping him together!

'Think not that I am come to send peace on earth: I came not to send peace, but a sword' – a man and his father, a mother and her daughter . . . My dear friends, let us examine ourselves. Do we know anything about this? If you can say, and say honestly, that Christ has become first to you, that he has affected even these most delicate relationships in life, then you need never have any doubt at all as to whether or not you are a child of God. You are!

However, let us go on with these tests of our love for our fellow-Christians. The next – the fourth test – is that we are conscious of the same family interests. Obviously! We have the same beliefs: 'One Lord, one faith, one baptism, one God and Father of all, who is above all, and through all, and in you all' (*Eph.* 4:5–6). It is inevitable – members of the same family always have the same interests. We have the same interest in the kingdom of God and in its success. We are naturally at one with Christian people in this. We see now that the most important thing in the world is the kingdom of God, and belonging to it, and the spread of this kingdom. Because of this, we are drawn together and attached to one another yet more deeply.

And then, of course, we all have the same hope of glory. 'If children, then heirs; heirs of God, and joint-heirs with Christ' (*Rom.* 8:17). We are going to the same eternal home. We are all away from home now. Heaven is our home. Our citizenship is in heaven, not here. We are therefore interested in the same hope of glory. We are looking forward to the same things; we are looking to a 'crowning day' that is coming. We all realize that we are but on a pilgrimage here, and that the realm of the reality is the unseen and the eternal. So, obviously, we are bound to our fellow-Christians in a way we are not bound to people who know nothing about that, and who ridicule it and dismiss it all, people who are bound only to this world and who live for this world.

So our interests are changed, but they are the same interests as those of other Christian people. As Jude puts it: '[I] write unto you of the

[same] common salvation' (*Jude* 3), and we are now concerned about this salvation, about defending it, and this brings us together. We see that we are a dwindling company in an evil world, and we feel that we must come still closer together, as the members of a family draw together when there is a threat from the outside. Whatever the differences, the family members all suddenly become one because of this common threat and their common interests. Is it not inevitable?

And then, as the fifth test, I would like to put it like this: we are aware that we speak the same language. This, again, is most interesting. Language is very interesting. There is such a thing as having the same idiom. People today say, 'We're on the same wavelength.' Quite right! There is a particular language within the common language. There is a specific terminology. I do not mean that we use clichés. That is abominable. Nor does it mean that we just address a man as 'Brother' every time we speak to him! No, no! That is not it at all. That is mere mechanics, not family feeling. I am talking about this depth of something that gives us the same language. We read in Malachi 3:16: 'Then they that feared the LORD spake often one to another.' Of course they did. They often spoke to one another because they were concerned about the same things, because they could make contact. There was something there that was binding them together.

Now I am interested in this particular aspect of the question of language. My point is that Christians recognize the language, they recognize the accent, if you like, the idiom. They recognize the manner of speech. And they can be very sensitive in their testing of this. There is a notable example at the end of Acts chapter 18 (verses 24–26):

And a certain Jew named Apollos, born at Alexandria, an eloquent man, and mighty in the scriptures, came to Ephesus. This man was instructed in the way of the Lord; and being fervent in the spirit, he spake and taught diligently the things of the Lord, knowing only the baptism of John. And he began to speak boldly in the synagogue

– now, notice this –

whom when Aquila and Priscilla had heard, they took him unto them, and expounded unto him the way of God more perfectly.

[429]

I think that is wonderful! Aquila and Priscilla were ordinary tent-makers, they had not had the educational advantages of the scholar, and here came this eloquent orator, this man 'mighty in the scriptures', and the two simple believers listened to him. And as they sat and listened, I can see them looking at one another, and what they said in their looks was this: 'There's something lacking here, he doesn't understand it properly. He's all right as far as he goes. He does have something and he can put it forth very eloquently, but there's a need here, there's something this man doesn't know.' Now that is what I mean. Aquila and Priscilla were not carried away by the eloquence.

I repeat that there is a language in the language. Apollos was 'mighty in the scriptures', he was instructed in the way of the Lord, and he was fervent in spirit. That did not matter – Aquila and Priscilla were missing this particular 'idiom'; they were waiting for it but they did not get it. So at the end of the service they went up to Apollos, and they spoke to him, I am sure, in a very sensitive and delicate manner. They did not attack him. They said, 'Can we have a quiet talk? Can we meet together?' And they did, and they just told him things that he had not heard before, for which he was very grateful. Then Apollos became a very much greater and better preacher; then his language was the full language of the gospel.

Let me give you a second example, from the very next chapter:

And it came to pass, that, while Apollos was at Corinth, Paul having passed through the upper coasts came to Ephesus: and finding certain disciples, he said unto them, Have ye received the Holy Ghost since ye believed? And they said unto him, We have not so much as heard whether there be any Holy Ghost (Acts 19:1–2).

When the apostle heard that there were some disciples in Ephesus, he immediately made for them and began to talk to them. But at once he recognized that there was something lacking. He said, 'What's the matter with these people?' And he put his question to them. When he heard their response, Paul said to himself, 'I thought not.' They seemed to be disciples, they seemed to have the language, but they did not have the real thing. The children of God have a sense of discrimination;

they cannot be misled by oratory, by mere eloquence, or a show of learning, or general statements about the gospel. There is something in particular that they want to hear and they are not happy unless they hear it. The children of God have the same language, the same sense of freedom and of understanding. They desire to know the same things and to increase in knowledge of them. Do you know anything about that, my friends?

But let me go on to the sixth test. 'We know that we have passed from death unto life, because we love the brethren' (*1 John* 3:14). Yes, and we prefer them to everybody else. This, again, is a very searching test. If, today, we were offered the opportunity either to spend our day in the highest circles in the land, but with people who were not Christians, or to spend our day with some humble Christians who speak our language, we would choose to be with the humble Christians. We would regard that as a greater pleasure, a greater honour, a greater enjoyment. David, even, felt it. He says in the eighty-fourth Psalm: 'I had rather be a doorkeeper in the house of my God, than to dwell in the tents of wickedness' (*Psa.* 84:10). I would prefer to be the merest underling in God's house, says David, than be at the very heart and centre of the world of the unbeliever. That is the thing! It is because we love the brethren. We like them; we like their company; we like their language; we like their outlook; we like everything about them. They are our people and we esteem them above everybody else.

So the last test is this: we are concerned about the welfare of our fellow-believers. That means a number of things. Here are some of them: 'Brethren, if a man be overtaken in a fault, ye which are spiritual, restore such an one in the spirit of meekness; considering thyself, lest thou also be tempted. Bear ye one another's burdens, and so fulfil the law of Christ' (*Gal.* 6:1–2). Because they are brethren and we are concerned about them, we are ready to bear with them; we will take more from them than from anybody else. You find the same teaching in Romans 15:

We then that are strong ought to bear the infirmities of the weak, and not to please ourselves. Let every one of us please his neighbour for his good to edification. For even Christ pleased not himself; but, as it is written, The reproaches of them that reproached thee fell on me (Rom. 15:1–3).

We are ready to help them. Obviously! If you are the older member of a family and have a little brother or sister who needs your help, you do not say, 'Carry on by yourself, I can't be bothered. I want to get on.' No, no! You love your brother or sister, so you wait and offer to help. It is instinctive. And that is true of the Christian. We not only bear with the weaknesses of our brethren, we go out of our way to help them; there is nothing we would not do for them.

This test also means that when our brethren suffer, we suffer with them, bearing the agony with them. We are troubled and unhappy and we give ourselves to praying for them. It is all in Acts 12:

Now about that time Herod the king stretched forth his hands to vex certain of the church. And he killed James the brother of John with the sword. And because he saw it pleased the Jews, he proceeded further to take Peter also . . . And when he had apprehended him, he put him in prison, and delivered him to four quaternions of soldiers to keep him; intending after Easter to bring him forth to the people. Peter therefore was kept in prison: but prayer was made without ceasing of the church unto God for him (Acts 12:1–5).

The believers were not physically in prison. It was only Peter who was literally in prison, but the rest were with him in spirit. They were bearing the burden, they were in trouble, and they gave themselves to unceasing prayer.

This is a very wonderful test. Are we concerned about our brethren who are less fortunate than ourselves? How often do we think of the lonely, faithful Christians who are in hamlets and villages and little towns about this country? How often do we think of those in other countries, and the lonely pioneer missionary? How often do we think of the suffering of other Christians? Do we feel it? Do we bear with it? Do we pray about it? How much of our time does it take? Do we ever shed a tear? All that is involved. We are members of a family together.

Think of the family in terms of a body. Paul says that if one member suffers, all the members suffer with it (*1 Cor.* 12:26). If your index finger hurts, you cannot say that there is only something wrong with that finger. If there is trouble in your index finger, there is trouble in you. If you have pain there, you will be in pain, you will have a headache and so on. It is because of the organic unity of your body. And it is the same with the church. We are all one. The apostle Paul was able to say without any hesitation at all that if anybody was in trouble, he was in trouble with them. Nothing could happen apart from his being involved at the same time in all the suffering. He says, 'Who is weak, and I am not weak? who is offended, and I burn not?' (*2 Cor.* 11:29). He was involved – 'the care of all the churches' (*2 Cor.* 11:28). He could not get rid of it.

Well, there are the tests. There are other tests, but these are the most important ones, it seems to me. 'We know that we have passed from death unto life, because we love the brethren' (*1 John* 3:14), and we know that we love them in those ways. God grant that we all may know beyond any doubt or peradventure that we are children of God. ❧

30

Our Relationship to the Devil: The Devices of the Devil

But as many as received him, to them gave he power to become the sons of God, even to them that believe on his name: which were born, not of blood, nor of the will of the flesh, nor of the will of man, but of God (John 1:12–13).

W e are still considering this great statement from the Prologue of John's Gospel because there is nothing more important than that we should realize the fundamental truth that in Christ Jesus we are made the children of God. There is nothing beyond that. We shall receive the inheritance, yes, but it is because we are 'children'. The fundamental fact is that by believing on him we are adopted into the family of God. Nothing is more vital for us than to make quite sure of this, and fortunately the New Testament provides us with many tests that we can apply to ourselves. Indeed, a very good case can be made for saying that the bulk of the New Testament was written in order to give Christian people a certain and sure knowledge of who and what they are.

We have been trying to apply these tests to ourselves. We do so in order that we may know the joy of salvation and also, and of even greater importance at the present time, in order that we may function truly as Christian people, because we can only do that when we have this assurance. 'The joy of the LORD is your strength' (*Neh.* 8:10). Without the joy there will not be much strength and without strength we shall fail in our representation of our Lord and Master and all he stands for and all he has to say to this world of ours at the present time.

These tests that we have been applying are mainly tests of *relation-ships*: our relationship to the Son, our relationship to the Father, our relationship to the Holy Spirit and our relationship to other members of the Christian family. In each case we have seen that we have been provided with a multiplicity of tests.

Never think that if you do not get a hundred per cent in every single one of these tests you are therefore not a Christian. Some of the tests are absolutes and you have to say either yes, that is true of you, or no, it is not. If you find yourself saying yes to these absolute tests, you know, beyond any doubt, that you are a child of God. But with regard to other tests, you may say, 'In a measure that's true of me, I wish it were more so.' That is all right. None of us is perfect. 'Not as though I had already attained, either were already perfect,' says the apostle Paul, 'but I follow after, if that I may apprehend that for which also I am apprehended of Christ Jesus' (*Phil.* 3:12). Sometimes you may even doubt whether a test is true of you at all. Well, that means still further self-examination and humbling and repentance and correction. The ideal is that we should correspond to all the tests in all their fulness. But we have deliberately taken time and have worked them out in detail in order that we all may see something, at any rate, that will lead us to a deeper and a firmer and a more settled and assured certainty.

And now we must go on. There is another element that we must consider. We do so because of our experience in life and also because of the plain, clear and unmistakable teaching of the Scripture. Having considered our relationship to the Son, our relationship to the Father, our relationship to the Holy Spirit and our relationship to our brothers and sisters, we turn now to our relationship to the devil. I wonder whether that comes as a surprise to any of you? Well, let me show you why it should not. According to the New Testament teaching, it is inevitable and, therefore, must of necessity be considered. Our relationship to the devil is also, I think you will agree, a most practical and most sensitive issue. And to me it is wonderful that we can turn even the attacks and the onslaughts and the opposition of the devil into a source of assurance and certainty – and that is what we must now try to show.

Why do I say that it is inevitable that we should discuss our relationship to the devil? Well, it is because of our Lord himself and our relationship to him. Here he is, the Son of God. The whole business of John's Prologue is to tell us about his incarnation, about how the Word was made flesh and dwelt among us, how he left the courts of heaven and came into this world of time and lived here, 'made in the likeness of sinful flesh' (*Rom.* 8:3); 'made of a woman, made under the law' (*Gal.* 4:4). But still more striking and remarkable is this: James tells us that 'God cannot be tempted with evil, neither tempteth he any man' (*James* 1:13), yet of the Son of God we read, '[He] was in all points tempted like as we are, yet without sin' (*Heb.* 4:15). And we can read the accounts in the Gospels of the particular temptations that he underwent in the wilderness directly at the hands of Satan.

Here, then, is the Son. The Son of God! And we are made sons by being made conformable to his image; we are partakers of his nature. He is the second man, the last Adam; he is the beginner of a new humanity; and 'he is not ashamed to call [us] brethren' (*Heb.* 2:11). The apostle John reminds us in his first epistle that 'as he is, so are we in this world' (*1 John* 4:17). So we are driven to think of ourselves, as we travel through the pilgrimage of this life, in terms of the Son of God himself. And there is nothing more striking in the four Gospels than the way in which he was subject to the attacks and the onslaughts and the temptations of the devil, this adversary, this enemy of our souls. After the temptations in the wilderness, the devil left him 'for a season' (*Luke* 4:13), but he continued to come back, especially in the Garden and upon the cross. So as we look at our Lord, knowing that we are now to conform to him, it becomes quite obvious and inevitable that we should be subjected to the same treatment that he received. And, therefore, the test comes in: if we are being subjected to the onslaught of the devil, it is proof positive that we have become the children of God.

But there is a second reason why it becomes quite inevitable that we should have to consider our relationship to the devil. Here in John's Gospel we are told that 'as many as received him, to them gave he power to become the sons of God . . . which were born, not of blood, nor of the will of the flesh, nor of the will of man, but of God'. That is what makes us children of God – the being born again. But, of course, when that happens to us, something else happens at the same time – and what is that? This is how our Lord himself put it to the apostle Paul on the road to Damascus at the time of Paul's conversion: 'I have appeared unto thee for this purpose, to make thee a minister and a witness . . . delivering thee from the people, and from the Gentiles, unto whom now I send thee' – what for? Well, here it is – '. . . to turn them from darkness to light, and from the power of Satan unto God' (*Acts* 26:16–18).

You cannot be born of the Spirit, you cannot be born again in the way described here, without at the same time being taken from the kingdom of darkness, from the power of Satan, into the kingdom of light, into the kingdom of God. Or, in the language of the apostle Paul in Colossians 1:13: 'Who hath delivered us from the power of darkness, and hath translated us into the kingdom of his dear Son.' Now this is very vital teaching. The position can be put like this. Non-Christians belong to the kingdom, the territory, the domain, the rule, of Satan. They are in his clutches, helpless victims in his hands. He has complete control over them. They are all the citizens of the kingdom of darkness. Our Lord said: 'When a strong man armed keepeth his palace, his goods are in peace' (*Luke* 11:21). So there they are. That is the position of everybody who is not a Christian, everybody who is not 'born again'. That is the plain teaching of the whole of the Bible.

Now in their position in the kingdom of Satan, non-Christians know nothing about the real temptations of the devil. There is no need for the devil to tempt them, they already belong to him. They are already his servants, and that means slaves, nothing less, his helpless, hopeless slaves. All he does is keep them going and if they show any tendency to rebel or to try to extricate themselves, they are struck down. That is the condition of all who have not been born of God. That is the position of all those who have simply been born of blood or as the result of the will of the flesh, of the will of man. There they are, almost automatic victims of the devil's way and rule.

But the moment people become Christians, the moment this rebirth takes place, they are taken right out of the devil's domain and are put into this new realm. And, of course, it follows without any need of any demonstration whatsoever that the devil is furious at this. The devil's one ambition from the beginning has been to ruin and to smash the kingdom of God. He fell because of that. His heart was lifted up with pride, we are told. He objected to being under God and he rebelled. He raised himself up, wanting to be as God. And the devil's activity from the moment of his fall has been designed to this one end: to bring ruination into the realm of God's kingdom. And, of course, when the Son of God came into the world, the devil redoubled his efforts. He tried to kill him when he was a babe; he followed our Lord all along. If only he could have brought him down! Having failed to do that, he is now exerting all his energies and all his powers – and all his followers are engaged to the same end – to ruin the church and the lives of those who belong to the Son of God.

It follows, of necessity, that for those who become Christians, who are born of God, born of the Spirit, their whole relationship to the devil is changed. This therefore becomes a very valuable way of testing whether or not we are the children of God. Are we in this entirely new relationship to the devil? It is a most wonderful and a most subtle test. In writing to the Romans, the apostle Paul says, 'But God be thanked, that ye were the servants [slaves] of sin, but ye have obeyed from the heart that form of doctrine which was delivered you' (*Rom.* 6:17).

The way we can know whether we are in this changed relationship is by testing ourselves in terms of the devil's behaviour with respect to us. How is he now treating us? What is his attitude towards us? What is he doing with respect to us? I have tried to divide it up like this: we must consider, first and foremost, what I may call the general attack of the devil upon the children of God. He is described as our 'adversary', and that is the role we are now considering – the devil as our adversary, the one whose whole object is to bring us down, to ruin the work of God and of Christ, to ridicule salvation, to say there is nothing in it. 'Your adversary the devil, as a roaring lion,' says the apostle Peter, 'walketh about, seeking whom he may devour' (*1 Pet.* 5:8).

How does the devil seek to destroy us? We could expand this greatly, but for now I am going to confine myself to just one point, and that is his use of persecution and opposition. Now the good, moral man or woman never knows anything about persecution. This is a most interesting point. The problem that many of us have is this: Can I be sure that I am a Christian and not just a good, moral, ethical person? There are such people. They are not Christians – they say so. But as regards their conduct, you cannot point a finger at them. Many Christians are tempted at this point. The devil comes and says, 'How do you know you are a Christian? Maybe you are just naturally good, like these others?' And at that point we are given one of the most valuable tests. Does the world persecute us? The world never persecutes moral people, in fact, it likes them, it honours them, it praises them. Why? For the obvious reason that it realizes that their lives are in many respects a compliment to humanity. Moral people are what they are because of their own efforts and nobody ever objects to that. But Christians, according to the teaching of the New Testament, not only are, but must always expect to be, attacked. And thus they are given, in a very wonderful way, a proof of the fact that they are indeed children of God. Listen to our Lord saying this in the Sermon on the Mount:

Blessed are they which are persecuted for righteousness' sake: for their's is the kingdom of heaven. Blessed are ye, when men shall revile you, and persecute you, and shall say all manner of evil against you falsely, for my sake. Rejoice, and be exceeding glad: for great is your reward in heaven: for so persecuted they the prophets which were before you (Matt. 5:10–12).

They have always done this, they are still doing it, they always will do it. There is our Lord's own teaching. We have a further illustration in John's Gospel:

If the world hate you, ye know that it hated me before it hated you. If ye were of the world, the world would love his own: but because ye are not of the world, but I have chosen you out of the world, therefore the world hateth you. Remember the word that I said unto you, The servant is not greater than his lord. If they have persecuted me, they will also persecute you; if they have kept my saying, they will keep your's also. But all these things will they do unto you for my name's sake, because they know not him that sent me (John 15:18–21).

And then we have the apostle Paul reminding Timothy of the same facts. Timothy was being persecuted, and he could not understand it, so he was grumbling and complaining and wondering what was going to happen. Listen, says the apostle Paul: 'Yea, and all that will live godly in Christ Jesus shall suffer persecution' (2 *Tim.* 3:12). It is inevitable. It happened to the Lord himself, and he said, 'The disciple is not above his master, nor the servant above his lord . . . If they have called the master of the house Beelzebub, how much more shall they call them of his household?' (*Matt.* 10:24–25).

Now we must be clear about this teaching. It does not mean that the Christian should be offensive. That is not what I am talking about at all. That is not what our Lord teaches. Some people get into trouble simply because they are foolish. They lack common sense, some of them; they ask for trouble. Here is our Lord – he never offended anybody: 'A bruised reed shall he not break, and smoking flax shall he not quench' (*Matt.* 12:20). He did not lift up his voice in the streets to cause commotion and riot. He was a friend of tax-collectors and sinners. He came to do good, he gave himself in doing good, there was nothing offensive in him, yet look how they treated him. And if you and I get into trouble because we are foolish or lacking in wisdom, or because we are indeed offensive, what I am now talking about has nothing to say to you. No, I am talking about being persecuted simply because you are like Christ, because you are what you are. Now according to the teaching of the New Testament, as I have shown you, and I could give you many other passages, that must happen to the Christian.

But why? Well, it works like this. Christians, because they are Christians, simply by being what they are and doing what they do, are an inevitable rebuke to everybody else. They cannot help it. They need not open their mouths. The devil and all who belong to him can sense who they are immediately. The devil hates them and is determined to get them down, and persecution is one of the methods that he uses. He raises up people to upset us and to malign us and to cause trouble in different ways. I say again, 'All that will live godly in Christ Jesus shall suffer persecution.' You may simply say about some activity, 'I'm sorry,

I can't, I don't', and you may say it with all the grace conceivable and in as polite a manner as possible, but the natural person hates it, as he hates Christ. 'This Christianity!' he says, though you are doing him no harm at all, though, indeed, you may be trying to do him good.

Evil hates holiness and the devil hates God and the Lord Jesus Christ and all who belong to him. There is no excuse for such an attitude; it is all evil. But it does happen and it always has happened. The prophets were persecuted. Why? Because they were trying to help Israel, because they were telling Israel the truth, because they were exhorting the people to righteousness, and Israel did not like it. And the world still does not like it. The world gloats in its evil, it rejoices in it, and if you are not with the world in it, it will hate you! People will suggest that you have become unnatural, that you have become cold. They will suggest that you are violating natural human feelings; they will try to break your heart and break your spirit. Persecution!

If you know anything about such persecution, it is very strong presumptive evidence that you are a child of God. If you find people are watching you and examining you and picking holes in everything you do and every word you utter, it is very good evidence that you are a child of God. As we have seen, if you were but a highly moral person, they would not do that at all. They would rather like you: you would still belong to them. But the moment you become a Christian, they are aware of this new something that has come in, and you become a marked man, a marked woman.

But now let us turn to the second main line of attack upon us. This time the devil is not so much our adversary as 'the accuser of our brethren'. This is a title that is given to him in Revelation 12:10. What does it mean? We can best illustrate it by looking at what happened to our Lord in the temptations in the wilderness because there we see the essence of this whole matter. Notice the phrase that the devil used twice in the course of the three temptations. He came and said to our Lord: '*If* thou be the Son of God' (*Matt.* 4:3, 6). That is it. *If* you really are the Son of God as you claim to be . . . now, then . . . He was testing our Lord; he was accusing him: Are you or are you not the Son of God? And in the same way he attacks us by accusing us.

The devil has two main methods. One is that he accuses in general. I am quite certain that he has been doing this with many of you, if not with all of you, as we have been considering this whole matter for so many Sunday mornings. I know for certain that he has come to many and has said, 'Are you still saying that you are a child of God?' Or when we fall into sin, or when something bad happens to us, he says, 'Do you still say, do you still think, that you are a child of God?' He makes a general accusation.

His second method, and the method he particularly uses, is to make specific accusations by quoting scriptures, and he has his favourites. Chief among them, beyond any question, are the beginning of Hebrews 6, the corresponding passage in Hebrews 10, and the statement in 1 John 5:16 that we are not to pray for those who have committed 'the sin unto death', the blasphemy against the Holy Spirit. And add to that, if you like, our Lord's teaching in Luke 12 and parallel passages about 'the sin against the Holy Ghost' (*Luke* 12:10). I say that these are the devil's favourite passages on the basis that he quotes them more frequently than any others. These are the scriptures that he puts before people.

For it is impossible for those who were once enlightened, and have tasted of the heavenly gift, and were made partakers of the Holy Ghost, and have tasted the good word of God, and the powers of the world to come, if they shall fall away, to renew them again unto repentance (Heb. 6:4–6).

The devil brings this verse, and the other verses, before people and he says, 'There you are, you've sinned. You've fallen out of grace, you've sinned against the love of God, and therefore you cannot renew yourself. You are lost and damned. You are absolutely hopeless. You might as well give up Christianity. You are a lost soul.'

Now I want to try to show you that if the devil is trying to accuse you, he is providing you with a most wonderful proof of the fact that you are a child of God. So you must learn how to recognize that attack and how to use it against him. How does it work out? Like this: the devil has never gone to any unbeliever to quote Hebrews 6 or Hebrews 10. Why not? Because they have never believed these things. They know nothing about being 'enlightened', they know nothing about tasting 'the powers of the world to come'. Moreover, they are not interested. The devil, therefore, does not quote these passages to them. It would be foolish and ridiculous for him to do that. I want to put it as strongly as this: whenever anybody comes to me in trouble and distress over Hebrews 6, Hebrews 10 and the rest, I know immediately that they are children of God. The devil himself has given me the proof. He would never have attacked them along those lines if they were not.

Now let me give you the statement of James that substantiates what I am saying. James rightly puts it in a very strong manner: 'Blessed is the man that endureth temptation: for when he is tried, he shall receive the crown of life, which the Lord hath promised to them that love him. Let no man say when he is tempted, I am tempted of God' – no, no! It is not God who does that, it is the devil, always (*James* 1:12–13). So James says, 'Blessed is the man that endureth temptation.' He has already put it like this: 'My brethren, count it all joy when ye fall into divers temptations' – which means, trials, tribulations, persecutions and so on, including these accusations of the devil. 'Count it all joy,' says James (*James* 1:2). The devil is giving you a proof that you are a child of God; he is attacking you as he only attacks the children of God. He does not need to attack his own people like that because they are not troubled. They never think about these things. They are not interested. They are not concerned. So, I repeat, the mere fact that you are assaulted in this way is a proof that you are a child of God.

But wait a minute. I would add, in the second place, that if we have any consciousness at all that the problem in our life is not merely a moral problem but that, over and above that, we are a part of a great spiritual conflict, then we know and can be certain that we are the children of God. To the natural man, however good and moral and ethical he may be, the problem is just a problem of conduct and behaviour – nothing more. But the moment people become Christians, they realize that they belong to a spiritual realm. They have an insight into the truth of the apostle Paul's words: 'We wrestle not against flesh and blood, but against principalities, against powers, against the rulers of the darkness of this world, against spiritual wickedness in high places' (*Eph.* 6:12). Now those who are not Christians know nothing about this spiritual conflict. They do not believe it. They are not interested. They ridicule it, in fact. They are only interested in their own conduct and behaviour, in moral principles, in how they can be better people. Nothing beyond that – they never go beyond themselves. But Christians realize that because they are Christians, they are a part of that battle; they realize that the real conflict is between God and the devil, heaven and hell, light and darkness – a great spiritual fight. The moment you are aware of anything of that, it is a proof that you are a child of God.

Or, in the third place, let me put it like this: the children of God alone have the feeling that their troubles come to them mainly from the outside. They know that there is much that is still wrong within them but their main feeling is that they are being attacked, that 'fiery darts' are being thrown at them. When they are reading their Bibles, evil imaginations, thoughts, desires, come to them and they are aware that these are not from within them but are being hurled at them. Now it is only the child of God who has an awareness of this external, objective attack, these powers outside us. I have never known an unregenerate person in trouble over that, never. Not a single time. It is impossible. Unbelievers do not need it, they are already the slaves of the devil. But Christians have been moved from the devil's kingdom of darkness, so the devil is hurling these thoughts at them. Everybody remembers the famous story about Luther in his study. So conscious of the devil was he that he took up that inkpot and threw it at him! And the moment you are aware that the attack is outside you, the moment you have any consciousness of the devil and the principalities and powers, you can be certain that the devil is giving you a proof that you are a child of God.

Then, further, can you say that you hate these thoughts? Can you say that you wish that you were left alone? Do you ever think, 'Oh, that he would leave me alone!'? Again, it is only the Christian who knows that. Non-Christians know nothing; they think the conflict is all in themselves, in their own natures, and they think they can get rid of it by reading good books and by mixing with good people and so on, building themselves up morally. They know nothing about this antagonist, this enemy, this accuser who is there, so they do not hate this evil in the way Christians do. 'Ye that love the LORD,' says the Psalmist, 'hate evil' (*Psa.* 97:10). And if you know anything about a hatred of evil, though you may still fall into it, if you really hate it, you are a child of God. The moment the hatred comes in, it is a proof of your rebirth.

And, in the fifth place, I take that a step further by putting it like this: anybody who is really troubled about these things is inevitably a child of God. What I mean, once more, is this: if passages such as Hebrews 6 and Hebrews 10 really do trouble you, if you are distressed about them, and are weeping, and say, 'Well, am I a Christian at all? It seems to me that I'm not, and if ever I was, that I've ceased to be one' – then, my dear friend, you need not go any further, you are a child of God. 'The natural man receiveth not the things of the Spirit of God: for they are foolishness unto him: neither can he know them' (*1 Cor.* 2:14). People as they are by nature are never worried about the fact that they are not 'born again'. The only people who are worried about not being born again are those who are born again! You have got to be alive before you can be worried. A dead person does not worry about anything, and the spiritually dead do not worry about the absence of spiritual life. It is an impossibility. It is the *child* who wants to know. It is the *lover* who wants to know that he or she is loved. So the very agony of soul, the anxiety and concern, are an absolute proof that is given to us by the devil that we are the children of God. He would not attack us along this line if we were not, and we would not be worried and anxious and disturbed and breaking our hearts about it if we were not already the children of God. It is an absolute, irrefutable argument.

And then, in the sixth place, I put it like this: the way in which we overcome these accusations and attacks of the devil can, again, give us absolute proof as to whether or not we are the children of God. Notice the way in which our blessed Lord himself dealt with the devil. The devil quoted Scripture, so did our Lord; that is how he answered him. Our Lord answered the devil by quoting the Scripture to him and he silenced him and he repulsed him. And if you find that you are doing the same thing, then you can be absolutely certain, again, that you are a child of God.

I mean something like this. The devil comes and says, 'You are not a Christian. You are not a child of God.'

'Why not?'

'Well, you've fallen into sin and the Scriptures say that anyone who belongs to God does not commit sin. Listen to 1 John 3:9: "Whosoever is born of God doth not commit sin; for his seed remaineth in him: and he cannot sin, because he is born of God." But you have fallen into sin, therefore you are not a Christian.'

Now, then, the answer is to do exactly what the Lord did, and reply with a scripture:

If we walk in the light, as he is in the light, we have fellowship one with another, and the blood of Jesus Christ his Son cleanseth us from all sin. If we say that we have no sin, we deceive ourselves, and the truth is not in us. If we confess our sins, he is faithful and just to forgive us our sins, and to cleanse us from all unrighteousness . . . My little children, these things write I unto you, that ye sin not. And if any man sin, we have an advocate with the Father, Jesus Christ the righteous: and he is the propitiation for our sins: and not for our's only, but also for the sins of the whole world (1 John 1:7–9; 2:1–2).

Now that is the way in which you answer the devil. He quotes a scripture and says you are not a Christian. You say, 'Wait a minute! You don't know the whole of Scripture, you only know just a few passages, like all your followers in the cults who only know certain particular texts, which they are always quoting like parrots. Yes, I've sinned but listen to the Scriptures . . .' And the devil is repulsed and defeated.

And the other scripture that I so constantly have to quote to friends who are in trouble about these questions is the one I have already quoted. They come and they say to me, 'I'm not a Christian' – and they are distressed and in agony. 'Wait a minute,' I say, 'do you know 1 Corinthians 2:14?'

'What's that?' they ask.

'"The natural man receiveth not the things of the Spirit of God: for they are foolishness unto him."' I say, 'Are these things foolishness to you? Is the teaching about God in the Bible foolishness to you? Is the teaching that the Lord Jesus Christ is the Son of God foolishness to you? Is the incarnation foolishness to you? Is his atoning death foolishness to you? Is the Person of the Holy Spirit folly? Is the rebirth foolishness to you? Are you ridiculing all these things? Is that your attitude?'

'Oh, no,' they say.

I say, 'Is it not true to say of you that your one concern is that you want to know these things and to be certain?'

'Yes!'

'Well, if they are not foolishness to you, you are not a "natural man". But you must either be a "natural man" or a "spiritual man". There is no no-man's-land. You are either natural or spiritual. You cannot be natural, since these Christian truths are everything to you. Therefore you are spiritual. The devil has given you proof that you are a child of God.'

Or you can add to that Romans 8:7: 'The carnal [natural] mind is enmity against God: for it is not subject to the law of God, neither indeed can be.' I say, 'Are you at enmity with God?'

'Oh, no!'

'Well, quite,' I say. 'Do you want above everything to know God?'

'Yes!'

'Very well, then, you don't have the natural mind, and if you don't have the natural mind, you must have the spiritual mind, and you cannot have that unless you are born of the Spirit, unless you are born of God, unless you are a child of God.'

And so the Christian defeats the devil by quoting the Scriptures to him. This becomes a very wonderful test. If you are doing what I have just been describing, then you have an absolute proof that you are a child of God. But perhaps you have not been doing it, and perhaps you came into this service distressed. Tell me, my friend, how have you been reacting as I have been working out the argument? Has it pleased you? Have you been jumping at it avidly, and saying, 'Thank God!'? If so, you are a child God. Children of God always respond with all their heart to this argumentation. Unbelievers do not know what I am talking about. It is all foolishness to them. Very well, then, in the very method whereby you repulse the attacks of the devil you are being given proof that you are indeed a child of God.

To complete this subject, let me just add two headings. Do you know what it is to undergo a satanic attack? Have you known periods in your life, hours, days, perhaps, when, as it were, you have been aware that the devil is constantly attacking you, marshalling his forces, surrounding you, giving you no rest, no peace, no intermission, so that you cannot get away? Satanic attacks! If you know anything about that, then I certify that you are a child of God. It is a terrible experience – there is nothing more terrible. But it does happen to be one of the highest proofs of all. The devil never has to do that to his dupes and slaves and victims. He has them already. This only happens to the saints.

And so my last word is this: Do you find, as you go on in the Christian life, that you are less and less surprised by the accusations of your adversary the devil and the manifestations of his opposition to you? Can you say that Hebrews 6 and Hebrews 10 are worrying you less and less as you go on? If so, it is a proof that you are a child of God. Are you less frightened by the devil, less alarmed? Can you say with the apostle Paul, 'We are not ignorant of his devices' (2 *Cor.* 2:11)? Do you have less and less craven fear or terror or alarm or frustration, and an increasing understanding of the devil's ways and methods? Do you find yourself standing back at times and saying, 'Oh, the subtlety of the devil!'? Before, you were just immersed in the situation; you were quarrelling with somebody and you just saw this person and yourself. Do you find more and more frequently that when this kind of thing happens, you say to yourself, 'Dear me, isn't the devil busy!'? You do not see the people so much as the hand behind, the devil. If you have an increasing awareness that an evil situation is of the devil and not simply from a human being, not flesh and blood, but the devil and the principalities and powers – if that awareness is increasing in you, if you see him rather than individuals and persons, it is a wonderful proof that you are a child of God.

'We are not ignorant of his devices.' No, no! says Paul. I have been fighting him for years and you good people at Corinth do not understand. You are not only ignorant of the grace of God, you are ignorant of the devices of the devil. But you will get to learn more about him as you go on. He will have to bring out his reserves and you will see his schemes in greater fulness, as our blessed Lord did before us.

So if we have this increasing knowledge of the devices of the devil, it is again an absolute proof of the fact that we are the children of God. The children of God are never presumptuous about this. They are never foolhardy. They never laugh at the devil. Anybody who laughs at the devil – oh, he may be a child of God but he is a very ignorant one! As we grow in grace, we never take anything for granted. We realize that we must watch and pray, that we must be 'strong in the Lord, and in the power of his might', and 'put on the whole armour of God' because we know that that is the only way whereby we can 'stand against the wiles of the devil . . . and having done all, to stand', even in the evil day (*Eph.* 6:10, 11, 13).

God grant that as we have been looking at these wiles and attacks of the devil, we may have had fresh and absolute proof of the fact that we are the children of God, 'born, not of blood, nor of the will of the flesh, nor of the will of man, but of God', that 'as Christ is in this world, so are we', and that the devil is giving us proof, though he does not realize what he is doing, of the fact that we are 'the children of God: and if children, then heirs; heirs of God and joint-heirs with Christ'. What a life! Everything in it, if we have understanding, can turn to give us assurance and certainty that we are what we are by the grace of God. ∾

31

Religion or True Faith?

But as many as received him, to them gave he power to become the sons of God, even to them that believe on his name: which were born, not of blood, nor of the will of the flesh, nor of the will of man, but of God (John 1:12–13).

*I*n order that we may be sure that we are the children of God, we have been looking at various tests that are provided for us in great profusion in the Scriptures. We have seen that it is by believing in the Son that we become the children of God. Let others call themselves Christians if they will – if they do not believe in him as the unique Son of God, if they do not believe in his Godhead, in the literal fact and miracle of the incarnation, in his miracles, in his atoning death and resurrection, they are just not Christians. I do not hesitate to assert that. Though they arrogate to themselves the name Christian, they are liars; they are deniers of the truth.

Now there must be no uncertainty about this. We must not fall into this modern error of imagining that Christians are nice but flabby people who agree with everybody and who never criticize anything. According to the New Testament, these 'antichrists' are not only to be avoided, they are to be denounced, and we are to say of them, as John says in his first epistle, 'They went out from us, but they were not of us' (*1 John* 2:19).

And for myself, I have no fellowship with and I do not belong to the same church as men who deny the very cardinal elements of the Christian faith and the plain teaching of the Word of God. So we must be certain, we must be sure, of our position. And, above all, we must be certain and sure that we are the children of God.

We have been considering the fact that we must know our relationship to the Son, our relationship to the Father, our relationship to the Holy Spirit and our relationship to the brethren, to one another – the 'brethren', I emphasize, not these others who call themselves Christians, but those who believe these truths, those who are ready, if need be, to die for them, those who really belong to Christ. Then last time we were considering how our very relationship to the devil can provide us with sure grounds of assurance. The devil tests the children of God in a way that he never tests anybody else.

But now I want to go on to another aspect of this matter. So far we have been, in the main, testing whether or not we are children of God in terms of our relationships. But now I want to look at this question in a more direct personal sense, because we can find proofs even here. We have already been applying this next test in part. You cannot consider relationships without inevitably considering yourself. Any relationship to another person tells you a great deal about yourself. Birds of a feather flock together, as the saying goes; you can tell a man by his company. So in dealing with the previous tests, which, generally speaking, are more objective, we have also, indirectly, been testing ourselves in a more subjective manner.

There is one very interesting thing about the tests we have been considering. They apply, of course, to all of us, but different tests come with more force to some people than to others. That, again, is to be expected. If we were to relate our experiences to one another, we would find a great variety in the details. There is only one way to become a Christian and that is to be born again. You cannot be a child of God without being born 'not of blood, nor of the will of the flesh, nor of the will of man, but of God'. The fact that your parents were Christians does not make you a Christian. There is a spiritual rebirth, which every one of us has to undergo. But looked at from the human, earthly standpoint, there is considerable variation in the details of our histories.

There are many here who have always been brought up in what we call a religious manner. They were always taken to a place of worship and may have been to Sunday school as children and have been taught the Scriptures from infancy. They have always been in a Christian atmosphere. That is the background out of which some of us have come. But there are others who became Christians in exactly the same way but whose backgrounds are very different. They did not know what it was to be in a place of worship at all. They were completely ignorant of the Scriptures and lived a life right out in the world without any knowledge of the gospel. But now they are members of the church side by side with the first group.

Now that broad distinction and classification can be subdivided, of course. But I am using it on this occasion simply to bring out the point that the devil knows all about our previous history and is always very ready to make use of it. So we do not all get tempted in the same manner – the details vary. We do all get tempted – the devil tempts each one of us, as we saw last time, on the question of whether or not we are the children of God – but having knowledge about our backgrounds, he knows our particular weaknesses, he knows how to attack us. And thus it comes to pass that very often the people who have the greatest difficulty about the question of assurance are the people who belong to my first group, those who were always brought up in a Christian atmosphere, in what is called a Christian way, because the devil says to them, 'You can't point to some dramatic change. You were always brought up in the church, you have always, as it were, believed in these things. With your intellect and intelligence, you have been able to absorb the teaching. So how do you know that you are not just carrying on with what you yourself have always done? How can you be sure that you are a child of God? As for that other person, of course, look at the great change! It is obvious. But you cannot say that about yourself.'

I feel, therefore, that the matter that is now before us has a very special reference to, and relevance for, those who, simply because of their background and upbringing within the realm of the Christian church, find it difficult to be quite sure of their salvation. My tests will apply primarily to them, though, at the same time, they are valuable tests for everybody. Let us not forget that complete outsiders can take up religion, as they can take up anything else, and they have often done so. So even they must test themselves with regard to these matters.

What, then, are these more direct and subjective tests that we can apply to ourselves to make sure that we are the children of God? One of them is our general relationship to the Christian message and to the life of the church. I remember reading, some time ago, a phrase about the Victorians that I felt was illuminating and that certainly helped me to understand this particular point. The author was writing about the Victorians, and in particular about Matthew Arnold, who was such a typical Victorian, and he said that the trouble with the Victorians was that their religion 'overshadowed them' instead of 'penetrating them'. That is a very profound remark. I think it is the key to the understanding of the so-called Victorian era; it really does tell us a great deal about them.

To the Victorians their religion, their Christianity, was, as it were, a kind of cloud in the heavens. It was always there, overshadowing them, but it was *there*, it was not here, it did not penetrate them. It was apart from them, external to them. They were very conscious of it, but it was a loose relationship. The author's expression puts it as accurately as it is possible to put it. Some of us perhaps know from experience exactly what he meant. You can be aware of Christian things but you are only aware of them as you are aware of the atmosphere, of a cloud in the sky keeping the sun away from you. You cannot do anything about it. You are walking along down here and there is this thing hanging over you, as it were. Now of those to whom religion is merely something that 'overshadows' them, I would say that there is no question at all but that they are not Christians. That is not the relationship of the true Christian, the one who is indeed a child of God, to these matters about which we are concerned.

Then let me take that further by putting it, in the second place, in this form: it is one thing to be religious, it is another thing to be Christian. Surely this does not need any proof or argument; it is quite basic. There are many religious people in the world today who tell you that they are not Christians. There are other religions: the Jews are religious, the Muslims are religious, and so on. The question is: Are we Christians? Are we truly the children of God? Because the Christian alone is the child of God according to the statement in John's Prologue. A very good test, then, is this: the difference between the Christian and the religious person is that the Christian is controlled by his faith; he does not control it. That is another valuable, broad distinction.

The man whose relationship to Christianity is external is a man who has to remind himself of it constantly. He reminds himself that it is Sunday – that is the day to be religious, perhaps in the morning only. He normally lives his life without thinking about the Christian faith, but there are certain set times or special occasions when he reminds himself of it or is reminded by something that takes place. In other words, his religion is almost like something that he has in a bag. He takes up his bag on Sunday morning and puts it down at Sunday lunchtime – that is it for the week. The point about him is that he is controlling it; he takes it up when he wants it and lays it down when he does not want it. If he is in trouble, of course, he prays and may read his Bible. If he is not in trouble, he does not dream of doing so. Now that is the typical religious person. His religion is occasional, a kind of addition to his life.

Even worse, religion may simply be a duty, a task to be performed. That was the trouble with those Victorians. The church was there, though many of them wished it was not. That was why they jumped with such avidity at the famous book of Charles Darwin, *On the Origin of Species*. They really did not like Christianity but they felt it was still there, like that cloud in the heavens. As long as they were not sure that it was not true, they felt that they had to keep in with it. So they did, but only as a duty, only because it was the right thing to do. To go to a place of worship and to call yourself a Christian was very much the thing to do in the Victorian era. But of course the Victorians did the minimum and no more, just enough to make them feel that they were safe, that they were all right.

Now I cannot see that any reason whatsoever is given in the Scripture for saying that such people have any right to regard themselves as children of God. So one of the greatest and best tests is this: that you have been taken hold of by the truth of the gospel. Read those words of the apostle Paul in Philippians 3:13 – what a perfect expression he gives there of this very matter – 'Brethren, I count not myself to have apprehended.' He is saying, in effect, 'I have not got full knowledge; I have not arrived at perfection.' So what is he doing? He says, 'If I may apprehend that for which also I am apprehended' (*Phil.* 3:12). In other words: 'I am trying to lay hold of that which has laid hold of me.' That is it! Christians are men and women who know they have been 'laid hold of'.

Christians do not have to remind themselves: they are not spasmodic, occasional. Their Christian faith is not something they pick up and put down. It is not like putting on a suit and taking it off again. No, no! It is not up in the skies any longer. It is not something that overshadows them. The whole analogy proves that. What makes you the child of your parents is that you have your parents' blood, the nature of your parents; you belong to their family. And this is true of Christians. They have their faith inside them and they know it and feel it. It is not a loose external relationship or a vague attachment. Christians are aware that it has taken hold of them. This is the biggest thing in their lives. They are no longer the master but have been mastered by this faith, this knowledge, this person in whom they believe.

It is difficult to put something like this into words and yet we all know exactly what I mean. What is your relationship to your faith, my friend? Are you mastered or are you the master? Are you in control or are you not? I say to you – it seems an astonishing thing to say and yet I say it honestly and sincerely – I am very glad I am preaching now and not a hundred years ago. We are facing basic questions today, rock bottom. Whatever else may be said about this present age, at any rate we can say that it is more honest; there is less pretence and sham. There is still some pretence remaining. Let us make quite sure that we ourselves are not just some hangover from Victorianism. At a time like this, God needs valiant soldiers of the cross, and we must know exactly where we stand. There may be testing times coming for us – there are some indications of that. There may be a tyranny arising in the form of a world church or a world government, so that those who refuse to say that Caesar is Lord may again have to answer for their faith. Let us make certain, let us make sure, and here is one of the tests: we have no choice if we are Christians; we do not have to persuade or force ourselves; we do not have to remind ourselves or be reminded. No, no! Our faith in Christ has taken hold of us.

The general relationship of Christians to their faith and belief is a most valuable test. But let us take this a stage further. Another test of whether or not we are the children of God or merely religious people is this: that we become less and less interested in the general aspects of religion. Now this is a very particular test for those who have been brought up in the Christian faith. Now I am speaking very largely from experience. There are religious people who are tremendously interested in the trimmings and trappings of religion. They delight to talk about denominations and denominational activities and interests. This was once rampant. There is much less than there used to be but there is still a great deal. I still see it occasionally when friends visiting here come to speak to me at the end of a service. Some betray themselves immediately. As they hold out their hand, they say, 'I'm a Methodist', or, 'I'm a Salvationist', or, 'I'm a Congregationalist', and so they tell me everything about themselves. I feel like saying, 'Well, yes, I'm sure you are and that's about all there is to it.' Because the Christian does not speak like that. But that is the big thing to them. They are probably very active church workers and they probably attend as delegates at conferences, so they are full of denominational affairs, and that is their conversation.

Then there are others who are tremendously interested in the social aspect of church-going, and in some sections of the church there is a kind of hierarchy, which becomes tremendously important. Different dress is worn, different terms and appellations are used, different titles are given, and there is a whole realm of interest in the working of the machinery. Who is going to be appointed to this or that position? And, ah, I hear that such and such a see is vacant. Who is going there? And people can be tremendously interested; indeed, that may be their sole interest. They generally stop at that. You see the danger.

And then – this, of course, was probably the greatest curse of all – a hundred years ago and, indeed, until comparatively recently, there was an interest in preachers and in talking about preachers and sermons. That can be exciting once you get into it. But you can have all that interest and still not be a Christian. It is like getting into any sphere, into any profession – you have your local interest, your professional interest and they can be most absorbing. I look back across my life and I feel ashamed of the hours I have wasted in talk about preachers, comparing them, contrasting them, stories about them. Well, it is all right, I am not here to say that it is sinful, but to the extent that you do that less and less, you have very good evidence that you are a child of God.

Of course, there has to be a machinery, a minimum of organization is necessary in any church, but those to whom the organization is everything are telling me that if they are Christians at all, they are very young and very small ones. The organization should be almost out of sight; it is not the main, the absorbing interest, it is not the one theme that excites and enthuses. What does, then? Oh, when people are true Christians and children of God, they are interested in the truth itself and in their relationship to it. What interests them now is the spiritual aspect – less and less the persons and the machinery, more and more the truth, its glorious character and their awareness of it. The whole of their emphasis shifts from the one to the other. Nothing is so dangerous to the life of the soul as professionalism, or, putting it the other way round, the less there is of that kind of thing, the more certain we can be that we are truly Christian. What is our main interest, my friends? What is it that we really are concerned about?

But let me go on – and this, I think, follows from the point I have just been making. A good sign, a good test, of the fact that we are truly the children of God is that we are more and more interested in the state of our hearts and in *being* something. Now you see the obvious contrast – the contrast between being and doing. The people who are religious are activists, doers. Of course, they must be because they believe they are making themselves Christians by their activities, they are justifying themselves by their works. If they stop, then they feel they are lost. But the children of God know that what matters is what they are, that they are 'born, not of blood, nor of the will of the flesh, nor of the will of man, but of God'. 'By the grace of God I am what I am' (*1 Cor.* 15:10). So they are now much more interested in being than in doing; they are more interested in being even than in having knowledge.

Now let us be fair! Let us not think that it is only the activist who is in error here. The religious person is often a great reader of religious books. You can be a great reader of the Bible itself, of theology and of doctrine and church history, and still not be a child of God. I know of no more intellectual pursuit than the reading and the study of theology. But, remember, the natural person can do that and has often done it. So in addition to activities and business and busy-ness, we put knowledge, reading, learning, intellectual interest in these matters. 'Knowledge', says the apostle Paul to the Corinthians, 'puffeth up' (*1 Cor.* 8:1). It always does. People become proud of what they know. They tell you what they have been reading and how much they read, and they let you see their libraries and so on. But they are betraying themselves. Those who are children of God are much more concerned about what they are, about the state of their hearts.

Oh, how subtle these things are, and how subtle is the devil! Even reading Christian biographies can be dangerous. Are these things not strange? I have spent most of my life in the ministry urging people to read. I have been urging them to read the great classics, the great, big books – and I still do. But I would be a very poor pastor if I did not give a warning at the same time. You can spend your time reading biographies and being moved as you read about what has happened to others, but it can be purely objective. You may live on their experiences and, because you are stirred by their experiences, you think they have happened to you. Now those who are truly the children of God read in order to help their spiritual growth, not that they may be among the learned ones. That is no better than being an unintelligent activist. Though I know that the one despises the other, there is, in fact, nothing to choose between them. Children of God are more concerned about the state of their hearts than about any knowledge that they may happen to possess. The Bible tells them, 'Keep thy heart with all diligence; for out of it are the issues of life' (*Prov.* 4:23), and they say, 'It doesn't matter that my head is packed with knowledge if my heart is wrong.'

So if you are more and more concerned about the state of your heart – observing it and watching it and testing it and examining it, it is a very good sign that you are a child of God. What concerns you more:

your knowledge or your spiritual condition? To what extent are we concerned about our growth in these matters? Look at the great apostle: 'Forgetting those things which are behind' – and they are tremendous things, remember, but he forgets them – 'I press forward' (*Phil.* 3:13–14). This is a very good test. There are some people who, when I meet them, start telling me about something that happened thirty years ago. And every time I meet them, they tell me again. Such people are living on some past experience. That is a very bad sign. I am not saying they are not Christians, but I am saying that they do not seem to have grown in thirty years. They are still exactly where they were at the beginning. Now an increasing concern about the state of the soul, my spiritual condition, my growth in grace and in the knowledge of the Lord, is an excellent test as to whether or not I am a Christian or merely a religious person who is perhaps afraid not to be religious.

That leads me to my next point. A sign that we are truly the children of God is that we become less and less negative and more and more positive in our relationship to our faith. To the religious person there is no question at all but that religion is merely a matter of restraint, a matter of prohibitions. That phrase about the Victorians shows it: religion 'overshadowed' them. It is interesting and illuminating and, at the same time, fascinating to read their biographies. They were a fearful people. They were trying to venture forward, trying, as they would put it, 'to shake off the shackles' of religion, but they could not and there it was, a perpetual shadow over them. Their attitude was entirely negative; their whole notion of Christianity was that it was – well, as Matthew Arnold, the high priest of it all, put it in that famous phrase: 'morality touched with emotion'. Mainly morality, but a touch of emotion that just lifts it up from the level of secular morality. In other words, religion was that which held them down, kept them back – John Stuart Mill and all the rest of them, the so-called 'great Victorians'.

At this point I really am with Mr Lytton Strachey: it is a good thing that all that harmful religious thinking has been exposed.[1] These leading Victorian thinkers and writers were the people who did the damage,

---

[1] Lytton Strachey (1880–1932) wrote critically and ironically about leading Victorians. His book, *Eminent Victorians*, was first published in 1918 by Chatto (London).

and you and I are living in an age that is reaping the results of what they sowed. That was not Christianity. It was a negative, a prohibitive, a restraining religion; it was a religion of fear, a fear of punishment. If only they could prove there was no God – and they believed that science was going to do that very soon – then they could really live. That was their attitude. And it is still the attitude of the religious person. There are still people whose main, if not sole, reason for attending a place of worship is that they are afraid not to. They know that the scientists, for all their discoveries, have not proved there is not a God; and though they may say in their arrogance that they do not believe in hell, and they do not believe this and that in the Thirty-nine Articles, they cannot prove anything, they only have their foolish opinions. So they play for safety. Religion, unfortunately, is still to many a kind of extra insurance policy.

In complete contrast are those who take a positive delight in the grace and the glory of God, and that is the proof that they are children of God. They believe, not because they are afraid, not because they are playing for safety, but because their Christian faith is their chief delight. Take Psalm 84. The Psalmist who wrote that Psalm was temporarily kept away from the house of God, and he was as miserable as a man could be. He thought of the people going up to the house of God and he looked at them as they went up in their processions. 'Oh, that I might be with them,' said the man. He did not have to force himself to go to the house of God, he did not have to compel himself, he did not have to remind himself – it was life to him. 'I had rather be a doorkeeper in the house of my God, than to dwell in the tents of wickedness' (*Psa.* 84:10). There was no difficulty about deciding, no constant wrangling and argument with ultimately a miserable, 'Well, on the whole I'd better do it!' No, no!

The Psalmist gloried in the house of God and its worship and he despised the tents of the ungodly with all their pomp and show and ceremony. He had seen through it and he delighted to say, 'My heart and my flesh crieth out for the living God' (*Psa.* 84:2). He longed to be in the house of God because he had seen something there of the grace and the glory of God, and he knew that God is 'a sun and shield' (verse 11). And, in any case, what can be more wonderful than to be in the presence of the living God! Even 'the valley of Baca' is turned into pools when God is present (verse 6). Yes, to him the house of God was what the nest was to that little bird (verse 3), it was the place he wanted to go to, it was the place to which he always returned. Everything else was an interlude. This was life to him; this was everything. Now that is the difference between the Christian and the religious person.

Or let me take it even a step further. If you find that you are less and less interested in the demands that you make of religion, if you are less and less interested in your rights and what you can get out of it, it is a good test and a good sign that you are indeed a child of God. This scarcely needs any demonstration. In a time of trouble – the world has been in great trouble this century – people are conscious of need and they look round for help. Where can they get it? Try the books, try philosophy, try the cults – 'Ah, the Christian church! I wonder whether the church can help me?'

All right, I am not criticizing this attitude; it gives us an opportunity. Thank God for anything that brings people to the gospel. But they must be rid of that mentality. They come with the idea that they want something. They want to get something. They are finding life difficult and have certain demands. So if you tell them that if they pray to God they will always have a direct and immediate answer, they say that is just what they want. They have come to get answers to prayers, to get guidance: 'How do I know what to do?' And if you tell them, 'All right, just begin to listen and you will get your guidance', they will say, 'How wonderful!' They come along in terms of their demands, their desires, their wants. These are the big things.

The extent to which that kind of 'I want' attitude is prominent in people, is the extent to which you are uncertain as to whether or not they are truly Christian, because when such people do not get the answer to their prayers that they want, they begin to grumble and complain and say that they doubt whether the gospel is true after all. 'Is God a God of love?' They have a grudge, a sense of complaint, almost of annoyance, and they do not know where they are. They are very enthusiastic if everything seems to work mechanically, if everything happens exactly as they have been told, but the moment things go wrong, they are bewildered. I met someone this last week who was in this very position – shattered, bewildered. Why? Because what she had was religion and not the true Christian faith. She was not really a child of God. She had felt that her prayers had been answered, that her demands had been satisfied, but suddenly it all stopped and she had nothing to fall back on. Now that is the position of those who are merely religious.

Children do not go home to their parents in order to get something but because they like being home. It is a wonderful thing, it is a privilege and a joy. They do not go home with a list of demands and requests – what they want and have been waiting for. Of course not! That whole attitude is foreign to the nature of a child. In the same way, the characteristic of children of God is this: they do not come for what they can get. Of course, they do receive, but they do not come for that reason.

When you are a child of God, the feeling that is uppermost in your mind and heart is, oh, you are in this wonderful, privileged position! And you are filled, not with a number of demands and then a complaint or a grudge if you do not get them, but with a sense of thanksgiving, a sense of praise. What amazes you is that God ever listens to you at all, miserable worm that you are, deserving nothing but hell. What demands, what rights, could you possibly have? And God in his glory in the heavens, in his holiness and purity and love – you are amazed that he even knows you and looks upon you. It is the most wonderful thing in life that he ever allows you into his presence at all. The privilege of being a child of God! You have forgotten all about your requests and demands and postulates – you just want to be there because he is there. You are like Mary:

> *O that I could forever sit*
> *With Mary at the Master's feet,*
> *Be this my happy choice;*
> *My only care, delight, and bliss,*
> *My joy, my heaven on earth, be this,*
> *To hear the Bridegroom's voice.*
>
> Charles Wesley

That is the test of the child. That is the test of the Christian.

And then let this be the last test we deal with for now: the desire for the food and drink. I have been hinting at it already. But this, too, is a very good test.

The more the Bible means to you, the more certain you can be that you are a Christian. The more prayer means to you, the more certain you can be that you are a Christian. How much do we pray, my friends? Do we find delight in prayer? Do we enjoy prayer? It is inevitable, is it not? God is our Father, we are his children. Well, the children like to be with their Father, and they do not do all the talking – they like to listen. They just like to sit in the presence of their Father, just to know that they are there. Nothing need be said. They are proud of it: they just lift up their heads now and again and look. Father is there. It is wonderful. Father and child together. They delight in this. And they delight in their Father's Word, they delight in meditating about him, taking their petitions to him when it is right to do so – and so on.

And there is the fellowship of the saints, too. These go together – it is quite inevitable. The prophet Ezekiel puts this before us in a very wonderful manner:

Moreover he said unto me, Son of man, eat that thou findest; eat this roll, and go, speak unto the house of Israel. So I opened my mouth, and he caused me to eat that roll. And he said unto me, Son of man, cause thy belly to eat, and fill thy bowels with this roll that I give thee. Then did I eat it; and it was in my mouth as honey for sweetness (Ezek. 3:1–3).

'Honey for sweetness'! Is God's Word honey to you? Do you enjoy it? Or do you just do your daily reading and feel very proud that you have done it, like the Boy Scout doing his daily good deed? So many people read their Scriptures like that. My friend, is it like honey to your mouth? When Samuel Rutherford was in prison, he wrote a letter in which he said, 'I have been tasting so much of the Heavenly Manna that my mouth is out of taste for the coarse brown bread of this world's enjoyments.' That is it! Tasting of the heavenly manna! Drinking of the heavenly wells of salvation, and enjoying it!

We must leave it at that for now. God willing, we will go on with this. But oh, God grant that we all may be able to say beyond any doubt that our faith is to us not something that only overshadows us, but that it is indeed *in* us. Remember our Lord's word to the woman of Samaria, who was very religious and who asked whether God should be worshipped on Mount Gerizim in Samaria or in Jerusalem. Our Lord pointed to that well about which she was arguing. Listen, he said, 'Whosoever drinketh of this water shall thirst again: but whosoever drinketh of the water that I shall give him shall never thirst; but the water that I shall give him shall be in him' – *in him!* – 'a well of water springing up into everlasting life' (*John* 4:13–14).

Is the well *in* you? Is the spring of eternal life *in* you? Is your faith *in* you, or is Christianity something that you take up and put down – something outside you? That is the question: It shall be *in you*, like a well of water springing up into everlasting life. Is the life of God in your soul? Have you been born 'not of blood, nor of the will of the flesh, nor of the will of man, but of God'? Do you know that the life of God has come into you? That is the question. ∾

32

'An Assurance Clear'

But as many as received him, to them gave he power to become the sons of God, even to them that believe on his name: which were born, not of blood, nor of the will of the flesh, nor of the will of man, but of God (John 1:12–13).

For some time now we have been considering together the statement that the Son of God came into the world that we might be made the children of God. We have seen that there is nothing more important for us in this life than to know that this is true of us. Any uncertainty about our relationship to God will affect our prayer life, it will affect our view of sickness, our view of death, our view of everything. Assurance of our position as children of God is essential to the full enjoyment of the Christian life. But it is equally, if not more, essential from the standpoint of our witness, our testimony to the world round and about us.

Now this is a matter that surely will commend itself to all of us, particularly on a Sunday like this, which is Whitsunday. This is the day that commemorates the events that took place in Jerusalem on the day of Pentecost so long ago in that first century, when the Christian church was constituted and started upon its great work and enterprise, which are still continuing until the present moment. We remember what our Lord said to his disciples after his resurrection, before his ascension and before he had sent down the gift of the Holy Spirit. We are reminded by his words of the real function of the Christian church, the function of every individual Christian: 'Ye shall be witnesses unto me both in Jerusalem, and in all Judaea, and in Samaria, and unto the uttermost part of the earth' (*Acts* 1:8).

If there is any call that should come to us with greater urgency than another at the present time, it is just this call to be witnesses. We see the state of the world, we see the sin and evil that are rampant all around us, we see the collapse of society in so many respects, and we believe that the only hope for the world is the hope that is found in this gospel that is committed to, and preached by, the church. Therefore I repeat that there is nothing more urgent than this call. And I remind you again that there is nothing else that can make the church a living witness, nothing else that can make us individually living witnesses, than an assured sense of our relationship to God through Jesus Christ our Lord.

Now the early church was turned into a powerful witness, of course, by what happened on the day of Pentecost. That is why our Lord had said, 'Tarry ye in the city of Jerusalem, until ye be endued with power from on high' (*Luke* 24:49). Now this is very remarkable. Our Lord had said those words to the men who had been with him during the three years of his ministry. You would have thought that they would have been the best conceivable witnesses. They had heard all his sermons, they had been present at his miracles and they had seen his death. They had witnessed the fact of his resurrection – he had been there with them, and so they had proof positive, infallible proof, that he had indeed risen from the dead. And yet our Lord had said to them, of all people, 'Tarry ye in the city of Jerusalem, until ye be endued with power . . .' Without this power, which can be given only by the Holy Spirit, even they would have been inadequate as witnesses and representatives of our Lord and his cause in all parts of the world. But the moment they were baptized by the Spirit, they became, as we see, living witnesses. So I now want to consider this whole question of assurance with you from that standpoint.

Assurance of salvation is obtained in two main ways, and it is very important that we should always be mindful of this. The first is the assurance that we obtain by means of a process of deduction. That is the approach we have been following so far in all our considerations. There are many specific statements in the Scriptures with regard to someone who believes on the Lord Jesus Christ. For instance, a typical statement from John's Gospel is: 'He that believeth on him is not condemned: but he that believeth not is condemned already, because he hath not believed in the name of the only begotten Son of God' (*John* 3:18). There is also the great statement in John 5:24: 'Verily, verily, I say unto you, he that heareth my word, and believeth on him that sent me, hath everlasting life, and shall not come into condemnation; but is passed from death unto life.'

One way of obtaining assurance, therefore, is this: to go through the Scriptures, look at such statements, and say, 'I do believe.' And then you say, 'So, because I believe, I must accept the argument, the logic of these statements. Because I believe, I am therefore forgiven, I've passed from death to life, I'm a child of God.' That is a process of deduction: you start with the explicit statements and then say to yourself, 'Do I believe? Am I a believer? If I am, then this must be true of me.' Now there is the first form of assurance. It is a satisfactory form of assurance – and it is with this that we all should always start.

You must start with Scripture. You do not start with yourself, you do not start with your feelings, but with the grand objective statements of the Scriptures, which have been written in order that we might have this assurance. John, in his first epistle, says: 'These things have I written unto you that believe . . . that ye may know that ye have eternal life' (1 *John* 5:13). Therefore you take the Scriptures and draw your deductions. But though that is an invaluable source of assurance, it obviously has its dangers. It is a very simple thing to say, 'I believe.' In order to have a sense of security, we say, 'All right, I'll say that.' In order to gain our end and object, we make the statement and thereby we obtain a sense of relief and satisfaction. And that is the danger. The Scriptures themselves are very careful to warn us not to rest on that alone because, as they say, 'The devils also believe, and tremble' (*James* 2:19). The devils believe in God; the devils recognized the Son of God; they were in no trouble about that, and yet they are devils.

In other words, there is always the danger of mere intellectual assent, a mere playing for safety, a decision to say certain things in order to put ourselves right. So the Scripture goes on and gives us a second type of statement from which we can draw further deductions, and it is with this second type that we have spent most of our time. Here we are dealing with the deductions that we draw from an examination of ourselves in the light of the teaching of Scripture. If you want a general or generic term to describe this type of assurance, you can say that it is assurance that is derived or deduced from our sanctification.

Now I have worked it out with you like this. We said that this whole question of being children of God obviously raises the subject of relationship. Those who are children of God are in a particular set of relationships. They are related to Christ – to the Son – as the one in whom they believe; they are related to the Father; they are related to the Holy Spirit; they are related to the brethren, the other children; they are related even to the devil in a new way; and they are aware of certain things within themselves. Now we have been examining all that. For instance, we are told: 'We know that we have passed from death unto life, because we love the brethren' (1 John 3:14). We therefore say: Do I love the brethren? What is my attitude towards my fellow-Christians? What is my relationship to them? Where do I put them on my list of values and of priorities? If I do love them, then I am a child of God.

Now this second approach is a more delicate test than that of mere believing because it tells me something about my nature. So we have spent most of the time in deducing our sonship, the fact that we are children of God, from this big argument of sanctification. When we are born, 'not of blood, nor of the will of the flesh, nor of the will of man, but of God', something happens to us. We have a new nature; we are given a new life. That must show itself, and it does in the various ways we have been considering. We have looked at ourselves honestly in the light of the plain statements of Scripture and have asked, 'Is that true of me?' Having a large variety of tests means that we have all been searched and examined and have thus been enabled to deduce whether or not we are in reality children of God.

So there is what I call assurance based upon deductions. But there is another form of assurance, and it is the highest form possible to men and women in this life. It is what we may call direct assurance. Now when I say 'direct', I mean that it is not deduced. It is not a mediate but is an immediate assurance. It is not something that you arrive at by means of the process through which we have been going but is something that is given to you, and given immediately and directly. No longer are we talking of argument and deduction but of being given an absolute certainty.

Now first of all, let me establish the fact that this immediate assurance is clearly and plainly taught in the Scriptures. It is not some figment of the imagination or some particular subjective state that only certain people know. Let me establish that it is possible for men and women to know directly and immediately and beyond any doubt whatsoever that they are the children of God. Let me give you some of the evidence. To start with, this certainty is promised. It was promised by our Lord himself on many occasions. There is that great statement in John's Gospel:

In that last day, that great day of the feast, Jesus stood and cried, saying, If any man thirst, let him come unto me, and drink. He that believeth on me, as the scripture hath said, out of his belly shall flow rivers of living water. (But this spake he of the Spirit, which they that believe on him should receive: for the Holy Ghost was not yet given; because that Jesus was not yet glorified) (John 7:37–39).

Now that is a clear and a specific and explicit promise. The same great promise is found in John chapter 14: 'He that hath my commandments, and keepeth them, he it is that loveth me: and he that loveth me shall be loved of my Father, and I will love him, and will manifest myself to him' (*John* 14:21). That is all in the context of the coming of this other Comforter, the Holy Spirit, this other Advocate from the Father.

There, then, is the promise. Then to see its accomplishment and fulfilment, you turn over into the book of Acts. 'Tarry ye in the city of Jerusalem,' our Lord had said, 'until ye be endued with power from on high' (*Luke* 24:49). The disciples knew the facts, but still they could not be living witnesses. But the moment they were baptized with the Holy Spirit on the day of Pentecost, they had a certainty that they had lacked and they spoke with a new authority. There is the fulfilment of the promise. And it was not confined to the disciples; about three thousand people were converted and baptized on the same day (*Acts*

2:41). It was the same with the people down in Samaria (*Acts* 8:14–17), with the household of Cornelius (Acts 10:44) and with those disciples in Ephesus (*Acts* 19:6). We can see it running right through the whole book of Acts.

And, of course, we cannot read the epistles without seeing that this immediate assurance is implicit everywhere. Look, for instance, at the apostle Paul's words in Romans 5:5: 'Hope maketh not ashamed; because the love of God is shed abroad in our hearts by the Holy Ghost which is given unto us.' Now the Greek word translated 'shed abroad' is a very strong word. It means an outpouring in great profusion. And that is what Paul assumes of all the members of the early church – that the love of God has been shed abroad in their hearts in this tremendous profusion.

Then you find a crucial statement in Romans 8:16: 'The Spirit itself beareth witness with our spirit, that we are the children of God.' Now that is it! That is what I mean when I speak of the direct, immediate assurance that is given by the Spirit. The same statement is made in Galatians 4:6: 'And because ye are sons, God hath sent forth the Spirit of his Son into your hearts, crying, Abba, Father.' Similarly, there is 2 Corinthians 1:21–22: 'Now he which stablisheth us with you in Christ, and hath anointed us, is God; who hath also sealed us, and given the earnest of the Spirit in our hearts'; and a parallel statement in Ephesians 1:13: 'In whom ye also trusted, after that ye heard the word of truth, the gospel of your salvation: in whom also after that ye believed, ye were sealed with that holy Spirit of promise, which is the earnest of our inheritance until the redemption of the purchased possession, unto the praise of his glory.'

Then listen to the apostle Peter. Here he is, not writing to apostles but to ordinary Christians, and this is what he says about their relationship to the Lord Jesus Christ: 'Whom having not seen, ye love; in whom, though now ye see him not, yet believing, ye rejoice with joy unspeakable and full of glory' (*1 Pet.* 1:8). Now that is a perfectly plain and explicit statement: you rejoice with a joy that is *unspeakable*, inexpressible, because it is so wonderful. That is the relationship of the Christian to the Lord Jesus Christ. Christians rejoice in him in that

[470]

way and to that extent. They cannot express it! It is a glorious joy, a joy full of glory; it is utterly incomprehensible to human thought and language. But though it cannot be put into words, they know that it is true of them. They have never seen him but that is their relationship to him. And there is only one thing that has brought them into that relationship, and that is the operation of the Holy Spirit.

There, then, is some scriptural evidence – and it is only a part of it – that shows us that there is the possibility of an immediate and direct assurance of salvation in all its fulness and in all its power. But this is not confined to the days of the early church, it is not confined to the New Testament. It is very interesting to notice from biographies and from the history of the Christian church how the devil has often tried to stand between people and the realization of this possibility by saying to them, 'Well, yes, that was all right, of course, at the beginning, but it is no longer true. It was just to start off the Christian church. That was something that was done two thousand years ago but you must not expect things like that to continue.' Now there is an abundant answer to that argument and it is very important that we should realize it on a Whitsunday like today.

In the whole of the New Testament there is not a single statement that tells us that immediate assurance was confined to the early church, not a single one. Indeed, it is the exact opposite. 'The promise is unto you, and to your children, and to all that are afar off' (*Acts* 2:39). It is all-inclusive. There is no greater lie of the devil than the suggestion that a distinction should be drawn between the early church and everything that has followed. The idea is totally unscriptural. No, no! We base what we expect in the Christian life upon the New Testament teaching. That is the pattern, the norm, the standard for all Christianity, always and at all times. And we have no right to be content with anything that is in any way short of what we find in the New Testament itself.

But, thank God, we have further evidence. Not only is it not scriptural to say that this immediate knowledge of God was only true of the early church, it is not true historically – and the testimony of history is very powerful. I am referring, first of all, to the great history of revivals of religion. Do you know something about the revivals of the past? I hope you do. I think it is most urgent that all Christian people should know something about past revivals. I say this because the Christian church today is weak and ineffective. What does she count for in this country? What does she count for in most countries? And yet there have been times when the church has counted above everything. When was this? Well, that is what happens when you get a revival of religion, which is a kind of repetition of the day of Pentecost.

A revival is the Holy Spirit coming again in tremendous power, coming upon a congregation, coming upon a church or a group of churches, coming upon a whole country, sometimes. There are the people gathered together in their usual humdrum, lethargic manner, not expecting anything to happen, when suddenly the Spirit of God comes down upon them and takes hold of them and possesses them and lifts them up and does wonders among them; and all the people are amazed, even as they were on the day of Pentecost. Revivals of religion! And there have been many, many such revivals, thank God. There has scarcely been a century but that there has been some kind of revival when God has again poured down his Spirit.

Now I know that there are many people today who say, 'The Spirit was given once and for all on the day of Pentecost, and all you do is draw on that.' Well, there is only one answer to that. It is to be found in Acts 4, where we read that the Spirit who had come in such power on the day of Pentecost came upon the believers again in a similar manner a few days later. And he has come like that in every revival that the church has ever been privileged to experience. This is not confined to the early church. I could easily tell you the stories of revivals, how the Spirit of God would suddenly come upon a church and lift the people up into the heavens until they did not know where they were. That is a revival of religion, a repetition of Pentecost.

But, again, thank God, the outpouring of the Spirit is not even confined to revivals. There is abundant testimony of his outpouring upon individuals, even when the church in general was not being revived. There are very many accounts of men and women who suddenly found themselves baptized with the Spirit of God. Now the point I am establishing is that it was not then that they came to believe: I am referring to people who had been believers for years. They had realized their sinfulness, they had realized that there was no hope except in Jesus Christ and him crucified, they had set their hearts entirely upon him, and yet they were lacking in a final assurance. They knew the Scriptures. They had drawn their deductions. They did love the brethren. They had applied the various other arguments and were persuaded that they really were the children of God. Yet there was in these people a kind of residual unhappiness, a lack of ease, a lack of absolute certainty. When they confronted 1 Peter 1:8, which says that the Christian is someone who rejoices in Christ 'with joy unspeakable and full of glory', they had to admit, 'It's not true of me. I do love him, and yet I don't love him as I ought.'

> *Lord, it is my chief complaint*
> *That my love is cold and faint;*
> *Yet I love thee, and adore,*
> *O for grace to love thee more!*
>
> William Cowper

That was their position. They were believers – certainly believers – and yet they had never had this immediate and direct assurance, which is given by the Spirit. But one day it came, and their testimony, every one of them, was that this meant more to them than everything else put together and multiplied many times. Direct, immediate assurance eclipses and surpasses everything else put together.

Now that is the kind of assurance of which I am speaking. That is what happened on the day of Pentecost. These believers were suddenly taken up and filled with joy! They were so joyful that some people looking on thought that they were drunk and said, 'These men are full of new wine' (*Acts* 2:13). It was the ecstasy of the joy of salvation, which had been brought to them by the baptism of the Spirit. This is, I repeat, the highest form of assurance. You are no longer deducing, you are given absolute certainty by the Spirit himself.

How does the Holy Spirit give this certainty? Well, I am trying to provide a comprehensive picture. He does it in two main ways. Perhaps the more frequent way is that he takes a certain word of Scripture. You may have read it a thousand times, you may know what it says, but never until this moment has it really spoken to you. Suddenly the Spirit takes a word and he brings it right to you. He says, 'I am saying this to you!' And you know that he is. He illumines a passage of Scripture. He takes his own Word and says, 'This is for you.' You knew it in general before; you know now that it is yours. But over and above giving you direct assurance by the Scripture, the Holy Spirit sometimes gives you assurance directly by just speaking to your spirit. This happens in a way that no one has ever been able to put into words, but he just makes an impression upon the spirit. He is a Spirit and he impresses our spirit.

And what is given to us? What does the Holy Spirit do? First of all, he gives us an absolute, personal sense that our sins are forgiven. Now when I say an absolute, personal sense, I am contrasting it with something else. There are many, many Christian people who come to the Communion table and see the bread and wine and say: 'The Lord Jesus Christ is the Lamb of God who takes away the sin of the world.' That is their assurance. They say, 'I believe in him, therefore I believe he has taken my sin away.' That is a deduction, is it not? I believe my sins are forgiven because John 3:18 tells me, 'He that believeth on him is not condemned.' And I do believe in him, therefore I am not condemned. I read, 'There is therefore now no condemnation to them which are in Christ Jesus' (*Rom.* 8:1). I am in Christ Jesus, therefore there is no condemnation. I am having to deduce it. I am having to argue it. I persuade myself. Now that is faith, and if you do that, you are a child of God. But that is not the assurance I am speaking about.

I am speaking about a personal assurance that he died for me individually and for my sins in particular. I am not deducing it but am being told by the Spirit that the Son of God loved *me* and gave himself for *me*. Down in the depths of my spirit and heart and soul the Spirit says, 'Yes, it was done for you!' It is an immediate, direct assurance of the pardon and the forgiveness of my sins.

And there is something added to that: the Spirit in this manner gives me a personal knowledge of God's love to me in particular. Take that phrase in Romans 5:5 about the love of God being 'shed abroad in our hearts'. That is not our love to God, that is his love to us, shed abroad in our hearts. You know what it is to be told by somebody that he or she loves you. You may have been able to deduce it, but that is very different from being told it. What each of us wants to know is that word of love, to be told that we are loved. Ah, it can be shown in many ways and, thank God, we can draw deductions from those ways. But all that is nothing. It is the word we want; it is the statement; it is the assertion. That is what the lover always longs for! The one who is loved wants to hear this!

> Tell me thou art mine, O Saviour,
> Grant me an assurance clear.
>
> William Williams

The Spirit does that. And when the love of God is shed abroad in your heart, there is no question about it, you do not have to deduce it any longer. You know it. You are overwhelmed by it. It is poured in upon you. And you can read in the lives of people individually, and in companies during revivals, of how this love of God came upon them and they were so certain of it that they were utterly transported. We are given a personal knowledge of God's love to us as individuals.

And then there is this further aspect: the Holy Spirit brings us to a personal knowledge of God and of the Lord Jesus Christ. 'This is life eternal, that they might know thee the only true God, and Jesus Christ, whom thou hast sent' (*John* 17:3). Now in the Scriptures, 'know' is a very strong word. Our Lord does not mean 'know about'. You can know about God – there are few who do not know about him. Anyone who believes the Bible at all knows a great many things about God. But: 'This is life eternal, that they might *know* thee . . .' That means a personal knowledge, an intimate knowledge. It means a realization of the reality of the Person.

Our Lord talks about that same personal knowledge in John chapter 14, where he says, in effect, 'I am going to leave you but you need not be troubled – I am going to come back to you in a much more real sense. I am going to be with you.' He even makes this extraordinary statement: 'If a man love me, he will keep my words: and my Father will love him, and we will come unto him, and make our abode with him' (*John* 14:23). 'Make our abode with him'! Father and Son dwelling within us; and we know that they do. That is what the Spirit gives, and there is no higher form of assurance than that. You are no longer in the realm of deductions. You know that the Father and the Son have taken up their abode in you. There was a statement that the great George Whitefield used to make very often. He said that no preacher should preach unless he could preach 'a felt Christ'. By that he meant that the preacher knows Christ, feels his presence and has felt his power. *A felt Christ.* It is the Spirit alone who can give that, and when you have that there is no need for deduction.

And this, in turn, leads to a great joy. I have already quoted the words in 1 Peter 1:8: 'Joy unspeakable and full of glory'. Let us be clear about this, my friends. You know when you get this love of God shed abroad in your heart. When the Spirit gives you this personal assurance, you are overwhelmed by a sense of God's love and of the glory of it all, and it leads to an element of ecstasy. Are we afraid of ecstasy? Have we become so polite that we are quenching the Spirit? Let me remind you again that when the Holy Spirit came upon those disciples and the others on the day of Pentecost at Jerusalem, the people looking on said, 'These men are drunk!' They were not drunk, of course. What had happened was that they had been filled with this glory and this joy, this happiness, and they were in a definite state of ecstasy, lifted up above themselves.

If you read the accounts of revivals, you will find men and women saying that they were given such a sense of the love of God to them that their bodies could not stand it and they literally fainted. Now I am not advocating phenomena; all I am saying is that there may be phenomena. What I am emphasizing is the joy and the happiness, the thrill, the ecstasy of it all. This is Christianity! This is what the Holy Spirit was sent to give us. This is what the early church rejoiced in. That is why Peter could write as he did. We need not bother about the gifts. Gifts may be given. They were given at the beginning; there have been gifts ever since. Do not worry about the gifts. What matters is that you know God's love to you, that he has told you that he loves you, that he has forgiven you, that you are his and that he will never let you go – that you are certain of this. That is what matters, whatever the accompaniments may be.

And then there is invariably a sense of eternity and, indeed, even a foretaste of eternity. Notice that expression in 2 Corinthians 1:22 and 5:5, 'the earnest of the Spirit'. The 'earnest' is a preliminary instalment; it is a foretaste, a tasting of the firstfruits. And those who have this assurance know that they belong to heaven. They are still on earth, but they belong there. They have 'the earnest of the Spirit' to assure them that they are but pilgrims and strangers in this world. Then they become detached from this earthly life. Having seen and felt something of the glory of heaven, that is what they want; they are people away from home and they are making their way home. That is what happens to all these people who get this assurance, this highest form of assurance, which is given by the baptism of the Spirit.

And then, in turn, this leads to a great sense within us of love to God. It is inevitable. You cannot help it. The moment you feel this love of God to you, you love him in return. 'Because ye are sons, God hath sent forth the Spirit of his Son into your hearts, crying, Abba, Father' (*Gal.* 4:6). That word 'Abba' was a familiar term – no longer God in some distant heavens, but God as my personal Father; a nearness, an intimacy, a knowledge. And a love for him wells up within us in response to his great love. My dear friends, the question is not, 'Do we believe in God?' but, 'Do we love him?' The church today is fiddling about *belief* in God, trying to *describe* God. That is not the thing. The church should be loving God, knowing him, beyond the realm of argument and disputation, basking in his love and loving him in return. 'Abba, Father'!

There, then, very hurriedly and inadequately, are some of the inevitable consequences of this assurance that is given by the Spirit. You are out of the realm of deduction: you are being told. God is telling you through the Spirit, and you are filled with this knowledge and you are rejoicing in it. Do you have this assurance, my friend? Do you know that God loves you? Do you know that your sins are forgiven? I mean, has he told you that? Are you absolutely certain of it? Do you know the love of God to you in particular? Do you know Christ as a living person, not as someone remote and distant whom you believe in by faith? Do you know him? Has the Father, has the Son, come and taken up their abode in you? That is what he promised. That is what happened to these people on the day of Pentecost. That is what has happened to so many throughout the centuries. Is there anything more important, I ask, than that we should all be knowing this and having it and rejoicing in it? I am not saying that you are not a Christian if you cannot say this but I am saying, oh, that you might rise to the full height of your sonship! Oh, that you might have this ultimate, this final assurance! It is meant for all. 'The promise is unto you, and to your children, and to all that are afar off' (*Acts* 2:39).

So how do we seek this assurance? How do we get it? The first thing, obviously, is to realize the possibility. To know that I am a child of God! That he is my Father, that he loves me individually! It is possible. We ought to realize this possibility, we ought to have it, and we should be content with nothing less. The moment we do realize that we can have this assurance, we begin to seek it. We seek it by obeying him: 'If ye love me, keep my commandments' (*John* 14:15). This is given, our Lord keeps on saying in John 14, to those who obey him and who keep his commandments. 'He that hath my commandments, and keepeth them, he it is that loveth me: and he that loveth me shall be loved of my Father, and I will love him, and will manifest myself to him' (*John* 14:21).

Has our Lord manifested himself to you? This is the way. Seek him! Seek him along the line of obedience: but go beyond that. Ask him to manifest himself to you. Pray to him to do this. Plead with him. Like a lover, write him letters, as it were! Ask him to tell you, ask him to grant you this 'assurance clear'. That is the hymn, as we have seen:

> *Tell me thou art mine, O Saviour,*
> *Grant me an assurance clear;*
> *Banish all my dark misgivings.*
> William Williams

Or, if you would like it in the form of a brief prayer, let me quote to you the little prayer that was found on a piece of paper copied out in his own hand by Hudson Taylor, the founder of the China Inland Mission. It was found after his death in the Bible that he used every day.

> *Lord Jesus, make thyself to me*
> *A living bright reality,*
> *More present to faith's vision keen*
> *Than any outward object seen;*
> *More dear, more intimately nigh,*
> *Than e'en the sweetest earthly tie.*
>
> Charlotte Elliott

That was his prayer – and his prayer was answered. The Lord Jesus, whom he had believed in and had worshipped at a distance, had manifested himself to him, and his prayer was that he might know this and enjoy this more and more day by day.

> *Lord Jesus, make thyself to me*
> *A living, bright reality.*

'I will manifest myself to him.' That is it! He becomes a reality.

> *More present to faith's vision keen*
> *Than any outward object seen.*

That the Lord Jesus may be more real to us than this building. That we may be more certain of his presence than we are of the presence of one another.

> *More dear, more intimately nigh,*
> *Than e'en the sweetest earthly tie.*

Let that be your prayer, and never cease to offer it until you know him, until he has manifested himself to you, until you know that he is dwelling within you, until you know something of being overwhelmed by his love and by the grace of his smile. And then you will be in a realm entirely above deduction. Then you will *know*, for he himself will have told you through his most blessed Spirit. ❧